THE CASKET LETTERS

A Solution to the Mystery of Mary Queen of Scots
and the Murder of Lord Darnley

BY

M. H. ARMSTRONG DAVISON

VISION

VISION PRESS LIMITED
Saxone House
74A Regent Street
London W1

N321940

First published in the British Commonwealth 1965
© Copyright 1965 by M. H. Armstrong Davison
All rights reserved
Printed in the U.S.A.
Bound in Great Britain
MCMLXV

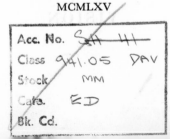

Ad Memoriam Rerum Gentiumque.

PREFACE

Although the whole idea of this work, the manner of presentation, and the conclusions are my own, I nevertheless owe a large debt of gratitude to a great number of people: first, to those authors on whose works I have so largely drawn for factual detail and for inspiration; secondly, to my wife who has patiently aided my labouring thoughts, typed much of the manuscript and helped largely with the proof-reading; and also, to my brother-in-law, Leslie M. Hopkins, Esq., of Devizes, Wiltshire, who gave me advice, both tactical and syntactical. Others whom I wish to mention are Dr. Doris Delacourcelle of the University of Newcastle upon Tyne, for advice on the translation of the mediaeval French; Dr. Palle Birkelund of the Royal Library of Copenhagen who provided me with a specimen of the handwriting of Anna Throndssen; and Dr. V. M. MacFarlane of Newcastle, who helped me in connexion with the nature of Darnley's illnesses. Many other people have encouraged and helped me, and to all of them I am grateful, whether I have accepted their advice or not. My gratitude is also due to the holders of copyright for permission to make use of illustrations, each of whom is individually acknowledged in the captions.

Finally, I wish to thank the publishers for their unstinted assistance and skilful work. If this book gives you pleasure, they must all share your gratitude; if it does not, let the blame lie with me.

M. H. ARMSTRONG DAVISON
Newcastle upon Tyne
November, 1964

CONTENTS

LIST OF ILLUSTRATIONS

INTRODUCTION

The mystery which surrounds the life of Mary Queen of Scots and the death of her second husband, Henry Lord Darnley, is one of unfailing interest to many different sorts of people. To the factual historian, the subject has proved a fascination for close on four hundred years; to the psychologist, it presents a series of absorbing emotional reactions; to the student of crime, it is almost the perfect murder story; while to the seeker after sensation, it abounds with violent and amorous incidents which have been exploited by novelist, poet, and playwright alike.

My interest in Mary Stewart began some twenty-five years ago, and, although it is only during the last ten years that I have made a detailed study of her life, I have, during that time, applied myself assiduously to reading and digesting almost everything of value which has been written about her and the Scotland of her age. When I began this study, I was disposed to accept the orthodox belief that Mary was a wanton and a murderess, but, as the facts marshalled themselves before my eyes, it became apparent that this view was untenable: there were too many improbabilities in the official story for it to be acceptable, and the reasons for its inconsistencies could only be the guilt of the prosecution and the innocence of the accused.

Personally, I have no axe to grind; being an Englishman who is neither a Roman Catholic nor a Calvinist, I had no desire to weight either side of the balance, and my conclusions were reached, so far as I am aware, by an unbiassed examination of the facts. Yet, having concluded that Mary Queen of Scots was innocent, this book cannot be considered to be unprejudiced: it is, in fact, the case for the defence, but I have tried to present it with a minimum of emotional rhetoric, and with reliance, wherever possible, on authorities which themselves depend upon immediately contemporary sources.

The so-called Casket Letters are the spear-head of the prosecution; if these documents be, in fact, what the Earl of Moray and his associates alleged them to be, there can be no doubt of the guilt of the Queen of Scots of the murder of her husband and of a criminal intrigue with the Earl of Bothwell. To prove that the Casket Letters are not what they seem does not prove the Queen to have been innocent, but it is an essential preliminary to an understanding of the events which surround the death of Darnley, and it is, therefore, to this problem that this book is particularly devoted.

If I should be blamed for following a practice which has become common of late, and should be accused of "white-washing", I would deny the charge. Crimes, such as the murder of Darnley occurred: all that I have tried to do is to apportion the guilt among those who deserve to bear it, which is not whitewashing, but mere justice.

The work is divided into four parts: an introductory section (Book I) which sets the stage, in which it is shewn that the actions of both Mary and Bothwell have been misrepresented, and in which the sinister activities of Darnley himself and of the Lords of the Congregation are brought into relief. The main section of the work (Book II) is devoted to an analysis of the Casket documents, sentence by sentence, together with an account of their appearance and production. The authorship and the manner of manipulation of the letters is made clear. It may be said that there is no unanimity about the numbering of the letters, nearly every author arranging the documents in a different order; I have followed the numeration used by T. F. Henderson in his "Casket Letters and Mary Queen of Scots". The third section of the work (Book III) is a chronological record of events from two months before the death of Darnley until four months after it. The book concludes with an Appendix on the medical aspects of the lives of Mary Queen of Scots and her three husbands, a subject which has hitherto been strangely neglected.

No new facts have been elicited in this enquiry, for I am not a palaeographer and I have worked exclusively from previously published material. Nevertheless, although no new facts have appeared, the conclusions drawn from the facts *are* new, and the story which emerges is one which has never been told before; Major-General R. H. Mahon came close to the truth in 1930, and Andrew Lang had glimpses of it as long ago as 1901. To these, and to many other authors who have prepared my path, I am duly grateful.

The reader is asked to remember that the actors in this drama are not fictitious, but are people who really existed: their characters did not vary from day to day. Because the following account shows each of them behaving in a consistent manner throughout, I am confident that, if this be not the whole truth, it is very close to it.

Great care has been taken to verify all references and dates. With regard to the latter, it should be noted that, during the period under review, the Julian Calendar was still in use, and, in the whole of Britain, the year legally ended on 24th March. It is usual, therefore, to express dates in the early part of the year with a double year number, e.g. 24th February, 1565–6: in the following pages, this clumsy convention has been eschewed, and all dates, whether in quotations or not, have been converted to the modern style in which the year ends on 31st December, the above date appearing as 24th February, 1566.

I have taken the liberty of modernizing the spelling of contemporary documents, even, very occasionally, altering an unfamiliar word, or one which has since changed its meaning, so as to preserve the original sense.

The Casket documents themselves, however, are given complete in their original orthography. One other point: Mary's Secretary of State, William Maitland, younger of Lethington, is here invariably referred to as 'Maitland'. To his contemporaries, although he had several nicknames, such as Michael Wily (Machiavelli) and the Chameleon, he was most frequently called Lethington, a title which correctly belonged to his father, Sir Richard. In order to avoid confusion, when quoting documents which refer to the Secretary as 'Lethington', I have changed the name and, in order to show that I have done so, I have placed it within brackets, thus, (Maitland); I have adopted a similar convention on some occasions in which a document refers to some person by an unfamiliar name or title.

Before discussing the true course of events, it is necessary to summarise the orthodox history of the life of Mary Queen of Scots, which is described in the text-books in the following way. The daughter of James V of Scotland and his second wife, Mary of Lorraine, Mary Stewart was born on 8th December, 1542, and she succeeded to the crown on the death of her father six days later. The kingdom was thus, once again, exposed to the perils of a long minority. Rival factions carried on a keen contest for superiority at home, while the independence of the country was threatened by the ambitious designs of Henry VIII, whose object was to marry his son Edward to the infant Queen. Eventually, the treaty of marriage which had been agreed between the Regent Arran (later Duke of Châtelherault, head of the House of Hamilton) and Henry VIII was annulled, not without cause, by the Scottish Parliament, and the ancient league with France was renewed. The result of these proceedings was a bloody and protracted war with England, with repeated invasions by the English forces, and the merciless devastation of large tracts of the country. This rough mode of wooing served only to exasperate the Scottish people, and to alienate them still farther from the alliance with England. After the disastrous battle of Pinkie (10th September, 1547), it was decided to provide for the safety of the young Queen by sending her to complete her education in France, and to affiance her to Francis the Dauphin, son of Henry II. Accompanied by her retinue, she reached the French shore in safety in mid-August, 1548. Her marriage to the Dauphin was solemnized with great pomp at Paris on 24th April, 1558. The terms of the union had been carefully considered in order to secure the independence of the kingdom of Scotland, but, a short time before the public ratification of the articles, Mary was induced by the French King and her uncles, the Guises, to subscribe three secret documents by which the kingdom of Scotland was to be conferred upon the King of France if Mary should die without issue. Soon after, Mary and her husband put forth pretensions to the throne of England on the ground of Elizabeth's alleged illegitimacy, an unfortunate step which excited the resentment of the English Queen. On the death of Henry II, Mary's husband became King of France, but her splendour was short-lived, and, by the death of Francis II on 5th December, 1560, Mary was left a widow at the age of eighteen. Invited to return to Scotland, although Elizabeth had not only refused the safe-conduct which she had sought, but had even sent some ships of war to intercept her on her voyage, Mary landed safely at Leith on 19th August, 1561.

Important changes had taken place in Scotland during the thirteen years of Mary's absence in France. The Roman Church had been overthrown, the authority of the Pope in Scotland abolished, the celebration of mass forbidden under severe penalties, the Protestant confession of faith and the Presbyterian system of church government established by the authority of Parliament. The Roman Catholics, however, were still a powerful party in the country, and entertained hopes of recovering their supremacy with the help of their young sovereign.

At the outset, Mary conducted herself with prudence. In her general policy, she favoured the Protestant party, and its leaders were entrusted with the management of public affairs. She manifested an earnest desire to secure the good-will of Elizabeth, and left no means untried to induce that Queen to recognize her claims to the right of succession to the English throne. Her straightforward, just and friendly policy at this period presents a marked contrast to the disingenuous and selfish policy of her "good sister" of England, who amused Mary with promises which, it is evident, she never intended to fulfil. The two Queens at length came into collision on the delicate subject of marriage. Elizabeth expressed her determination to oppose an alliance between the Scottish Queen and every foreign potentate; Mary declined the proposals of the various continental aspirants to her hand, and manifested a desire to consult the wishes of the English Queen. Elizabeth insinuated that, if Mary's choice should fall on one of her subjects, she would immediately recognize her right of succession to the English throne, and at length proposed for her acceptance her own favourite, Robert Dudley, whom she created Earl of Leicester. So anxious was Mary to secure the friendship of Elizabeth and the sanction of her claims that she expressed her willingness to acquiesce in this proposal on the conditions specified; but, in the end, after many evasions, Elizabeth declared that she would not bind herself to recognize the pretensions of the Scottish Queen. Mary, provoked beyond measure, withdrew her confidence both from Elizabeth and from her Protestant advisers, Moray and Maitland, who had strongly recommended a union with England, and threw herself into an affair which was bound to raise their opposition. Lord Darnley, eldest son of the Earl of Lennox, who, through his mother, was, after Mary, next in succession to the English throne, and, through his father, was also high in line for the crown of Scotland, had recently visited Scotland with the hope of gaining the Queen's affections, and had favourably impressed her by his personal appearance. Although he was a young man of weak intellect and passionate temper, and had made himself many enemies at court by his overbearing behaviour, the Queen determined to marry him. The opposition both of Elizabeth and of Moray and the Protestant party to this match only caused Mary to adhere more firmly to her resolution; accordingly, on 29th July, 1565, they were married at Holyrood.

Scarcely had the marriage taken place, when the Queen was called upon to suppress the insurrection which it had created, and which is known to history as the Chase-about Raid. Moray, Argyll, Châtelherault and other powerful barons, encouraged by Elizabeth, appeared in arms, in defence, as they alleged, of the Protestant religion, which the marriage of the Queen with Darnley, a Roman Catholic, had seriously imperilled. Mary, with the utmost promptitude, raised an army and chased the rebels out of the kingdom. They took refuge in England, where, to add to their troubles, Elizabeth, who had sent them money and encouragement, now shamelessly disavowed them, and even rebuked Moray publicly for his rebellious conduct. The Earl, in the extremity of his desperation, even stooped to solicit the intercession of the secretary, Riccio, with the Queen of Scots.

Mary had decided against proceeding to extremes against her rebels, but was unfortunately induced to change her mind by the arrival of a French envoy, who brought a copy of the league which had been drawn up at Bayonne for the extirpation of the Protestant religion. Mary, signed the league and resolved to take steps at the next meeting of Parliament for the forfeiture of Moray and his associates. Meanwhile, Mary's weak, headstrong and vicious husband had taken deep offence at her refusal to bestow on him the crown matrimonial, and had contracted a bitter hatred for Riccio, whom he blamed for the Queen's reluctance to comply with his demands, and whom he later also accused of a criminal intimacy with the Queen. The result was a conspiracy for the assassination of Riccio, which was subsequently joined by Morton and others of the Protestant party, for the purpose of restoring the banished Lords and averting the dangers which threatened the cause of the Reformation. This plot, carried into effect in circumstances of peculiar atrocity on 9th March, 1566, recoiled on the heads of its authors, who were compelled to flee the country, and were outlawed and forfeited.

Mary now acted with prudence: she pardoned Moray and some of his associates of the Chase-about Raid on condition that they would detach themselves from the murderers of Riccio: she restored Moray to some part of the power which he had formerly possessed, and laboured to reconcile him to Bothwell and Huntly, with whom he had been at feud. On 19th June, 1566, Mary was safely delivered of that son in whom the two crowns were ultimately united. The foolish conduct of Darnley now thwarted all her efforts to secure tranquillity for her kingdom, and rendered him so obnoxious to Mary and her nobility that Maitland, Moray and other leading nobles proposed to free her from her misery by a divorce, a project which was soon to be exchanged for one of assassination. Meanwhile, the profligate and unscrupulous Earl of Bothwell rose rapidly in Mary's confidence and esteem. At what precise period he conceived the audacious project of gaining the hand of the Queen, it is impossible to say, but it led him soon after to enter into a conspiracy with Maitland and the other Lords for the murder of the King. The atrocious plot was carried into effect during the night of 9th–10th February, 1567. While Mary was by his bedside, for Darnley was recovering from smallpox in a house at Kirk o'Field on the outskirts of Edinburgh, gunpowder was placed in her bedroom, which was immediately below his own. Presently, she departed to attend the wedding masque of two of her servants, Sebastian Pages and Christina Hogg, at Holyrood: the wretched Darnley was strangled during her absence, and the house was blown up. Whether or not this murder was perpetrated with the Queen's complicity, there can at least be no doubt that she regarded it with no feeling of disapprobation after it was accomplished.

Although the public voice accused Bothwell of the murder, the Earl was heaped with honours; in spite of the pathetic appeals for justice on the part of the father of the murdered King and the vehement reproaches of Elizabeth, Mary could not be induced to take a single step to bring the murderers of her husband to justice. She was at length driven to save herself from obloquy by a mock trial of her favourite which ended in a collusive acquittal. When Parliament assembled a few days later, Bothwell was selected to bear the crown and sceptre before her at its opening. He was scarcely ever absent from her side, and his complete ascendancy over her was obvious to all. It soon became evident that, hurried along by her passion, she was bent on bestowing her hand on the murderer of her husband, and she had actually decided upon this step, as is shewn by a contract of marriage which she had signed on 5th April, seven days before Bothwell's trial and acquittal.

By a combination of force and fraud, Bothwell secured the signatures of the leading nobles and ecclesiastics to a paper recommending him as a suitable husband for the Queen. The seizure of her person, with her own consent, took place five days later, on 24th April, 1567, and was followed by Bothwell's divorce from his Countess, which was hurried through the courts with indecent haste. In spite of the disgust of the public, the remonstrance of the French Ambassador, and the solemn warning of Craig, John Knox's colleague, Bothwell was married to the Queen at Holyrood on 15th May, 1567, little more than three months after the murder of her second husband. Several weeks before the marriage, a party had been secretly organised among the nobles for the protection of the infant Prince against the suspected designs of the unscrupulous favourite. Within a few weeks of their sovereign's marriage, they took up arms and declared their determination to separate the Queen from her husband, and to seize and punish him as the murderer of the King. Mary and Bothwell retired to Borthwick and thence to Dunbar, and, in a few days, found themselves strong enough to confront the confederates at Carberry Hill, six miles from Edinburgh, on 15th June, 1567. The royal army, reluctant to fight in such a quarrel, soon began to melt away; in the end, the confederates promised to return to their allegiance if Bothwell were dismissed and the Queen would follow them to Edinburgh. To these terms Mary gave her consent: Bothwell was permitted to ride off the field, and the Queen surrendered to the insurgents on the agreed terms. Within an hour, she found that she was in the hands of her enemies: they conducted her to Edinburgh where she was treated with indignity, and thence she was conveyed to Lochleven, where, by violent threats, she was induced to sign documents by which she resigned the crown in favour of her son, nominated the Earl of Moray as Regent, and appointed a temporary Council of Regency until Moray should return from France, whither he had retired shortly before Bothwell's trial. The coronation of James VI, the arrival of Moray and his assumption of the Regency soon followed.

Moray had not been many months in the possession of his new dignity, when Mary escaped from Lochleven on 2nd May, 1568, and took refuge in the fortress of Hamilton. A strong body of the nobles joined her standard, and she soon found herself at the head of a considerable army. While on the march to Dumbarton, she came into conflict with the Regent's forces at Langside near Glasgow; her army was completely defeated, and she herself made all haste to Dundrennan, whence she crossed the Solway and landed in England on 16th May, 1568.

The rash resolution of Mary to take refuge in the kingdom of her rival enveloped her future in disaster. Elizabeth might have restored her to her throne, or have granted her asylum in England, or have permitted her to retire to France, but all three courses seemed to be fraught with danger to the Queen of England and her throne. In violation, therefore, of the principles of justice and humanity, she resolved to detain Mary a prisoner in England. It was necessary, however, to provide a pretext for this behaviour, and Mary was therefore induced to submit her cause to the arbitration of her crafty rival; and the Scottish Regent, in compliance with the summons of Elizabeth, but with reluctance, brought forth his charges against his half-sister before a commission which sat first at York and later at Westminster and Hampton Court, and he attempted to substantiate his case by producing the Casket documents, letters which he affirmed to be in the handwriting of Mary, and which she had sent to Bothwell: if these were genuine, they were conclusive of her guilt. In the end, after an investigation lasting four months, from October, 1568, to January, 1569, the conference terminated without any definite decision in favour of either party, and the only result was to provide the English Queen with a pretext for retaining her rival in captivity.

The remainder of Mary's long imprisonment in England was little other than a series of abortive intrigues for the recovery of her crown and liberty. Her party in Scotland was eventually completely crushed by the Regent Morton, but she remained a source of danger to the security of Elizabeth's throne. The Roman Catholic party regarded her as the rightful heir to the English Crown, and various plots arose with the object of dethroning Elizabeth and transferring the throne to Mary. The activity of the English ministers led to the discovery of all the intrigues. In 1572, the English envoy to Scotland was instructed to propose to the Earl of Mar, then Regent, and to Morton that Mary should be delivered up to them, in order that she might be immediately put to death, but the exorbitant demands of Morton led to the abandonment of this unscrupulous project.

At last, in 1586, the Scottish Queen having been accused of complicity in Babington's conspiracy, the object of which was the assassination of Elizabeth and the restoration of the Roman Catholic religion, she was brought to trial, found guilty and condemned to death. Mary defended herself with great courage and ability, and she protested against the illegality of the proceedings. Elizabeth was, however, reluctant to incur the odium of putting the sentence into effect, and even attempted to induce Sir Amyas Paulet, Mary's keeper at the time, to poison her. Eventually, she signed the death warrant, which was carried into execution on 8th February, 1587, in the Great Hall of Fotheringhay Castle.

So runs the orthodox account. It is the object of the following pages to show that this story is a travesty of the truth, at least in regard to the central period of Mary Stewart's life.

The nursery rhyme so familar to us all, "Mary, Mary, quite contrary," was originally a political jibe: the silver bells and cockle-shells were the signs and symbols of Roman Catholicism, the former being the mass-bell and the latter the badge of the pilgrims, especially those to the shrine of St. James of Compostela. The pretty maids were the "four Maries", girls of Mary's own age and daughters of the houses of Beaton, Seton, Fleming and Livingstone, who were brought up with her in France, and acted as her main companions. My object in this book has been to answer the question of the anonymous, yet immortal, composer of these lines, and to explain exactly what fruit grew in the Queen's garden of Scotland, and how it was that she came to eat of the bitter, leaving the sweet to others.

BOOK I
"Silver Bells & Cockle Shells"

CHAPTER I

Mary and Religion

During the course of the five and a half years in which Mary Stewart reigned as Queen in Scotland, she was opposed by the Protestant Lords in three great rebellions: the Chase-about Raid which ensued on her marriage with Henry, Lord Darnley; the murder of Riccio; and the final revolution which overwhelmed her at Carberry. Apart from the question of her alleged complicity in the murder of her second husband, which later provided a convenient justification for the third revolution, the attitude of the Protestant Lords is condoned in the accepted histories, because they had opposed her on the ground of religion.

Mary was a Roman Catholic: she returned in 1561 to a country in which the mass had been overthrown and in which the Reformed Faith had been established, and the story goes that, lacking the power at first to restore her people to the Church of Rome, she carefully bided her time, ceaselessly working for the re-establishment of the mass, and the overthrow of the Lords of the Congregation.

It is undoubtedly true that at least two of the great European powers, the Vatican and Spain, would have been glad to further such a scheme. When Mary returned to Scotland, England had lapsed from Rome only three years before, until which time Philip II of Spain had been titular King of that country. In the eyes of many Catholics, Mary was the rightful sovereign of the whole of Britain, since Elizabeth was to them, clearly illegitimate: the Pope had never sanctioned the divorce of Catherine of Aragon (although he had offered to allow Henry VIII two wives!), and Catherine was still alive at the time of Elizabeth's birth. Furthermore, the number of Catholics in both England and Scotland was probably not inferior to the number of earnest Protestants. If, therefore, the Roman religion could be restored in Scotland, the return of England to the Papal fold would be likely soon to follow, and this would offset, and perhaps even reverse, the cataclysmic Protestant upheaval in the Spanish Netherlands. Moreover, if Philip II played his cards aright, his son might become

1

King of a united and Catholic Britain: Mary had already made overtures for the hand of Don Carlos.

Mary, then, and the ardent Catholics had much to win by playing such a game, and as has been said, the action of the Protestant Lords in opposing her, even with armed force, and the duplicity of Elizabeth in supporting them, has been justified on the assumption that they believed that religion was at stake. But was there, in fact, any intention on the part of Mary to play such a game? We shall review carefully, as the importance of the subject merits, the details of Mary's religious policy, from which it will become clear that, devout as she undoubtedly was in her personal life, her whole, unchanging policy in religion was one of toleration, an attitude which could only fail at such a period.

Before we examine Mary's own acts in connexion with religion, it may be well to point out that her claim to the throne of England during Elizabeth's life was announced on only one occasion: on the death of Mary Tudor, when Mary Stewart was herself less than 16 years old. The claim was made by the French King, Henry II, Mary's father-in-law, and she herself cannot be considered responsible. She being at that time the wife of the Dauphin Francis, it is easy to imagine that the claim would arouse little response in Spain. Secondly, there is no doubt that the Pope accepted Elizabeth, not only as *de facto*, but also as *de jure*, Queen of England until long after the battle of Carberry, and it was, at least in part, Elizabeth's treatment of Mary which led to the Bull of Excommunication against her. Finally, Philip II never agreed to the marriage of Mary with his son Don Carlos, although negotiations were repeatedly opened on her account.

From France, Mary could hope for nothing: the country was distracted by the opposition of Catherine dei Medici to the house of Guise, which led to the repeated outbreak of civil war. It would seem certain, therefore, that there was not, and never could have been an international cabal for the restoration of the Roman religion in the British Isles, and, had Mary hoped for such a *bouleversement*, the forces for it must have been raised at home. As we shall now see, there is no evidence of any such attempt on her part.

Francis II died on 5th December, 1560. By that date, the Lords of the Congregation were in control of the whole of Scotland. A parliament, which had been agreed at the Treaty of Edinburgh, was held in that city towards the end of January, 1561, but it was clearly *ultra vires*, the treaty not having been ratified by the King and Queen of Scots. On 27th January, the Book of Discipline, the statement of the comprehensive scheme for a new church and for a system of education, was signed in Parliament by a large number of Lords and gentlemen, including the Duke of Châtelherault, leader at that time of the Protestant party, and his son, the Earl of Arran; other signatories were the Earls of Argyll, Glencairn and Rothes, and Mary's illegitimate half-brother the Lord James Stewart, Prior of St.

Andrew's; others signed later. Thus was the Reformed Faith established in Scotland, and although the legality of the proceeding was extremely questionable, we shall see that Mary never interfered with its enactment.

On 24th March, 1561, the following proclamation was made in Edinburgh (342):

"I command and charge in our Sovereign Lady's name, and in name and behalf of the Lords of Secret Council, Provost and Baillies of this burgh, that within 18 hours next hereafter, all priests, monks, friars, canons, nuns and others of the ungodly sects and opinions, which heretofore has enjoyed the privilege and liberty above written, and has not given their repentance of their former iniquities and opinions: as also, all mass-sayers and mass-maintainers, whoremongers, adulterers, and fornicators, dispatch them of this town, freedom, liberty, bounds and suburbs thereof, and that they neither haunt, resort nor frequent, so long as they remain obstinate ...."

The godly were declaring war on the religion of Rome, in Mary's own name, and they were adding insult to injury by bracketing mass-sayers with whoremongers. Later, Mary was to react strongly to a reiteration of this insult, as will presently be seen (page 7).

About this time, Mary received an invitation (596), dated 6th March, to send ambassadors to the Council of Trent. Her reply is lost, but judging by the Pope's rejoinder of 3rd December (597), he was not very well satisfied with it. After an encomium on Mary's constancy in religion, there are three paragraphs of encouragement which show quite clearly that Pius IV thought Mary not likely to do much for the Church without pushing. These paragraphs are as follows:

"But because not he who begins, but he who perseveres unto the end shall be saved, therefore persevere with the utmost constancy in imitating your fore-fathers, those most Christian, Catholic kings, in their tenacity to the Catholic faith. As they ever showed to the Apostolic See due devotion and affection, so did they ever find that See acting towards them as an affectionate kindly mother. If hindrances be thrown in your way, waver not in your resolution. You know that he is not crowned who has not striven lawfully, wherefore conquer every obstacle by valour and greatness of soul. Let no fear of any danger scare you from the defence of the holy faith, the Catholic religion, the honour of God Almighty, which you are contending for while protecting His churches and His clergy. He will guard your life and realm, if you will guard His honour and His priests. Never will He fail His faithful servants. To say nothing of the distant past, did you not see how, a few years since, His Divine Majesty rescued with most mighty hand, from out of dangers great and many, your neighbour, Mary of pious memory, then Queen of England? Although she was destitute of all human aid, He set her free, overthrew her enemies in a way that brought her great glory. She surely did not defend the cause of God timidly, nor hesitate in withstanding the foes of the Catholic religion. As in her case, so in yours, the divine assistance will ever respond to your devotedness.

Our assisstance also, and that of the Holy See, both spiritual and temporal, shall be ready, and not ours only, but that also of all princes and of all our sons, who remain devout and obedient to the See Apostolic.

Whatever authority we have with them shall be yours. We shall undertake the guardianship of your interests, if need arise, not less zealously than if they were our own. Courage, then, most dear daughter in the Lord, be firm and constant! In all your needs assure yourself of our readiness and good offices: count confidently on whatever can be expected from a most affectionate father".

The final paragraph announces the mission of Nicholas de Gouda, whom the Pope is sending to Scotland to encourage Mary to send representatives to the Council of Trent.

To return to the period before Mary's departure from France: on the 14th April, 1561, while on her way towards Joinville, she was overtaken at Vitry by John Lesley, Parson of Oyne, later Bishop of Ross. Lesley had been sent by the Earl of Huntly to seek Mary's return to Scotland as the avowed supporter of the Roman Church; Lesley warned her of the ambition of the Lord James Stewart, impressed upon her the loyalty and Catholicism of Huntly, and the latter's ability to restore the religion by force of arms. Mary, however, would have none of this. It is almost certain that she would have objected to a reopening of civil war and, further, she must have known that Huntly was little more loyal than her other Lords, for he had joined the Congregation during the rebellion against her mother, and had also shared in the spoils of the Church.

On the following day, 15th April, the Lord James Stewart, emissary of the Protestant party, overtook Mary at St. Dizier. He had no difficulty in persuading her that, when she should return to her realm, she should depend upon the Protestant party for her support, and this was, in fact, what she ultimately did.

Sir Nicholas Throckmorton had audience of Mary at Paris on 18th June, 1561, and, on that occasion, she revealed her views on religion succinctly (334): she believed her religion to be the only true one, and nothing would make her change it. She would constrain none of her subjects, but she hoped that Elizabeth would not aid them to constrain her. Mary's every action until Carberry showed that this was to remain her policy, and that, as she had promised Lord James Stewart at St. Dizier, she would tolerate the Reformed Faith in Scotland, provided that she might continue her own faith within her own household.

Soon after this declaration of her opinions, Mary left Paris. She sailed presently from Calais, and arrived at Leith on 19th August, 1561. She had not been long in her new abode when the godly attempted to impose their religion on her. A tumult was raised within the precincts of Holyrood House, when mass was about to be said, on her first Sunday in Scotland (24th August). However, the disturbance was quelled by the Lord James Stewart, and, the following day, proclamation was made at the Mercat Cross (387):

"For so much as the Queen's Majesty has understood the great inconvenience that may come through the division at present standing in this realm, for the difference in matters of religion, that her Majesty is most desirous to see it pacified by a good order, to the honour of God and tranquillity of her realm, and means to take the same by the advice of her Estates as soon as conveniently may be, and that her Majesty's godly resolution therein may be greatly hindered in case any tumult or sedition be raised amongst the lieges if any alteration or innovation be pressed at or attempted before that the order be established. Therefore, for eschewing of the said inconvenience, her Majesty ordains letters to be directed to charge all and sundry her lieges by open Proclamation at the Mercat Cross of Edinburgh, and other places needful, that they and every one of them contain themselves in quietness, keep peace and civil society amongst themselves; and, in the meantime, until the Estates of the Realm may be assembled, and that her Majesty have taken a final order by their advice and public consent, which her Majesty hopes shall be to the contentment of the whole, that none of them take upon hand, privately or openly, to make any alteration or innovation in the state of religion, or attempt anything against the same, which her Majesty found publicly and universally standing at her Majesty's arrival in this Realm, under pain of death. With certification that, if any subject of the Realm shall come in the contrary hereof, he shall be esteemed and held a seditious person and raiser of tumult, and the said pain shall be executed upon him with all rigour, to the example of others. Further, her Majesty, with the advice of the Lords of Secret Council, commands and charges all her lieges that none of them take upon hand to molest or trouble any of her domestic servants or persons whatsoever come forth of France in her Grace's company at this time in word, deed or countenance, for any cause whatsoever, either within her Palace or without, or make any division or invasion upon any of them, under whatsoever colour or pretence, under the said pain of death. Albeit, her Majesty be sufficiently persuaded that her good and loving subjects would do the same, for the reverence they

bear to her person and authority, not withstanding no such commandment were published".

This proclamation was to give a further expression of what Mary had
told Throckmorton in June; it could in no way be construed into a threat
against the Reformed Kirk, and it was a public announcement of the
agreement which had been reached between the Queen and Lord James
Stewart at St. Dizier. Nevertheless, the Earl of Arran gave in a formal
protestation (387) threatening death "against idolators, wherever they
may be apprehended, without favour". This was merely to deny Mary's
authority, spurn the action of the Estates, and call upon mob law. It
would not be surprising if the Queen were exasperated by such open
contumely.

Less than a fortnight later, on 6th September, 1561, Mary chose her
Privy Council. Those chosen were the Duke of Châtelherault, the Earls
Huntly, Argyll, Bothwell, Errol, Marischal, Athol, Morton, Montrose,
Glencairn, the Lords James Stewart and Erskine, the Treasurer (Rich-
ardson), the Secretary (William Maitland, younger of Lethington), the
Clerk Register (Macgill) and the Justice Clerk (Bellenden). Of these,
Huntly, who was Chancellor, was a Roman Catholic, but had already
joined the Lords of the Congregation; Errol and Montrose were also of the
Old Religion, but neither seems to have taken much part in the affairs
of the time. Athol, too, was a papist, but he was a close friend of Maitland.
The privy council thus consisted of four Roman Catholics, of whom one
was a Member of the Congregation, and twelve Protestants. Of the whole
Council, Maitland and Lord James appeared to have most influence with
Mary, and there can be no doubt that, once again, she was showing that
she had no intention of oversetting the religion "which she found publicly
and universally standing" at her arrival in Scotland.

Mary left Edinburgh on a "progress" on 10th or 11th September, 1561.
On the 14th, there was some disturbance which Randolph, the English
resident in Edinburgh, who is not always to be trusted in matters of this
kind, reports thus (25): "On Sunday eight days, viz. the 14th instant, her
Grace's devout chaplains in the Chapel Royal, by the good advice of her
trusty servant Alexander Erskine, would have sung a High Mass. Argyll
and Lord James so disturbed the choir that some, both priests and clerks,
left their places with broken heads and bloody ears. It was sport for some
that beheld it, others shed a tear or two and made no more of it". It has
always been assumed that this took place in Stirling, where the Queen was
on that date, but such a *volte-face* on the part of Lord James, who had
quelled a similar disturbance three weeks before, seems most unlikely. It
is more probable that this outbreak occurred in Edinburgh in the Queen's
absence, and that Lord James Stewart was demonstrating that the mass
would only be tolerated for her and her immediate household, not for her

retainers in her own palace when she was elsewhere. At any rate, Mary appeared to take no notice of the affair.

The Queen had returned to Edinburgh by 2nd October, on which date the town authorities saw fit to renew their proclamation of 24th March, (page 3). The matter is recorded in the register thus (342): "The which day, the Provost, Baillies, Council and whole Deacons, perceiving the priests, monks, friars and others of the wicked rabble of the Antichrist the Pope to resort to this town, in contrary the tenor of the Proclamation made in the contrary; therefore ordains the said proclamation to be proclaimed of new, charging all monks, friars, priests, nuns, adulterers, fornicators and all such filthy persons to remove themselves of this town and bounds thereof within 24 hours, under the pain of carting through the town, burning on the cheek and banishing the same for ever".

Mary was not slow to respond to this insult, but she responded in a much more restrained manner than either Knox or Buchanan states. She merely insisted on the Provost (Archibald Douglas of Kilspindie) and the Baillies being deprived of their offices for one year, as is shown by the town register (343). On Mary's request, Douglas of Kilspindie was restored to the Provostship in the following year.

On 22nd December, 1561, the Queen, with the advice of her Lords of Secret Council and others, passed an Act for the financing of the new Kirk out of the revenues of the old. Certain of the Bishops (including the Archbishop of St. Andrews) voluntarily gave up a portion of the rents of their benefices, and it was decided that (122):

"if the fourth part of the fruits of the whole benefices ecclesiastical within this Realm may be sufficient to sustain the Ministry through the whole Realm, and support the Queen's Majesty to entertain and set forward the common affairs of the country, failing thereof, the third part of the said fruits, or more, until it be found sufficient to the effect foresaid, to be taken up yearly in time coming, until a general order be taken therein: so much thereof to be employed to the Queen's Majesty for entertaining and setting forward of the common affairs of the country, and so much thereof unto the Ministers and sustenation of the Ministry, as may reasonably sustain the same, at the sight and discretion of the Queen's Majesty and Council foresaid: and the excrescence and superplus to be assigned unto the old possessors".

The up-shot was that the Romish clergy retained two-thirds of the rents of their benefices; of the remaining third, half went to the Ministers of the Reformed Kirk, and half to Mary, admittedly for public expenditure. Since, however, there was at that date no distinction between privy and public purses, it appears that Mary was not sufficiently devout to refrain from enriching herself out of the spoils of the Church. The astonishing thing is that the Roman clergy were allowed to retain such a large proportion of their rents.

On 12th January, 1562, Pius IV wrote to Mary a letter which indicates that he had been completely misinformed concerning the state of affairs in Scotland, and, whoever had caused the misunderstanding, Mary did not apparently see fit to correct his Holiness's impression. The first paragraph of the letter refers again to de Gouda, and then it continues (598):

"The news we hear of you is this, that, as soon as you re-entered your realm, you began straightway to take pains to set up anew religion, which had been there cast down, and the Catholic faith, and prepared to retain your people in the unity of the Catholic Church, and in obedience to the Holy See.

The pious zeal and religious solicitude of yours can in no wise be praised enough. Nobly do you prove yourself mindful of your father's blood and of your mother's race. Admirably do you understand wherein lies the secret of the stability and intangibility of kingdoms, to wit, in the worship and fear of Him 'through whom kings reign', in whose hand it lies to give and take crowns and kingdoms".

There is much more in similar strain, and the letter concludes with exhortations for representatives to be sent to the Council of Trent.

On the 31st May, 1562, the Privy Council re-issued the proclamation of 25th August, 1561 (page 5), against any alteration in the state of religion with a forceful addition, which concludes (388):

"Certifying them that, as her Majesty will embrace all her subjects obeying her commandments, so can she not of her honour and duty but hate and punish the contemners and transgressors thereof, especially in this point where the matter concerns the keeping of good order, common peace and mutual society, whereof they may most certainly assure themselves when they shall fail the same, and obtain the reward that is due unto subjects that makes any defection from their Sovereign's obedience".

In the General Assembly of the Church of Scotland, held in Edinburgh at the end of June, 1562, a strongly worded, if not frankly treasonable, "supplication" to the Queen was prepared. The matter is described in full by Knox (118): the requests were for the removal of the Mass ("that idol and bastard service of God") from the Queen and her household, for the "punishment of horrible vices, such as adultery, fornication, open whoredom, blasphemy, contempt of God, of his Word and Sacraments", and, finally and with better reason, for the proper support of the ministers and the kirk, since the half of a "Third" was evidently not proving sufficient. Maitland succeeded in having the Supplication re-drafted in milder terms, much to the annoyance of the Reformer. In the course of the debate, Maitland, as reported by Knox, used these words, "But above all others, that was most offensive that the Queen was accused, as that she would raise up Papists and Papistry again. To put that in the people's head was no less than treason; for oathes durst be made that she never meant such thing". So the influential and Protestant Maitland, who knew more of the Palace secrets than anyone, save perhaps the Lord James Stewart (now Earl of Mar), did not believe that Mary had any intention of trying to restore Scotland to the Papal fold.

Father de Gouda, the Pope's nuncio, arrived in Scotland secretly on 18th June, 1562. It was not, however, until 24th July that he succeeded in obtaining an audience, and even this was conducted in a hole-and-corner manner. De Gouda reported (30th September) to his superior, from which letter are taken the following paragraphs, Nos. 7–10 (599):

"She began by excusing herself for not receiving the Pope's nuncio in another way and with greater honour, which, she said, was owing to the disturbed state of the kingdom. Having read the apostolic brief, she answered that she hoped the Supreme Pontiff would have regard to her ready will, rather than to anything she had actually done since her return, and much wished that his Holiness knew what the troubles were in which she found her kingdom. To save a spark of the old faith, and the germs of future Catholicism, to wit, herself and the others who even now adhered to the orthodox religion, she had been obliged unwillingly and perforce to bear many things, which she would not otherwise have borne. The Pope exhorted her in defending the faith to follow the example of Queen Mary of England, now departed in Christ; but the position, and that of the kingdom and of the nobility of the English Queen were very different from hers. To the request that some of her subjects should be sent to the Council of Trent, her reply was that she would consult her bishops to see how it could be done, but under present circumstances with little hope of success. For herself, she would rather die forthwith than abandon her faith.

Such was her first reply to the main subject of my negotiations and to the papal brief. I noticed her anxiety about the time, and her fear lest the courtiers should come back from the sermon, and so made no further proposals about religion for the moment, but mentioned the subject of the papal letters addressed to the bishops, asking advice, as it were, how these could best be delivered. Would she send for some of them and give the letters to them herself, or should I visit each in turn? She said that my delivering them was out of the question, adding after a moment that it could not be done without causing disturbance, for she feared their delivery would be a sign for a revolution. I said my orders were to deliver them, but she again replied that it was impossible, except perhaps in the case of one bishop. She alluded to the Bishop of Ross, the president of the Council, or of the Parliament, who was then in town. The Queen herself sent her secretary to him the same day, requesting him to confer with me, and his answer may be more conveniently related further on.

My next proposal was to ask her approval for an interview with her brother, the Lord James, Earl of Mar (who albeit illegitimate governs almost everything in the realm), as I wanted to lay before him the object of my embassy, lest he should suspect me of any designs against himself or against any of the great nobles. She said she would enquire whether he would admit me to an interview; but I heard no more of it, and learnt afterwards that it would never have done for me to have met him, they are so prejudiced and embittered against the Pope. I then asked for a safe-conduct or security for such time only as I remained in the kingdom. She answered that she thought no one would do me any injury in public, while, as for the secret attempts of miscreants, she could not hinder them, even by the law. 'If I did give you one', she added, 'I should rather be betraying you, and greater danger would threaten you when known. You are safer unknown. Wherefore do not go abroad, but keep in some secret chamber'

Lastly, I said that I had been anxious to treat with her, had time allowed, on the best terms of succouring her people, now so miserably led astray; but, as it did not permit further discussion, for it was necessary that she should dismiss us before the return of the courtiers, that is, her brother and his followers, from the sermon, I said in brief that the most easy and fitting method was that followed by the emperor and most of the Catholic princes, secular and ecclesiastical, including her uncle, the Cardinal of Lorraine, namely, to establish a college where she could always have pious and learned men at hand, who might instruct in Catholicism and piety both the people and the young, who were the hope of the commonwealth. She replied, in one word, that this might come in due time, but was impracticable just then, and so dismissed us".

It is impossible to read into this account anything other than that de Gouda and the Pope were being put off: Mary could not have been less encouraging without causing an open rupture between herself and the Holy See. De Gouda had been kicking his heels for six weeks, and his presence could not but be known to the Protestants, as in fact it was. When he ultimately was received, it was under a pretended secrecy, and the insecurity of his position was magnified by the Queen, whose safe-conduct could not possibly have increased his danger. That his presence was known is proved by the fact that Mary sent her secretary, who can hardly have been anyone except Maitland, to the Bishop of Ross on his account, that she also agreed to mention him to the Lord James; and, finally, because the affair is reported by Randolph, the English Ambassador, in two letters to Cecil (26th June and 1st August, 1562). In the earlier of these (30), the arrival of the nuncio is mentioned, and the knowledge of it by Randolph is said to be known to the Queen, while, in the second (31), the "secret" meeting is described, although Randolph was ignorant of what was actually said at it.

It is clear that all the Pope's suggestions were negatived, and de Gouda achieved nothing, coming away with the conclusion (600) "Although religion is most dear to her, yet, as I said before, she cannot execute the holy desires of her heart, because she is alone and is well-nigh destitute of human aid".

On the 4th September, 1562, Knox was visiting the West of Scotland and, under his aegis, the 'band of Ayr' was signed by more than 80 people of standing, including the Earl of Glencairn and Lords Cathcart and Ochiltree. The bond was an oath to maintain the Holy Evangel and to assist each other "in all lawful and just actions". It could hardly be considered treasonable in a country in which the Holy Evangel was upheld by law.

About a month before this, Mary left Edinburgh on a progress to the North. Her visit was a long one and culminated in the defeat and death of the Earl of Huntly at Corrichie on 28th October, 1562. The causes which led to the overthrow by Mary of the most powerful Catholic nobleman of her country are very obscure. In spite of his religion, Huntly had agreed to join the Lords of the Congregation in 1560, but his participation had been half-hearted, and he was certainly mistrusted by the Protestants; furthermore, Mary had turned down his offer to restore her to a Catholic realm by force of arms, made to her by Lesley, now Bishop of Ross, at Vitry (page 4): Huntly probably felt that he was mistrusted by both sections of the nobility, and may, whether with good cause or not, have dreaded the arrival of the Queen and her half-brother in his own territory. The final spur seems to have been given to his rebellion by the double refusal of his son, Sir John Gordon, to put himself in ward after a brawl in Edinburgh in which Lord Ogilvie of Airlie was wounded by him. The dispute arose over the ownership of the property of Findlater, which Sir John claimed as his own. On the other hand, the Protestants had, no doubt, good reason for the wish to neutralise the power of this powerful Roman Catholic nobleman, and it is certainly true that the Lord James Stewart wished to exchange his Earldom of Mar for that of Moray, which latter had been vested in the Earl of Huntly since 1549. It may also be noted that Ogilvie of Airlie was a staunch Protestant, so that he would have the sympathy of the Lord James in any dispute with the Gordons. There was also a rumour that Huntly wished to kidnap the Queen and marry her to one of his sons, but there seems to be no evidence of this, and it may well have been Protestant propaganda: if there were any truth in it, Huntly would appear to have gone about this affair in a singularly inefficient manner.

Whatever the cause, the result was definite enough. Huntly's forces were defeated at Corrichie (28th October, 1562) near Aberdeen, and he himself died of apoplexy, immediately after the battle. His son, Sir John Gordon, was executed a few days later, and the Lord James became Earl of Moray. The Chancellorship was given to James Douglas, Earl of Morton, another 'precise Protestant'. Lord George Gordon, the eldest surviving son of the Earl of Huntly, was warded in Dunbar Castle after reprieve from sentence of death: it is relevant to point out in this connexion that he was a Protestant. He was released in August, 1565, during the Chase-about Raid, and re-instated in the lands of his father, as 5th Earl of Huntly; his forfeiture was reversed by Parliament in April, 1567. Whether Mary was acting on her own initiative, which seems unlikely, or not; and whether the action against Huntly was justified, as seems quite possible, or not, the result was to place the Queen still more firmly in the hands of the Lords of the Congregation. Once again, this action, in which she certainly concurred, weakened the chances of a Roman Catholic revival.

The year 1562 came to an end with Knox trying to stir up trouble and Randolph, the English Resident at Edinburgh expressing his contentment with the affairs in Scotland. That Knox's fears were unjustified, he explained in a letter to Cecil (34):

"He (Knox) hath no hope (to use his own terms) that she will ever come to God or do good in the commonwealth; he is so full of mistrust in all her doings, words or sayings, as though he were either of God's privy council, that knew how He had determined of her from the beginning, or that he knew the secrets of her heart so well that neither she did or could have for ever one good thought of God or of His true religion. Of these matters we commune oft; I yield as much as in conscience I may unto him, though we in some things differ in judgment. His fear is that new strangers be brought into this realm. I fear and doubt the same, yet see no likelihood, nor can give any reason why, more than he. Whom she shall marry, I cannot think, nor hear of none that go about her. Those that talk with me of Spain can never make it sink into my head; for the Swede, she says herself, she will not; and the others farther off are like to take great pains for little profit. So that, by marriage, I see not what number shall come to possess this realm again as before, or able to make party against so many confirmed Protestants as are now here. If the Guisians be victorious in France, the matter is more to be doubted, and that we fear most, but God, I trust, hath stirred up such a party against him (the Duke of Guise) that shall pass his power, and no less befall him than in the end God sendeth unto all such bloodthirsty tyrants as he is. As Mr. Knox hath opined unto your honour his fear, so am I bold also to let your honour wit my opinion, both what cause he hath not so deeply to fear, nor so far to mistrust in the goodness of God, but that this woman may in time be called to the knowledge of His truth, or, at the least, that she have not that force to suppress his Evangel here, or to break that amity and concord that is so well begun, and I trust shall take such progress that His glory may be known and the posterity of both the realms rejoice for ever and give Him thanks for the workers of the same".

So Randolph, in the furtherance of his country's policy, was quite ready to support Knox against Mary, although he did not believe that she either would or could overset the Protestant religion.

On 30th and 31st January, 1563, respectively, Mary wrote to the Cardinal of Lorraine and to the Pope. Although she tells his Holiness that she is trying to send representatives to the Council of Trent, it is clear from her letter to the Cardinal, that she is not going to do so. The following analysis of the letters is taken from Papal Negotiations (601):

"To the Cardinal of Lorraine—Cardinal Granville having promised to send you my letters safely, I send you this, together with a letter for the Pope. I beg you to accompany it with assurances of my constancy in the Catholic Faith. The misery of this country grieves me, and I would give my life for it and for my faith if need were. Excuse me to his Holiness if I have failed in my duty to religion, for you know more about my wishes and my power than any other. I also beg you to let me know what is resolved in the Council. From Edinburgh, 30th January, 1563".

"To the Pope—We have always wished to do our duty towards our religion and our country, but the evil times have prevented us. We are now doing our best to make a number of our prelates go to the Council. The Cardinal of Lorraine will explain these points more amply. Edinburgh, 31st January, 1563".

On 18th March, Mary sent a somewhat similar letter (602) excusing her inability to send representatives, addressed to the Council of Trent.

At Easter (11th April, 1563), the Old Religion took steps to assert itself: mass was said publicly in various places, a frank breach of Mary's proclamations of 25th August, 1561, and 31st May, 1562. The situation was not improved by the fact that some of the Lairds, notably in the West part of Scotland, took the law into their own hands and imprisoned the offending priests. Mary was tactless enough to protest to Knox at their action, and received a rebuff which she ought to have expected (585). Forty-nine of the priests were brought to trial at Edinburgh on 19th May, 1563 (167); five were convicted by a jury, and were committed to ward.

The remaining forty-four put themselves in the Queen's will and, of them, thirteen were warded, eight discharged on finding caution not to offend again, and twenty-three were remitted; the Archbishop of St. Andrews was one of those who had put himself in the Queen's will, and was warded in the Castle of Edinburgh. He was released after nine weeks, on finding caution that he should "not contravene the Ordinance and Proclamation made by Her Grace anent the Religion which her Majesty found publicly and universally standing at her arrival within this realm".

It cannot be held that Mary had in any way supported her co-religionists: not only did she mark her approbation of the trial, for (661) she "came to a house not far from the place where the Lords sat in judgment, supped and remained there till all was ended, near unto 8 p.m.", but also no action was taken against those who had illegally enforced the law.

On 18th March, 1564, Mary again issued a Proclamation declaring her determination to support the religion as she found it on her arrival in Scotland (723).

On 15th June, 1564, Pius IV sent Mary the Decrees of the Council of Trent by the hands of a Scotsman, who does not seem to have been sent to Rome by Mary and may well have been a chance visitor (592). The Pope's letter (603) is merely an exhortation to further the cause of the Roman Church. Mary replied on 20th October (416); her letter is very short and is written in French, which, as Mahon points out (557), is unusual in letters to the Pontiff, but which may be accounted for by the letter being in Mary's own hand: her Latin was not good enough for her to compose a letter unaided. If the sentiments in the letter were genuine, there was no reason why her then secretary, the Catholic Riccio, should not have put it into Latin; that he did not, suggests that she had no intention of fulfilling her words, and they were, as Mahon says, "common formulae of devotion". The words in question are "We shall work more and more for the growth and unity of our Mother the Holy Church, and make our subjects obey her, if God by His grace can overcome and destroy the heresies (as I hope), together with the good order and reformation which your Holiness will be able to give".

On 4th December, 1564, Parliament, which had assembled to reverse the forfeiture of the Earl of Lennox, who had recently been allowed to return to Scotland at the request of Queen Elizabeth, passed an act against the mass (724):

> "To be present at its celebration was made punishable by the loss of lands, goods, and even life, if the prince should think fit; nor were any excepted from the full penalties of the statute, except the Queen and her household. This confirmation of a severe and unjust law might, at least, have convinced the more rigid Protestants that Mary remained true to the promise she had made on her first arrival;

while her continued favour to Moray, and the parliamentary sanction given to the late grant of his new earldom, manifested the sincerity of her dealing towards him to whom she committed the chief management of her affairs".

Thus Frazer Tytler, and his opinion has the more weight since he can hardly be described as a partisan of Mary.

In February, 1565, Henry Stewart, Lord Darnley, came to Scotland, and it was soon apparent that he would become Mary's husband. In spite of numerous statements that it was a love match, there is good reason to believe that there was, to say the least, a strong political background in favour of such a marriage, and it had been bruited as a possibility since early 1561. Darnley, son of the Earl of Lennox, was descended from Margaret Tudor, widow of James IV, who had married the Earl of Angus: he thus stood high in line for both the English and Scottish thrones; indeed, after Mary, the next heir to the Scottish throne was either Lennox whom the Hamiltons claimed to be of bastard descent because Angus had been "handfasted" to another woman before he married Queen Margaret, or the Duke of Châtelherault, head of the Hamiltons, whom Lennox claimed to be equally illegitimate, since his father had "put away" his first wife and married Châtelherault's mother during her lifetime. The only possible valid reason for disallowing Mary's claim to the English throne, should Elizabeth die without issue, was that she was born outside the realm, but this objection did not apply to Darnley, whose mother, by a strange chance, and he had both been born in England. Thus Mary, by marrying Darnley, strengthened her claim to be next in succession after Elizabeth, without noticeably weakening her hold on Scotland. The religious aspect of the marriage was equally complicated. Châtelherault and Lennox were both Protestants, but the former was an active member of the Congregation, while the latter had been absent in banishment for treason since 1545. Lady Lennox was a Roman Catholic, and had brought her son up in this faith, which, however, he had not held openly at the court of Queen Elizabeth. After his arrival in Scotland, he wooed the Protestant party and attended the Kirk until he was offended, not surprisingly, by one of Knox's outspoken sermons. He married Mary (29th July, 1565) by Catholic rites, but joined with the Protestants in the murder of Riccio. It is obvious that his religion was like his clothes, to be changed according to the occasion.

On 18th April, 1565, Randolph wrote to Cecil (41) to confirm the rumour that the marriage would take place. It is interesting that, as usual, the religious side of the affair is brought up to bolster the political. He writes,

> "With the Duke (of Châtelherault) I spoke not long since: he takes his house quite overthrown, and with heavy heart beholds the sight of

them that he fears shall be his confusion. He trusted much in the Queen's favour, now he sees his undoing and all his adversaries' fetches tending to that end. The Godly cry out that they are undone— no hope now of the sure establishment of Christ's true religion, but all turning to confusion".

Yet the Protestant laws were still observed. On 23rd April, 1565, Randolph wrote to the Earl of Leicester (42),

"On Palm Sunday there was a priest taken at mass in Edinburgh: he was brought in his vestments to the Market Cross, tied there with a rope 3 hours for 3 several days. The boys of the town cast so many eggs upon him that he hardly escaped with life".

On 1st May, 1565, the Pope replied to Mary's letter of 20th October, but only in terms of weary exhortation (604).

The General Assembly of the Church of Scotland, meeting when the marriage of Mary and Darnley was imminent, saw fit to renew the demand that the Queen should suppress the mass "not only in the subjects, but also in the Queen's Majesty's own person", and that "the sincere Word of God and His true religion now presently received" might be established throughout the whole realm "as well in the Queen's Majesty's own person as in the subjects' " (133). The demand was carried to Mary at Perth by the Earl of Glencairn (725) on 1st July. Hay Fleming castigates Mary for failing to make an immediate reply. He writes (134), "The Queen's Majesty, however, was not disposed to give a prompt assent to such a demand; and by her delay the Protestant Lords felt constrained to convene in Stirling, to consider what they should do, if she endeavoured to over-throw their religion, or gave occasion to Elizabeth to invade Scotland". In fact, a copy of her reply had reached Cecil by 29th July, and we know from Randolph's letter to Cecil of 16th July (651) that she intended to give her response on the 25th; the matter had been "in long consultation, nothing could be resolved upon, and so were they commanded to return upon Sunday next, which is this day 8 days". Mary's reply was sweetly reasonable when it came. She said that she would not leave the religion in which she had been nourished and brought up, as she would thereby wound her own conscience and lose the amity of the King of France and of her other friends; she prayed all her loving subjects that, as she intended to press the conscience of no man, they would not press her to offend her own conscience; that she would establish religion throughout the realm when the three Estates of Parliament were agreed; and that she would "always make them sure that no man shall be troubled for using themselves in religion according to their conscience, so that no man shall have cause to doubt that for religion's sake men's lives or heritages shall be in hazard" (164). This last clause, of course, only referred to Protestants: the Papists were still debarred from following their own rites. She was also willing to hear a disputation on the Scriptures, and even preaching, provided that it was "out of the mouth of such as pleased her Majesty", and she named Erskine of Dun as a suitable man (135).

The convention of the Lords at Stirling was, of course, an act of treason, and was the first overt act of the Chase-about Raid. The leaders were Moray, who feared to lose his power in the event of the Queen's marriage; Argyll, his brother-in-law; and the Duke of Châtelherault, who was not prepared to see his chance of the throne disappear without a struggle. These three, therefore, enhanced their already treasonable act by sending the following letter (346) to Queen Elizabeth, who responded, according to Knox, by sending them £10,000 sterling (120).

"May it please your Majesty. Understanding by your Highness's ambassador, Sir Nicholas Throckmorton, and also by the information of your Majesty's servant, Master Randolph, here resident upon your Majesty's affairs, the good and gracious mind your Majesty with continuance beareth to the maintenance of the Gospel, and us that profess the same in this Realm, has thought expedient to let your Majesty understand that lately we have presented the Queen's Majesty, our Sovereign, certain Articles for establishing of the Evangel in this our native country. Whereof, as the answer is long delayed, so hope we but very slenderly thereof: and herefore, fearing that our earnest suit, joined with the profession of the said religion, shall at length provide unto us no good will of our sovereign, without our meriting; and, seeing it hath pleased God to bless your Majesty with that most honourable title to be under God, Protectrix most special of the professors of the religion, and, having in ourselves experimented most amply your Majesty's gracious liberality in that behalf, can do none other in time of necessity, nor with thankful hearts for the past, and good hope for that shall come, have recourse to your Majesty's accustomed bounty, with the which your Highness embraced us and many others in our and their most extremity; which we remember with thankfulness, and shall while through our lives (which God by your Majesty hath redeemed) shall endure; and, for that cause, would be most sorrowful to see any occasion fall out that might trouble the mutual amity of these two nations, so happily and upon so good ground founded and begun by your Highness' liberality, to your immortal praise. And for this cause has commanded the bearer to declare our good wills and best affection to the preservation thereof to your Majesty, to whom therefore it may please your Majesty, give credit on our behalf as to ourselves. And thus, after our most humble

commendation of our service unto your Majesty, we commit your
Highness to the protection of God. From Stirling, the 18th July, 1565.
Your Majesty's most humble servitors,
James Hamilton.
Ar. Argyll.
James Stewart."

Treason could not well go further. Even if "religion" had been in
danger, and there is absolutely no reason to think that it was, to have
called upon help from a foreign prince was an act which no government
in the world, past or present, could fail to regard as a heinous offence.

As early as 6th July, Argyll had started to gather troops (112), and
Elizabeth sent a strong warning to Mary and encouragement to her rebels
in a letter dated 10th July (46). In order to allay the fears of the people
and to expose the behaviour of the rebellious Lords, Mary issued, on 12th
July, the following proclamation anent religion (393):

"For so much as divers evil-given persons, subjects of this Realm,
irked of the good tranquillity which, since the arrival of our Sovereign
Lady, the Queen's Majesty, within the same, and during her gracious
government, has continued; wickedly and ungodly has pretended by
untrue reports to alienate the hearts and love of the good subjects
from her Highness, and that her Majesty had begun, or intended to
impede, stay, or molest any of them in using of their religion and
conscience freely; which, as indeed it never entered in her Majesty's
mind, so cannot her Highness marvel enough of it, seeing the bruit
spread so far, contrarious to her expectation, and good proof that all
her Highness' lieges has had of her clemency in time bypast; wherefore, and to the effect that none of her Majesty's good subjects, either
by their vain bruits, or by any seditious persons' solicitation, suffer
themselves to be persuaded otherwise nor the very truth is, ordains
letters to be directed to Officers of the Queen's Sheriffs in that part,
charging them to pass to the Mercat Crosses of all burghs of this
Realm and other places needful, and there, by open proclamation,
make publication of this, her Majesty's mind and meaning; certifying
and assuring all her good subjects that, as they, nor none of them, has
hitherto been molested in the quiet using of their religion and conscience, so shall they not be disquieted in that behalf in any time to
come, but, behaving themselves honestly as good subjects, shall find
her Majesty their good Prince, willing to do them justice, and to show
them favour and clemency, without innovation or alteration in any
sort".

On the 15th July, a similar proclamation was made, with the addition
that the lieges were called to arms, an act which was overdue, and which
was perhaps stimulated by Elizabeth's letter of 10th July, which would,

probably have arrived in Edinburgh on that day. On 16th and 17th July Mary wrote personal letters to many of her Lords, Barons and gentlemen, repeating the promise of freedom in conscience and religion, and calling them to arms in her protection (47 & 345).

Meanwhile, realising the desperate situation in which she was now placed, and fearing that the forthcoming civil war would be seized on by Elizabeth as the moment for attack, Mary wrote to Philip II for aid (24th July). As Mahon says (558), this letter cannot be regarded as free from equivocation, yet it was obviously impossible for her to tell Philip II that she had confirmed freedom of conscience to all. What she said was (421):

"I have always resisted as much as possible those of a faith contrary to my own, and, in order to have the more means to do so, I am resolved, with the advice of my subjects, to marry the son of the Earl of Lennox. I am assured that your ambassador (in London), who must take part in all this, in order to stop the progress of the new sect, will already have told your Majesty the reasons which have decided me. They wished to force me to renounce going to hear mass; I having been forbidden and having resolved to persist in it until death, have warned your ambassador of all that has happened, assured as I am that, having so great need of your aid and assistance, your Majesty will accord me it to maintain the faith, for the support of which you are arming so many of the forces against the Turks. And, as I can emphasize that there is hardly anything more dangerous to Christianity and more pernicious to the obedience due to princes than that of these new evangelists . . . I beg your Majesty . . . to be good enough to order your ambassador to support the rights which the said Earl of Lennox and I have in England, and order him to declare to the Queen of England that your Majesty will not permit anything to be done to our prejudice".

Mary was in desperate need of foreign assistance, and this could only be obtained on the grounds of religion and by posing as a champion of the Roman Church, an attitude belied by her public acts; nevertheless, her letter is less emphatic than it might have been, and she seems to limit herself to asking for some kind of warning to be sent to Elizabeth from whom she feared an attack.

On 29th July, Mary married Henry, Lord Darnley, recently elevated to the title of Duke of Albany, and, the previous evening, proclaimed by the title of King of Scots. There is no doubt that parliamentary sanction was necessary for the conferring of this dignity, and that the proclamation was illegal; however, almost no one in Scotland raised this particular objection, and Darnley is nearly always referred to as King Henry by contemporary writers. The marriage was solemnized early in the morning by the Dean of Restalrig; the ceremony, which followed the rites of the Roman Church, took place in the Chapel of Holyrood House, Mary according to the custom for widows, being dressed in mourning: Darnley did not attend the mass after the ceremony.

For a full understanding of Mary's attitude to her religion, it is important to appreciate that, although Darnley and she were within the degrees of consanguinity which, by the laws of the Roman Church, made marriage illegal, she did not await the arrival of a dispensation before hurrying through the ceremony. No doubt the circumstances were unusual, with rebellion afoot, but it was a step which no really 'good' Catholic could have taken. She had dispatched the Bishop of Dunblane to Rome with a request for the dispensation at the end of June, 1565, but the document was not signed until 24th September, (592) and can hardly have reached Scotland before the end of November, if so soon.

The course of the Chase-about Raid does not concern us here, save to mention that the rebels were finally driven over the English border early in October, 1565. During the affair, Mary repeated her assurances to the country regarding religion. On 22nd August, 1565, (165) she reminded the lieges that none could pretend ignorance of the fact that she had forbidden any alteration or innovation in religion, but that those who were now rebels were trying to cover their rebellion by persuading the good subjects that she and the King were attempting "the plain subversion of the estate of religion", and, "by such untrue reports to alienate the hearts of the good subjects from the obedience of their Highnesses". A substantially similar proclamation was again made on 13th September (347), and, on 10th December, the same attitude is made clear in a proclamation which Mignet describes thus (577):

" 'Certain rebels', she said, 'the authors of this uproar lately raised up against us, have given the people to understand that the quarrel they have in hand is only religion, thinking with that cloak to cover their ungodly designs, and so to draw after them a large train of ignorant persons, easy to be seduced'. She then declared that, on the contrary, they were actuated only by ambition, and accused them of being as insatiable as they were ungrateful, since, although she had bestowed upon them all kinds of honours and benefits, they had rebelled against her. 'Their ambition', she continued, 'could not be satisfied with heaping riches upon riches, and honour upon honour, unless they retain in their hands us and our whole realm to be led. used and disposed at their pleasure. We must be forced to govern by council, such as it shall please them to appoint us, . . . and what other thing is this, but to dissolve the whole polity, and (in a manner) to invert the very order of nature, to make the prince obey, and subjects command? The like was never demanded by any of our most noble progenitors heretofore, yea, not of Governors and Regents,

When we ourselves were of less age, and at our first returning into this our realm, we had free choice of our council at our pleasure, and, now when we are at our full maturity, shall we be brought back to the state of pupils, and be put under tutelage? This is the quarrel of religion they made you believe they had in hand; this is the quarrel for which they would have you hazard your lands, lives and goods, in the company of a certain number of rebels against your natural prince. To speak in good (plain) language, they would be Kings themselves, or at the least leaving to us the bare name and title, and take to themselves the credit and whole administration of the kingdom'. She concluded by promising her subjects the peaceable possession of their goods, and entire liberty of conscience, and demanded in return their loyal obedience and continued fidelity".

Could any sovereign ever have gone back on such promises so publicly and so frequently renewed?

Before the end of the rebellion, Mary and Darnley again sought aid from Philip II: they were of course aware that the rebels were receiving help from Elizabeth, and it was quite possible that they would be involved in open war with their more powerful neighbour; preparations had been on foot on the English border, for, as Bedford had written to Cecil on 18th August (652) "the Queen's Majesty's (Elizabeth's) pleasure was to have all things in readiness as if it were wars". This move on the part of Mary and Darnley is described thus by Mahon (559):

"It was about this time that Francis Yaxley arrived from Flanders . . . He was a servitor of the Lennox, an ardent plotter in the cause of Rome, and had been appointed secretary, so it is said, to Darnley, who met him with rejoicing. He came secretly at the end of August, 1565, and was despatched again almost immediately on a mission to Philip, to whom he carried letters dated 10th September, from both Mary (402) and her husband. Darnley's letter is not recorded, but in her letter Mary says:

'Your desire to maintain religion, caused me lately (page 19) to seek your favour and aid, foreseeing that which has now happened in our kingdom, tending to the ruin of the Catholics and the establishment of these unhappy errors. My husband and I, in attempting to resist, shall be in danger of losing our crown, and at the same time the rights we have elsewhere, if we do not obtain aid from one who is a great prince of Christendom .. . We have chosen to appeal to you before all others for your counsel, and we count upon your support; for the which purpose we send this English gentleman (Yaxley), Catholic, and 'faithful servitor' of the King and me, with ample credit to explain our situation . . Send him back soon for the matter is urgent .. .'

Looked at dispassionately, this letter might have been so much more vehement that it might almost be called restrained. There is in it no repudiation of her own moderation, the note is of the attempt to overwhelm both freedom and the State. To describe Yaxley as her 'faithful servitor' shows clearly enough that she alone was not behind the pen, for she had never seen him until some ten days previously".

Phillip II responded by sending 20,000 crowns, but the ship in which Yaxley returned was wrecked, he was drowned, and the money fell into the hands of the Earl of Northumberland.

Pope Pius IV died on 9th December, 1565. The new Pope, who took the name of Pius V, sent a letter of exhortation and congratulation to Mary on 10th January, 1566. On 31st January, Mary and Darnley appointed the Bishop of Dunblane as their orator at the Holy See. The Queen wrote (417) that she wished for temporal and spiritual assistance "in order to change the deplorable and unfortunate state of our kingdom. The moment is propitious because our enemies are partly banished and partly placed within our hands . . . . If God and your Holiness, whose cause we maintain, come to our aid, with such assistance we shall overcome all obstacles". Again, the letter is about as restrained as it well could be: although Mary was desperately anxious to obtain financial help.

Randolph, hand-in-glove with the Protestant elements, and not unmindful of the brewing revolution which led to the murder of Riccio (9th March, 1566) wrote to Cecil on 5th February (203):

"The Queen of Scots hath said openly that she will have mass free for all men that will hear it. Her husband, his father, Lord Athol and others now daily resort to it. The Protestants are in great fear and doubt what shall become of them. The wisest so much mislike his state and government that they design nothing more than the return of the Lords (Moray, Argyll and Châtelherault), either to be received in their own rooms, or once again to put all in hazard".

There is no other evidence that Mary was plotting any change in religion. However, Randolph followed this by a letter to Cecil on 7th February, 1566, (653) in which he raises the question of a Catholic League:

"There was a band lately devised in which the late Pope, the Emperor, the King of Spain, the Duke of Savoy, with divers Princes of Italy, and the Queen Mother (Catherine dei Medici) suspected to be of the same confederacy, to maintain papistry throughout Christendom. This band was sent out of France by Thornton and is subscribed by this queen, the copy whereof remaining with her, and the principal to be returned very shortly, as I hear, by Mr. Stephen Wilson, a fit minister for such devilish devices; if the copy hereof can be gotten, it shall be sent as conveniently I may".

The Earl of Bedford, writing also from Berwick a week later, is less assured on this subject (654),

"There is a league concluded between the King of Spain, the Duke of Savoy and divers other papist Princes for the overthrow of religion, as you shall hear more by other, which is come to this queen's hand, but not yet confirmed".

The whole idea of a Catholic League as described never has been confirmed, and no record of any such league is to be found in any collection of diplomatic documents: there was no substance in the report of either Randolph or Bedford (590), and we hear no more of the matter in subsequent letters.

There followed the next great rebellion of Mary's reign: the murder of her secretary, David Riccio, which took place on 9th March, 1566, and, although it masqueraded somewhat half-heartedly as a religious move, and opportunity was taken to murder one Roman Catholic priest, John Black, this was obviously a purely political *coup d'état*. The blow, however, miscarried, and Mary almost miraculously recovered her ascendancy, mainly by her clear-headedness, but also with the aid of the Earl of Bothwell and a few other loyal subjects. We shall deal later (page 26) with Darnley's part in this affair, and the subsequent and very natural estrangement between him and his wife.

As soon as the Pope heard of the murder, and of Mary's triumphant return to Edinburgh (18th March, 1566), he hastened to write to her a letter of congratulation, dated 12th May, 1566, (605) which is noteworthy mainly for the fact that he attributes the whole rebellion to the machinations of Elizabeth, and perhaps he was not wholly wrong: whether or not the device was of English origin, it was certainly nurtured in England, and could have been prevented by a timely warning from thence, for Cecil, at least, knew of the rising and the intended murder well before the blow fell. De Silva, the Spanish Ambassador in London, writing to Philip II on 6th April, 1566, definitely says that Cecil told the Countess of Lennox of the murder the night before it occurred (555).

The Bishop of Dunblane who, as we have seen, had been appointed Orator to the Holy See for Mary, was in Paris when he received his instructions: he reached Rome about 26th April, by which time he was aware of the recent events in Scotland. After his call for assistance, the Pope not only appointed a nuncio, Vincenzo Laureo, newly-made Bishop of Mondovi, and made funds available for Mary's use, but also sent a brief full of fervent zeal and encouragement, which was dated 6th June, 1566 (607). The nuncio, in fact, never got further than Paris, but Mary's attitude to his coming was at first mildly encouraging. She wrote to the Pope on 17th July (606), saying "His (the nuncio's) arrival, and that of the money you have liberally granted, we look forward to with no little longing".

Ultimately, however, Mary refused to accept the nuncio or his money, because she was unwilling to carry out the conditions which went with papal assistance; what those conditions were we learn from letters of the nuncio in Paris to the Cardinal of Alessandria, dated 21st August, (608) and 12th November, 1566 (609). The former, after dealing with the state of affairs in Scotland, goes on, "These difficulties might be obviated if the King of Spain should come, as it is hoped, with a strong force to Flanders, or, as certain persons of weight believe, if justice were executed against six rebels, who were leaders and originators of the late treason against the Queen, and whose deaths would effectually restore peace and obedience in that kingdom". The six are then named as being Moray, Argyll Morton, Maitland, Bellenden, and Macgill. In the second letter, after informing the Cardinal that Mary has made up her mind "with great difficulty" to accept him, after the arrival at her court of Archibald Beaton, bearing 4,000 scudi, which "were not to be employed in any way for any other end except for that of holy religion. The Queen, finding herself in great straits, was advised by the Lords of her Council to get me to come to Scotland in order to avail herself of the rest of these monies". He is of the opinion "that there ought not to be further delay in doing something signal for the service of God in Scotland . . . There seemed to be no more expeditious remedy . . . than the punishment of a few seditious wretches (as I informed the Pope in the seperate leaf of 21st August); the Queen should execute with a brave heart this most just punishment for God's glory".

Mary's refusal to comply with these terms was transmitted to the nuncio by Stephen Wilson, who left Edinburgh on or about 8th November, 1566 (567).

Mary's son, Charles James, later James VI and I, had been born on 19th June, 1566. The christening, which was conducted with the full rites of the Catholic Church, save that the priest was forbidden to spit in the child's mouth, took place on 17th December, 1566: once again, Mary was demonstrating that she was a Catholic, but not completely at one with her Church.

On 23rd December, 1566, Mary took the dubious step of restoring the Archbishop of St. Andrews to his consistorial jurisdiction (430). We have no means of knowing the reason for her action, but it has laid her open to the charge of having already determined to marry Bothwell, for it was before the consistorial court that Bothwell obtained annulment of his marriage to the Lady Jane Gordon. It is, however, just as likely, as will be shown later, that the Queen was considering severing her matrimonial bonds with Darnley, for which she had ample reason. Whatever the cause, Mary soon thought better of her action: the General Assembly of the Church of Scotland petitioned on 27th December (392) for the Lords of Secret Council to stay the appointment, and, on 7th January, 1567, the Queen transferred the nomination of the Commissaries from the Archbishop to the civil Court of Session (372).

After the murder of Darnley (10th February, 1567), the Earl of Bothwell became the leader of the government. In the Parliament, held 16th to 19th April, an act was passed anent religion which declared that "the Queen had attempted nothing contrary the estate of religion which her Majesty found publicly and universally standing at her arrival". The act was so thorough, says Keith (369), that the Parliament held in the following December by the Protestant rebels could devise nothing stronger, and they contented themselves with repeating it.

Mary's last religious act as a Queen Regnant was to marry the Earl of Bothwell, which she did by Protestant rites on 15th May, 1567, the Bishop of Orkney performing the ceremony. Once again, according to the custom for widows, she was married in mourning, as she had been when she had wedded Darnley. It is important to appreciate that, according to the laws of the Roman Church, the marriage of Bothwell to anyone was quite illegal, since his previous wife, the Lady Jane Gordon, was still alive. Furthermore, his marriage had also been annulled on the ground that he and the Lady Jane were within the forbidden degrees of consanguinity and that no dispensation had been obtained. This last was untrue: a dispensation had been obtained, and Mary was aware of it, for she had signed the contract of marriage (699), and that dispensation had been granted by the very Archbishop whose Court now agreed to annul the union. Mary had travelled a long road since the Pope had awarded her the Golden Rose in 1560 (595).

The Pope thought so too. On 2nd July, 1567, the Cardinal-Secretary wrote to the Bishop of Mondavi (623):

"In answer, he (Pius V) commissions me to write in the following manner, to wit, that, whereas his Holiness has never hitherto dissembled about anything, he will not begin to do so now, especially in this all important matter of religion. Wherefore, with regard to the Queen of Scots in particular, it is not his intention to have any further communication with her, unless, indeed, in times to come he shall see some better sign of her life and religion than he has witnessed in the past".

We have reviewed exhaustively the religious acts which Mary carried out while she was Queen-Regnant in Scotland. It cannot be claimed that she was a champion of the Roman faith, and it is clear that she had never any intention of abrogating, or being forced from, the attitude of toleration which she had taken up at St. Dizier in April, 1561. Later, the hardships of imprisonment were to confirm her in the faith; she then re-opened communications with the Pope, became truly devout, and finally died on the scaffold believing herself to be a martyr to her religion.

CHAPTER II

Darnley and the Crown

The behaviour of King Henry, or, as he is more usually known, Lord Darnley, during the year before his death (10th February, 1567) is of paramount importance for the understanding of what did in fact occur at Kirk o'Field. On his arrival in Scotland in February, 1565, he flirted with the Protestant religion, although he was, nominally at least, a Roman Catholic; and when the wedding between the Queen and him took place, he refused to accompany his bride at mass. The Chase-about Raid ended with the rebels (Moray, Argyll and Châtelherault) being chased into England. The murder of Riccio (9th March, 1566) was part of a plot for their return, and, as such, was organised between Morton, who had not joined the rebels, in Scotland, and Moray in England.

There was, however, a second thread in the causation of the *coup d'état.* Darnley had been proclaimed, albeit illegally, King, and he had been joined with Mary in equal authority with herself. This, however, did not satisfy him: he wished to have the Crown Matrimonial bestowed upon him (348). The Crown Matrimonial would not have increased his authority or lessened Mary's position, but it would have carried with it succession to the throne, should Mary die childless.

A Parliament was to be held on 12th March, 1566, and, as the forfeiture of the exiled nobles would certainly be enacted in it, it was imperative that the government should be subverted before the session opened. Darnley was won over to the plot by the promise that the Crown Matrimonial should be his, although it can have been of no value to him, if the Queen, who was six months pregnant, should bear a living child. Mahon (554) says that the murder of Riccio was Darnley's own addition to the plot, and this certainly fits in with Ruthven's account (395). If Darnley himself decided that the murder of Riccio should be carried out in the very presence of the Queen, this fact, taken with the Queen's state of health and the insistance on the Crown Matrimonial would lead one irresistibly to the conclusion that the death of the Queen as a result of a miscarriage

26

was looked for, it being remembered that miscarriage was a very dangerous illness in those days and that doctors were not always scrupulous. Such a slow death would give opportunity for Mary to be 'persuaded' to give the Crown Matrimonial to her husband. For what it is worth, it is interesting that the first news of the affair which reached the Spanish Ambassador in Paris was that Darnley "had murdered his wife, admitted the exiled heretics, and seized the kingdom" (627).

Randolph, too, knew in advance of the intended murder of Riccio, and of the danger to Mary's life, for, on 14th February, 1566, three weeks before the assassination, he wrote to Leicester (743), "I know that there are practices in hand, contrived between the father (Lennox) and the son (Darnley) to come by the crown against her will. I know that, if that takes effect which is intended, David (Riccio), with the consent of the King, shall have his throat cut within these ten days. Many things grievouser and worse than these are brought to my ears, yea, of things intended against her own person". It may be noted that neither Randolph nor Leicester, nor any member of the English government, thought fit to warn Mary of her danger.

In this connexion, it is not without interest that Nau, in the memoirs which he wrote while Mary was a prisoner at Sheffield, tells a highly relevant story (667). Describing the escape to Dunbar which followed the murder of Riccio, he writes:

"As soon as he had cleared the town, the king began to gallop, and Arthur Erskine after him, until they reached the outskirts of Seton. Here some soldiers had been posted on guard by the nobles of the Queen's party, to let them know when she had passed. When the King saw them, he took it into his head that they belonged to the enemy, and, goaded on by the dread which he felt that he might fall into their hands, he spurred on his horse with increased energy. At the same time, he tried to make the Queen's horse go faster by flogging it on the hind-quarters, crying out 'Come on, come on! By God's Blood, they will murder both you and me, if they can catch us'. Worn out by the fatigue which she had already endured and in great suffering, the Queen dreaded a miscarriage, and entreated him to have some regard to her condition. She said she would rather expose herself to any danger than deliberately imperil the life of their child. Hereupon, the King put himself into a fury. 'Come on!' said he, 'in God's name, come on! If this baby dies, we can have more'."

Was Darnley really such a coward? Shallow and fickle, yes, but not necessarily a poltroon. Judging by the stakes for which he was soon to play, and the risks which he ran in breaking faith with the rebellious Lords, he must have had some courage. It is at least possible that, in spite of the collapse of his plot with the Lords, he saw once again a chance for him to come to the throne, and played the coward deliberately in order to cause the miscarriage which the murder of Riccio had failed to bring about.

On the 18th March, Mary entered Edinburgh in triumph, and the murderers of Riccio scattered like chaff before the wind. On the following day, Morton, Ruthven and 67 others were summoned to appear before the Council on pain of outlawry (139), while, on the 20th, Darnley published a solemn declaration at the Mercat Cross, denying all knowledge of or complicity in the Riccio conspiracy, merely owning that he had consented to the return of Moray without Mary's knowledge (138). According to Mary (403), he went through this deplorable piece of hypocrisy at his own desire.

At this juncture, Lord Gordon, who had been released from Dunbar Castle and created Earl of Huntly during the Chase-about Raid, was invested as Chancellor in place or Morton (349).

Randolph reported to Cecil on 21st March (50):

"The Queen, to be revenged on the Lords who slew David, is content to remit to the former Lords (i.e. the Chase-about Rebels) with whom she was so grievously offended, all they had done. Who, seeing this offer, were all content to leave the other lords that were the occasion of their return, and took several appointment as they could get it—the first being Glencairn, next Rothes and Argyll—and so every one after other, saving Moray, with Pitarrow and Grange, who, standing on their honours and promise, will not leave the others. So the lords of this last attempt, viz. Morton, Ruthven, Lindsay and (Maitland), seeing these men fall away in whom they had trusted so much, and ventured themselves so far, found it best to save themselves in time, and, on Sunday last (17th March), all four went their ways: Morton to the West Border, Ruthven through Teviotdale to Wark and to this town (Berwick) yesterday—Lindsay to Fife, (Maitland) to Athol to be saved by my lord there, or purchase his pardon of the Queen—which is thought will be as hard as may be, so he is looked for shortly here, if he can escape. Besides these principal takers in hand, there are also the Laird of Ormiston; Hawton, his son-in-law; Calder, his nephew; Brimston; Whittingham; Andrew Ker of Fawdonside, Justice-Clerk's brother; George Douglas (Darnley's bastard uncle) and others. Divers of Edinburgh, so I judge as many like to take hurt as were in the former action. Andrew Ker has come here with Ruthven and his son. On Monday last (18th March), the Queen returned to Edinburgh—in her company were Bothwell, Huntly, Marischal, Home and Seton, with all the men they could bring. Where she was wont to be carried in a chair by four of her guard, she is yet able to ride on a horse, though by her own account, within six weeks of her time. She lodges not in the Abbey

(Holyrood House), but a house in the High Street. Her husband has disclosed all he knew of any man, and yet hath given his hand and subscribed divers bonds and writings, testifying that to be his own deed, and done by his command. It is said he gave him (Riccio) one blow himself, and, to signify the deed was his, his dagger was left standing in the body. Their mind was to have hanged him (Riccio), but because business arose in the court between the Earl Bothwell and such as were appointed to keep the house, they went the next way to work with him. How Moray stands, we know not as yet: he went to meet Argyll at Linlithgow, and both, we hear, are come to the Queen. The Lords of this last attempt have written to him no longer to forbear for their cause to agree with the Queen, and seeing that the other have left both them and him, that he do not further endanger himself for their cause. Lennox remains sick at Dunbar, much offended with his son".

The same day, Bedford wrote similarly to Cecil (735), and added, "Their king remaineth utter enemy to those Lords now abroad, notwithstanding his former doings with them".

It was about this time that news arrived that Yaxley, who had been sent on a mission to Philip II, and had returned with a large sum of money, had been drowned. It will be recalled (page 21) that he had carried a letter from Mary to Philip, and another, which has been lost, from Darnley to the King of Spain. The King replied in a letter to Darnley, in which he expressed his affection to Lennox, and his hopes that the marriage of Darnley to the Queen would further religion (579).

Whether or not by Darnley's own desire, for he seems to have been given to moods of sulkiness, Mary adopted, at about this time, a new form of signing documents, to some of which she affixed her own name with the word "fiat" after it, omitting Darnley's signature, as in her grant to Hugh Lauder of 26th March, 1566. The practice was not, however, invariable, says Hume (335), since many documents after this period bear both Mary's and her consort's signatures: that of the Queen first, and usually in similar ink to the body of the document, that of Darnley frequently in different ink, and evidently signed on a subsequent occasion.

Meanwhile, active steps were taken against the traitors. Morton and several others were outlawed on 29th March, and Ruthven and others on 2nd April (171). Both the Lords in question were in England, where Ruthven died about six weeks later. Four persons, Thomas Scott of Cambusmichael, and three others, were convicted of treason for their part, and were condemned to death. Scott and a man called Yair were hanged, but the other two were spared "at the intercession of the Earl of Bothwell" (587). Various other persons had to find surety for their good behaviour.

On the 4th April, 1566, Randolph wrote to Cecil (53). After mentioning some of the trials for treason which had been taking place, he continues:

"The King of all others is in worst case, for the Queen has no good opinion of his attempting anything against her will, nor the people, that he hath denied so manifest a matter being proved to be done by his commandment, and now himself to be the accuser and pursuer of them that did as he willed them. Scott that was executed, and Murray that was arraigned yesterday were both accused by him; and it is written to me for certain by one that spoke with the Queen last Monday (1st April), that she is determined the house of Lennox shall be as poor as ever it was. The Earl (Lennox) continues sick, sore troubled in mind, and lies in the Abbey (Holyrood House). His son has been once with him, and he once with the Queen in the Castle. She has now seen all the covenants and bonds that passed between the King and the lords, and finds that his declaration before her and the Council of his innocency of the death of David was false, and is grievously offended that, by their means, he should seek the Crown Matrimonial".

The bonds which Mary had seen (396), one of which was signed by Darnley, and the other by Moray, Argyll, Glencairn, Rothes, Lords Boyd and Ochiltree and others, exposed the whole treason, and Mary could no longer give any trust to her husband; many a Queen would have dealt severely with her consort for such an offence, and Darnley was lucky to find himself merely in disgrace. One wonders whether she had just seen the bonds on that day, 26th March, on which she omitted Darnley's name from the grant to Hugh Lauder, and on which she also retired to Edinburgh Castle (52), to remain there until after the birth of her son (19th June, 1566).

Rumours of Darnley's dislike of Bothwell reached Drury about now (307), and he reported that "the displeasure abates not between the King and the Queen, but rather increases, insomuch that Darnley had with thirteen or fourteen horse ridden towards Stirling with the purpose of renewing the conspiracy with Argyll and Moray". This had occurred on Good Friday, 12th April, when the two lords were on their way to Edinburgh to obtain reconciliation with the Queen, which was duly accorded them, for they took their seat at the Council board on 29th April, 1566 (172). Darnley's meeting with Argyll and Moray was frustrated, because the Queen, says Hay Fleming, sent to warn them against dealing with him (140), but they were hardly likely to need the warning, seeing how Darnley had betrayed them.

By 21st April, the day on which Argyll and Moray arrived in Edinburgh, both Mary and Darnley were lodged in the Castle (196), but the King was very much in disgrace. Randolph, who had been at Berwick ever since he fell out of favour shortly before the Riccio affair, writes to Cecil on 25th April, 1566 (54):

"Moray, Argyll and Glencairn are come to court. I hear his credit shall be good. The Queen wills that all controversies shall be taken up, in special that between Moray and Bothwell. Argyll and Athol are almost agreed . . . There is continued speech of the discord between the Queen and her husband—so far, and it is commonly said and believed of himself, that Mr. James Thornton is gone to Rome to sue for a divorce (sic) between them. It is very certain that Mauvissière (the French Ambassador, who had arrived at Easter) has not spoken with him these three days. He is neither accompanied nor looked upon of any noble men, attended by certain of his own servants and six or eight of the guard, at liberty to do and go where and what he will. There is yet no great hope of quietness among them".

That Mary was unhappy and worried at this time is shown in that, according to Maitland, she wished to withdraw permanently to France, but the truth of the matter was reported by Mauvissière: that she hoped to take a three month holiday in France after her confinement (726 & 504). It is not surprising that her thoughts should have turned to the country in which she had been brought up, after all her tribulations, but it also shows that her mind was not taken up with thoughts of revenge against the husband who had wronged her so cruelly. On 6th May, 1566, Darnley wrote to Catherine dei Medici (662), and also to the King of France, Charles IX (55), thanking them for their letters and protesting his innocence of the murder of Riccio, saying "I have been much grieved to perceive how wrongfully common fame would make me chargeable with such a horrible crime". But Darnley's propaganda could have little effect on the Protestant Lords, and Randolph on 13th May (56) says, "They have such a misliking of their king as never was more of man".

About this time, there arose a rumour that Darnley was intending to leave the country (727): this story was reported by Foster at Berwick to Cecil on 16th May. It would not have been surprising that he should have desired to leave the neighbourhood of the men whom he had betrayed, but there was probably a much deeper reason which will become apparent as the tale unfolds, for the story of his determination to go to Flanders is repeated from time to time and is, finally, a theme of one of the Casket Letters (page 151). Thus, on 24th May, Morton at Newcastle writes to Bedford (57), "The King is minded to depart to Flanders and such other places as he thinks will best serve for his purpose to complain upon the Queen our Mistress, for the evil handling and entreatment that the Queen makes him". Naturally, Darnley was not entirely without support in such a factious country as Scotland, and Mahon (541) shows that there are indications that Sir James Balfour was hand-in-glove with him at this time.

Shortly before the birth of her son, Mary made a will, which has unfortunately failed to survive. It would have been a valuable indication of her feelings towards her husband and her nobles. Fortunately, we have something nearly as good; an inventory of her jewels on which she has scribbled instructions for their disposal, should she die (640). Many of the jewels are bequeathed to members of her mother's family, and others are left to the crown. Moray, his wife and daughter; her half-sister, the Countess of Argyll; Lady Huntly, Lady Seton, her nephew Francis (later 5th Earl of Bothwell—he was the son of Mary's bastard half-brother, Lord John Stewart, and Bothwell's sister); the four Maries and others were remembered. Bothwell was to receive one bequest (a table-diamond enamelled black). Darnley, however, was to be given five items (or, possibly, eleven); in any case, more than anyone else. Opposite one item, a diamond ring enamelled red, she had written, "C'est celui de quoy ie fus espousee. Au Roy qui la me donne" (sic). At the bottom, she had written a note to the effect that all the bequests were to be cancelled should her child live, in which case he was to inherit all. Two things are obvious from this inventory: that Mary still retained some affection for the husband who had treated her so badly, and that she had no exaggerated fondness at that time for the Earl of Bothwell. It may be recalled that Lennox was later to claim that Mary's infatuation for Bothwell had arisen at this very time, a statement which was absurd, since Bothwell was not permitted to lodge in the Castle during the time when the Queen had retired thither (504).

On the 19th June, 1566, Mary successfully gave birth to her son. On the same day, Darnley wrote to Mary's uncle, the Cardinal of Guise (687), "Sir My Uncle, having so favourable an opportunity of writing to you by this gentleman, who is on the point of setting off, I would not omit to inform you that the queen my wife has just been delivered of a son, which circumstance, I am sure, will not cause you less joy than ourselves". There is no indication here that Darnley had any doubt as to the paternity of the child, who must have been conceived about the middle of September, during the height of the Chase-about Raid, probably while they were at St. Andrews and Dundee together.

But Darnley had other reasons for rejoicing, for, on or about that date, Yaxley's servant, Henry Gwynne, joined him in Edinburgh. Now, Philip's reply to Darnley had not been sent with Yaxley who had been drowned, but had reached de Silva, the Spanish Ambassador in London, in January, 1566 (560). Presumably because of the state of affairs in Scotland, de Silva retained the letter, and it was not until now that it came to Darnley's hand. It is a legitimate conclusion that, with the encouraging letter to Darnley, quoted by Mignet (580), there was some very special message for Darnley's ear alone, especially since de Silva's excuse, that no safe messenger was available until then, was palpably false: Thornton had passed through London at the end of January, and he would have been an ideal messenger, if what was to be sent was to be given to both the King and the Queen, and there had been other and later messengers of equal integrity. Gwynne, who was one of Darnley's English retainers and who had been with Yaxley in Spain, had returned to Scotland via Flanders, and would, of course, be able to tell Darnley all that Yaxley would have had to say. No wonder the King was jubilant.

On 24th June, Killigrew, Elizabeth's ambassador who had been sent to Edinburgh to congratulate Mary on the birth of her son and heir, when writing to Cecil (60), gives us an interesting account of the factions in the country,

"I find here an uncertain and disquiet sort of men—especially the nobility divided in factions whereof I will write more again. Argyll Moray, Mar and Athol, at present at Court, be linked together, and Huntly and Bothwell with their friends on the other side. Bothwell and the Master of Maxwell are both on the borders, bearing the Queen in hand that there is a practice to bring in Morton during her child-bed: but the truth is that Bothwell would not gladly be in the danger of the four above-named that lie in the Castle. Yet it is thought and said that his credit with the Queen is more than all the rest together. The Queen's husband lies also in the Castle, but his father in the town. Methinks, for all the young prince, there is small amount made of them . . . Grange is gone home to his house, and (Maitland), being ready for Flanders, and warned that Bothwell (Admiral of Scotland) laid wait for him at sea, has gone into Argyll with little hope to return to court. Balfour's credit decays, and the Bishop of Ross, called Mr. John Lesley, manages all her affairs of state."

When one remembers the respective parts played by Moray, Argyll, and Athol on the one hand, and Bothwell on the other, both in the Chase-about Raid and in the Riccio affair, it is not surprising that "his credit with the Queen is more than all the rest together".

It should be remembered that, while affairs were in this state of unstable equilibrium in Scotland, the rebellion in the Spanish Netherlands was in full swing. Oppression was the key-note of Philip's policy, and his armies there had been reinforced. It seems to have been his intention to go in person to Flanders at the head of a large army and take order with his offending subjects. Thus Alva, presently to become the Spanish Governor of the Netherlands, wrote to Philip II on 29th June, 1566 (720), "Your Majesty being in Flanders could more easily encompass that which would further her (Mary's) interests". Whatever it was that was to be done, it was all to be kept profoundly secret from Mary's uncles and the Queen Mother (Catherine dei Medici).

This letter must be read in conjunction with another of the same date from de Silva in London to Philip II (563), in which he mentions that the

English ambassador in Paris had expressed surprise at Darnley's friendship with Alava, the Spanish Ambassador in Paris. This 'friendship' must not be taken too literally, for, as Mahon shows, Darnley had never met Alava.

In his letter of 24th June, 1566, to Cecil which we have quoted above (59), Killigrew mentioned that Gwynne had lately arrived with letters and tokens out of Flanders, and also that a man called Rogers was "in secret" in Edinburgh. On 5th July, 1566, this same Rogers, then at Oxford, wrote a remarkable letter to Cecil (61):

> "One Master Poule (Paul?) that has been at sea before, which Poule and divers gentlemen in his company are looked for shortly in Scotland, offering to serve the King (Darnley) at their own charges. The King said this before twenty gentlemen, that he was not so ill-loved in England, but that forty gentlemen there would so serve him, and more soon after conveyance of my Lady's (the Countess of Lennox's) letters . . . . One Martin Dare (Dacre?) which hath been a captain at Scilly, keeps Poule company. There are in the North that practice with him to take Scarborough (where there was an important castle), and have all the North at his command. Gentlemen of the West Country have sent him the map of Scilly, which is an island in the sea; and the King looking at it saw some ordnance (cannon) in it, and said he took possession of his own; and naming a place of his father's, said he would have them thither . . . . I have learned all this at the Standens' hands (servants to Darnley) who, knowing I am an offender of the laws, professed great friendship".

Rogers reiterated and amplified this story at a later date (16th January, 1567) (66).

From this combination of events we see a certain pattern taking shape. Bothwell has most credit, but the other Lords are in a fair way to regain theirs: they are lodged in the Castle with their Queen, and Maitland was soon restored to favour. There is friction between Bothwell and Huntly on the one hand and Moray and the Lords of the Congregation on the other. Perhaps the latter are plotting for the restoration of Morton, of which Bothwell evidently disapproves. Darnley is in disgrace and Sir James Balfour with him, but he is evidently in correspondence with Philip II, a correspondence to which Mary is not admitted, concerning a secret which must not come to the ears of her uncles. Philip II has long been expected to send his forces to the Netherlands, and if he were there, he could do something for Mary—or for her husband. Darnley has been considering retiring to Flanders; he is claiming the royal cannon of England as his own, on account of his royal descent; he is trying to raise a faction on his own behalf in England; and he is contemplating the seizure of Scarborough directly opposite Flanders, and of the Scilly Isles, a convenient outpost on the route from Spain to Scotland and Ireland, in which latter country, O'Neill is causing trouble, much to Darnley's content and with his assistance (62). There can be no doubt that the man who had formerly planned his wife's death and his own succession to the Scottish throne with the aid of the Protestants, was now plotting to place himself on the English throne with the assistance of the Catholic Philip II. What his attitude was to the Scottish throne and the wife who was his sovereign will become clear in the sequel.

At this very time, Randolph was saying that "the Queen does everything in her power to oblige Darnley, but cannot prevail on him to do the least thing to oblige her" (692).

On the 28th July, five and a half weeks after the birth of her son, Mary paid a visit to the Earl and Countess of Mar at Alloa. Darnley followed her by land, for Mary had gone in a ship, naturally provided by Bothwell as Great Admiral of Scotland. Some disagreement seems to have occurred on Darnley's arrival, and he departed at once to Dumferline (141). Mary remained at Alloa until the end of the month, and returned to Edinburgh on 31st July, but paid another visit to Alloa on 3rd August, when she stayed several days. Darnley's movements at this time cannot be ascertained (350).

Bedford at Berwick, writing to Cecil on 3rd August, 1566, (655) announces the reconciliation of Maitland with the Queen, and two others of the Riccio rebels had "by the Earl of Moray's means gotten their release". Home, Scott of Buccleugh and Ker of Cessford, all borderers, are forming a confederation against Bothwell, and Bedford will do "as much as we may do without breach of amity and as the treaty will in any wise bear . . . and they shall find with favour". Bothwell is now at feud also with the Master of Maxwell, and he "continueth the most hated man of this realm". He goes on, "The Queen and her husband agree after the old manner, or rather worse; she eateth but very seldom with him, but lyeth not nor keepeth no company with him, nor loveth such as love him. He is so far out of her books as at her going from the Castle of Edinburgh (to Alloa) he knew nothing thereof. It cannot for modesty nor with the honour of a Queen be reported what she said of him". He then goes on with a tale of how Sir James Melville had offended her by giving a dog to Darnley, and had said that "she could not trust him who would give any thing to such one as she loved not". Bedford's informant was Grange, a spy in English pay, who was also a prominent member of the Congregation, and this story must be equated with Bedford's report of 9th August (398), that Mauvissière had told him as he passed through Berwick on leaving Scotland, that the Queen and her husband had been together these two nights, and that he has used his efforts to reconcile them. One wonders what on earth that thing could be "which could not for modesty" be told by Bedford: he was not usually squeamish. Anyway, on 13th August, 1566, Darnley obtained a large cash payment from the treasury (353), and the following day, he and his wife went hunting in the Meggatland with

Bothwell, Moray and Mar in attendance. According to Nau (668), Darnley treated the Queen very badly on at least one occasion during this outing, which ended with their return to Edinburgh on 20th August.

Meanwhile, Bedford was reporting (742), "I have heard that there is a device working for the Earl of Bothwell, the particularities whereof I might have heard, but because such dealings like me not, I desire to hear no further thereof". Bedford was even too scrupulous to send a warning to Bothwell, who, unlike Moray and his other enemies of the Congregation, had repulsed attempts to bribe him, and was not on Elizabeth's secret pension list. An "Advertisement out of Scotland" sent, perhaps by Bedford, about 31st August (631) reports a dispute occurring from Darnley's threat to kill Moray, a threat which Mary is said to have reported to the Earl. Darnley apparently apologised, and the affair was smoothed over, but must, if there be any truth in the matter, have left further cause for strife.

About the end of August, the infant James was removed to Stirling Castle and placed under the care of the Earl and Countess of Mar. Presumably, Margaret Beaton, wife of Arthur Forbes of Reres and aunt to one of the Queen's Maries, accompanied the Prince, as she was his nurse. Mary and Darnley went with them, and then hunted for a few days in Glenartney (117). They returned to Stirling, where they arrived on 31st August, and where Darnley received another supply of money (353). There, on 4th September, Maitland dined with the Queen, and the Secretary's reconciliation with her was complete: he was reinstated in his old office (173). Mary returned to Edinburgh on 6th September (197), but Darnley seems to have remained at Stirling.

In Edinburgh, Mary busied herself in organizing her finances for the coming baptism of her son, spending much of her time at the Exchequer; and Buchanan relates a very nasty story of Mary's adultery with Bothwell at this time, Lady Reres acting as procuress. There is no contemporary evidence of this; Buchanan's story, which, he says, is based on a most improbable confession of Mary's to Moray and his mother, was written when the Protestants were doing all in their power to blacken both Mary and Bothwell. Buchanan, as a further proof, relies on the confession of Dalgleish, Bothwell's servant, which is yet upon record, and makes no reference to any such affair.

Mary returned to Stirling on 21st September, where John Beaton arrived from Paris with the first instalment of the Papal subsidy (610). Before her return thither, Mary had reconciled Bothwell and Maitland (63), and, when Mary went back to Edinburgh on 23rd September, Darnley refused to accompany her (564). It was now that he told du Croc, the French Ambassador who had arrived with Beaton, that he intended to leave the kingdom. Lennox visited his son at Stirling on or about 26th September (435). On his return to Glasgow, the Earl announced this intention of Darnley and his own inability to dissuade him from it, in a letter to Mary which she received on 29th September, and laid before the Privy Council (351).

That same evening, Darnley arrived in Edinburgh; he refused to enter the palace where the Lords were, and Mary had to go outside and take him to her room. He spent the night with her, and, when she asked why he had formed the plan to leave the country, he refused to answer and denied that he had any cause for discontent. The following morning, the Lords and du Croc approached Mary and Darnley and "with all humility" asked if he had decided to cross the sea, and, if so, what cause had they given him for discontent. They pointed out the unfortunate consequences which would ensue to the realm, should he absent himself without obvious cause, and offered to comply with any reasonable suggestion. Mary then spoke to him "most graciously" and asked him, since he had refused her request the previous night to open his heart to her in private, at least to declare in this company in what way she had offended him. She had never, she said, done anything to his prejudice, and if there was any cause for his displeasure, he should reveal it without dissimulation. Darnley again denied that he had any cause whatsoever for discontent, refused to give any reason for his intended voyage, took his leave and departed to Peebles. He then sent a letter to Mary in which he reiterated his intention to leave the realm, and the Lords learned that he had a ship in readiness. In this letter, Darnley complained, first that Mary was not giving him full authority and was not honouring him as much as formerly; secondly, that he had no following and all the nobles had abandoned him. Mary, in reply, reminded Darnley that she had at first honoured him and had been rewarded by his leadership in the murder of Riccio, and that, if he had no following it was his own fault. However, she had never accused, but had always excused, him. If the Lords had abandoned him, it was because he had given them cause: if he wished to be loved, he must first make himself lovable, otherwise it would be impossible for her to put the management of affairs into his hands. All these details about the 30th September, 1566, are taken from a letter from the Lords of Secret Council to Catherine dei Medici of 8th October, 1566, (715), which was written at Mary's request.

Mary also wrote to Lennox, saying that Darnley had no cause for discontent, "but his speaking is conditional, so that we can understand nothing of his purpose" (174). From a letter of Robert Melville to the Archbishop of Glasgow, Mary's ambassador in Paris, dated 22nd October, 1566 (354), we learn that Darnley had used his threat to leave the country as a demand for the dismissal of Maitland, Bellenden and Macgill, all strong Protestants; while du Croc, writing to the Archbishop of Glasgow on 13th October (352), after corroborating the events of 26th to 30th September above set out, mentions Darnley's jealousy of certain nobles (Moray, Argyll and Morton presumably). We thus see that Darnley's "black list", as Mahon points out (565), was the same as that of the papal nuncio, referred to in a previous chapter (page 24): the objects of Darnley and the Pope were identical. Taking all these events together, it becomes clear that the letter from Lennox to Mary, which she received on the morning of the 29th September, and which was soon followed by the arrival of her husband, was, in effect, a threat or attempt to blackmail the Queen into acceding to Darnley's request for the dismissal of the Protestant junta.

It seems that Darnley's behaviour caused a considerable flutter in the ministerial dovecote: Moray, Huntly, Bothwell and Argyll apparently signed a bond, or Moray (691) says that they did, to fortify and support each other in all their undertakings against all opponents.

The time for the Justice Eyres to be held at Jedburgh was approaching. Bothwell, in preparation for the assizes, set off to Liddesdale on 6th October, to round up some notorious thieves, perhaps those whom we have previously seen were seeking help from Bedford. On 7th October, he was seriously wounded by Jock Elliott of the Park.

On 7th or 8th October, Mary left Edinburgh for Jedburgh, where she arrived on 9th October, 1566 (197). The assizes were completed on 15th October, and either on that or the subsequent day, Mary, accompanied by Moray, visited Bothwell, who was lying convalescing at Hermitage Castle in Liddesdale, some 18 miles from Jedburgh. Mary returned to Jedburgh the same day, and, on the following day, was taken seriously ill, nearly dying from haemorrhage from a gastric ulcer, a condition often caused and always aggravated by worry.

About this time, du Croc seems to have met the King somewhere between Edinburgh and Glasgow: Darnley shewed clearly enough that he wished the Queen to reopen negotiations with him, but du Croc assured him that this was impossible (690).

Meanwhile, Mary's illness continued. Bothwell was brought in a litter to Jedburgh on 21st October (143), by which time she was somewhat better, but she had a severe relapse on 25th October, and very nearly died. It was not until 28th October, that Darnley visited his wife at Jedburgh, when she had already been ill eleven days. He was not pleased with his reception, which was doubtless cool, and he stayed only one night, leaving for Stirling the following day (176). Events thus bore out what Maitland had written less than a week before to the Archbishop of Glasgow (429):

"The occasion of the queen's sickness, so far as I understand, is caused of thought and displeasure, and I trow by that I could wring further of her own declaration to me, the root of it is the king. For she has done him so great honour without the advice of her friends and contrary to the advice of her subjects, and he on the other part has recompensed her with such ingratitude, and misuses himself so far towards her, that it is a heartbreak for her to think that he should be her husband, and how to be free of him, she sees no outgate .... I see between them no agreement, nor no appearance that they shall agree well thereafter".

Early in November, Mary had recovered sufficiently to make a slow progress along the borders. On 5th November, the day she left Jedburgh and came to Kelso, Mary received a letter, said to be from Darnley, the receipt of which is related in Buchanan's 'Detection' thus, "which, when she had read in the presence of the (Earl of Moray), the Earl of Huntly and the Secretary, she cast a piteous look, and miserably tormenting herself, as if she would have fallen down again into her former sickness, she plainly and expressly protested that, unless she might by some means or other be despatched of the King, she should never have a good day. And if by no other way she could obtain it, rather than she would abide to live in such sorrow, she would slay herself" (562). This later account by Mary's enemy bears all the stamp of truth, but, that the letter really came from her husband, is less certain, for de Brienne, representing Charles IX at the forthcoming baptism, arrived in Edinburgh on 3rd November (566), and a letter might well have been brought by him from, for example, one of her uncles, and it would obviously have been delivered on 5th November.

Up to this time, Mary had been playing with the idea of accepting the nuncio, had had a subsidy from him, and was contemplating demonstrating her faith by celebrating the baptism of her son with full Catholic rites. With the Pope and Spain behind her, in spite of her toleration of the Protestant Lords, she could hold her own in her kingdom. But now, whatever it was that she had learnt from the letter, she at least knew the extent of Darnley's duplicity, and of his intrigues with Philip II and the Pope, and she knew that her husband had told them that she was far from being a champion of the Roman Church. She at once broke off negotiations with the nuncio; her messenger, Stephen Wilson, must have left Edinburgh not later than 8th November, for he had arrived in London by 13th November, on which date, de Silva, the Spanish Ambassador, wrote to Philip II (567) "He (Wilson) has been instructed to tell me that the Queen had heard that her husband had written to your Majesty, the Pope, the King of France and the Cardinal of Lorraine that she was dubious in the faith". It follows that Mary must have reached her decision on or about 5th November, the day on which she received the letter at Kelso. The disintegration of her plans must have been a severe blow to a woman recovering from an illness of which she had almost died but ten days before. Can we wonder if she wished to slay herself?

It is obvious that Darnley, who had plotted to seize the throne of Scotland in March, 1566, was now, eight months later, deep in an intrigue which had as its object the raising of himself to the throne of a United Catholic Kingdom of Britain and that this goal was to be achieved by the destruction of the Protestant Lords and, with them, of the wife who had endeavoured to excuse his former treachery.

Mary continued her progress along the borders, visited Berwick, and finally withdrew to Craigmillar, where she arrived on 20th November, 1566. Here, Darnley visited Mary for a short while, leaving for Stirling on 3rd December (693). Du Croc described the state of affairs in a letter to the Archbishop of Glasgow, dated 2nd December (339),

"The Queen is for the present at Craigmillar, about a league distant from this city (Edinburgh). She is in the hands of the physicians, and, I do assure you, is not at all well: and I do believe the principal part of her disease to consist in a deep grief and sorrow, nor does it seem possible to make her forget the same. Still she repeats these words, 'I could wish to be dead'. You know very well that the injury she has received is exceeding great, and her Majesty will never forget it . . . . To speak my mind freely to you, but I beg you not to disclose what I say in any place that may turn to my prejudice, I do not expect for several reasons any good understanding between them, unless God effectually put to His hand; I shall only name two. The first is, the King will never humble himself as he ought, the other is, the Queen cannot perceive any nobleman speaking with the King, but presently she suspects some contrivance among them".

When we recall what Mary had learnt since she last saw her husband, we can hardly be surprised at her attitude when he came to Craigmillar.

Sometime between 20th November and 5th December, and most probably on the 4th of that month, that is, the day after Darnley's and the day before Mary's departure from Craigmillar, occurred the incident which has led to the belief that a bond for the murder of Darnley was signed at this time. The evidence that such a bond existed rests mainly on the confession of Ormiston (21), made in 1573, in which he said that Bothwell shewed him a paper with four or five signatures, which the Earl said were those of Huntly, Argyll, Maitland and Sir James Balfour. This paper had been drawn up, said Ormiston, "a quarter of a year before the deed was done", i.e. about the beginning of November, so the bond he saw could as well have been the association which Moray spoke of as being signed at the beginning of October, and which we have mentioned above (page 38). But, whether there was such a bond for the murder of Darnley signed at this time, the question of his future place in the realm was certainly discussed. In January, 1569, Mary, then in captivity at Bolton, sent a declaration to Huntly and Argyll, asking them to alter what they found wrong and then to sign and return the declaration. The Earls never received the paper, which was intercepted by Cecil's agents. That part which touches the events at Craigmillar runs thus (248),

"In the year of God 1566 years, in the month of December, or thereby, after her Highness's great and extreme sickness, and returning from Jedburgh, her Grace being in the castle of Craigmillar, accompanied by us above-written (the Earls of Huntly and Argyll), and by the Earls of Bothwell, Moray, and Secretary Lethington (Maitland), the said Earl of Moray and (Maitland) come in the chamber of us, the Earl of Argyll, in the morning, we being in our bed; who, lamenting the banishment of the Earl of Morton, Lords Lindsay and Ruthven, with the rest of their faction, said, that the occasion of the murder of David (Riccio), slain by them in presence of the Queen's Majesty, was for to trouble and impede the parliament; wherein the Earl of Moray and others should have been forfeited and declared rebels. And seeing that the same was chiefly for the welfare of the Earl of Moray, it should be esteemed ingratitude if he and his friends, in reciprocal manner, did not enterprise all that were in their power for relief of the said banished; wherefore they thought, that we, of our part, should have been as desirous thereto as they were.

And we agreeing to the same, to do all that was in us for their relief, providing that the Queen's Majesty should not be offended thereat; on this (Maitland) proposed and said that the nearest and best way to obtain the said Earl of Morton's pardon was to promise to the Queen's Majesty to find a means to make divorcement between her Grace and the King her husband, who had offended her Highness so highly in many ways.

Whereunto, we answering, that we knew not how that might be done, (Maitland) said, the Earl of Moray being ever present, My Lord, care you not thereof. We shall find the mean well enough to make her quit of him, so that ye and my Lord of Huntly will only behold the matter, and not be offended thereat. And then they send to my Lord of Huntly, praying him to come to our chamber.

This is as they dealt with us particularly. Now let us shew what followed after that we were assembled. We, Earl of Huntly, being in the said chamber, the said Earl of Moray and (Maitland) opened the matter likewise to us in manner foresaid, promising, if we would consent to the same, that they should find the mean to restore to us in our own lands and offices, and they to stand good friends unto us, and cause the said Earl of Morton, Ruthven and all the rest of that company, to do the like in time coming. Our answer was, it should not stop by us, that the matter come not to effect, in all might be profitful and honourable both for them and us, and specially where the pleasure, weal and contentment of the Queen's Majesty consisted. And thereon, we four, viz. Earls of Huntly, Argyll, Moray and Secretary (Maitland), passed all to the Earl of Bothwell's chamber, to understand his advice on these things proposed; wherein he gainsaid not more than we. So thereafter, we passed all together towards the Queen's Grace; where (Maitland), after he had remembered her

Majesty of a great number of grievous and intolerable offences, that the King, as he said, ungrateful of the honour received of her Highness, had done to her Grace, and continuing every day from evil to worse, proposed, that, if it pleased her Majesty to pardon the Earl of Morton, Lords Ruthven and Lindsay, with their company, they should find the means with the rest of the nobility, to make divorcement between her Highness and the King, her husband, which should not need her Grace to meddle therewith. To the which, it was necessary, that her Majesty take heed to make resolution therein, as well for her own easement, as well of the realm; for he troubled her Grace and us all; and remaining with her Majesty, would not cease till he did her some further evil turn, when her Highness would be much impeded to put remedy thereto. After these persuasions, and others divers, which the said (Maitland) used, besides these that every one of us shewed particularly to her Majesty to bring her to the said purpose, her Grace answered, that under two conditions, she might understand the same; the one, that the divorcement were made lawfully; the other, that it were not prejudice to her son; otherwise, her Highness would rather endure all torments, and abide the perils that might chance in her Grace's lifetime. The Earl of Bothwell answered that he doubted not but the divorcement might be made without prejudice in any way to my Lord Prince; alleging the example of himself, that he ceased not to succeed to his father's heritage without any difficulty, albeit there was divorce between him and his mother. It was also proposed, that after their divorcement, the King should be him alone in one part of the country, and the Queen's Majesty in another, or else he should retire him in another realm, and hereon her Majesty said, that peradventure he would change opinion, and that it were better that she herself for a time passed into France, abiding till he acknowledged himself. Then (Maitland) taking the speech, said, Madame, fancy ye not; we are here of the principal of your Grace's nobility and council, that shall find the means, that your Majesty shall be quit of him without prejudice of your son. And albeit that my Lord of Moray, here present, be little less scrupulous for a Protestant, nor your Grace is for a papist, I am assured he will look through his fingers thereto, and will behold our doings, saying nothing to the same. The Queen's Majesty answered, I will that you do nothing whereunto any spot may be laid to my honour or conscience, and therefore, I pray you, rather let the matter be in the state it is, abiding till God of His goodness put remedy thereto; that ye, believing to do me service, may possibly turn, to my hurt and displeasure. Madame, said (Maitland), let us guide the matter amongst us, and your Grace shall see nothing but good, and approved by Parliament".

Pasted on the back of this protestation, is a reply to it by the Earl of Moray, dated 19th January, 1569 (249), which is a very equivocating document. He denied that he "was ever present when any purpose was held at Craigmillar in his audience, tending to any unlawful or dishonourable end", or that he ever signed any bond at that place. He had, he confessed, signed a bond with Huntly, Argyll and Bothwell at the beginning of October (mentioned above, pages 38 & 40), which he was forced to do, or the Queen would have shewed him no favour (she had, however, already done so, before the bond was signed), and he had never at any other time, before or after the murder of Darnley, signed any bond whatsoever.

The so-called 'Huntly Protestation', of course, derived from Mary, who was one of the principals in the incident described: Huntly and Argyll never saw it, but, since Mary expected them to be able to sign it, with only minor corrections, as a true and correct record of the events of that day it must be reasonably near the truth.

It will be noticed that there is here no suggestion of any bond between the Earls concerned, but it is nevertheless possible that one was signed after the conversation with Mary had shewn them that she was not averse to being quit of Darnley, provided that it could be done without a spot on her honour, and without illegitimating her son. As a good Catholic, Mary ought never to have considered the possibility of a divorce, but it is possible that the fact that she had been married before the dispensation had been signed by the Pope, could have been twisted into a justification for an annulment. If any bond were signed, it may have been the same as the paper which we read of in the Second Casket Letter, where Darnley speaks of some of her Council asking her to sign a warrant to have him arrested, and killed if he resisted (page 155). It is to be noted that Mary had refused to sign that warrant.

On 5th December, Mary moved to Holyrood, proceeding thence on 10th to Stirling, which she reached on 12th (359 & 198). While at Holyrood, a grant of the Provostry of Kirk o'Field to Robert Balfour, brother of Sir James Balfour, passed under the Privy Seal (527), so that the place in which Darnley was so soon to die was now in the hands of the brother of the man with whom Darnley had plotted for the downfall of Riccio and whose fortunes were so linked with his that his "credit decayed" while the King was in disgrace.

Bedford, Elizabeth's representative at the baptism, arrived at Stirling, and was presented to Mary on 16th December (663). He had brought with him a costly present from Elizabeth as Godmother: it was a golden font weighing 333 oz., valued at more than £1,000 sterling (356); but Bedford had an even better present than that for the Queen of Scots: he had brought nothing less than the offer from Elizabeth to name Mary as her successor to the throne of England.

When, in July, 1560, a treaty (called the Treaty of Edinburgh) had been agreed between the English, the French and the Scottish Protestant Commissioners, one of the articles had been so worded as to imply the perpetual exclusion of Mary and her heirs from the throne of England. Mary had consistently refused to ratify the treaty for this reason, and she had been supported in this by her secretary, Maitland. Bedford's instruction from Elizabeth (357) contained the words,

> "And, as yourself know, how we sent you to France to that Queen, to require the confirmation of the Treaty of Edinburgh, and the same being since deferred, upon account of some words therein prejudicial to the Queen's right and title, before all others after us, our meaning is to require nothing to be confirmed in that Treaty, but that which directly appertains to us and our children, omitting anything in that Treaty that may be prejudicial to her title, as next heir after us and our children: all which may be secured to her by a new treaty betwixt us. And, for her security, she may have from us an engagement that we will never do or suffer anything which may be to the prejudice of her title, and shall declare against any who shall invade the same"

Nothing could be more definite than that; it was a natural and friendly action on the part of the sister Queen, already in her thirties and unmarried, who would naturally wish her cousin to succeed her. But there are two facts which make us look askance at this open-hearted proposal: first, that Elizabeth, neither previously nor subsequently, even to the day of her death, ever did name a successor, and always expressed the greatest repugnance to doing so; and, secondly, that these instructions to Bedford are dated 7th November, 1566. Only two days before that, on 5th November, Elizabeth had uttered an harangue to thirty members of each of the two Houses of Parliament in answer to a petition on this very point, and in the course of her vehement and outspoken remarks, she had said (581), "Your petition is to deal in the limitation of the succession. At this present, it is not convenient; nor never shall be without some peril unto you and certain danger unto me".

What faith, then, can be put in the sincerity of the offer which Bedford was to make? The answer must be "None"; the offer, like the costly present was a blind; it would not have been a bribe, for the gage would never be paid. But, if a blind, a blind for what? Surely, nothing else than so much dust to throw in the eyes of foreign princes. For example, should Mary die by violence in the near future, Elizabeth could point to her actions, and explain that she was on better terms with her "Sister" than she had ever been, and that, who ever might benefit, she was in no way responsible. This is as much as to say that Elizabeth, or Cecil, expected such an event to take place, but no one can imagine for one moment that Elizabeth was in league with Darnley, or the papal nuncio: her intelligence must have been with another party.

On 17th December, the baptism of the baby Prince was celebrated with all pomp at Stirling, the Earl of Bedford with Moray, Huntly and Bothwell standing at the door because of their Protestant rectitude (145). There were many festivities for the assembled nobles: de Brienne represented the King of France, but Moretta, the ambassador of the King of Savoy and representing also the King of Spain, was late, perhaps intentionally (561 & 568). The important absentee, however, was the infant's father; although Darnley was resident in Stirling, he attended neither the baptism nor any of the entertainments, but not, apparently, because he feared being insulted by Elizabeth's ambassador (177).

On 23rd December, 1566, du Croc wrote to the Archbishop of Glasgow, Mary's ambassador in Paris (340),

"The King had still given out that he would depart two days before the Baptism, but when the time came on, he made no sign of removing at all, only he still kept close within his own appartment. The very day of the Baptism, he sent three several times, desiring me either to come and see him, or to appoint him an hour that he might come to me in my lodgings; so that I found myself obliged at last to signify to him that, seeing he was in no good correspondence with the Queen, I had it in charge from the most Christian King (Charles IX) to have no conference with him; and I caused tell him likewise that it would not be very proper for him to come to my lodgings, because there was such a crowd of company there; also, he might know that there were two passages to it, and, if he should enter by the one, I would be constrained to go out by the other. His bad deportment is incurable, nor can there be ever any good expected from him, for several reasons, which I might tell you, were I present with you. I cannot pretend to foretell how all may turn, but I will say that matters cannot subsist long as they are without being accompanied by sundry bad consequences". The Queen, he says, continues pensive and melancholy. "She sent for me yesterday, and I found her laid on the bed weeping sore; and she complained of a grievous pain in her side".

There is an indication in the Second Casket Letter that Darnley and Moray had quarrelled at about this time:

"He schawit, amangis uther purposis, yat he knew weill aneuch that my brother had schawin me yat thing which he had spoken in Striviling, of the quhilk he denyis ye ane half, and abone all, yat ever he came in his chalmer";

which may be translated,

"Darnley told me (Mary), amongst other talk, that he well knew that Moray had told me what he (Darnley) had said at Stirling, of which Darnley denies half, and above all that he went into Moray's bed-room".

As Mahon points out (556), a quarrel arose in Stirling between Moray and Darnley concerning the number of his retainers: the Earl of Lennox had, in fact, appointed certain gentlemen to resort to Stirling, and it would seem that Moray insisted on a reduction in the size of his train.

With this is to be taken the affair of Walker and Highgate, mentioned in the Second Casket Letter, and referred to by Mary in a letter to the Archbishop of Glasgow, dated 20th January, 1567 (406). Walker had told Mary of reports that "the King, by the assistance of some of the nobility, should take the Prince, our son, and crown him; and, being crowned, as his father, should take upon him the government". These events may well have been connected, the more so since Walker's alleged informant was the Town Clerk of Glasgow (436), the Lennox stronghold. The fact that Mary restored the Archbishop of St. Andrews to his Consistorial jurisdiction on 23rd December, could be construed into indicating that Mary, overwhelmed by this last and, to a young mother, most heinous treason, had decided to pave the way for her own divorce. If so, she repented, for, as we have seen, the Archbishop's new powers were transferred to the Reformed Kirk only a fortnight later. Perhaps she had formed a resolution to take a step which must have presented itself to her or to her advisers in view of the menace of the militant Catholic Darnley, not only to herself, but also to her Protestant Privy Council; namely, to arraign her husband for high treason at the forthcoming Parliament, which was to be held in April. That there is no record of such a suggestion being made is strange indeed, for Darnley was undoubtedly committing high treason and the device of an arraignment must have suggested itself to the minds of more than one of her Lords; then indeed, "her Grace would see nothing but good, and approved by Parliament".

If, however, some of those same Lords had already decided on the death of Darnley in such a way as to throw suspicion on the Queen, the absence of any official record of the suggestion could be understood.

Furthermore, there may have been another reason for some of the Lords to dispose of Darnley by some means other than arraignment. The next parliament would be the last before the Queen reached her twenty-fifth birthday, and at it, by the law of the country, Mary could revoke all gifts of crown lands and property made up to that date. Although it was not likely that Moray would be affected by this law, the absent Morton would certainly suffer, and he was the ally of Moray and the others. It might well be to their advantage, therefore, to prevent, somehow or other, the holding of this Parliament, but the question of Darnley was a pressing matter, and would therefore need another approach for its solution.

The 24th December was the culminating day of the troubled period which surrounds the christening of the Prince. On that day, Mary, relenting at last when the entreaties of Bedford were added to those of her

Protestant Lords, pardoned the Earl of Morton and some 76 others, members of the Riccio conspiracy (147): later the same day, she set off for Drymen.

Also on 24th December, Andrew Ker of Fawdonside was pardoned, but his relaxation passed the Privy Seal separately from those of Morton and the others, and it is known that Mary had refused to restore this man who had treated her particularly outrageously at the murder of Riccio, and had then threatened her with a pistol (537). It seems not impossible that Darnley used his royal authority after Mary's departure, before he, too, made his way from Stirling to Glasgow, which he did unostentatiously the same day.

An English ship, perhaps Master Poule's, was waiting for him in the Clyde, but, before his preparations were complete, or before he had finally decided on an irrevocable step, he became ill: he was still only convalescent when he was visited at Glasgow by Mary towards the end of January, 1567, and, having now abandoned the earlier plan of departing to Flanders, he returned with her to Edinburgh, to the house which the Balfours now owned, and there, on 10th February, 1567, at about two o'clock in the morning, he expiated a life of treachery and dishonour, which his ambition and accomplishments seemed to darken rather than to relieve.

CHAPTER III

Bothwell and the Queen

The criminal attachment of Mary to the Earl of Bothwell has always been said, by those who believe in the complicity of the Queen in the murder of Darnley, to have been the mainspring of that affair; and the fact that they were married such a short time (three months) after the events at Kirk o'Field is certainly, on the face of it, a highly suspicious circumstance. It is therefore important to examine the evidence for this attachment, to see what sort of a man Bothwell was, and to try to form a judgment, not merely whether such an intercourse might have occurred, but whether there are sufficient indications to shew that it was probable: for we must make clear at the outset that there is absolutely no immediately contemporary evidence of any such improper intimacy between the Queen and this important nobleman: all the direct evidence makes its appearance after the death of Darnley, and the various ambassadors and spies resident in Scotland make no report of any undue familiarity between these two, who, necessarily, were under the constant supervision of all who were interested in the affairs of the kingdom.

As is well known, Mary, after the defeat at Langside which terminated her short spell of freedom, entered England on 16th May, 1568. She had escaped from Lochleven a fortnight before; after the ten and a half months' captivity which had ensued on the "battle" of Carberry. Until Mary had passed from their keeping into the protection of a foreign power, the Lords of the Congregation had no worries about their position, and they seem to have been content to keep her in captivity, satisfied with her demission of the crown, and unwilling to proceed to sterner measures. It is an open question whether this inactivity was due to the brotherly affection of the Earl of Moray, then Regent, or to a preference for letting a sleeping dog lie: a public trial might have been an awkward affair to handle.

However, as soon as Mary appeared in England, matters took on a different complexion. Warned by Cecil, who wrote to him on 20th May, 1568 (499), Moray immediately communicated with Buchanan, who set about preparing the indictment known as the 'Book of Articles'; for it was obvious that Mary's voice would be heard in England; some sort of inquisition would have to take place, and the one line of defence open to the Lords was to accuse their Queen of tyranny and worse.

Darnley's father, the Earl of Lennox, had withdrawn from Scotland in April of the preceeding year and, as soon as Mary's arrival became known, he, too, prepared an independent series of charges against the Queen (502), but, as Mahon has pointed out ("Mary Queen of Scots"), this set of charges differs in some very material points from that of Buchanan, and in none more than the time and place of the inception of the criminal intercourse of Mary and Bothwell.

According to Lennox, they had become lovers by April, 1566, less than two months before the birth of her child (511). "They (Mary and Darnley) passed to the Castle (26th March, 1566) . . . . She (Mary), forgetting her duty to God and her husband, and setting apart her honour and good name, became addicted and wholly assotted unto the said Bothwell. Not only for lust of the body, but also . . . ." Then he continues, "After her deliverance etc.", thus clearly indicating, for his narration is in chronological sequence, the date of this surrender. Furthermore, while Lennox mentions the visit to Jedburgh for the Justice Eyres, he does not suggest that Mary committed adultery at that place, and he is ignorant of anything occurring at the Exchequer (mid-September, 1566). Indeed, Lennox's evidence of adultery is woefully thin, the more so because, as we have already seen (page 32), Bothwell was not admitted to the Castle of Edinburgh at the relevant time, although Darnley, Moray and Argyll were lodged therein. Thus, while it is extremely improbable that, given the opportunity, any woman in the later stages of pregnancy would accept a lover, it would also appear that the opportunity did not in this case present itself.

Buchanan, on the other hand, places the first act of adultery at the Exchequer House, in mid-September (12), telling a particularly revolting story in which Lady Reres (Margaret Beaton) is made to play the part of Doll Tearsheet. He relies on the confession of Dalgleish, which, he says, "yet remains of record", as indeed it does, and it makes no mention of this incident. Our prosecutor then continues (13),

". . . . when the Queen determined to go to Jedburgh, to the Assizes there to be held about the beginning of October, Bothwell makes his journey into Liddesdale; there behaving himself neither according to the place whereto he was called, nor according to his nobility of race and estimation, he was wounded by a poor thief, that he himself was ready to die, and carried into the castle called the Hermitage, with great uncertainty of his recovery. When news hereof was brought to (Borthwick) to the Queen, she flings away in haste like a mad woman, by great journeys in post, in the sharp time of winter (early October), first to Melrose and then to Jedburgh. There, though she heard sure news of his life, yet her affection, impatient of delay, could not temper itself, but she must needs bewray her outrageous lust, and in an unconvenient time of the year, despising all discommodities of the way and weather, and all danger of thieves, she betook herself head-long (she arrived at Jedburgh 9th October and, on conclusion of the Assizes, visited Hermitage a week later) to her journey, with a com-pany as no man of any honest degree would have adventured his life and his goods among them (her half-brother, the Earl of Moray accompanied her, as we know from a letter of Scrope to Cecil, 23rd October, 1566 (227 & 728)). Thence, she returns to Jedburgh, and with most earnest care and diligence provides and prepares all things to remove Bothwell thither. When he was once brought thither, the company and familiar haunt together was such as was smally agreeing with both their honours. There, whether it was by reason of their nightly and daily travails, dishonourable to themselves, and infamous among the people, or by some secret providence of God, the Queen fell into such a sore and dangerous sickness, that scarcely there remained any hope of her life".

As we have already seen, (page 38) Mary fell ill the day after her visit to Jedburgh (16th or 17th October), and Bothwell did not arrive there until 21st. It is as well to say that, from the letter of Scrope mentioned above, we learn that Mary only stayed two hours at the Hermitage and transacted some important business with Bothwell, who, as her Lieutenant-General of the Marches, was a key-man. It is also important to stress that Maitland and du Croc, the French Ambassador, who were both at Jed-burgh, give not the slightest hint in their letters of this period of any such behaviour, nor does anyone else mention it. Buchanan further alleges acts of impropriety between Mary and Bothwell at Tullibardine, where she went at the end of December, 1566, and again at Seton after the death of Darnley. Once again, it can only be said that no contemporary writer or diarist alleges similar behaviour.

It can be seen by this that the prosecution woefully fails to produce anything approaching proof, and, in a Court of Law, no action for divorce could be won on such evidence: indeed, the case would be completely discredited by the obvious falsehoods on which it depends. However, the Court of History has other conventions than the Courts of Justice, for we must attempt to reach a conclusion, even though direct evidence be lacking or distorted, or if witnesses be perjured; and we must found our judgment on probability and presumption.

James Hepburn, fourth Earl of Bothwell, Hereditary Great Admiral of Scotland, was born almost certainly in 1535 (252). He was thus seven years older than Mary and, at the time of Darnley's death he was about 31. There was therefore no incompatibility in ages between the Queen and him. Bothwell's father, always a turbulent spirit, can have seen little of him, and some of his youth was spent at Spynie, the home of his debauched great uncle, the Bishop of Moray (253), but he was also 'at the schools' in Paris, and apparently returned to Scotland soon after the death of his father in September, 1556 (254). He wrote excellent French in a very good Italianate script, as his "Affaires du Comte de Boduel", written in his captivity in Denmark, reveals, and he was addicted to reading works of military history and strategy (255)—four of his books on this subject have survived; they are well-bound and bear his coat of arms on the boards. Here again, we can see no incompatibility between Mary and the Earl; indeed she, who was virtually a Frenchwoman and who had been brought up in France, must have been pleased when, in her barbarous kingdom, she could discourse of the pleasanter life in the country of which she had once been Queen with one who knew it well.

The Earl was undoubtedly a man of warlike spirit. He distinguished himself in a border raid as early as March, 1558, was thereon given the keeping of the important Castle of Hermitage, by the Queen-Regent, Mary of Lorraine, and, soon after, was promoted Lieutenant of the Borders (256). The Queen-Regent continued to place her trust in this young man, and he seems to have carried out his duties well and faithfully; it is particularly to be noted that, unlike Moray, Châtelherault, Argyll, Maitland, Grange and many other important men, his name appears on none of the lists of "pensioners" of Elizabeth, a fact the more exemplary since his estate was impoverished and his father had been more accommo-dating in the matter of bribes. He did, however, inherit some at least of his father's turbulence, and we find him delivering cartels of defiance on at least three occasions (after the sack of his house of Crichton in 1559, after his trial in April, 1567, and during the affair of Carberry, June, 1567).

Bothwell's first big blow for Mary of Lorraine against her Protestant rebels occurred when, on 31st October, 1559, he ambushed and wounded Cockburn of Ormiston and relieved him of the sum of £1,000 which he had obtained at Berwick for the support of the rebel cause (259). This attack on his co-religionists, for Bothwell was firm in the reformed faith, was never forgiven by them, and, by demonstrating Elizabeth's part in the rising, he also earned the undying hatred of the English government. Bothwell had retired to his Castle of Crichton after his escapade, and the Earl of Arran and Lord James Stewart promptly set out from Edinburgh, where they were engaged in besieging the Queen-Regent in Leith, to revenge themselves: Bothwell escaped with the money, but the Lords contented themselves by sacking the Castle of Crichton. While they were thus engaged, the French sallied from Leith and scored a notable success on the remaining beseigers (114).

Bothwell chose, perhaps rightly, to blame the despoiling of his house on the Earl of Arran, and thus began a feud which was to have considerable repercussions on himself. This feud was set on foot by a cartel of defiance to Arran, issued on 7th November, 1559 (23), to which Arran replied in suitably vigorous terms, and the matter was allowed to rest at that point.

The war dragged on; Mary of Lorraine became ill and was received into the Castle of Edinburgh. Shortly before she died, she sent Bothwell to France to help in raising an army for her defence, and to Denmark, to obtain the assistance of Frederick II in providing a fleet for its transportation to Scotland (97).

Bothwell seems to have gone direct to Denmark: while he was there, Mary of Lorraine died, the Treaty of Edinburgh was agreed (6th July, 1560), and the rebellion was over. The Earl abandoned his mission and went to France, where he was received at Court. Through all these troubles, Bothwell had been a staunch supporter of his benefactress, the Queen-Regent; and her daughter, Mary, must have heard good reports of the young and effectively courageous nobleman. Mary must, therefore, have been prepared to think well of the Earl and to put her trust in him.

Throckmorton, the English Ambassador in Paris, saw fit to warn Elizabeth of Bothwell's intended return to Scotland. Writing on 28th November, 1560, (578) he says, "He is a glorious, rash and hazardous young man, and therefore it were meet his adversaries should both have an eye to him, and also keep him short". Bothwell did return to Scotland for a short time at the end of February, but was back in France by 5th July, 1561 (158), and he almost certainly was one of the company who brought the Queen back to Scotland, arriving at Leith on 19th August, 1561; he was chosen a member of the Privy Council on the following 6th September.

Arrived in Scotland, Bothwell soon shewed his natural turbulence. On 19th December, 1561, a riot between Bothwell, the Lord John Stewart, one of the Queen's bastard half-brothers, and the Marquis d'Elboeuf, the Queen's uncle, on the one side, and the servants of Arran on the other, was narrowly averted by the intervention of Huntly, Argyll and the Lord James Stewart (160). The cause of the uproar was the irruption of Bothwell and the other two noblemen into Cuthbert Ramsay's house, where lived Alison Craig; Knox says (115), "this was done in despite of the Earl of Arran, whose whore the said Alison was suspected to have been". The Lords were reproved by Mary, but, on Christmas Eve, the Hamiltons attempted to carry the feud further, and bloodshed was only just avoided (264). Bothwell was sent to his house of Crichton to ease the tension.

On 11th January, 1562, the Lord John Stewart, Commendator of Coldingham, married Bothwell's sister, Janet; the ceremony, which took place at Crichton, was attended by Mary (195).

Not long after this, Arran began to shew signs of insanity, which was soon to lead to his permanent incapacity. On 21st February, 1561, Randolph writes to Cecil (26) "always as something there was that I found strange in my Lord of Arran, so did I not wonder though other men marked as well as I the same". Again, a week later, speaking of the Hamiltons, he writes (27) "The father (the Duke of Châtelherault) is so unconstant, saving in covetousness and greediness, that in three moments he will take five purposes; his son so drowned in dreams, and so feedeth himself with fantasies, that either men fear that he will fall into some dangerous and incurable sickness, or play one day some made part that will bring himself to mischief". Prophetic words.

About 21st March, 1562, Bothwell was attacked and fired on by Cockburn of Ormiston's son (28). The Earl took the youth prisoner to Borthwick, but "gently enough sent him back again" (116). Soon after this, Bothwell seems to have made overtures to Arran, by letter, according to Randolph (28), through the agency of Knox, according to the Reformer (116). Whatever the means, a reconciliation was brought about, and, on 26th March, the two Earls dined together, and Bothwell then paid a visit to Kinneil, home of Arran's father (117). On the following day, after sermon, Arran arrived at Knox's house and declared that Bothwell had drawn him into a plot to kidnap the Queen, place her in Dumbarton Castle, kill the Earl of Mar (Lord James Stewart, afterwards Earl of Moray), and seize the government. Arran, next, himself withdrew to Kinneil, where he wrote to Mary, and then, letting himself out of a window by means of a rope made from his bed-clothes, he walked to Grange's house in Fife (161). On his arrival there, he was obviously stark mad, "he began to rave and speak strange purposes, as of devils, witches and such-like, fearing that all men about came to kill him" (29). Bothwell immediately repaired to St. Andrews, where the Queen was, and where Arran was already under arrest, "to purge himself, who was also put in ward, being found guilty on his own confession in some points", says Randolph writing to Cecil. The two Earls and Gavin Hamilton, Commendator of Kilwinning, were presently transferred as prisoners to Edinburgh Castle; Arran never recovered from his insanity and was kept in some measure of restraint for the remainder of his life.

It is very difficult to believe that Bothwell would have broached such a plot to the already half-mad Arran on the very day of his reconciliation with him, in spite of Randolph's remark that Bothwell was "found guilty on his own confession in some points". Both Randolph and Mar (Moray) were the Earl's enemies as the former himself confesses (35), and we can well imagine that Moray would seize such an opportunity for placing him in ward, and that Randolph would not put the best construction on his acts. It is to be noted also that, only a few months previously (16th November, 1561), there had been a near-panic at Holyrood on a rumour that Arran was even then marching to seize the Queen (584); in his crazy state, with perhaps some regret for being reconciled with his former enemy, it would be a natural step for him to accuse Bothwell of what was, in fact, his own intention. On the other hand, it is worth remembering that, in the end, Bothwell did kidnap his Queen (24th April, 1567), but this was five years later, when circumstances had greatly altered and when this action, as will be shewn, was probably forced on him to save his own life. This remark is premature, but it is inserted to explain, not to condone, Bothwell's treason at a later date; whether condonation is possible will appear further on in this history (page 198).

Bothwell remained in ward in the Castle of Edinburgh until 28th August 1562, on which date he escaped. Knox hints that Mary connived at his liberation (119), but she was on her northern progress and in the thick of Huntly's rebellion, when she would have had other things to think about. The Earl lingered in Scotland, probably at the Hermitage, until the end of the year, and then set out by sea towards France. His vessel was forced to put in at Holy Island (Lindisfarne) on account of a storm; Bothwell landed and lay low in a village. Here, however, he was discovered and, on 7th January, 1563, he was arrested (265) and presently confined in Tynemouth Castle.

By the middle of the year, Bothwell was released on parole (36), but was not permitted to leave England. Mary eventually asked Elizabeth to allow him to continue his journey into France (39); after some delay, he received a safe-conduct, and reached France at the beginning of November, 1564 (267). In February of the following year, he seems to have been appointed Captain of the French King's Scottish Bodyguard (268), but he apparently relinquished this post, for he had arrived in Scotland by 5th March, 1565 (268). Randolph writes to Cecil on 15th March (40). "The Queen altogether mislikes his home-coming without her licence, and has already sent a sergeant-of-arms to summon him to underlie the law, which, if he refuse to do, he shall be pronounced rebel". Randolph also mentions that the Earl is "charged by Murray (of Purdovis, brother of Murray of Tullibardine and a Lennox supporter) of speaking dishonourable words against this Queen, and threatening my lord of Moray and (Maitland) that he would be the death of both when he returned to Scotland". Whatever the truth of this allegation, Bothwell decided not to stand trial, perhaps wisely, since Moray and Argyll, says Gore-Browne, led 6,000 men into Edinburgh the day before the assize (271). On 2nd May, 1565, Bothwell was "put to the horn" (586): he withdrew to France once again.

With the outbreak of the Chase-about Rebellion, Bothwell received remission for breaking ward from the Castle of Edinburgh, and his outlawry was reversed (698). Mary, whose position was parlous and who needed all the help she could get, released Lord Gordon (Huntly) from Dunbar, and recalled Bothwell, who landed at Eyemouth on 17th September, 1565 (136), in spite of an attempt by the English navy to arrest him (48). Three days later, he was received at Holyrood and created Lieutenant-General of the East, Middle and West Marches (166). The royal army had driven the disintegrating rebel forces over the border by 10th

October (394): Bothwell was left at Dumfries in command of a considerable force, while Mary and Darnley returned to Edinburgh and disbanded the rest of their army (137).

On 24th February, 1566, Bothwell cemented his friendship with Huntly by marrying his sister, Lady Jane Gordon (701); as will later appear (page 189), this was a purely political marriage, neither bride nor groom having much interest in the business. A fortnight later (9th March, 1566), came the murder of Riccio. Bothwell and Huntly, who were in the Palace of Holyrood at the time, escaped that night, but, with the aid of the Dowager Countess of Huntly, they made an unsuccessful effort to rescue the Queen on the following day (273). When Mary did escape (12th March), she was joined by Huntly, Bothwell, Fleming, Seton, and Livingstone (274), and their combined forces were too strong for the rebels; they led her back to Edinburgh in triumph on 18th March, 1566. It may not be amiss to recall that two of the rebels, Mowbray and Harlaw, condemned to death for their part in the Riccio affair, were reprieved at the "intercession of Earl Bothwell" (588).

Randolph (21st March, 1566) (51) says that Bothwell was rewarded with "all that belonged to (Maitland)", who was now in disgrace; but, as we have seen (page 32), the Earl was refused entry to the Castle of Edinburgh (58), whither Mary withdrew on 26th March. Randolph also states that soon afterwards Bothwell was made Keeper of the royal castle of Dunbar (58); by 24th June, Killigrew reports to Cecil (60) "that his credit with the Queen is more than all the rest together". Friction between Moray and Maitland on the one side, and Bothwell on the other continued, but they were ostensibly reconciled by the Queen in September (63). On 7th October, Bothwell was wounded in Liddesdale. He seems to have recovered his health reasonably soon, and we have seen (page 42) the part which he played in the conference at Craigmillar (circa 4th December, 1566). By now, he was certainly in good credit with Mary, for he was appointed by her to receive the ambassadors who came to the christening of Prince James; was, with Moray and Argyll, presented with a suit of clothes (178); and was present at the baptism and the subsequent festivities.

From the above, it is clear that Bothwell's record was by no means a bad one. Apart from his broils with Arran and the extremely doubtful question of a plot with that nobleman to kidnap the Queen, his history is one of useful, even devoted, service to Mary's mother and to herself; it would have been a strange Queen who failed to bear him at least some gratitude.

When, however, we glance, as is necessary, at Bothwell's *affaires du coeur*, we find that his record is far less praiseworthy. We have already noticed that he spent at least part of his youth at Spynie, the home of the Bishop of Moray, his great-uncle. This gentleman had at least ten illegitimate children by different mothers (253), and was hardly the best person to stand *in loco parentis*. However that may be, Bothwell's first recorded entry into the lists of love occurred in 1559, when he was about 24. He apparently fell in love with Janet Beaton, the widow of Scott of Buccleuch, known to history as the Wizard Lady of Branxholm (257): she was 43 at this time, and had had three husbands and seven children. Whether or not the two were betrothed ("handfasted") is not known, but certainly such a union was commonly believed to have been made between them (258). "Handfasting" was considered to be as binding as marriage, and we have already seen that an attachment of this sort on the part of Angus before he married the widow of James IV, was claimed by Châtelherault to illegitimate the Countess of Lennox, and, therefore, Darnley (page 15). Whatever the union, when it came to an end, the lady apparently bore no ill will to her young lover.

A more important liaison was formed by Bothwell when he visited Denmark in 1560, on embassy from Mary of Lorraine. Here again, we are in doubt as to the nature of the union which he formed with Anna Throndssen, but Randolph reported to Cecil (23rd September, 1560) (24) that he was married. The lady in question was the daughter of a Norwegian admiral; she was probably but poorly endowed, for she had a brother and six sisters (260).

When news reached the Earl of the Treaty of Edinburgh and the end of the rebellion, he abandoned his now useless embassy, and departed to France, taking Anna Throndssen with him. He left her in Flanders (261), either because he was short of money or because she was expecting a child. As we have seen, Bothwell left the French Court shortly before the death of Francis II, for his intended departure was notified by Throckmorton on 28th November, 1560 (578), and surprise was expressed that he should have gone to Flanders (263). He did not appear in Scotland until February, so presumably the intervening period was spent with the lady of his choice for the moment.

Whether Anna returned to Scotland with Bothwell in February, or whether she joined him there later is unknown. Her presence in Scotland is absolutely ignored by all the correspondents and diarists, so she must have been kept very much in the shade: perhaps she was installed at the Hermitage or, less likely, obtained some minor court employment. That she was in Scotland, however, is proved by her passport (263 & 266) which is yet recorded in the register of the Privy Council; it is dated 17th February, 1563, at which time Bothwell, having escaped from Edinburgh Castle, was in captivity in England, and his return to Scotland must have seemed very remote. The passport authorises Anna Throndssen to dwell in Scotland, with freedom to leave and return at will, and a specific mention is made of a voyage to Norway. Whether she actually made this journey, and if so, whether she returned to Scotland, is unknown; but the belief that she went to Norway seems to receive support from a letter of Randolph to Cecil of 3rd June, 1563 (36), in which he writes,

"We hear that Bothwell is at liberty upon his faith. I think it the best way to make him a very beggar, stark naked, naught. His substance is consumed there more than ninety days since, saving a Portuguese piece, which he received for a token out of the North, from a gentlewoman, that, if ever she be a widow, shall never be my wife. I advise all my friends to take heed how they lodge such a guest. I beseech your honour, put him where you will, saving in Dover Castle: not for fear of my old mother, but my sister is young and hath many daughters. He has sought to borrow money from his countrymen merchants lately there, but can get none".

This letter clearly shews Randolph's ill-will to the Earl, and the reference to the "token out of the North from a gentle-woman" whom he apparently believes to be Bothwell's wife, could well mean that Anna had in fact reached Norway. Had she gone to her native land in an attempt to raise money for the Earl, and was the token a maravedi, which as Barham says, is worth so little that a shovel-full go to a halfpenny, to indicate her failure in getting supplies? Or was it a signal with a pre-arranged meaning which could only be understood by Bothwell?

As we have seen, Bothwell eventually received permission to continue to France; returning to Scotland without licence, he once again fled to France on receiving the summons for treason, and he remained in exile until he was recalled to assist Mary against the Chase-about rebels. There is a vague rumour that, before his recall, he took "another wife" in France (272), but whether this was a Frenchwoman or whether he had merely been rejoined by Anna is purely speculative.

Returned to Scotland and once again to be numbered as a loyal subject, Bothwell became intimate with Lord Gordon, now Earl of Huntly, who had been released from Dunbar about the time Bothwell had been recalled to Scotland; and this intimacy, which surely depended upon political necessity, both Earls being Protestants in the Marian camp, was soon cemented by the marriage of Bothwell to Huntly's sister, Lady Jane, on 24th February, 1566 (702). The latter was believed to be in love with Alexander Ogilvy of Boyne, whom she married *en troisième noces* (December, 1599) (707), the Earl of Sutherland intervening (December, 1573) (706): Boyne had filled in the interval by being married to Mary Beaton, one of the Queen's Maries (May, 1566) (700).

The marriage of Bothwell and Lady Jane was solemnized according to Protestant rites at the Canongate Church in Edinburgh; Knox says "that the Queen was desirous that the marriage might be made in the Chapel (of Holyrood) with the mass, which the Earl Bothwell would in no wise grant" (401). Because the couple were within the forbidden degrees of consanguinity, a dispensation was granted by the Archbishop of St.

Andrews (711) on 17th February, for Lady Jane was a Roman Catholic. The contract of marriage had been signed on 9th February (712), Mary herself being one of the witnesses.

The honeymoon, if such it can be called, was interrupted by the murder of Riccio on 9th March, 1566. We have already mentioned the part played by Bothwell and Huntly in restoring the Queen's fortunes (page 55). Bothwell, being refused lodging in the Castle of Edinburgh, betook himself and his bride to Crichton about 17th May, 1566. Within a short time, he had committed adultery with a servant, one Bessie Crawford, who was cited as co-respondent in the action for divorce (275) led by the Countess of Bothwell at the end of April, 1567 (703), although the existence of a charter conferring the lands of Nether Hailes and others on his wife, dated 11th June, 1566, (713), is highly suggestive of condonation of the adultery on her part. It is pretty clear from the fore-going and from subsequent events that the Earl and his Countess were not head over heels in love with each other.

Darnley died at Kirk o'Field on 10th February, 1567. The government virtually fell into Bothwell's hands, and it soon became obvious that he would marry the Queen. Drury, writing to Cecil on 29th March, 1567 (103), says, "The judgment of the people is that the Queen will marry Bothwell", but, suspicious as this early intimation is of an affair between Mary and the Earl, it must be remembered that there might well be other causes, and, as will be made clear later (page 198), these were probably very strongly operative. The Earl was an ambitious man and he was in power; the Queen was almost friendless and probably very ill (see Appendix A); most important of all, the enmity of the Lords of the Congregation and of the English to Bothwell made his position, and that of the Queen highly precarious. Marriage to his sovereign would strengthen his hold on the common people, confirm him in government, and definitely turn any opposition into rebellion, thus placing the law on his side.

On 12th April, 1567 (589), Bothwell was tried and acquitted, through failure of the prosecution to present any evidence, of the murder of Darnley. Exactly a week later, he obtained from the assembled Lords, on the occasion known as Ainsley's Supper, a bond promising their assistance and support in his marriage to the Queen (10). Later, the Lords were to claim that they had signed this bond for two, apparently incompatible, reasons, one being that the tavern was surrounded by 200 hackbutters under Bothwell's orders, and the other, that Bothwell produced a warrant, signed by the Queen, authorizing them to sign the bond. It is noteworthy, as to the first reason, that Grange writing to Bedford the following day (75) says that "Bothwell called most of the noblemen to supper, to desire their promise in writing and consent to the Queen's marriage", but says nothing of the hackbutters. As to the second reason, Moray late in 1569, says that he produced the warrant before Elizabeth's commissioners at

York (210), Norfolk, Sussex and Sadler, who also stated that such a document was shewn to them privately by Moray (215). Nevertheless, it is an extraordinary circumstance that, when the Scottish Commissioners proceeded, in December, 1568, to bring proof of Mary's complicity with Bothwell, this warrant, which would indeed have been a trump-card, was not put in evidence. It must therefore be highly doubtful whether the document originally produced at York was genuine.

Two days after "Ainsley's Supper", Mary left Edinburgh (21st April, 1567) to visit her son at Stirling (200). On all previous occasions, she had travelled by way of Linlithgow, breaking her journey for a night at that town, her birth-place, but on this occasion, she may have completed the 36 miles in one day. She left Stirling on 23rd April, spent the night at Linlithgow, and, the following day, was kidnapped by Bothwell at the crossing of the Almond about 6 miles west of Edinburgh (284).

Mary, with Huntly and Maitland, who were in her company, was taken to Dunbar. What happened there is doubtful, but Mary claimed that Bothwell used gentle words, persuasion and, at last, even force to extort a promise of marriage (413), while Grange (104) declares that the "ravishment" (abduction) was with Mary's own consent. On 26th April, 1566, Lady Bothwell, a Roman Catholic, began her suit for divorce against the Earl in the Commissary (Protestant) Court of Edinburgh, on the ground of his adultery with Bessie Crawford; she obtained judgment on 3rd May (703). However, she had been intending the divorce for more than a month, for the first procuratory for her was signed on 20th March (186), and by 30th March she had gained her brother's apparently reluctant consent to the divorce (540).

On 27th April, Bothwell, a Protestant, led a suit for annulment of his marriage with Lady Jane Gordon in the Roman Catholic Consistory Court on the ground of consanguinity. Although a dispensation had been given, the Earl obtained judgment on 7th May (705). Since the consistorial jurisdiction had been taken from the Archbishop early in January, the court must have been an illegal one. Nevertheless, it sufficed of its purpose for, by the Catholic Canon Law, a divorced adulterer was forbidden to marry again during his wife's lifetime: annulment of the marriage removed this obstacle to his further progress.

Bothwell had brought Mary back to Edinburgh on 6th May, and, on the day after he had obtained judgment, a proclamation was issued announcing that the Queen had resolved to marry the Earl (704). That same day, Grange wrote to Moray, who had departed to France early in April, to hold himself in Normandy, ready for a return (444).

The banns of marriage were called on 9th May, not without demur by Craig, a minister who refused to publish them (187). On 12th May, 1567, Mary appeared before the Lords of Session and declared that she was a free agent (9); two days later, the marriage contract was completed and

Bothwell was created Duke of Orkney (151). The marriage was solemnised on the following day, 15th May, by Protestant rites (151), du Croc, the French Ambassador refusing to attend (630), since France was much opposed to Bothwell (375). Already a confederacy had been formed by Mar, Argyll, Morton and Athol against the new Duke; others were to join soon, said Grange in a letter which he wrote to Bedford on this date (375). In this he requested a direct promise of assistance, in default of which the Lords would seek help from the French. This confederacy gathered strength, and soon led to the overthrow of the government.

Meanwhile, Mary does not seem to have been happy with her third husband, although he "openly uses great reverence to the Queen" (107) Du Croc, in his letter to Catherine dei Medici of 18th May, 1567 (716) says, "On Thursday (15th May, her wedding-day), Her Majesty sent for me, when I perceived something strange between her and her husband; she asked me to excuse it, saying that, if I should see her sad, it was because she never wished to rejoice, as she said she never would, desiring nothing but death. Yesterday, being secluded all day with the Earl of Bothwell, she cried out aloud for someone to give her a knife so that she could kill herself".

The confederacy of the nobles opposed to Bothwell was mentioned by Grange as gaining strength: on 28th May, Mary called the lieges to arms, making the excuse that a raid into the borders was afoot (377). The proclamation evidently roused mutterings, for she found it necessary to issue a further one on 1st June, 1567 (378), denying that she had any intention of subverting the laws, and emphasizing her love and care for her son.

Probably on 6th June, Mary and Bothwell attempted to withdraw to Edinburgh Castle, but were refused admittance by Sir James Balfour, who had become Keeper on 8th May (543 & 544). On the following day, they left the capital, Bothwell for the last time, and retired to Borthwick, some 12 miles South of Edinburgh, and there, on the evening of 10th June, the Lords led by Morton, Mar, Home and Lindsay (380) surrounded the castle. Bothwell had already departed to Dunbar before the attack developed, but whether on that day or the previous one is not certain; when his absence became known, the attack was called off, and the confederates returned to Dalkeith, and thence to Edinburgh. Bothwell apparently returned on 11th June and took Mary to Dunbar, while, on the same day, Huntly was received into Edinburgh Castle (121).

The rest is soon told; Mary and Bothwell met the insurgent forces at Carberry on 15th June. After protracted negotiations, Mary gave herself into the hands of the Lords, and Bothwell was allowed to withdraw to Dunbar. As soon as they had got the Queen into their hands, the Lords broke their promise to treat her as their sovereign, and she was imprisoned with indignity in a house in the High Street, whence she was taken to

Lochleven on the night of 16th–17th June (154). The Lords maintained that they took this course because Mary would not agree to divorce Bothwell, and had even written a letter, which they had intercepted, in which she had declared her intention never to abandon him (382). This letter was never produced and it is almost certainly mythical.

Bothwell seems to have left Dunbar about 27th June, 1567 (688). He was outlawed on 17th July (156) and, after a short stay at Spynie, departed to his Dukedom of Orkney. Thither he was followed by Tullibardine and Grange, who sailed with four ships on 19th August, 1567 (190). Bothwell's own small flotilla was dispersed, and the Earl sailed to Norway, arriving on 2nd September at Bergen (286), where he found himself in the hands of Erik Rosenkrantz, Viceroy of Norway and cousin of Anna Throndssen, who promptly filed a claim for the return of monies which she had lent him in 1560. It was the end: a detention in an inn was exchanged for imprisonment in a castle; transferred in turn to Copenhagen, to Malmö and to Dragsholm, the Great Admiral of Scotland had seen the last of freedom: as could be expected of such a turbulent spirit, confinement wore him down, his exertions to obtain his liberty gave place to the ceaseless and aimless motions of insanity, and he died after eleven years, in the country of his first 'wife', and in the prison to which his affair with her had led him. No Greek tragedian could have provided him with a more fitting end.

History records only one illegitimate son of James Hepburn, Earl of Bothwell, but we know nothing of him, other than that his name was William and that he became heir to the Earl's mother. We have no indication of the date of his birth or the name of his mother. For one who was so ready for the adventures of love, Bothwell seems to have been singularly unprolific.

So much, then, for the dominant and forceful Earl. What of the other partner in a possible and passionate love affair, such as is suggested in the Book of Articles and, more particularly, in the Casket Letters? First of all, it is fair to say that there are some symptoms in Mary's medical history (see Appendix A) which are at least compatible with a degree of hysteria, and such a diagnosis would suggest that she was not a highly sexed woman. This is borne out by at least some aspects of her three marriages. She was still a child (15½) when she married Francis the Dauphin, but women were expected to mature early in those days, and no breath of scandal was ever whispered of her by the authors of memoirs, such as Brantôme, who were only too eager to spread salacious stories of people in high position, and her fame remained untarnished as long as she lived in France. Her marriage with Darnley may have had an element of affection, soon to be destroyed by his treacherous behaviour, but was, at any rate largely, a political measure. Her third marriage, short as it was, seems not to have been a success, although the turbulence of affairs would certainly undermine her feeling of security. A woman who had married her lover, urged thereto by lust, and stopping not even at the murder of her husband, would hardly be sad on her wedding day and one would not expect her to be ready to commit suicide two days later.

The breath of scandal, in fact, only touches Mary at two points, other than in connexion with Bothwell: in the cases of Châtelard and of David Riccio. The Châtelard incident occurred on 12th February, 1563; Mary had held a long meeting with Maitland, Moray and two other members of her Council. The Frenchman, who had been treated to a good deal of kindness by the Queen, took the opportunity to hide, armed, beneath her bed, where he was discovered by two grooms of the chamber. The next day, when she was told about this incident, she ordered him out of her presence. The following night (14th February), he found his way into her room when only her gentlewomen were with her. He tried to excuse his previous offence, but this intrusion was too much for the Queen: Châtelard was arrested, condemned and executed. As Hay Fleming justly points out (163), his rash conduct was, of course, exaggerated at the time in the rumours which found currency. Maitland informed de Quadra, the then Spanish Ambassador in London, that, on being discovered, Châtelard had tried to pass it off as a joke, but later had said that he had tried to damage the Queen's honour by staying all night under her bed, intending to leave in the morning in such a way as to be certain that he was observed. It is difficult to see anything to reproach in the Queen's behaviour.

The question of Riccio is more serious, for it was certainly rumoured in later years that James VI was Riccio's son. "Come down, thou son of Signor Davie, thou hast slain an honester man than thyself", cried the people of Perth to His Majesty after the Gowrie affair (5th August, 1600). Appointed Mary's Secretary in 1564, Riccio soon had considerable influence over her, and was a strong supporter of Mary's marriage with Darnley.

In September, 1565, Bedford was alleging that there was improper familiarity between Mary and Riccio; and Elizabeth made similar insinuations to the French Ambassador in October (169), but the English Queen's information came from Tamworth, who, being imprisoned by Mary for what she considered insolence, and being detected in passing money to her rebels, was naturally spiteful. Further, it must not be forgotten that, at this very time, the Chase-about Rebels were being driven out of Scotland and Elizabeth's "diplomacy" had received a sharp check: a counter-blast was needed, and the only one which could be produced was a campaign of vague innuendo. Randolph, also, hinted at unmentionable things ("not to be named for reverence' sake") in October (168), but he, too, was seeing the collapse of his efforts to destroy Darnley, and similar considerations apply to him as to Elizabeth and Bedford.

As the time for the murder of Riccio, about which they had fore-knowledge, approached, Bedford and Randolph, now at Berwick, became more outspoken. Because the *coup d'état* by Moray, who was in league, at least for the time being, with Darnley, was approved by the English government, jealousy of Riccio provided a suitable motive, and this was announced by the two Englishmen in their letter three days before the murder (170): "Darnley", they say, "hath assured knowledge of such usage of herself as altogether is intolerable to be borne . . . . he is himself determined to be at the execution of him whom he is able manifestly to charge with the crime, and to have done him the most dishonour that can be to any man". De Foix, the French Ambassador in London, reported to Catherine dei Medici on 20th March, 1566 (714), that the principal cause of Riccio's murder was that Darnley had found him alone with Mary, in her room, at one in the morning, the secretary being clad only in a shirt and a furred robe. This was said to have occurred "some days before". It is surprising, if this were true, that Darnley himself never alluded to it again, when he needed all the excuses he could find to justify his conduct, and even more surprising that he did not run the cowering Riccio (he was said to have been found hiding in a cupboard) through with his sword on the spot. But de Foix's information must have come from English, and therefore tainted, sources.

It would be difficult to believe that James was the son of any other than Darnley: he was conceived during the Chase-about Raid when the Queen and he were constantly in company, were on good terms and had not long been married. It is noteworthy that all the evidence of guilty intrigue comes from English sources, and even Maitland, himself one of the plotters and with a grudge against Riccio who had obtained his post as Secretary in effect, if not in name, never hints at this affair. The 'Book of Articles' itself, the Lords indictment of Mary, avoids the Riccio affair, although it would have been, if true, useful corroborative evidence of Mary's incontinence.

In fact, the main difficulty in accepting the allegation of a violent love affair between the Queen and the Earl of Bothwell is the virtual impossibility of constructing a chronology which will bring them together at the appropriate time, but will also separate them sufficiently for the whole series of the Casket Letters to be comprehensible. No one will place the commencement of the *affaire* before Bothwell's return to Scotland during the Chase-about Raid. It cannot have begun immediately: Mary and Darnley were constantly together at this time, and Bothwell was at least left behind at Dumfries when Mary and Darnley returned to Edinburgh; the presence of troops and officers would have made an incident then impossible. After this rebellion, English scandal couples Mary's name with Riccio; and when Bothwell had taken his wife, and when the Secretary had been murdered, Mary, now advanced in pregnancy, retired into the

Castle of Edinburgh, while Bothwell went to Crichton, and to his *amour* with Bessie Crawford. After the birth of James, Mary visited Alloa (end of July, 1566); Darnley followed her, but did not remain with her. There is no evidence that Bothwell was also at Mar's on this occasion. During the middle part of August, Mary and Darnley, with Bothwell and others, went hunting; it is difficult to imagine much opportunity for love in these circumstances. As soon as the hunting of Meggatland was over, the King and Queen took James to Stirling and continued to hunt in Glenartney, returning to Stirling, where Darnley remained, while Mary repaired to Edinburgh about 6th September. Apart from a flying visit which Mary made to Stirling about 21st to 23rd September, Bothwell and she were both in Edinburgh until 6th October, on which day the Earl set off for Liddesdale, where he was wounded. Buchanan places the Exchequer House incident during this time, and, if there really were an affair, it must have begun about now; the prosecution's case, however, is ruined by the silence of everyone at the time, and by its reliance upon perjured evidence. Buchanan himself seems to realise that the story is somewhat unlikely, and describes the rape of the Queen by Bothwell, assisted by Lady Reres, which the Queen evidently found so much to her liking that she sent the lady to bring Bothwell back to her on the following night. From late October, when the Queen had recovered from her illiness, and Bothwell from his wounds, Mary and the Earl were together, in company with other Lords, until after the christening. On 24th December, the day of Darnley's flight to Glasgow, they visited Drymen together, and here, as a few days later at Tullibardine, Buchanan alleges that the *amour* was renewed. We know however, that on each visit, a certain amount of public business was transacted, and we may presume that the Queen and her escort were not unattended, perhaps by other Lords. They returned to Stirling on 28th December, no doubt having heard of Darnley's evasion, and, on 30th December, paid a one-day visit to Tullibardine, where James Murray, a Lennox supporter, lived. This visit is suggestive of an attempt to open negotiations with the Lennox faction, among whom Darnley now was. Within two days (2nd January, 1567), Bothwell had left Mary, and he was away at Whittinghame, waiting for the Earl of Morton until about 14th January. On 20th January, or thereabouts, Bothwell accompanied Mary as far as Callendar House on her way to visit Darnley at Glasgow; the Earl seems to have returned to Edinburgh, and left again for Liddesdale on 24th January. By 30th January, Darnley, Mary and Bothwell were all in Edinburgh, the King at Kirk o'Field, and Mary and the Earl at Holyrood.

After the death of Darnley, Bothwell had continual access to Mary, save for the period of her visit to Stirling, 21st to 24th April. It is, therefore, extremely unlikely that the opportunity for a love affair had presented itself, the only possibility before the climax of Darnley's flight being the mid-September or Exchequer House period, and Darnley himself was certainly ignorant of that event when he was approached by the Lords and du Croc on 30th September. However, it is still more difficult to fit the Casket Letters into the scheme of events: the greatest difficulty is with Letter III, which the prosecution did not attempt to date. Letters IV and V were supposed to have been written about 7th February, 1567, and the problem of Letters VI, VII and VIII was only solved by alleging that all three (and the love-ballad) had been written at Stirling on the 22nd and 23rd April. Such an interpretation stretches credulity beyond the measure of possibility.

The conclusion which seems to be justified by the events which we have been considering is that Bothwell had a strong character of a nature typically attractive to women, the more so since he was perhaps less unlettered than many of his peers. Mary must have felt gratitude to him and, when her second husband betrayed her so horribly, and Bothwell made such efforts in her behalf, it would indeed be likely that her gratitude would grow into affection. It is, however, most unlikely that there was any criminal association between them, especially when there is no hint of this at the time from their companions, many of whom were prepared to make a veritable mountain out of the smallest molehill. It would even be most unlikely that any criminal assault was made by him on Mary at the time of her abduction, for he was actuated, it would seem, partly by ambition, and partly by the desire for self-preservation, in his desire to marry her, and a criminal assault would, more probably, have lost rather than gained, his ends. For those to whom these conclusions seem insufficient it may be fair to add that many a woman falls in love without committing adultery, and that an adulteress does not necessarily commit murder. If the story were simply that Darnley had wished to leave the country, surely a passionate woman and an ambitious lover would have let him depart, and would have abandoned themselves to their lust, without risking the consequences of an unnecessary assassination.

BOOK II
"Pretty Maids All in a Row"

CHAPTER I

The Casket Documents

The documents in the silver casket are the only direct proof, apart from the highly dubious second deposition of French Paris, of Mary's complicity in the murder of her second husband, Henry Stewart. The facts that they were alleged to have been found at a most auspicious moment for the Lords, that they were retained virtually unseen in their hands for more than a year before they were produced and read, and that they are, as we have seen, difficult to correlate with the circumstances in which they are alleged to have been written, allow us to examine them, as it were, as hostile witnesses.

First of all, it may be said that no one who had read only the documents which have come down to us from the period up to the death of Darnley would have the slightest suspicion that the Queen had murdered her husband or was in love with the Earl of Bothwell. Secondly, it is right to say that none of the casket documents which have come down to us would bear the slightest weight in a Court of Law, for all, with one possible exception, are copies or translations of the original French, yet at least half of the proof depends upon the handwriting: the one possible exception is one of the contracts of marriage which, if it be one of the original Casket Documents, is certainly a forgery. Furthermore, none of the letters, that is to say, epistles, is signed, one is partially dated, while the remainder bear no date or place of origin.

Perhaps it is wise to explain that, in the Scots language of the period, the word "letters" was applicable to any document in manuscript, while what we now call "letters", would have been described as "letters missive". The "Casket Letters" actually consist, as produced in 1568, of eight "letters missive", two contracts of marriage, and a love-ballad of twelve verses, often referred to as "sonnets", although the verses are not in sonnet form, and the whole constitutes a single continuous poem.

The documents were alleged to have been first seen four days after the incarceration of Mary in Lochleven. As we have seen, she was sent there during the night of 16th/17th June, 1567, arriving on the 17th, two days after the affair at Carberry. According to Morton, the Earl of Bothwell sent his servant, Dalgleish, from Dunbar to Edinburgh Castle to obtain the Casket which Bothwell had left there, and it is important to realise that Bothwell had left Edinburgh for the last time on 7th June: he had apparently been refused admittance to the Castle on the previous day (544), so the Casket must have been deposited there before 6th June, 1567. Sir James Balfour, the Keeper of the Castle, gave Dalgleish the box, but warned Morton of what had happened. This is Morton's own account, which was read in Commission at Westminster on 9th December, 1568 (87 & 90):

"The true declaration and report of me, James Earl of Morton, how a certain silver box, overgilt, containing divers missive writings, sonnets, contracts and obligations for marriage between the Queen, mother to our sovereign Lord (Jmes VI), and James sometime Earl of Bothwell, was found and used.

Upon Thursday, 19th June, 1567, I dined at Edinburgh, (Maitland) with me. At time of my dinner, a certain man came to me and, in secret manner, shewed me that three servants of the Earl Bothwell, viz. Mr. Thomas Hepburn, Parson of Auldhamstocks; John Cockburn, brother to the Laird of Skirling; and George Dalgleish, were come to the town, and (had) passed within the Castle. Upon which advertisement, I, on the sudden, sent my cousin, Mr. Archibald Douglas, Robert Douglas his brother, and James Johnston of Westerrow, with others my servants to the number of sixteen or thereby, towards the Castle, to make search for the said persons, and, if possible were, to apprehend them. According to which my direction, my servants passed, and at first missing the fore-named three persons, for that they were departed forth of the Castle before their coming there, my men then parting in several companies, upon knowledge that the others whom they sought were separated, Mr. Archibald Douglas sought Mr. Thomas Hepburn, and found him not, but got his horse. James Johnston sought for John Cockburn and apprehended him. Robert Douglas, suiting for George Dalgleish, after he had almost given over his search and inquisition, a good fellow, understanding his purpose, came to him, offering for a mean piece of money to reveal where George Dalgleish was; the said Robert, satisfying him that gave the intelligence for his pains, passed to the Potter-row beside Edinburgh, and there apprehended the said George, with divers evidences and letters in parchment, viz. the Earl Bothwell's infeftments of Liddesdale, of the lordship of Dunbar, and of Orkney and Shetland, and divers others, which all, with the said George himself, the said Robert brought and presented to me. And the said George, being examined of the cause of his direction to the Castle of

Edinburgh, and what letters and evidences he brought forth of the same, alleged he was sent only to visit Lord Bothwell his master's clothing, and that he had no other letters or evidences, but those which were apprehended with him; but his report being found suspicious, and his gesture and behaviour ministering cause of mistrust, seeing the gravity of the action that was in hand, it was resolved by common assent of the noblemen convened, that the said George Dalgleish should be surely kept that night, and, in the morning, should be had to the Tolbooth of Edinburgh, and there be put in the 'jayne' (i.e. gêne or seat for torture) and torments, for furthering of the declaration of the truth: wherein being set, upon Friday, 20th June, before any rigorous demeaning of his person, fearing the pain and moved of conscience, he called for my cousin, Mr. Archibald Douglas; who coming, the said George desired that Robert Douglas should be sent with him, and he should shew and bring to light that which he had. So, being taken forth of the 'jayne', he passed with the said Robert to the Potter-row, and then, under the foot of a bed, took forth the said silver box which he had brought forth of the castle the day before, locked, and brought the same to me at 8 o'clock at night. And because it was late, I kept it all that night. Upon the morrow, viz. Saturday, 21st June, in presence of the Earls of Athol, Mar, Glencairn, myself, the Lords Home, Semple, Sanquhar, the Master of Graham, (Maitland) and the Laird of Tullibardine (controller), and the said Mr. Archibald Douglas, the said box was stricken up, because we wanted the key: and the letters within sighted, and immediately thereafter delivered again in my hands and custody. Since which time, I have observed and kept the same box, and all letters missive, contracts, sonnets and other writings contained therein surely, without alteration, changing, eking or diminishing of anything found or received in the said box. This I testify and declare to be undoubted truth".

There are one or two points in this declaration which deserve to be considered, as touching the Earl of Morton's credibility in a matter of such importance. First of all, the statement is unsupported by any collateral evidence. It would, one would have thought, have been an obvious move to obtain a deposition, at least from Robert Douglas, but this was not done. Still more surprisingly, the deposition of George Dalgleish (19), dated 26th June, deals solely with the question of the murder of Darnley; he was not apparently asked a single question about the Casket or its contents, or concerning his movements and actions at or about the time of his arrest. He had been executed before the Commission sat, but the narrowness of his deposition did not apparently cause any surprise to the English Commissioners. We may add that Morton's list of the parchments in Dalgleish's hands is evidently inaccurate, for Bothwell had his patent to the Dukedom of Orkney with him when he arrived in Norway (286). Next, it is difficult to understand how the proceedings described as occurring on 20th June could take so long. If it were true that Dalgleish gave up his attitude of reticence "before any rigorous demeaning of his person", the box should have been in Morton's hands by midday at latest. How could the delivery of the box be delayed until 8.0 p.m.? Moreover, it must be appreciated that the proceedings of the Commission were strictly secret and, on the date that this above declaration was made, no one other than the English Commissioners, Moray, Morton and their colleagues (Maitland, Macgill, Buchanan, John Wood, the Bishop of Orkney, Lord Lindsay and the Abbot of Dunfermline—if they were all present) was there to hear it, and the English Commissioners were there only to receive such proof as Moray and his colleagues would offer; they were not themselves going to test any evidence produced. It is therefore wrong to suppose that, in Henderson's words (296), "it would have been egregious folly in Morton to have inserted in the list of those present at the sighting of the documents the names of any who were not present, or who were not prepared to assert that they were present. Such a fraud would inevitably, sooner or later, have been detected". There is no reason why it should ever have been detected: the English Commissioners were merely acting as judges of the evidence produced, they did not inform Mary's commissioners of all that Moray and his colleagues had laid before them, and there was no reason why this matter should have been disclosed. The Lords named may have been present when the Casket was opened, but Morton's declaration is otherwise so suspicious, as we have seen, that his statement can hardly be relied upon in this matter.

A certain importance attaches to the use of the word "sighting". It is true that the word is used in a legal sense, meaning 'to examine closely', but it is also used in the more ordinary sense of 'to see' or 'to glance at'. The phrasing, "the letters within sighted, and immediately thereafter delivered again in my hands and custody" does not suggest more than that the documents were seen; reading all of the documents would have been a lengthy affair and some allusion to the length of time and the reactions of the readers would have been a natural thing to insert.

Finally, Morton's account either shews that the Casket Documents were not produced in Parliament on 15th December, 1567, as it is commonly believed that they were, or else an important episode in their history was neglected, which again renders the declaration an object of suspicion.

Morton's statement concludes with the assertion that he "kept the same box, and all letters missive, contracts, sonnets, and other writings contained therein surely, without alteration, changing, eking (adding) or diminishing of anything found or received in the said box".

Black (93), following Chauviré, (98) considers that eight letters, two contracts and a poem of twelve verses (which he calls "twelve sonnets or fragements of sonnets") could be considered as twenty-two documents. Such a position is quite untenable, but the importance of the actual number of documents in the Casket is that, although Moray and his colleagues produced to the English Commissioners the eleven documents mentioned, yet Morton, proceeding on embassy to England early in 1571, at that time gave a receipt for twenty-one documents. This receipt is so important that it must be given in full (212):

"At Edinburgh, 22nd January, 1571. The which day, in presence of the right honourable Matthew Earl of Lennox, Lord Darnley, grandfather, lawful tutor and Regent to our Sovereign Lord (James VI), his realm and lieges, and Lords of Secret Council; James Earl of Morton, Lord of Dalkeith, Chancellor and Great Admiral of Scotland, being in readiness to pass to the Queen's Majesty of England, as one of our sovereign Lord's Commissioners, for divers great and weighty matters, concerning his Highness and his estate, granted and confessed him to have received from the said Lord Regent a silver box, overgilt with gold, with the missive letters, contracts or obligations for marriage, sonnets, or love-ballads, and other letters therein contained, to the number of twenty-one, sent and passed between the Queen, our said Sovereign Lord's mother, and James sometime Earl Bothwell: which box, and whole pieces within the same, were taken and found with the deceased George Dalgleish, servant to the said Earl Bothwell, upon 20th June, 1567, and were delivered by the said James Earl of Morton to the deceased James Earl of Moray, Lord Abernethy, uncle and Regent to our Sovereign Lord for the time: after whose decease, the same box and letters were recovered, out of the hands of his servants, by the said Earl of Lennox, now Regent, which letters, being authentically copied, and subscribed with the hands of his Grace and Lords of Secret Council, the same copies were left to remain with his Grace *ad futuram rei memoriam:* and also the said Earl of Morton promised and obliged him to bring again and deliver the said box, and principal letters, to the said Lord Regent, at his returning from this present legation".

It is therefore quite definite that the Casket contained twenty-one documents. The fact that only eleven were shewn raises two possibilities: that some of the documents were not produced, and that some separate documents may have been dovetailed into each other in such a way as to seem to be one.

Assuming that there is at least some truth in Morton's declaration, and that the Lords possessed themselves on or about 21st June, 1567, with some letters and other documents which had either been written, or which they believed to have been written, by Mary, we should expect to see some reflection of this in letters and policy, and for this we must now look.

On 25th June, 1567, Drury at Berwick wrote to Cecil (108): "There is here that the Queen had a box wherein are the practices between her and France, wherein is little good meant to England", which is, perhaps, the sort of rumour that might seep out after the discovery of the Casket. The following day, the Lords of Secret Council issued a proclamation offering 1,000 crowns reward for the arrest of Bothwell (383), and they state that they have evident proof "as well of witnesses as of writings" that he was the principal deviser of Darnley's murder (289). On 29th June, Drury again mentioned a box, and the manuscripts in it, "part in cipher deciphered" (442), but none of these references is sufficiently certain to convince the sceptic. On the whole, however, the balance of evidence is in favour of a casket being found at about the date which Morton mentions, but the manner of its discovery, and the nature of its contents remain unknown.

The French ambassador, du Croc, left Edinburgh on 29th June. It has been asserted, on the strength of a statement by the Spanish Ambassador in London, that he carried copies of the letters with him. The whole question is discussed by Mahon (520), who considers it unlikely. On 9th July, someone, who may have been John Wood (445), left Scotland carrying letters to Moray, who had retired to France in the previous April. The letters were obviously important and it is possible that they contained some account of the finding of the Casket. About this time, Moray's secretary, Nicholas Elphinstone, passed from France to Scotland, which he reached about 14th July, or soon after (734). He was in London on 8th July (732), and on 12 July, de Silva, the Spanish Ambassador in London, wrote to Philip II (520): "The Queen's adversaries assert positively that they know that she had been concerned in the murder of her husband, which was proved by letters under her own hand, copies of which were in 'his' possession". The pronoun seems to refer to the French Ambassador in London, de la Forrest, who might have got the copies from du Croc, but, since the latter was on his way to France, where no more of the letters was heard, the probability is that de Silva or his decipherer has made some mistake; perhaps the 'his' should be 'their', the Queen's Adversaries.

Throckmorton, Elizabeth's ambassador to Scotland, had arrived in Edinburgh by 13th July, (733), and he wrote to Elizabeth on 14th July, 1567 (83). The Lords have told him that

> "the principal cause of her detention is, these Lords seeing her fervent of affection to (Bothwell), fear, if put at liberty, she would so maintain him, that they should be compelled to be in continual arms against him. They also mean a divorce between them, which cannot take place if she were at liberty and had power in her hands. But they do

not intend to touch her in surety or honour, for they speak of her with respect and reverence, and affirm that, the conditions aforesaid accomplished, they will restore her to her estate".

This is strange language on the part of those who, "from letters under her own hand", knew that their Queen was a murderess, but it is just possible that they were waiting to see what attitude Throckmorton, or the English Government, was going to take concerning the imprisonment of their Sovereign. It must have been known that Elizabeth had very strong views on the untouchability of queens. However, even four days later, the Lords still adopted the same attitude (84);

"though these lords and councillors speak reverently, mildly and charitably of their Queen", writes Throckmorton, "so that I cannot gather from their speech any intention to cruelty or violence, yet she is in very great peril of her life, for the people at this convention mind vehemently her destruction. It is public speech of all estates (saving the councillors) that she has no more privilege to commit murder nor adultery than any other private person".

On 21st July, the Lords still apparently believed that Mary had been "led captive" by Bothwell, "and by fear, force, and, as by many conjectures may well be suspected, other extraordinary and more unlawful means (i.e. by witchcraft), compelled to become bed-fellow to another wife's husband" (85).

As we have seen, de Silva in London had heard of the Casket Letters as early as 12th July (page 79). On 21st, he writes to Philip II (443);

"I mentioned to the Queen (Elizabeth) that I had been told that the Lords held certain letters proving that the Queen (Mary) had been cognisant of the murder of her husband. She told me that it was not true, although (Maitland) had acted badly in the matter, and, if she saw him, she would say something that would not be at all to his taste".

Lang (445) thinks that Elizabeth's informant was Robert Melville who had left Edinburgh for London on the day the Casket was opened, but the fact is not proved to demonstration; perhaps du Croc or even Elphinstone was her informant, but it is noteworthy that Mary's confessor, Roche Mameret, arrived in London at about this time (446).

On 24th July, Mary signed instruments of abdication, and, on the following day, Throckmorton wrote to Cecil (109),

"If they cannot by fair means induce the Queen to their purpose, they mean to charge her with tyranny for breach of those Statutes which were enacted in her absence. Secondly, they mean to charge her with incontinence with Bothwell and others. Thirdly, they mean to charge her with the murder of her husband, whereof they say they have proof by the testimony of her own handwriting, which they have recovered, as also by sufficient witnesses".

Who the witnesses were to have been was never disclosed.

On 26th July, de Silva, who had seen Mary's confessor, wrote to Philip II (446) that Mameret was much grieved by Mary's marriage with Bothwell, which, he had told her, was illegal. "He swore to me solemnly that, until the question of the marriage with Bothwell was raised, he never saw a woman of greater virtue, courage and uprightness . . . She swore to him that she had contracted the marriage" with the object of settling religion by that means. This can only mean that she was hoping that she would be able to overcome the rebels who were opposing her, as they always had done, under the banner of religion. No one could have believed that the staunchly Protestant Bothwell would have taken any pains to restore the "auld religion".

On 29th July, Mary's son was crowned in the parish church at Stirling, and the Lords could now at least pretend that they were on the right side of the law, for they had been careful to insert a clause to the effect that the Queen was giving up her crown voluntarily, being "so vexed, broken and unquieted" that she could no longer endure to govern (155).

Moray had arrived in London on his way back to Scotland from France on 23rd July, 1567 (316), and, on 31st July, he also saw de Silva, and told him a story which the Spanish Ambassador detailed to Philip II in a letter of 2nd August (447). Mary's complicity in the murder of Darnley, said Moray, was

> "proved beyond doubt by a letter which the Queen had written to Bothwell containing more than three sheets of paper, written with her own hand and signed with her name; in which she says in substance that he is not to delay putting into execution that which he had been ordered, because her husband used such fair words to deceive her, and bring her to his will, that she might be moved by them if the other thing were not done quickly. She said that she herself would go and fetch him (Darnley), and would stop at a house on the road where she would try to give him a draught; but if this could not be done, she would put him in the house where the explosion was arranged for the night upon which one of her servants was to be married. He, Bothwell, was to try to get rid of his wife, either by putting her away or poisoning her, since he knew that she (the Queen), had risked all for him; her honour, her kingdom, her wealth which she had in France, and her God; contenting herself with his person alone".

Moray had added that he had heard of this letter from a man who had read it.

For the moment we will only say that the letter which Moray described bears a certain superficial resemblance to the first part of Casket Letter Letter II, but, as will later be seen (page 162), some of the statements have been grotesquely altered or inverted, and Moray describes some remarks which do not occur at all in the letter as produced to the Commission. Three possibilities present themselves as to Moray's source of information about this letter: he might have seen it before he left Scotland (two months before the Casket was opened); the messenger sent by the Lords to Moray on 9th July, 1567, may have taken an account of it: or Moray, who had been in London for eight days when he saw de Silva, may have there received some messenger from Scotland who gave him an account of the letter. The third possibility can be eliminated: the subject was so important and so secret that there would have been no point in sending a messenger to London to describe a letter, whether it existed or not, when Moray was already on his way to Scotland. The same argument holds with only slightly less force against the sending of the information to France, for Moray had been warned to be ready for a return as early as 8th May (444). We are therefore probably right in deciding that, if this letter did exist, Moray saw it before he left Scotland in April, 1567. It follows with reasonable certainty that the letter was not in the Casket and, indeed, that it was not addressed to Bothwell. We shall return to this question later (pages 162 & 163); meanwhile, we may notice that Lennox, when he prepared his supplication in May, 1568, also describes this identical letter (516). Lennox was in or near London during Moray's visit, and we may be quite sure that they met, and one can be certain that Lennox received his information of this letter from Moray: it was not a communication which would be easily forgotten by the father of the murdered King. Moray presently departed for Scotland: he arrived in Edinburgh on 11th August, and eleven days later was proclamed Regent.

It is tantalising, but also significant, that no further mention of the Casket or its contents occurs until 28th November, 1567, when Drury wrote from Berwick to Cecil (290), "The writings which did comprehend the names and consents of the chiefs for murdering of the King are turned to ashes, the same that concerns the Queen's part kept to be shewn". The references here are not very conclusive; the first one is obviously to the bond of Craigmillar (circa 4th December, 1566) or the Association of early October, 1566. This is the bond which, according to Nau, was given to Mary by Bothwell at Carberry (669):

> "At parting from the Queen, Bothwell wished to ease his conscience by making known to her the wicked design of her enemies. He told her Majesty that the Earl of Morton, secretary (Maitland), James Balfour and some others, who at that moment were on the opposite side, were guilty of the death of the late King, the whole having been executed by their direction and counsel. He shewed her their signatures to the bond agreed upon among themselves, and told her to take good care of that paper".

Now Nau's narrative may not have been obtained entirely at first hand from the Queen; he had entered her service in 1575, and, when he decided to write a history of Scotland, he no doubt incorporated much that he heard from Mary in conversation, and other parts which he elucidated from her companions. Certainly, there are some errors in his account, and it seems possible that Bothwell let Mary see the bond, but did not give it to her, asking her, not 'to take good care of that paper' ('garder'), but 'to look well at it' ('regarder'). If Mary did have the bond, or Bothwell's copy of it, for the principals would surely have exchanged copies, it would have been taken from her before she reached Lochleven.

On 4th December, 1567, Moray, the Lords of Secret Council and others, "men of judgment", considered the action which was to be taken in the forthcoming Parliament (301). They decided that "the cause of the apprehension and retaining of the Queen" must be opened in Parliament, and action taken to safeguard the rebels against a charge of treason. The only way was, they said, to reveal the whole matter, which they were most loath to do, for the love they bear unto the Queen's person. They desired the estates to exonerate the Lords from all their actions since 10th February, 1567, the date of Darnley's death, because these were all due to the "Queen's own default, in as far as by divers her privy letters written and subscribed with her own hand, and sent by her to James Earl Bothwell, chief executor of the said horrible murder, as well before the committing thereof as thereafter, and by her ungodly and dishonourable proceeding in a private marriage with him suddenly and unadvisedly thereafter, it is most certain that she was art and part of the actual devise and deed of the fore-mentioned murder of the King".

Accordingly, in the Parliament which met on 15th December, 1567, the following act was passed (302),

"that the cause and occasion of the convention and messages of the said Earls, Lords, Noblemen, Barons and other faithful and true subjects, and, consequently, their taking of arms, and coming to the fields with open and displayed banners, and the cause and occasion of the taking of the said Queen's person, upon the said 15th day of June last bypast, and holding and detaining of the same within the house and fortalice of Lochleven, continually since then, presently and in all time coming, and generally all other things invented (begun), spoken, written or done by them, or any of them, to that effect, since the 10th day of February last bypast, upon the which day the deceased Henry, King, then the said Queen's lawful husband, and our Sovereign Lord the King's dearest father, was treasonably, shamefully and horribly murdered, unto the day and date of this present act, and in all time to come, touching the said Queen and detaining of her person. That the cause, and all things depending thereon, or that anyway may pertain thereto, the intromission or disposing upon her property, casualties or whatsoever thing pertaining, or that anyway might pertain to her, was in the said Queen's own default, in so far as, by divers her privy letters written wholly with her own hand, and sent by her to James sometime Earl of Bothwell, chief executor of the said horrible murder, as well before the committing thereof as thereafter; and by her ungodly and dishonourable proceeding to a pretended marriage with him, suddenly and unadvisedly thereafter, it is most certain that she was privy, art and part, of the actual devise and deed of the fore-named murder of the King, her lawful husband, and father to our Sovereign Lord, committed by the said James sometime Earl of Bothwell, his accomplices and part-takers, and therefore justly deserves whatsoever has been done to her in any time by-gone, or that shall be used towards her, for the said cause, in time coming, which shall be used by the advice of the Nobility in respect that our said Sovereign Lord's mother, with the said James sometime Earl of Bothwell, went about by indirect and coloured means, to colour and hold back the knowledge of the truth of the committers of the said crime. Yet all men in their hearts was fully persuaded of the authors and devisers of that mischievous and unworthy fact, awaiting until God should move the hearts of some to enter in the quarrel for revenging of the same. And, in the meantime, a great part of the nobility, upon just fear to be handled and demeaned in similar manner as the King had been of before, perceiving also the Queen so thrall, and so blindly affectionate to the private appetite of that tyrant, and that both he and she had conspired together such horrible cruelty, being therewith all garnished with a company of ungodly and vicious persons, ready to accomplish all their unlawful commandments, of whom he had a sufficient number continually waiting upon him for the same effect, all noble and virtuous men abhorring their tyranny and company, but chiefly suspecting that they, who had so treasonably put down and destroyed the father, should make the innocent Prince, his only son and the principal and almost only comfort sent by God to this afflicted nation, to taste of the same cup, as the many invented purposes to pass where he was, and also where the noblemen were in, by their open confession gave sufficient warning and declaration. Wherethrough, the said Earls, Lords, Barons and other faithful and true subjects taking arms, or otherwise whatsoever joining and assisting in the said action and in the said conventions, displaying banners, and coming to the fields, taking and retaining of the Queen's person, as well in times by-past as hereafter, and all others that has thereafter or shall in any time coming adjoin them, and all things done by them, or any of them, touching that cause, and all other things depending thereon, or that anyway may appertain thereto, the intromission or disposing upon her property or casualties or whatsoever other things pertaining, or any way might appertain to her, was in default of herself, and the said James sometime Earl of Bothwell, and by the horrible and cruel murder of our said Sovereign Lord's deceased dearest father, conspired, devised, committed, concealed and coloured by them, and not condignly punished according to the laws. And that the said Earls, Lords, Barons and other true and faithful subjects, convening at any convention bygone, and now presently after the said murder, for furthering of the trial thereof, and also they, and all others that were on the fields, took arms, apprehended, held, kept or detained, or presently holds, keeps or detains her person, or shall thereafter, or that has joined or assisted, or shall in any time hereafter join to them in that quarrel, touching the premises, are, were and shall be innocent, free and acquit of the same, and of all action and cause criminal and civil that may be intended or pursued against them or any of them there-for in any time coming. And that a part of the Three Estates fore-said, Prelates, Bishops, great Barons and burgesses, give their seals upon, to be used as shall be thought most expedient by them, for the honour of the realm and security of the noblemen and others having interest in the said cause. And decerns this declaration to be no way prejudicial to the issue of our Sovereign Lord's mother, lawfully coming of her body, to succeed to the crown of this realm, nor their heirs".

A great deal of ink has been spilt on the difference in phrasing between the decision of 4th December, in which mention is made of "her privy letters written and subscribed with her own hand and sent by her to James Earl Bothwell", and the Act of 15th December, in which the appropriate sentence appears as "her privy letters written wholly with her own hand, and sent by her to James sometime Earl of Bothwell". It seems more than probable that the earlier decision, which, by the way, is not recorded in the register of the Acts of the Privy Council, was somewhat hurriedly written, and served merely as a frame-work on which the actual act of Parliament was woven, greater care being taken to get the details correct; witness the alteration of Bothwell's title from "James Earl Bothwell" to "James sometime Earl of Bothwell", and also the fact that the former document is so worded as to imply that Mary was one of the actual murders of Darnley, while in the later one this inaccuracy is corrected. More important is the question whether the letters were or were not actually produced in either the meeting of Council or Parliament, and if so, whether they were read or merely displayed to the casual glance. Morton's declaration, as we have seen, suggests that they were not so produced. On the other hand, the declaration of the Queen's nobles convened at Dumbarton on 12th September, 1568, states (251),

"And if it be alleged that her Majesty's writing, produced in Parliament, should prove her Grace culpable, it may be answered, that there is in no place mention made in it by the which her Highness may be convicted; albeit it were her own hand-writing, as it is not. Also, the same is devised by themselves in some principal and substantial clauses. And such alleged privy writings can make no probation in criminal causes, which will be clearer nor the light of the day. And so, by the said writing, nothing can be inferred against her Majesty".

This declaration was signed by seventeen lords, including Argyll and Huntly. From this, it might be a tenable theory that only one letter was produced, or at any rate read, and that this was not taken from, or at that time kept in, the Casket.

Another point of importance is that, at last, the Lords had taken the stand fore-shadowed by Throckmorton on 25th July, and they no longer claimed, as they had done until 21st July, that Mary had been acting under the tyranny and forceful persuasion of Bothwell in marrying him. Until that date, they had repeatedly asserted that the detention of the Queen was caused entirely by her refusal to denounce her husband. It should also be noticed that they stated in definite terms that "the cause and occasion of the taking of the said Queen's person upon the said 15th day of June" was her own default, since she was guilty art and part in the murder of her husband, as shewn by her privy letters. Yet, according to their own account, those letters had not come into their possession until nearly a week after the taking of the Queen.

Having protected themselves with the mantle of legality as much as was possible, and having justified the continued detention of their Queen in Lochleven, the Lords were apparently prepared to let the issue rest. Nothing much more was done, although various suggestions were considered from time to time. However, the escape of Mary from her prison on 2nd May, 1568, quickly followed by her defeat at Langside (13th May) and her flight into England (16th May) necessitated that they should be prepared to justify themselves by some sort of legal process which would, almost certainly, take place under the aegis of Elizabeth. No one could say exactly how the Queen of England would react, she was always touchy about the status of royalty, and it would seem that her first response was one of friendliness towards her "dearest Sister and Cousin".

Lennox, presumably warned by Cecil, immediately prepared his first indictment. As Mahon clearly shows, this document was written by him between 22nd and 28th May, for, on the latter date he had audience of Elizabeth, and the 'Supplication' was almost certainly handed to her at that time (503). His reference to a letter is almost exactly the same as that which de Silva had described on 2nd August, 1567, citing Moray as his authority. This is what Lennox said (515),

"But, before we proceed any further in this matter, I cannot omit to declare and call to remembrance, her letter written to Bothwell from Glasgow before their departure thence, together with such cruel and strange words unto him (Darnley), which he, her husband, should have better considered and marked than he did, but that the hope that he had to win her love did blind him, together that it lieth not in the power of man to prevent that which the suffering will of God determineth. The contents of her letter to the said Bothwell from Glasgow was to let him understand that, although the flattering and sweet words of him with whom she was then presently, she meaning the King her husband, had almost overcome her, yet she remembering the great affection which she bear unto him (Bothwell), there should no such sweet baits dissuade her or cool her said affection from him, but would continue therein, yea, though she should thereby abandon her God, put in adventure the loss of her dowry in France, hazard such titles as she had to the crown of England as heir apparent thereof, and also the crown of her realm. Wishing him then presently in her arms. Therefore bade him go forward with all things according to their enterprise, and that the place and everything might be finished as they had devised against her coming to Edinburgh, which should be shortly. And, for the time of execution thereof, she thought it best to be the night of Bastian's marriage, which indeed was the night of the King, her husband's murder. She wrote also in her letter that the said Bothwell should in no wise fail in the meantime to despatch his wife, and to give her the drink as they had devised before".

Now, these statements bear only a superficial resemblance, as we have said (page 76), to Casket Letter II, and we shall later see that this cannot be an honest description, even a garbled one, of that letter. It is noticeable that Lennox emphasizes that this letter was written at Glasgow, while, in de Silva's account, we read that "she said that she herself would go and fetch him", indicating that the letter was written before her journey to Glasgow. This may, however, be a slip on de Silva's part.

Meanwhile, as soon as the Regent learnt that Mary was in England, John Wood was sent to London. Leaving Scotland on 21st May (493), he would arrive about 26th or 27th May. His purpose was "to resolve her Majesty (Elizabeth) of anything she stands doubtful to". Having received a communication from Cecil (499), Moray, on 27th May, instructed Buchanan to prepare the 'Book of Articles'. The Latin version was completed early in June, 1568 (494), and an English translation was prepared in September or October of that year, and this was the one produced to the Commission. Now, the Latin version only contains one short reference to the letters (494).

"She prepared herself from Edinburgh to ride to Glasgow in the end of January to visit the King her husband, that almost by the space of a month had continued there in sickness uncouth and marvelous to behold, of mind, as well appears by her letters, to bring him to Edinburgh to his fatal end and final destruction" (Buchanan's own translation). Now, this short description of the Casket Letters corresponds better with the letter described by de Silva and Lennox than with the actual Casket Letter II, especially if we remember that the English word "letters" is a translation of the Latin "litterae", which can mean "letter" or "letters"; indeed, the plural form was frequently used with a singular meaning in English; an example occurs in the first paragraph of the letter of Norfolk and others to Elizabeth on 11th October, 1568 (214) (page 86). When Buchanan made this English translation (September or October, 1568), he know more about the Casket Documents than when he prepared his indictment, for he added a postscript, in which we read (496),

"Whereby, as also by her own handwriting in many and sundry letters sent between them during the course of that wicked time, it is most patent, true and evident that she was not only privy of the same horrible and unnatural murder, but also the very instrument, chief organ and principal causer of that unnatural cruelty, perpetrated in the person of him that was her lawful husband and, by God's law, one flesh with herself; before the committing whereof (as plainly appears) she, not only by words, but by writing, promised to take the Earl Bothwell to husband, wherein, albeit for a colour she disdainfully calls the King, the deceased Henry Stewart of Darnley, her late husband, yet it appears well, because the letter (document) is without a date, that it has been written and subscribed before the murder, for, on 5th day of April thereafter, notwithstanding the marriage standing between him and his wife, she entered in a plain and a new contract with him, as the same writing by the Earl of Huntly and subscribed with both their hands proports, so that there lacks no proof, and testify a multitude of infallible presumptions".

We have seen that John Wood arrived in London from Moray about 27th May, 1568 (page 82), in order to let Elizabeth understand the Lords attitude and, no doubt, to try to win her to their side, and on both 30th May and 6th June, Drury forwarded packets (500 & 501), one of which may have contained the Scotch translation of the Casket Letters, for Moray's letter of 22nd June, 1568, refers to what he has sent to Wood, and then, further on in the same letter, says that Wood has such translated copies. This is strange, for, as we have seen, Buchanan, instructed to prepare the indictment on 27th May, apparently only knows of one letter, although by 22nd June Moray is speaking of a number of letters.

The second packet forwarded by Drury at Berwick would reach London on 9th or 10th June, and on 11th, Lennox wrote letters to Scotland asking for information against Mary and, in his letter of that date to Moray, he says (448) of Mary, "there is sufficiency in her own handwriting, by the faith of her letters, to condemn her". Lang shews conclusively that Wood and Lennox had met before this was written. We see, therefore, that the intention of using, in case of need, one letter of Mary's held good until at least 27th May; but, by 5th June at latest, a number of letters, almost certainly those which we now know as the Casket Letters, were being used as evidence against the Queen. If these documents were to be forged, there was not much time for it: had the decision to compose and prepare in suitable form the eight letters, the poem and the two contracts, been taken immediately after sending the despatch to Buchanan, there would still have been less than eight days, and, while this might just possibly be time enough, the odds are greatly against it.

On 22nd June, 1568, Moray, replying to a demand for an explanation of his conduct towards Mary, which had been sent by Elizabeth, wrote (207),

"And for our offer, to make her Majesty (Elizabeth) declaration of our whole doings, anent that wherewith the Queen, our Sovereign Lord's mother, charges us and others joined with us, we have already sent unto our servant, Mr. John Wood, that which, we trust, shall sufficiently resolve her Majesty of anything she stands doubtful unto; and yet, if her Highness will that we send other for more special information of the case, we shall gladly follow her pleasure. with as great haste as possible we can.

But, because we perceive the trial, which the Queen's Majesty (Elizabeth) is minded to have taken, is to be used with great ceremony and solemnities, we would be most loath to enter in accusation of the Queen, mother of the King our Sovereign, and afterwards to enter in qualification with her: for all men may judge how dangerous and prejudicial that should be. Always, in case the Queen's Majesty (Elizabeth) will have the accusation directly to proceed, it were most reasonable we understood what we should look to follow thereupon, in case we prove all that we allege, otherwise we shall be as uncertain after the cause concluded as we are at present. And therefore, we pray you, require her Highness, in this point to resolve us, at least that my Lords of the Council will assure us what we shall trust to.

Farther, it may be that such letters as we have of the Queen, our Sovereign Lord's mother, that sufficiently in our opinion proves her consenting to the murder of the King, her lawful husband, shall be called in doubt by the judges to be constituted for examination and trial of the cause, whether they may stand or fall, prove or not. Therefore, since our servant, Mr. John Wood, has the copies of the same letters translated in our language, we would earnestly desire that the said copies may be considered by the judges that shall have the examination and commission of the matter, that they may resolve us this far, in case the principal (i.e. the originals) agree with the copy, that then we prove the cause indeed. For when we have manifested and shewn all, and yet shall have no assurance that it we send shall satisfy for probation, for what purpose shall we either accuse, or take care how to prove, when we are not assured what to prove, or, when we have proved, what shall succeed?"

This letter must go down in history as the most extraordinary overture by an interested party to a judicial tribunal; yet Moray had reason to be careful, for, if he accused his Queen of murder, all chance of a compromise between them was past, and if, in spite of such proofs as he had, Elizabeth should refuse to pronounce sentence on the Queen, she would have a stranglehold over Scottish policy, for, at a moment's notice she could oust the Regent, or even the King (James VI), and restore the captive Queen "without a stain on her character". This, of course, was how Elizabeth finally played the game; no wonder that, even after Mary's condemnation in 1586, she hesitated to sign the warrant, and execution was delayed for more than three months: once Mary was dead, Elizabeth's hold over Scottish policy was gone.

However, the value of Moray's huckstering epistle as regards the Casket Letters is obvious, for this is the first unequivocal mention of them, and we can be sure that, when the copies were sent to Wood, about 5th June, 1568, the final selection of *piéces de conviction* had been made.

It having been decided that the Commission assembled by Elizabeth with the avowed purpose of arranging a compromise between Mary and her dissident subjects should meet at York early in October, Moray took charge of the Casket and its contents, giving a formal receipt on 16th September, 1568, to the Earl of Morton (211). The Casket is described as "a silver box overgilt with gold", and its contents are named as "all missive letters, contracts or obligations for marriage, sonnets or love-ballads, and all other letters contained therein, sent and passed between the Queen, our Sovereign Lord's mother, and James sometime Earl Bothwell". The box is also said to have been found with Dalgleish on 20th June, 1567. Moray acknowledges that Morton had kept the contents unchanged, which was something altogether outside his own knowledge, but perhaps he only meant to record Morton's asseveration to that effect.

Early in October, the Commission began its work. The details of the sessions are complex, and need not detain us here. Suffice it to say that, without the knowledge of Mary's Commissioners, and purely extra-judicially, Moray's Commissioners shewed the Scotch translations of the Casket Letters to the English Commissioners. The account of this transaction is given in a letter from the English Commissioners, the Duke of Norfolk, the Earl of Sussex and Sir Ralph Sadler, to Queen Elizabeth, dated 11th October, 1568 (214):

"Please it, your most excellent Majesty, to understand, that, since our last dispatches, the Earl of Moray and his colleagues, to occupy

the time, have put in their answer to the complaints exhibited by
their adverse party, the copy of which answer we send herewith to
your Majesty. And, albeit they have in the same touched nothing
plainly in the cause of the murder, whereupon they stay and suspend
their proceedings until they may be resolved in their articles proposed
unto us, which we sent in our last letters to your Majesty, yet the
said Earl hath been content privately to shew us such matter as they have
to condemn the Queen of Scots of the murder of her husband, to the
intent they would know of us how your Majesty, understanding the
the same, would judge of the sufficiency of the matter, and whether,
in your Majesty's opinion, the same will extend to condemn the
Queen of Scots of the said murder. And so they sent unto us (Maitland), James Macgill and Mr. George Buchanan and (John Wood),
which in private and secret conference with us, not as Commissioners,
as they protested, but for our better instruction, after declaration of
such circumstances as led and induced to vehement presumptions to
judge her guilty of the said murder, shewed unto us a copy of a bond,
bearing date 19th April, 1567, to the which the most part of the
Lords and Councillors of Scotland have put to their hands, and, as
they say, more for fear than any liking they had of the same. (This
was the bond signed at "Ainsley's Supper"). Which bond contained
two special points, the one a declaration of Bothwell's purgation
of the murder of the Lord Darnley, and the other a general consent
to his marriage with the Queen so far forth as the law and her own
liking should allow. And yet, in proof that they did it not willingly,
they procured a warrant, which was now shewed unto us, bearing
date 19th April, signed with the Queen's hand, whereby she gave
them licence to agree to the same, affirming that, before they had
such warrant, there was none of them that did or would set to their
hands, saving only the Earl of Huntly. There was also, in the copy of
the bond, a copy of a warrant following much to that effect, saving
that the one did licence to do and the other seemed to discharge and
pardon that (which) was done, which bears date 14th May. It appeared also, that the self-same day of the date of this bond, being
19th April, the Earl of Huntly was restored by Parliament: which
Parliament was the occasion that so many Lords were thus assembled,
which, being all invited to a supper by Bothwell, were induced after
supper, more for fear than otherwise, to subscribe to the said bond,
two hundred hackbutters being in the court and about the chamber-
door, where they supped, which were all at Bothwell's devotion,
which the said Lords so much misliked that, the next morning by
4 o'clock, few or none of them were left in the town, but departed
without taking their leave.

There was also a contract shewn unto us, signed with the Queen's hand and also with Bothwell's, bearing date 5th April, written, as it is said, with the Earl of Huntly's own hand, who, with one Thomas Hepburn, were the only witnesses to the same. Which contract beareth date, before Bothwell's purgation of the murder, whereof he was not tried nor purged before 12th April following, and also before the process of divorce began between Bothwell and his wife, which was not begun before 1st May, and yet with speed ended within eight days, and the ungodly marriage between the Queen and him solemnised 15th May after; and also 15th June following, the Queen herself was taken by her Nobility (Carberry). The counterfeit and colourable taking of the Queen by Bothwell, when he carried her to Dunbar, was 24th April after the death of her husband, who was murdered 10th February, 1567.

There was also a contract shewn unto us of the Queen's own hand of the marriage to be had between her and Bothwell, bearing no date, which had not *verba de praesenti*, as the other had bearing date 5th April. It appeared also unto us by two letters of her own hand, that it was by her own practice and consent that Bothwell should take her and carry her to Dunbar, of policy, as (Maitland) told us, because else there could be no device in law to pardon his foul fact of the murder, affirming that, by the laws of that realm, a pardon for great offences includeth all lesser facts and offences, but extendeth to none greater than that which is pardoned; and, therefore, except he should commit the highest offence, which is treason, as he did in laying violent hands upon his Sovereign, no pardon could serve to excuse him of the murder, and, having his pardon for the treason, it sufficeth also for the murder. A fit policy for a detestable fact".

One may interject here, however, that Bothwell or Mary would have needed considerable legal knowledge to think of such a recondite stratagem, and yet, paradoxically, they must at the same time have been unaware that no man could be tried twice for the same crime. Bothwell had already stood trial for the murder of Darnley on 12th April, 1567. In the absence of any evidence for the prosecution, he had been acquitted; therefore he needed no pardon.

The letter continues,

"After the device of the murder was determined, as it seemed by the sequel, they inferred upon a letter of her own hand that there was another mean of a more cleanly conveyance devised to kill the King, for there was a quarrel made between him and the Lord Robert of Holyrood House (one of Mary's illegitimate half-brothers) by carrying of false tales between them, the Queen being the instrument, as they said, to bring it to pass, which purpose, if it had taken effect, as it was very likely, for the one giving the lie to the other, they were at daggers drawing, it had eased them of the prosecution of the devilish fact which, this taking none effect, was afterwards most tyrannously executed.

Afterwards, they shewed unto us one horrible and long letter of her own hand, as they say, containing foul matter and abominable to be either thought of or to be written by a Prince, with divers fond ballads; which letters, ballads and other writtings before specified, were closed in a little coffer of silver and gilt, heretofore given by her to Bothwell. The said letters and ballads do discover such inordinate love between her and Bothwell, her loathing and abhorrence of her husband that was murdered, in such sort as every good and godly man cannot but detest and abhor the same.

And these men here do constantly affirm the said letters and other writings which they produce of her own hand, to be her own hand indeed, and do offer to swear and take oathes thereupon, the matter contained in them being such as could hardly be invented or devised by any other than by herself, for that they discourse of some things which were unknown to any other than to herself and Bothwell; and it is hard to counterfeit so many, so the matter of them, and the manner how these men came by them is such, as it seemeth, that God, in whose sight murder and bloodshed of the innocent is abominable, would not permit the same to be hid or concealed.

In a paper here enclosed, we have noted to your Majesty the chief and special points of the said letters, written, as they say, with her own hand, to the intent it may please your Majesty to consider them, and so to judge whether the same be sufficient to convict her of the detestable crime of the murder of her husband, which, in our opinons and consciences, if the said letters be written with her own hand, is very hard to be avoided. Most humbly beseeching your Majesty, that it may please the same to advertise us of your opinion and judgement therein, and to direct us with such speed as to your Highness shall be thought convenient how we shall proceed further in this great matter".

Which letter having been written by Norfolk and his two colleagues, the astonishing contradiction follows that within a few days the Duke was considering marriage with the captive Queen (449). This, however, *might* be the decision of a gambler, risking his life by marrying a murderess to obtain a crown, but it may suggest that Norfolk did not take the documents very seriously. Perhaps more surprising is a letter by another commissioner, who had seen all the above papers and also signed the letter of 11th October, namely Sussex, who, on 22nd October, 1568, wrote to Cecil (324),

"This matter must at length take end, either by finding the Scotch Queen guilty of the crimes that are objected against her, or by some manner of composition with a shew of saving her honour. The first, I think, will hardly be attempted for two causes; the one, for that, if her adverse party accuse her of the murder by producing her letters, she will deny them, and accuse most of them of manifest consent to the murder, hardly to be denied, so as, upon trial on both sides, her proofs will judicially fall best out, as it is thought".

Yet he says further in his letter,

"I think the best in all respects for the Queen's Majesty (Elizabeth), if Moray will produce such matter as the Queen's Majesty may, by virture of her superiority over Scotland, find judicially the Scotch Queen guilty of the murder of her husband, and therewith detain her in England at the charges of Scotland".

This, although he thought Mary's proofs would fall out best!

Presently, for reasons which need not detain us here, the Commission was transferred to Westminster, where the first session was held on 25th November, 1568, at which Moray received assurances as to the future should he embark on the perilous sea of direct accusation of his Queen (217). With the position thus clarified, the Accusation was presented on 26th November in form of a document, known as the "Eke" (218), in which it is affirmed that

"as James sometime Earl Bothwell was the chief executor of the horrible and unworthy murder, perpetrated in the person of the deceased King Henry of good memory (!), father to our Sovereign Lord, and the Queen's lawful husband; so was she (Mary) of the fore-knowledge, devise, persuader and commander of the said murder to be done".

The Commission met again on 29th November, on which occasion Lennox appearing in person, put in as evidence "in writing, briefly and rudely, some part of such matter as he had conceived to be true for the charging the Queen of Scots with the murder of her husband, his son" (219).

On 1st and 3rd December, Mary's Commissioners, stressing the fact that Moray was allowed access to the tribunal, requested that Mary also should be permitted to attend in proper person (220 & 221) and to speak in her own defence before Elizabeth, her Privy Council, her nobility and such foreign Ambassadors as were then present in England. Elizabeth refused this request on 4th December (222), and Mary's Commissioners then made the mistake of offering a compromise (223), although Moray's "Eke" had been an open accusation of the Queen, and refusal to answer it or, still worse, to offer a compromise, naturally implied that the Queen was guilty. It is important to realise, however, that the offer came from Mary's Commissioners without her knowledge and sanction, and in spite of her instructions that, should any accusation be made, she must either answer it personally or the Commission must be broken off. By failing to follow their Mistress's orders, her Commissioners had taken a seriously false step. However, at the next session, 6th December, 1568, an attempt was made to remedy this, and Mary's Commissioners asserted their intention of breaking off the sittings, producing a document to this effect. By some means not stated in the Journal Book, Mary's Commissioners were held in play and the Commission continued in being. Moray was then pressed into adducing proof of the accusations in his "Eke" (225). The Regent complied by producing the Act of Parliament of 15th December, 1567, and the 'Book of Articles' (Buchanan's indictment of the Queen) (226). The text of this latter document is given by Hosack (325), and it contains five references to the Casket Documents. The first reference is to Casket Letter II, "And she (Mary) being at Glasgow, travailing to bring the King with her, she wrote to Bothwell to see if he might find out a more secret by medicine to cut him off nor that way which between them they had conspired and devised of his destruction before her coming from Edinburgh". This is not an unfair gloss on the text, but the next reference seems to be unsupported by evidence, "And from Glasgow by her letters and otherwise, she (Mary) held him (Bothwell) continually in remembrance of the said house". The third reference is to the Contract of Marriage of 5th April, 1567, pointing out that this was dated before Bothwell's divorce, and the fourth is to both Contracts of Marriage. The final reference describes the finding of the Silver Casket on the arrest of George Dalgleish, as set out in Morton's declaration.

On 7th December, 1568, the Casket was itself produced, those present being the English Commissioners and Moray and his associates: Mary's Commissioners were not present; the Journal of the Commission for that day runs (326),

"And so they produced a small gilded coffer of not fully one foot long, being garnished in many places with the Roman letter 'F' set under a royal crown, wherein were certain letters and writings, and as they said and affirmed to have been written with the Queen of Scots own hand to the Earl Bothwell, which coffer, as they said, being left in the Castle of Edinburgh by the said Earl Bothwell before his flying away, was sent for by one George Dalgleish, his servant, who was taken by the Earl of Morton, who also thereto, sitting presently as one of the Commissioners, avowed upon his oath the same to be true, and the writings to be the very same, without any manner of change, and before they would exhibit the sight of any of those letters, they exhibited a writing, written in a Roman hand in French, as they said and would avow by the Queen of Scots herself, being a promise of marriage to the Earl Bothwell, which writing being without date, and, although some words therein seem to the contrary, they did suppose so to have been made and written by her before the death of her husband, the tenor whereof thus followeth, Nous, Marie, par la Grace de Dieu, etc.

They also exhibited another writing in Scottish which they avowed to be wholly written by the Earl of Huntly, dated 5th April, containing a form of a contract for marriage between the said Queen and Earl Bothwell, subscribed Mary, which they avowed to be the proper hand of the said Queen, and, underneath it, James Earl Bothwell, which they also avowed to be the proper hand of the said Earl Bothwell. At which time he was commonly defamed, and not cleansed, as they termed it, which is, not acquitted, before 12th April following, the tenor of which contract thus ensueth, At Seton the 5th day of April, etc.

After this, they shewed the Acts or Records of the Justice Court held at Edinburgh the said 12th April, signed by John Bellenden, Justic-Clerk, among which followed dittay, otherwise called the indictment, in this sort following, James Earl Bothwell, Lord Hailes and Crichton, etc. And in another place amongst the said Acts and Records, the names of the Lords of High Assizes, with their answer to the said dittay, as hereafter followeth, Assize Andrew Earl of Rothes, etc.

To which, they added this in defence of the said verdict (of acquittal of Bothwell for the murder of Darnley), besides the matters contained in the later part of the protestation made by George Earl of Caithness, Chancellor of the said Assize (i.e. Foreman of the jury), that the said dittay was not in this point true, alleging the murder to be committed the 9th day of February, which was . . . . . . for that indeed the murder was committed on the next day, being the 10th in the morning before at 2 hours after the midnight preceding, which in law was and ought to be truly accounted the 10th day, and so the acquittal not in that point untrue.

They also required that consideration might be had of certain words in divers places of the contract made at Seton, 5th April, 1567, whereof the tenor is above inserted, whereby is by express words mentioned that, before 5th April, a process of divorce between the Earl Bothwell and Dame Janet Gordon, his wife, was intended, that is to say begun, for that they alleged that at the same time the process of the said contract was made not only when the said Earl was undivorced, but before any such process or suit was intended; for which purpose, the said Earl and his colleagues produced forth before the several ordinary ecclesiastical judges, two acts of the whole judgment of the divorce, wherein appeared that the process of the one began 25th April, and the other 27th, as further may appear by the tenor of the said process hereafter following''.

At this point, we must interject a few remarks concerning this part of the proceedings. First, from the definite wording of the phrase, ". . . . .before they would exhibit the sight of any of those letters" (in the casket), it is obvious that the two contracts of marriage were not "casket documents", yet, prior to this, Moray had given a receipt for the Casket (16th September, 1568) "with all missive letters, contracts or obligations for marriage, sonnets or love-ballads, and all other letters contained therein" (211). Were these, then, other contracts? Or did it seem more politic at that moment to produce the contracts as official documents along with the Acts and Records of the Court of Justice and of the Ecclesiastical Courts? Secondly, the protestation of the Earl of Caithness referred to was simply a formal matter, almost universal at that time, declaring that, should the acquittal of Bothwell not be acceptable to the authorities, no blame should attach to the jury: the reason for such a protestation was to prevent the presentation of a writ of error with consequent punishment of the jurors for a wrongful verdict. The Lords here excuse the Earl and his fellow-jurors on the ground that the indictment was laid for murder on the wrong day, a point of which no notice seems to have been taken at the trial; perhaps this argument might have been used to justify a fresh trial of Bothwell had he fallen into the hands of the Lords at a subsequent date. Finally, it was not true that the divorce between Bothwell and his wife had not begun by 5th April; as we have seen (page 59), Lady Jane took out a procuratory for the divorce on 20th March.

The Journal of the Commission continues,

"After this, the said Earl (Moray) and his colleagues offered to shew certain proofs, not only of the Queen's hate towards the King, her husband, but also of inordinate love towards Bothwell, for which purpose they first produced a letter written in French and in a Roman hand, which they avowed to be a letter of the said Queen's own hand to Bothwell, when she was at Glasgow with her husband, at the time she went to bring him to Edinburgh, the tenor of which letter hereafter followeth, Il semble que avecques vre. absence, etc. (Casket Letter I).

After this, they produced for the same purpose one other long letter, written also with the like hand and in French, which they also avowed to be a letter written with the said Queen's own hand to Bothwell from Glasgow. Upon the reading whereof, they did express their own knowledge of certain matters concerning doubtful speeches in the same letter contained, of one William Highgate, and . . . and also of the Laird of Minto, by which they intended to make it plain that otherwise was doubtful (i.e. obscure), the tenor of all which letter followeth hereafter, Estant party du lieu, etc." (Casket Letter II).

On the following day, the examination of the Casket Letters proceeded (227):

"This day (8th December, 1568), the Earl of Moray, according to the appointment yesterday, came to the Queen's Majesty's (Elizabeth's) Commissioners, saying that, as they had yesternight produced and shewed sundry writings tending to prove the hatred which the Queen of Scots bore towards her husband to the time of his murder, wherein also, they said, might appear special arguments of her inordinate love towards the Earl Bothwell; so, for the further satisfaction both of the Queen's Majesty (Elizabeth) and their Lordships, they were ready to produce and shew a great number of other letters written by the said Queen, wherein, as they said, might appear very evidently her inordinate love towards the said Earl Bothwell, with sundry other arguments of her guiltiness of the murder of her husband. And so, thereupon, they produced seven several writings written in French in the like Roman hand, as others her letters which were shewed yesternight, and avowed by them to be written by the said Queen. Which seven writings, being copied, were read in French, and a due collation made thereof as near as could be by reading and inspection, and made to accord with the originals, which the said Earl of Moray required to be redelivered, and did thereupon deliver, the copies being collationed. The tenors of all which seven writings hereafter follow in order, the first being in manner of a sonnet, O Dieu, ayez de moy, etc."

From this it appears that the originals were forthwith returned to Moray, the English Commissioners keeping the copies of, presumably, the six letters and the ballad shewn on this day and of the two letters shewn on the previous day, but the whole transaction is not quite as clearly described as we could wish.

Moray and his colleagues then produced other evidence; the examinations, processes, verdicts and judgments of Hay, Hepburn, Powry and Dalgleish, all servants of Bothwell who had been executed for the murder of Darnley. They also produced the decision of the Parliament of December, 1567, to condemn Bothwell, Ormiston and others for the same murder, and the protestation made by Huntly, Argyll and Herries which at least shewed acquiescence in the proceedings of that Parliament by some of Mary's supporters.

On the following day, 9th December, Mary's Commissioners again tried to withdraw, but were again frustrated (228), because the English Commissioners found the document of withdrawal unsatisfactory in some parts, and asked for it to be redrafted. By this means, the Commission was kept in being while Moray produced further evidence against Mary, whose Commissioners were, of course, ignorant of the proceedings which had been continuing in their absence. Since the Commission was thus still legally in session, the Protestant Lords continued their case against the Queen. The Journal for that day reads (229), "The Queen's Majesty's (Elizabeth's) Commissioners, being occupied in perusing and reading certain letters and sonnets written in French, being duly translated into English", Mary's Commissioners requested to see them for the purpose which we have mentioned above. Later the same day, Morton made a declaration concerning the apprehension of Dalgleish and the opening of the Casket (230), and which he put in writing on the following day (213). and other evidence was also produced: a statement by the Queen that she was a free agent, made on 12th May, 1567, immediately before her marriage to Bothwell (242); the instrument of abdication by the Queen (234); the evidence of Darnley's servant, Thomas Nelson, who was present when the house at Kirk o'Field blew up and was somewhat miraculously preserved from death by the town wall (232), and the evidence of Thomas Crawford (234), a gentleman of the Earl of Lennox,

"who was, as they said, the same party of whom mention is made in in a long letter in French and exhibited the 7th of this month (Casket Letter II), when it is said, about the beginning of the same letter, that a gentleman of the Earl of Lennox met the party that wrote the letter about four miles from the place where the letter was written, as in the copy of the same letter may appear. Whereupon the said Thomas Crawford, coming before the Commissioners, he did present a writing, which he said he had caused to be made according to the truth, of his knowledge, which being read, he affirmed upon his corporal oath then taken to be true, the tenor whereof hereafter followeth, The words between the Queen, etc.

After this was read, the said Crawford said that, as soon as the Queen of Scots had spoken with the King, his Master, at Glasgow from time to time, he, the said Crawford, was secretly informed by the King of all things which had passed between the said Queen and the King, to the intent he should report the same to the Earl of Lennox, his Master, because the said Earl durst not then, for displeasure of the Queen, come abroad, and that he did immediately at the same time write the same, word by word, as near as he possibly could carry the same away; and sure he was that the words now reported in his writing, concerning the communication between the Queen of Scots and him, upon the way near Glasgow, are the very same words, on his conscience, that were spoken, and that of hers, being reported to him by the King are the same in effect and substance as they were delivered by the King to him, though not perhaps in all parts the very words themselves. The confession of the said Thomas Crawford in writing hereafter followeth thus, The words between the Queen and me, etc.".

This document, consisting of two parts, "These are the words I remember were between the King and the Queen in Glasgow when she took him away to Edinburgh" and "The words between the Queen and Thomas Crawford, the Queen and me by the way as she came to Glasgow to fetch the King, when my Lord my Master (Lennox) sent me to shew her the cause why he came not to meet her himself", is given complete by Henderson (313): we shall discuss it in connexion with Casket Letter II (page 163): for the moment it is only necessary to say that it is quite impossible that both Letter II and this evidence can be genuine, for their correspondence, even as to what Mary thought that Darnley was thinking, is too exact. It is certain that Crawford's evidence was compiled from the letter, from which it is virtually copied.

On 13th December, Elizabeth decided to enlarge her Commission (235), which hitherto had comprised Norfolk, Sussex and Sadler, to whom Sir Nicholas Bacon, Leicester, Lord Clinton and Cecil had already been added when the venue was removed from York to Westminster (216). On 14th December the first session of the enlarged Commission was held at Hampton Court, the Earls of Northumberland, Westmoreland, Shrewsbury, Worcester, Huntingdon and Warwick being present. The state of affairs up to that date was laid before the Commission in considerable detail and (236)

> "there were produced sundry letters written in French, supposed to be written by the Queen of Scots own hand to the Earl of Bothwell, and therewith also one long sonnet, and a promise of marriage in the name of the said Queen with the said Earl Bothwell. Of which letters the originals, supposed to be written with the Queen of Scots own hand, were then also presently produced and perused, and, being read, were duly conferred and compared for the manner of writing and fashion of orthography with sundry other letters long since heretofore written and sent by the said Queen of Scots to the Queen's Majesty (Elizabeth). And next after these, was produced and read a declaration of the Earl Morton of the manner of the finding of the said letters, as the same was exhibited upon his oath, 9th December; in collation whereof no difference was found. Of all which letters and writings, the true copies are contained in the memorial of the acts of the sessions of 7th and 8th December".

If it be accepted, and it is not quite clear that this is so, that the words "in collation whereof no difference was found" refer to the "conferring and comparing for the manner of writing and fashion of orthography" of Mary's previous undoubted letters, it would appear that some attempt was made to test the claim that the letters were in the Queen's own handwriting. On this point, however, three things must be said. First of all, the contemporary copies in French of four of the Casket Letters (Nos. III, IV, V and VI) and of the love-ballad, have come down to us, and in these the

orthography is notably different from that commonly used by Mary.
Secondly, most of the Lords were almost illiterate, but, even if they had
been accomplished with the pen, the comparison of handwriting is a
science which was not understood until the present century, and the mis-
takes of so-called experts in this matter are a byword. In this connexion, it
should be borne in mind that the English and Scottish Lords almost all
wrote Gothic script, while Mary, having been brought up in France,
wrote a "Roman", or as we should now say, an Italianate hand. The
difference between these two forms was greater than the difference between
English and Continental handwriting of the present day; yet anyone who
receives an occasional letter from the Continent will agree that, to the
Englishman, all foreign writing appears the same. It is more than probable,
it is certain, that any documents written in Italianate script would all be
ascribed to the same author, in this case, the Queen of Scots; and no
reliance can be placed on this inspection by the unskilled lords. Finally,
it must be remembered that Norfolk continued with his plan to marry the
Queen of Scots, in spite of the production of this evidence, and the letters
did not deter Northumberland and Westmoreland from rising in rebellion
on Mary's behalf within a year from this session.

The re-examination of evidence was continued on the following day
(15th December, 1568), and the process occupied the whole day. Now that
the evidence against Mary had been produced, the Commission was
allowed to go into a decline. On 10th December, Elizabeth gave Mary
three choices (237): she might answer the accusation by her Commissioners; she might answer by writing; or she might answer to some nobles
sent to her for that purpose. If she refused all of these "it will be thought as
much as she were culpable". Mary's Commissioners repulsed these suggestions (238), and asked for leave for the Queen to pass to either Scotland
or France. The proceedings dragged on: on 25th December, Mary replied
to Moray's "Eke" (239), accusing the Lords of the murder which they had
imputed to her and offering to prove the case, meanwhile asking Elizabeth
to cease from giving them support. Mary asked also for "such writings as
were produced against her", which Elizabeth thought reasonable, but
nevertheless failed to supply. She repeated this request for the writings or
copies of them on 7th January, 1569, when she stated that she was ready to
answer the accusations and to accuse her rebles (240), whereupon Elizabeth, still refusing to allow Mary to see the evidence produced against
her, then asked the Queen of Scots to abdicate (241), which Mary refused
(242).

On 10th January, 1569, Moray was given leave to return to Scotland,
"for so much as there has been nothing deduced against them as yet that
may impair their honour or allegiances; and, on the other side, there had
been nothing sufficiently produced nor shewn by them against the Queen
their Sovereign, whereby the Queen of England should conceive or take

any evil opinion of the Queen her good sister, for anything yet seen" (243). This must not be taken as representing Elizabeth's real feelings in the matter: it was merely a declaration of policy. With an unjudged Queen in Elizabeth's hands, the Government of Scotland must pursue a course agreeable to her. Mary's Commissioners tried to prevent Moray's return to Scotland by now accusing him once again in Mary's name of the murder of Darnley (244), but without avail: Moray and his associates were not only permitted to depart, but also received a loan of £5,000 from the generous Queen of England (247). Elizabeth now delayed the withdrawal of Mary's Commissioners by offering to let their mistress have copies of the writings produced against her, provided that she would promise to answer them (245), but this offer was refused on the ground that the Commission, which had never been regarded as judicial and was avowedly for the purpose of making a compromise between Mary and the Regent, had now ceased to exist, since Moray had retired (246). It was not until 31st January that the Queen of Scots' Commissioners were given licence to depart (250), by which time Moray was safely in Scotland and in full command of the Government.

One other item of importance needs to be related. On 15th October, 1570, Randolph wrote to Cecil (291) concerning the alleged bond for the murder of Darnley, "This bond was kept in the Castle (of Edinburgh) in a little box covered with green cloth, and, after the apprehension of the Scottish Queen at Carberry Hill, was taken out of the place where it lay by (Maitland), in presence of James Balfour, the Clerk of the Register and keeper of the keys where the registers are". Yet another casket; or was it the same one?

When Moray returned to Scotland in January, 1569, he presumably took the Casket Documents with him, with the possible exception of one of the Contracts of Marriage. As we have seen, they passed into the hands of Morton on 22nd January, 1571, when copies were made *ad futuram rei memoriam;* unfortunately, these copies have never been seen again. On Morton's execution, 2nd June, 1581, the letters passed to the Earl of Gowrie (292), who likewise perished on the scaffold, 3rd May, 1584, since when all trace of the letters has been lost, for both Esmé Stewart and Elizabeth seem to have failed to get possession of them, although they tried repeatedly to do so (293).

The Silver Casket has also disappeared, although the one in the possession of the Hamiltons and exhibited at the Lennoxlove Museum is traditionally accepted as the identical box. It is about the right size (8 inches long), of silver, with gilded scroll-work; the lock has been "stricken up", but there are no crowned 'F's. The provenance of this box is not above suspicion, and the identity is made even less likely by the presence of a key.

The contents of the letters became known by publication. In 1571, Buchanan's 'Detectio' was published, and three of the letters appeared in

Latin translation (294); the Scotch version of the 'Detection' also appeared in this year, and Wilson's English edition in the year following: Both contained translations of all eight letters, the first sentence being given in French. Wilson's version of the letters is only an anglicised version of the Scotch, and cannot be considered as a separate translation. A French edition appeared in 1573 (295), and this had appended French translations of seven of the letters; this version, the so-called Published French, was completely dissimilar from the original French, and was prepared by re-translation from the English; it does not purport to be original and may be neglected.

The Documents are thus available to us in the following forms: Letter I in the Published Scotch translation, in the English Translation (Record Office), presumably in the form read at the session of the Commission on 9th December, 1568, and in the Published Latin and Published French translations. Letter II in Published Scotch, in English Translation (State Papers) and in Published Latin and French Translation; Letter III in a contemporary copy of the original French (Record Office) and in the Published Scotch version; Letter IV in a contemporary copy of the original French (Hatfield House), in English Translation (Hatfield House), and in Published Scotch, French and Latin; Letter V in a contemporary copy of the original French (Record Office), and in Published Scotch and French; Letter VI in a contemporary copy of the original French (Hatfield House), in English Translation (Hatfield House), and in Published Scotch and French; and Letters VII and VIII in Published Scotch and French Translations only. The love-ballad, which consists of twelve unequal verses, is also only available in the Published French, which may, however, be a copy of the original, and Published Scotch Translation. The French Contract of marriage exists in contemporary form in the Cotton collection, while the Scotch Contract (5th April) appears only to be available in published form.

	Original French. (copy)	Contemporary Scotch.	Wilson's Anglicised Scotch.	Contemporary English.	Published French.	Published Latin. (Buchanan's)
Letter No. I	—	Yes.	Yes.	Yes.	Yes.	Yes.
,, II	—	Yes.	Yes.	Yes.	Yes.	Yes.
,, III	Yes.	Yes.	Yes.	—	—	—
,, IV	Yes.	Yes.	Yes.	Yes.	Yes.	Yes.
,, V	Yes.	Yes.	Yes.	Yes.	Yes.	—
,, VI	Yes.	Yes.	Yes.	Yes.	Yes.	—
,, VII	—	Yes.	Yes.	—	Yes.	—
,, VIII	—	Yes.	Yes.	—	Yes.	—
Love-ballad.	?	Yes.	Yes.	—	Yes.	—

Unfortunately, the French copies of Letters III, IV, V, and VI are obviously somewhat inaccurate, and we have no means of knowing whether the original spelling has been retained: if it has, these letters were certainly not written by Mary, whose idiosyncrasies of orthography (such as 'é' for 'ai') are not reproduced.

A decision on the authorship of the letters can therefore only be made by textual criticism, and the next ten chapters of this book are devoted to this approach. It is necessary, however, to anticipate the conclusions of the enquiry to this extent, that it will become apparent that Letters III, IV, V, VI, some parts of Letter II, and the Love-ballad are all by one person, while Letters I, VII, VIII and the greater part of Letter II are by another, who is undoubtedly Mary Queen of Scots; furthermore, it is possible, from internal evidence, to date these four "authentic" letters accurately, and to prove that the dates of three of them are other than those suggested by Moray and his associates, and even that Letters VII and VIII could not have been placed in the Casket by Bothwell.

When comparing the two sets of letters as differentiated above, the reader is asked to notice that, in genuine Marian productions, as in her autograph letters printed in Labanoff, and in Letters I, II, VII and VIII the sentences are short and direct; occasional obscurity occurs from failure to qualify pronouns, but the style is completely different from Letters III, IV, V and VI, in which the author is at pains to be affected, uses long and complicated constructions, and breathes a completely different literary spirit, being also addicted to flowery terms of endearment, such as "My dear life". Finally, Mary, in her Casket Letters refers to the Earl of Huntly as "your brother", or "your brother-in-law that was", while the other lady invariably denounces him as "your false brother" (or "brother-in-law").

With these few observations on style and a reminder that the letters deserve to be examined as hostile witnesses, we can proceed to their scrutiny.

CHAPTER II

Casket Letter No. III

This letter is taken first for two reasons: it is perhaps the finest example of a letter by the "other woman", as unlike anything by Mary as could be imagined, and besides it is utterly impossible to find a suitable date for its composition by the Queen. It seems probable that it was written to Bothwell, but at what date is not certain. The Lords who shewed it to the Commission made no attempt to date it, and the copy in the Record Office is endorsed by a clerk "To prove the affection". The letter has considerable felicity of expression and is eminently French in spirit.

Original French (89)

"Monsieur, si lenvy de votre absence celuy de vostre oubli la crainte du dangier tant promis d'un chacun a vostre tant ayme personne peuvent me consoller Je vous en lesse a juger veu le malheur que mon cruel sort et continuel malheur mavoient promis a la suite des infortunes et craintes tant recentes que passes de plus longue main les quelles vous scaves mais pour tout cela Je me vous accuserai ni de peu de souvenance ni de peu de soigne, et moins encores de vostre promesse violee ou de la froideur de vos lettres mestant ja tant randue vostre que ce quil vous pleust mest agreeable et sont mes penses tant volonterement, aux vostres a subjectes que je veulx presupposer que tout ce que vient de vous procede non par aulcune des causes de susdictes ains pour telles qui son justes et raisonnables et telles qui Je desir moy mesme qui est lordre que maves promis de prendre final pour la seurete et honnorable service du seul soubtien de ma vie, pour qui seul Je la veus conserver et sens lequel Je ne desire que breve mort et pour vous tesmoigner combien humblement sous vous commandemens Je me soubmets Je vous ay envoie en signe d'homage par paris lornement du cheif conducteur des aultres membres inferant que vous investant de sa despoille de luy qui est principal le rest ne peult que vous estre subject et avesques le consentement du cueur au lieu du quel puis que le vous ay ja lesse Je vous envoie un sepulcre de pierre dure

100

peinct de noir seme d'larmes et de ossements, la pierre Je la compare
a mon cueur qui comme luy est talle en un seur tombeau ou receptacle
de voz commandements et sur tout de vostre nom et memoire qui y
sont enclos, comme mes cheveulx en la bague pour Jamais nen sortir
que la mort ne vous permet fair trophee de mes os comme la bague en
est remplie en signe que vous aves fayt entiere conqueste de moy, de
mon cueur et iusque a vous en lesser les os pour memoire de vre
victoire et de mon agreable perte et volontiere pour estre mieux
employe que ie ne le merite Lesmail demiron est noir qui signifie la
fermete de celle que lenvoie les larmes sont sans nombre ausi sont
les craintes de vous desplair les pleurs de vostre absence et le desplaisir
de ne pouvoir estre en effect exterieur vostre comme je suys sans
faintise de cueur et desprit et a bon droit quant mes merites seront
trop plus grands que de la plus perfayte que Jamais feut et telle que je
desire estre et mettray poine en condition de contrefair pour digne-
ment estre emploiee soubs vostre domination. reseves la donc mon
seul bien en aussi bonne part, comme avecques extreme Joie Jay fait
vostre mariage, qui jusques a celuy de nos corps en public ne sortira
de mon sein, comme merque de tout ce que Jay ou espere ni desire de
felicite en ce monde or craignant mon cueuer de vous ennuyer autant
a lire que je me plaise descrir Je finiray apres vous avoir baise les
mains daussi grande affection que je prie Dieu (o le seul soubtien de
ma vie) vous la donner longue et heureuse et a moy vre bonne grace
le seul bien que je desire et a quoy je tends Jay dit a ce porteur ce que
Jay apris sur le quel Je me remets sachant, le credit que luy donnes
comme fait celle qui vous veult estre pour Jamais humble et obeis-
ante loyalle femme et seulle amye qui pour Jamais vous voue entierement le cueur le corps sans aucun changement comme a celuy
que Je fait possesseur de cueur du quel vous pouves tenir seur
Jusques a la mort ne changera car mal ni bien onque ne estran-
gera".

Contemporary Scotch Translation (298)

"My Lord, gif the displesure of zour absence, of zour forzetfulness,
ye feir of danger sa promisit be everie ane to zour sa luifit persone may
gif me consalatioun, I leif it to zow to juge, seing the unhap that my
cruell lot and continuall misadventure hes hitherto promysit me,
following ye misfortunes, and feiris as weill of lait, as of ane lang tyme
bypast, the quhilk ze do knaw. Bot for all that, I will in na wise accuse
zow, nouther of zour lytill remembrance, nouther of zour lytill cair,
and leist of all of zour promeis brokin, or of ye cauldness of zour
wryting, sen I am ellis sa far maid zouris, yat yat quhilk pleisis zow is
acceptabill to me; and my thochtis ar sa willingly subdewit unto
zouris, that I suppois yat all that cummis of zow proceidis not be ony
of the causis foirsaid, but rather for sic as be just and ressonabill,

and sic as I desyre myself. Quhilk is the fynal order that ze promysit to tak for the suretie and honorabil service of ye only uphald of my lyfe. For quhilk alone I will preserve the same, and without the quhilk I desyre not but suddane deith. And to testifie unto zow how lawly I submit me under zour commdementis, I have send zow, in signe of homage, be Paris, the ornament of the heid, quhilk is the chief gude of the uther memberis, inferring thairby that, be ye seising of zow in the possession of the spoile of that quhilk is principall, the remnant cannot be bot subject unto zow, and with consenting of the hart. In place quhairof, sen I have ellis left it unto zow, I send unto zow ane sepulture of hard stane, colourit with blak, sawin with teiris and bones. The stane I compare to my hart, that as it is carvit in ane sure sepulture or harbour of zour commandementis, and abone all, of zour name and memorie that ar thairin inclosit, as is my hear in this ring, never to cum forth, quhill deith grant unto you to ane trophee of victorie of my banes, as the ring is fullit, in signe that yow haif maid ane full conqueis of me, of myne hart, and unto yat banes my banes be left unto yow in remembrance of your victorie and my acceptabill lufe and willing, for to be better bestowit then I merite. The ameling that is about is blak, quhilk signifyis the steidfastnes of hir that sendis the same. The teiris ar without number, sa ar the dreddouris to displeis yow, the teiris of your absence, the disdane that I cannot be in outwart effect youris, as I am without fenzeitnes of hart and spreit, and of gude ressoun, thocht my meritis wer mekle greiter then of the maist profite that ever was, and sic as I desyre to be, and sall tak pane in conditiounis to imitate, for to be bestowit worthylie under your regiment. My only wealth, ressaif thairfoir in als gude part ye same, as I have ressavit your marriage with extreme joy, the quhilk sall not part furth of my bosum, quhill yat mariage of our bodyis be maid in publict, as signe of all that outher hope or desyris of blis in yis world. Zit, my hart, feiring to displeis you as mekle in the reiding heirof, as I delite me in ye writing, I will mak end, efter that I have kissit zour handis with als greit affectioun as, I pray God (O ye only uphald of my lyfe) to gif yow lang and blissit lyfe, and to me zour gude favour, as the only gude yat I desyre, and to ye quhilk I pretend. I have schawin unto this beirer that quhilk I have leirnit, to quhome I remit me, knawand the credite that ye gaif him, as scho dois that will be for ever unto zow humbill and obedient lauchfull wife, that for ever dedicates unto zow hir hart, hir body, without ony change, as unto him that I have made possessour of hart, of quhilk ze may hald zow assurit, yat unto ye deith sall na wayis be changeit, for evill nor gude sall never mak me go from it".

Using these two versions of the letter, we shall now try to produce an acceptable modern English translation, commenting where necessary on any points which seem significant.

> "Monsieur, if grief at your absence and of your forgetfulness and the fear of danger so spoken of by everyone to your so loved person can console me, I leave you to judge;"

This letter, therefore, is written to Bothwell as is proved by the reference to Paris, but when the Earl had been absent for some time, long enough for him to have proved himself an inadequate correspondent, and when he was in a position of some danger.

> "Seeing the misfortune that my cruel destiny and continual misfortune have brought upon me, according to the bad luck and fears, recent as well as a long time past, of which you are aware".

The double use of "malheur-misfortune" in this sentence, and the clumsy statement, that misfortune has brought misfortune upon her, is typical of our author. It is clear that the attachment between her and Bothwell has existed for a long time, and that we are dealing with a passionate and highly-strung individual.

> "Concerning all that, I shall not accuse you . . ."

"me" has been written in error for "ne"

> ". . . nor of your forgetfulness, nor little care, nor still less of your broken promise, nor of the coldness of your letters, I being already so far rendered yours that what pleases you is agreeable to me, and my thoughts are so willingly submissive to yours that I want to assume that everything that comes from you proceeds, not from any of the fore-said causes, but rather from such as are just and reasonable, and such as I desire myself . . ."

The lady has evidently put up with a great deal from Bothwell; she is still prepared to regard his actions as dictated in her best interests, but she knows in her heart that this is not true.

> ". . . which is the course which you promised to take for the safety and honourable service of the only support of my life, for whom alone I want to preserve it, and without whom I only wish for sudden death".

This sentence is not clear, either grammatically or in the train of thought. The word "final" ought, one feels, to follow "l'ordre", not "prendre", in which place it is decidedly an intruder. It has been neglected in making the translation. However, even so, there is a false sequence of ideas, or, rather, an over-leaping of them. What was meant was, of course, "...which is the course which you promised to take for my safety and honourable service, for you are the only support of my life, for whom alone I want to preserve my life . . . ", but the feeling of submission was too strong, and the "honourable service" had to be given to him, which is grammatically nonsense.

"Now, to witness to you how humbly I submit myself to your orders, I
have sent you, in sign of homage, by Paris, the ornament of the head".

The ornament is, of course, a lock of hair. Paris was, presumably,
Nicholas Hubert, otherwise French Paris, a servant of Bothwell. In the
deposition which he made on 10th August, 1569, he stated that he first
entered into credit with the Queen at Callendar when she was going to
Glasgow, and that she gave him a purse of gold at that time to give to
Bothwell (208). If therefore he was the bearer of the present letter and
gift, either they came from Mary after 22nd January, 1567, or else they
came from someone else. The former seems to be quite impossible, for
Bothwell was never absent from her for more than a few days thereafter,
and we are forced to conclude that the letter came from another hand.

". . . the ornament of the head, conductor of the other members,
implying thereby that, in investing you with the fruit of that which is
principal, the remainder cannot but be subject to you, and with the
consent of the heart, in place of which, since I have already relinquished it to you, I send you a sepulchre of hard stone, painted black
and strewn with tears and bones".

Once again, the sequence of thought 'o'erleaps its sell', for, if Bothwell
already had her heart, she had no need to send him something in place of
it. This "sepulchre of hard stone, strewn with tears and bones" has been
identified with the table diamond enamelled black which, shortly before
the birth of her son, Mary bequeathed to Bothwell, but, as will appear,
the "sepulchre" was evidently a locket, large enough to contain a lock of
her hair, and there is no need to suppose that the stone was precious or
even semi-precious.

"The stone, I compare with my heart, which, like it, is fashioned
into a sure tomb or receptacle . . ."

So it is, certainly, a locket of sorts.

". . . for your orders and, above all, of your name and memory, which
are enclosed therein, like my hair in the trinket, never to come forth
until death permits you to make a trophy of my bones".

The word "bague" has always been translated "ring", but here it undoubtedly refers to the stone, in which she has sent her hair; furthermore,
in the inventories of Mary's reign which Robertson printed the word
'bague' occurs frequently, indicating various jewels and ornaments other
than rings.

"Thus the trinket is filled therewith, in sign that you have made an
entire conquest of me, of my heart . . ."

This expresses the meaning, but the construction shews the lost train of
thought which we have noted before, and the word "comme", which is
here translated "thus" was incorrectly chosen. Once again, "trinket"
is the obvious translation of "bague". A ring could not be filled with

anything—except a finger. Similarly, the "therewith" must mean hair, but seems to refer to the writer's bones.

"... and, until death has left you my bones in memory of your victory, and my agreeable and willing loss, to be better used than I deserve".

Once again, the sentence has lost its end, for the first "and" is left hanging and neglected.

"The enamel round about ('emiron' for 'environ') is black, which signifies the steadfastness of her who sends it; the tears are without number, as are the fears of displeasing you, the tears for your absence, and the displeasure that I cannot be in outward appearance yours, as I am without scruple in heart and spirit and in deed (à bon droit), even if my merits were much greater than those of the most perfect person who ever was, and such as I desire to be, and whom I shall take pains to imitate in character (or station: 'condition' can mean either), in order to be employed worthily under your domination".

This apparently means that, even if she were a much more worthy person, she would still not scruple to be Bothwell's wife, and, in fact, she will try to behave as if she were perfect, in order to be employed worthily under his domination. It is extremely difficult to imagine a Queen, however much in love, penning this sentence to a subject; even if we translate 'condition' as 'character'. Clearly the other reading of 'station' would be ludicrous in a Queen writing to an Earl.

"Receive it then, O My Only Wealth, in as good part as I have received your marriage with extreme joy, which, until the public one of our bodies will ever be hidden in my breast . . ."

There is no need to postulate here, as does Lang, that the writer was carrying about a contract of marriage stuffed in her corsage: the meaning is obviously that she will keep their "marriage before God", as such deluded girls usually term it, secret, until their union has been sanctified by holy matrimony.

". . . (and) as a mark of all that I have or hope for of happiness in this world. Now, My Heart, fearing to bore you in the reading as much as it has pleased me in the writing, I shall finish after having kissed your hands with such great affection that I pray God (O the Sole Supporter of My Life) to give to you a long and happy life, and to me your good grace, the sole wealth that I desire and at which I aim".

The reader will probably be as much in doubt as the writer whether the words in parenthesis are addressed to the Deity or to the Earl.

"I have told the bearer what I have learnt, I trust him (or, I remit myself to him), knowing the credit (i.e. credence) which you accord to him, as does she who wishes to be for ever your humble, obedient and loyal wife, and only friend, who forever vows to you entirely her heart and body, without any alteration, as to him whom I make possessor of my heart, of which you can be sure that it will not change until death, for no evil or good whatsoever will estrange it".

The letter is not signed or dated, but we can nevertheless be sure that the text is complete; one may well think, however, that such a letter could not have been allowed to end unsigned, and the absence of a signature is a suspicious occurrence, suggesting that the document produced was not an original.

On the other hand, we can be equally sure that this letter is not forged; it bears all the stamp of a genuine love letter; no forger would have taken so many words to say so little. If we assume that this letter is written by some deluded girl who believes herself to be married to the Earl in all but name, who, after a passionate love-affair now feels herself somewhat neglected, and who perhaps imagines that the Earl is of a rather higher station of life than she, we shall probable not be far from the truth. Such a woman, possibly French and certainly foreign, might be secreted at the Hermitage, unknown to the frequenters of the Court, having been lured thither under promise of marriage, which, she might be told, could not be solemnized yet for weighty political reasons. We cannot be certain of the date, Bothwell has been away a long time, his letters to her are cold and infrequent, but since she sends his servant to him, he is probably in the same country. Furthermore, he is in some personal danger. It is not impossible that the letter dates from the months before his marriage to Lady Jane Gordon (Feburary, 1566), perhaps during the Chase-about Raid, in which case, the letter is to be dated between about 20th September, 1565, for Bothwell arrived in Scotland on 17th of that month, and 10th October, when the rebellion ended. As a tentative suggestion, the theory that Bothwell brought a "wife" with him from France when he returned secretly to Scotland early in March, 1565, is worth bearing in mind. He landed on the West coast of Scotland, which gave easy access to Liddesdale, and, although he certainly went to Edinburgh, he soon took up residence at the Hermitage (269 & 270), but had to flee the country hurriedly when he was summoned for treason (2nd May, 1565). Did he leave the lady behind at the Hermitage, and, if so, had she still not seen him when, having been recalled to Scotland, he helped to overthrow the Chase-about Rebels?

CHAPTER III

Casket Letter No. I

This letter was alleged to have been written by Mary to Bothwell during her visit to Glasgow in January, 1567, while Darnley was lying ill; since the letter is dated "From Glasgow this Saturday morning", the only possible date, if it be genuine, is 25th January, 1567. The English copy of the letter is endorsed by Cecil's clerk, "A short letter from Glasgow to the Earl Bothwell. Proves her disdain against her husband". The first sentence in the original French is preserved; it runs, "Il semble qu'avecques vostre absence soit joynt l'oubly, veu qu'au partir vous me promistes de vos nouvelles. Et toutesfoys je n'en plus apprendre, etc."

Contemporary English (88)	*Contemporary Scotch* (204)
It seemyth that with your absence forgetfulnes is joyned, consydering that at your departure you promised me to sende me newes from you; nevertheless I can learn none. And yet did I yesterday looke for that that should make me meryer than I shall be. I think you do the lyke for your returne, prolonging it more than you have promised.	It appeiris, that with zour absence thair is alswa joynit forzetfulnes, seand yat at zour departing ze promysit to mak me advertisement of zour newis from tyme to tyme. The waitting upon yame zisterday causit me to be almaist in sic joy as I will be at zour returning, quhilk ze have delayit langer then zour promeis was.
As for me, if I heare no other matter of you, according to my commission I bring the man Mondaye to Cregmiller, where he shall be upon Wednisdaye. And I to go to Edinboroughe to be lett blud, if I have no word to the contrayry.	As to me, howbeit I have na farther newis from zow, according to my commissioun, I bring the man with me to Craigmillar upon Monounday, quhair he will be all Wednisday; and I will gang to Edinburgh to draw blude of me,

107

He is the meryest that ever you sawe, and doth remember unto me all that he can to make me beleve that he loovith me. To conclude: you wold saye that he makith love to me, wherein I take so much plesour that I never com in there but my payne of my syde doth take me; I have it sore to-daye. Yf Paris doth bring back unto me that for which I have sent, it shuld much amend me.

I pray you send me word from you at large, and what I shall doo if you be not returned when I shall be there; for if you be not wyse, I see assuredly all the wholle burden fallen upon my shoulders. Provide for all, and consider well.

First of all, I send this present to Ledinton to be delivered to you by Beton, who goith to one day a law of Lord Balfour. I will saye no more unto you, but that I pray God send me good newes of your voyage.

From Glasgo this Saterday morning.

gif in the meane time I get na newis in ye contrary fra zow.

He is mair gay than ever ze saw him; he puttis me in remembrance of all thingis yat may mak me beleve he luifis me. Summa, ze will say yat he makis lufe to me: of ye quhilk I tak sa greit plesure, yat I enter never where he is, bot incontinent I tak ye seiknes of my sair syde, I am sa troubillit with it. Gif Paris brings me that quhilk I send him for, I traist it sall amend me.

I pray zow, advertise me of zour newis at lenth, and quhat I sall do in cace ze be not returnit quhen I am cum thair; for, in cace ze wirk not wysely, I se that the haill burding of this will fall upon my schoulderis. Provide for all thing, and discourse upon it first with yourself.

I send this be Betoun, quha gais to ane day of law of the Laird of Balfouris. I will say na farther, saifing that I pray zow to send me gude newis of zour voyage.

From Glasgow this Setterday in the Morning.

The English and Scotch translations shew some discrepancies, which we must try to reconcile in constructing a modern version. It may be helpful to remember that the Scotch translation was made first, and that the English translation was made in some haste, with the Scotch version available for confirmation of difficult points. Let us take the letter phrase by phrase, and first, we must notice that there is no form of address at all. This suggests, either that the opening part of the letter is missing, or that what we have is the postscript to an official document. There can be no doubt that the letter is by Mary herself, or that it was sent to the Earl of Bothwell: the mention of Paris may be taken as conclusive on the latter point. Now, it was frequently Mary's custom to send an official letter, written, sometimes in Scotch, by her Secretary or clerk, which was properly addressed and dated, and which she then signed, adding a postscript in her own hand. Several examples will be found in Labanoff's collection. Sometimes the postscript begins with a short address, "Mon compère", "Monsieur de Foix"; at other times, no address is made, and the autograph postscript commences with the message. Sometimes the letter was signed, and the postscript then added without further signature, in other cases, the message was added first, and the signature was appended below it. Since this letter is obviously complete in itself, it seems reasonable to suppose that it is such a postscript, appended to an official letter which had been signed, and this would account for the absence of both address and signature.

"It seems that, with your absence, there is also joined forgetfulness, seeing that, at your departure, you promised to send me news, nevertheless I can learn none".

So far as the latter part of this sentence is concerned, the English version has been followed, since one might expect that, with the Scotch and French versions before him, the English translator was less likely to omit a phrase than the Scottish, who worked from the French document only. It follows, from this sentence, which is clearly an opening one, that Bothwell has departed from Mary, not the reverse, and that he has been away for some days. Obviously, the Earl's mission is one of importance, for the Queen is worried by the absence of news.

"The expectation of news (French, "nouvelles", plural, hence "yame" = "them" in the Scotch) yesterday caused me to be almost as merry as I shall be at your return, which, like your news, you have delayed longer than you promised".

This sentence is a compromise, but it seems to express the meaning fairly. Mary is certainly anxious for the Earl's return.

"As for me, if I hear no other news from you, according to the orders which I have given, I shall bring the man with me on Monday to Craigmillar, where he will be on Wednesday".

If, then, she learns nothing from Bothwell to make her think that the journey is unwise, Mary will bring "the man" to Craigmillar, leaving on Monday and arriving on Wednesday; the word "all" before Wednesday in the Scotch version would appear to be an error. "According to my commission" (French, 'selon ma commission'), of course means, "according to my orders, or the orders which I have given": if the orders were Bothwell's, as the Published French translation is made to say, this would have read, "according to your commission". Now, who is "the man"? If Darnley, the arrangements do not hold good, for, although Mary may have started from Glasgow with Darnley on Monday, 27th January, 1567, since they did not reach Edinburgh until 31st January or 1st February, (199) (Friday or Saturday), it seems more likely that they left on Tuesday, 28th; in any case, they did not proceed beyond Edinburgh to Craigmillar, and could hardly have reached there by Wednesday from Glasgow, especially since Darnley was still unwell.

As was pointed out by Mahon (508), the following paragraph shews quite clearly that "the man" was her son, and no one will be surprised at such a designation by a proud mother of her only child. The fact becomes all the more clear when we recall that Mary left Stirling on Monday, 13th January, 1567, bringing James with her to Craigmillar, where they arrived on Wednesday, 15th January, the journey from Stirling taking the usual two days(199).

"And I will go to Edinburgh to be bled (?) if I have no word to the contrary".

Naturally, Mary could not remain away from the seat of government, but, if it were a question of blood-letting, as it may have been, for we know that she was ill when this letter was written, and bleeding was a panacea in those days, why should she not have this done at Craigmillar? Is it to be supposed that the surgeon was too busy to visit her? The answer is that, as in one version of Casket Letter II, the translator has read 'saigner' for 'signer', thus accounting for the clumsy Scotch form, in which, the verb having been used actively in the original French, the phrase has been rendered actively, "to draw blood of me", while the later English translation corrects this to the passive, "to be let blood", no doubt because the "of me" was an interpolation rendered necessary by the wrong translation of the verb. The sentence should then be rendered, "And I will go to Edinburgh to sign (state documents), if I have no word to the contrary". Presently (page 113) we shall see why Mary was hesitant in returning to Edinburgh and even thought it possible that Bothwell might send her some news which might prevent her from going thither.

"He is the merriest that ever you saw, and brings to my mind everything possible which makes me believe that he loves me. Summa, you would say that he makes love to me, in which I take so much pleasure, that I never come in where he is, but I get the pain in my side: I have it badly to-day".

Can anyone read the above and not believe that this is a mother, ill of body and worried in mind, speaking of her loved and only child? The Prince was, at this time, seven months old. That it is not Darnley of whom she writes, we can tell by comparing this passage with the comparable one in Casket Letter II, where Darnley's behaviour is shewn to be very different, for he "used many small flatteries so coldy and so wisely that you would wonder at it". 'Summa' (French, 'en somme' or, simply, 'somme') was a common expression of the time, and frequently used by Mary. The pain which Mary had in her side was undoubtedly caused by the gastric ulcer of which she nearly died in October, 1566. She was still suffering pain from it in December, as du Croc mentioned, and it would not be surprising if it were still present a fortnight later. We may notice, however, that there is no sign or mention of it in the long Casket Letter II, which is another reason for thinking that the present letter precedes the visit to Glasgow by a fortnight or so. The passage about the pain is, however, conclusive evidence that this letter is by Mary herself.

"If Paris brings back that for which I send, it should do me much good". This reference to Paris is important. If Paris's deposition be correct, in that he first 'entered into credit' with the Queen on or about 22nd January, this sentence would, at first sight, suggest that this letter is posterior to that date. But there is another explanation. Although Paris had not yet earned Mary's confidence (i.e. "entered into credit with her"), she would very likely know his name as Bothwell's constant attendant. Since Bothwell was intending to send Mary news of importance, nothing is more likely than that he should take Paris with him on this mission, intending to employ him as the messenger. If, as has been thought, Mary had sent for some drug to ease her pain, not Paris, but her apothecary would have been the obvious person to send. It may be noted that, while the English version uses the past tense, "that for which I have sent", the Scotch uses the present, and also adds a 'him' which is omitted in the English, "that which I send him for". A possible reading of the original might therefore be "that for which I (now) send". Mary knows, as all sufferers from peptic ulcer know, that her condition is aggravated by worry, and that, if Paris, at present with Bothwell, should bring back the good news for which she now sends, "it should much amend" her.

"I pray you, send me your news at length, and (tell me) what I should do if you have not returned when I arrive at Edinburgh, for, unless you are careful, the whole burden of this affair will fall upon my shoulders. Be prepared for everything, and think well about your business before you act (or come to a decision)".

This seems to be the sense of the message. As the Scotch version shews, the "first of all' belongs to this sentence and not, as in the English, to the following one. The "burden" of the affair seems to be the general situation which may well lead to Mary's ruin, not any specific event, for, in the English translation it is described as "all the whole burden".

"I send this present (letter) to Lethington to be delivered to you, by Beaton, who goes to a day of law with the Laird of Balfour'.

We need not look for any sinister meaning in the failure of the Scotch version to mention Lethington: it was probably a simple error. If Mary were in Glasgow and Bothwell in Edinburgh, there would be no problem about the sending of the letter, for there must have been frequent messingers travelling between the two towns when the Queen was thus separated from her Government. If, however, Bothwell were at that time in the Eastern Marches, but his exact whereabouts were unknown, it would be quite natural to send the letter to Lethington, the seat of Mary's secretary's father, situated on the Leader. Presumably, Beaton's "day of law", or the civil case in which he and the "Laird of Balfour" were interested, was to be held somewhere in that area, and the Laird of Lethington, Sir Richard

Maitland, would provide one of his servants to convey the letter to Both-well, who was perhaps keeping him informed of his movements. The Laird of Balfour was, like the bearer, a Beaton: the latter was probably John Beaton, Master of the Queen's Household.

"I will say no more, but that I pray God (or you) to send me good news of your journey.

From Glasgow, this Saturday morning".

If the above interpretation be accepted, which seems difficult to be avoided, it will be seen that the last five words were the addition of a forger. Mahon (510) seems to think that the date is genuine, but that the place of origin has been added. This would be more comprehensible if the date had preceded the place, for the forger would be more likely to add something at the end rather than insert words where the obvious space might be lacking. However, if this letter were really the postscript to an official document, thus explaining the absence of an address, the official document would be dated and the place of signature would be named in it; thus the addition after the postscript would be supererogatory.

In order to understand the background to which this letter properly belongs, it is necessary to remind the reader that the Earl of Morton and many of the Riccio rebels were pardoned on 24th December, 1566, the day on which Darnley removed himself to Glasgow. Mary had gone to Drymen, and she returned to Stirling on 28th December, leaving for Tullibardine with Bothwell on 30th December. It should be remembered that the Laird of Tullibardine, Murry, was a Lennox follower, and this latter visit suggests that Mary was anxious to obtain news concerning the implications of Darnley's flight, or even to arrange for the opening of negotations with him through one of the family supporters. She was back in Stirling with Bothwell by 1st January, 1567, at latest, and the following day there was a meeting of the Privy Council at that place: the name of Bothwell is absent from the sederunt (507). It is obvious that he had de-parted in some haste, and his destination was the Eastern March, for, on 23rd January, Drury wrote to Cecil (315): "The Lord Morton lyeth at the Lord of Whittinghame's, where the Lord Bothwell and (Maitland) came of late to visit". Now, Morton, who was at Newcastle at the time of his pardon, might well have been expected to enter Scotland early in January: for some reason or other, he delayed his entry, for he was in Berwick on the 10th January (66).

That Mary should wish to get in touch with this powerful representative of the Douglases was natural. Darnley's action indicated the likelihood of imminent rebellion, and, although she might well expect that Morton would be ranged against her husband, who had betrayed him in the Riccio affair, yet this was not absolutely certain, for Morton had sided with Darnley on that occasion, and no doubt would again if it could be shewn to be worth his while. Almost as bad, he might decide to be neutral, being a 'precise Protestant', and withold his powerful help from the Queen.

We now understand Mary's anxiety lest the whole burden fall upon her, her desire for news, delayed beyond expectation because of Morton's slowness in entering Scotland. Perhaps the official letter to which this was the postscript was one of additional instructions as to the extent of the concessions which Mary was prepared to make in the event of Morton being unwilling to side with her, but this is pure hypothesis. Since Edinburgh was, *par excellence*, the home of the Protestant faction, we can appreciate that the nature of Morton's reply might well influence a decision on whether it were wise for Mary to take up residence at Holyrood at such a critical juncture.

In his confession before execution in 1581 (517), Morton said that, at the meeting at Whittinghame, Bothwell had proposed the murder of Darnley, but that he, Morton, had refused to "meddle in that matter". We can be sure that this is untrue, for, had such a subject been broached, it would certainly have been alluded to at the proceedings in Westminster in December, 1568, in which Morton himself took part.

The conclusion is inevitable that Casket Letter I was written from Stirling between Tuesday, 7th January, and Saturday, 11th January, 1567, for only then would the allusion to 'bringing the man to Craigmillar on Monday where he would be on Wednesday' fit the facts. It follows that the last line of the letter, "From Glasgow, this Saturday morning" is a forgery, and, it may be pointed out, that it was the minimum addition necessary to produce the required effect. It was no mean intellect which conceived this simple subterfuge.

It may be remarked in parenthesis that this explanation also resolves the problem of the date of the long Casket Letter II, which, from internal evidence, is usually believed to have been begun before and to have been finished after 25th January, thus embracing the apparant date of this present letter. As will appear (page 115), this problem never had any real existence, even if Letter I had been written on the day ascribed to it.

The reader is now asked to re-read one of the versions of Casket Letter III, avoiding all comments, and then to read this letter of Mary. The differences in style will at once be apparent, and an appreciation of these differences will be helpful to an understanding of what follows. Letter III is affected, the sentences are involved, there is a sprinkling of flowery terms, and the spirit is one of submission and, almost, of despair. Conversely, the Marian letter is composed in short, simple sentences, without affectation, there are no terms of endearment, and the spirit is one of an anxiety not unnatural in the circumstances, but quite unmixed with servility, submission or resignation.

CHAPTER IV

Casket Letter No. II

Darnley departed from Stirling on 24th December, 1566, and he seems to have gone direct to Glasgow, where presently he fell ill. The exact nature of the disease is not certain, nor do we know the date of its onset. The first mention of his sickness is by Bedford, who, writing from Berwick to Cecil on 9th January, 1567 (65), says that Darnley has smallpox and that Mary has sent her physician to him.

Mary eventually decided to visit Darnley at Glasgow. She left Edinburgh on or about Monday, 20th January (148), stayed one or two nights at Lord Livingstone's seat, Callendar House, and probably arrived at Glasgow about 22nd January. Bothwell accompanied her as far as Callendar, and then returned to Edinburgh. On 24th January, Bothwell paid a short visit to Liddesdale, for Scrope mentions his presence there in a letter of 28th January, 1567 (729); the Earl was back in Edinburgh on 30th January (513). Mary and Darnley presumably left Glasgow on Monday, 27th or Tuesday, 28th January, for they arrived in Edinburgh on 31st of that month, or the day before or after: there is no certainty of these dates, but they are not important to the argument. Mary's delay in visiting Glasgow is quite understandable. She knew that Darnley was meditating the seizure of the throne by one or other of his two plans: with Spanish assistance obtained by crossing to Flanders, or by abducting the Prince and ruling in his name. She knew that Glasgow was the stronghold of the Lennox faction, and she may well have felt considerable trepidation in putting her head into such an obvious noose. She evidently took a strong escort of Hamiltons, the hereditary enemies of the Lennox, with her, but nevertheless she was acting very courageously. We can be certain that she would not prolong her visit for a day more than was absolutely necessary. However, go she must, for her own personal intervention and her influence on the fickle youth who was her husband, were the only means of averting a resort to arms, and this must be avoided at all costs: the fanatical Catholics would be likely to follow the Lennox, and the fanatical Protestants would not aid Mary. Furthermore, peace must be maintained until the friendly offers of Elizabeth, brought by Bedford at the time of the christening, could be implemented. The position was critical: if rebellion could be staved off for a few months, or even weeks, until Mary, as she believed, would have Elizabeth's full support, her crown and future would be secure.

Darnley was still convalescent from his illness on his return to Edinburgh and he was therefore lodged in a separate house, the old Provost's House of Kirk o'Field, next door to the house recently acquired by Sir James Balfour's brother; the convalescence would end with the bath, no doubt prepared with sweet-smelling herbs, which was to mark the end of the course of medical treatment.

The English version of the letter is endorsed by Cecil's clerk, "The long letter written from Glasgow from the Queen of Scots to the Earl Bothwell". The first sentence of the original French has been preserved, and runs, "Estant partie du lieu ou javoye laisse mon coeur, il se peut aisement juger quelle estoit ma contenance, etc."

In order that the letter which follows may be read with understanding, it is necessary to anticipate in general terms the conclusions to be drawn from it. These are, first, that the letter is not one, but two, the first part being of later date than the second, as is conclusively shewn by the two references to the bracelets; which, in the first reference have been completed, but, in the second, are still unfinished. It will also be seen that the two letters described, with differing emphasis, the same series of events, and we may therefore conclude that they are to two different persons, the first or later part being for the information of Mary's chief minister, the Earl of Moray, the second or earlier being sent to Bothwell. Secondly, there are some additions to these two letters which will easily be recognised as coming from the same pen as Casket Letter III, the "other woman". There is no address or signature, a circumstance which is in itself suspicious. The reader is reminded that the punctuation, paragraphing and use of capital letters are all supplied arbitrarily and do not reflect the originals, in which capitals are few and punctuation almost non-existent.

Contemporary English Translation (88)	*Contemporary Scotch Translation* (456)
1. Being gon from the place where I had left my harte; it may be easily judged what my countenance was, consydering what the body may, without hart, which was cause that till dynner I had used lyttle talke, neyther wold any body advance him selfe therunto,	*1.* Being departit from the place quhair I left my hart, it is esie to be judgeit quhat was my countenance, seeing that I was evin als mekle as ane body without ane hart; quhilk was the occasion that quhile denner tyme I held purpois to na body; nor zit durst ony

thinking that it was not good so to doo.

2. Fowre myles from thence a gentleman of the Erle of Lennox cam to made his commendacions and excuses unto me, that he cam not to meete me, because he durst not enterprise so to doo, consydering the sharp wordes that I had spoken to Conyngham, and that he desyred that I wold com to the inquisition of the facte which I did suspecte him of. This last was of his own head without commission.

3. and I tolde him that he had no receipte against feare, and that he had no feare, if he did not feele himselfe faulty, and that I had also sharply aunsweared to the doubts that he made in his lettres, as though ther had bene a meaning to poursue him. To be short, I have made him hold his peace; for the rest, it weare to long to tell you.

4. Sir James Hamilton cam to meete me, who told me that at another tyme he went his waye when he hard of my comming; and that he sent unto him Houstoun to tell him that he wold not have thought that he wold have followed and accompany him selfe with the Hamiltons. He aunsweared that he was not com but to see me, and that he wolde not follow Stuard nor Hamilton, but by my commandement. He prayed him to go speake to him: he refused it.

5. The Lard Lus, Houston and the sonne of Caldwell, and about XLty hors cam to meete me, and he ld me that he was sent to one

present thameselfis unto me judging yat it was not gude sa to do.

2. Four myle or I came to the towne, ane gentilman of the Erle of Lennox come and maid his commendatiounis unto me; and excusit him that he came not to meit me, be reasoun he durst not interpryse the same, becaus of the rude wordis that I had spokin to Cuninghame: and he desyrit that he suld come to the inquisitioun of ye matter yat I suspectit him of. This last speiking was of his awin heid, without ony commissioun.

3. I answerit to him that thair was na recept culd serve aganis feir; and that he wold not be affrayit in cace he wer not culpabill; and that I answerit bot rudely to the doutis yat wer in his letteris. Summa, I maid him hald his toung. The rest wer lang to wryte.

4. Schir James Hammiltoun met me, quha schawit that the uther tyme quhen he hard of my cumming, he departit away, and send Howstoun, to schaw him that he wald never have belevit that he wald have persewit him, nor zit accompanyit him with the Hammiltounis. He answerit that he was only cum bot to see me, and yat he wald nouther accompany Stewart not Hammiltoun but be my commandement. He desyrit that he wald cum and speik with him: he refusit it.

5. The Laird of Lusse, Howstoun and Caldwellis sone, with XL hors or thairabout, come and met me. The Laird of Lusse said, he was

day a lau from the father, which shuld be this daye, against the signing of his own hand which he hathe; and that knowing of my comming he hath delayed it, and hath prayed him to go see him, which he hath refused, and swearith that he will suffer nothing at his handes. Not one of the towne is com to speake with me, which makith me to think that they be his, and then he speakith well of them, at leaste his sonne.

7. The King sent for Joachim and asked him why I did not lodge nighe to him, and that he wold ryse sooner, and why I cam, whither it wear for any good appoyntment that he cum, and whither I had not taken Paris and Guilbert to write, and that I sent Joseph. I wonder who hath told him so muche, evin of the mariage of Bastian. This bearer shall tell you more upon that.

8. I asked him of his lettres, and where he did complayne of the crueltye of som of them; he saide that he did dreme, and that he was so glad to see me that he thought he shuld dye. Indeed, that he had found faulte with me . . . . . .

9. I went my waye to supper. This berer shall tell you of my arryv . . . praied me to come agayne, which I did, and he told me his grefe, and that he wold make no testament, but leave all unto me, and that I was cause of his sicknes for

chargeit to ane day of law be the Kingis father, quhilk suld be this day, aganis his awin hand-writ, quhilk he hes, and yit notwithstanding, knawing of my cuming, it is delayit. He was inquyrit to cum to him, quhilk he refusit, and sweiris that he will endure nathing of him. Never ane of that towne came to speik to me, quhilk causis me think that they ar his, and neuertheles he speikis gude, at the least his sone.

6. I se na uther gentilman but thay of my company.

7. The King send for Joachim zisternicht and askit at him, quhy I ludgeit not besyde him, and that he wold ryse the soner gif that wer, and quhairfoir I come, gif it was for gude appointment, and gif I had made my estait, gif I had takin Paris. This bearer will tell you sumwhat upon this; and Gilbert to wryte to me, and that I wald send Joseph away. I am abaschit quha hes schawin him so far; zea, he spak evin of ye mariage of Bastiane.

8. I inquyrit him of his letteris, quhairintill he plenzeit of the crueltie of sum; answerit that he was astonischit, and that he was sa glaid to se me that he belevit to die for glaidnes. He fand greit fault that I was pensive.

9. I departit to supper. Yis beirer wil tell yow of my arryving. He prayit me to returne, the quhilk I did. He declairit unto me his seiknes, and that he wald mak na testament, bot only leif all thing to me, and that I was the caus of his

the sorrow he had that I was so strange unto him.

10. And, said he, you asked me what I ment in my lettre to speake of cruelty: it was of your cruelty, who will not accepte my offres and repentance. I avowe that I have don amisse, but not that I have always disavowed. And so have many other of your subjectes don, and you have well perdonid them. I am yong. You will saye that you have also perdonid me many tymes, but that I returne to my faultes. May not a man of my age, for want of councell, fayle twise or thrise, and mysse of promes, and at the last repent and rebuke him selfe by his experience? Yf I may obtayn this perdon, I protest I will never make faulte agayne; and I aske nothing but that we may be at bed and at table togither as husband and wife. And if you will not, I will never rise from this bed. I pray you, tell me your resolution heerof. God knowith that I am punished to have made my God of you, and had no other mynd but of you. And when I offende you som tyme, you are cause therof, for, if I thought when any body doth any wrong to (me) that I might for my refuge make my mone therof unto you, I wold open it to no other. But when I heare any thing, being not familiar with you, I must keepe it in my mynde, and that troublith my wittes for anger.

11. I did still answear him, but that shall be to long. In the end, I asked him why he wold go in the maladie, becaus of the regrait that he had that I was sa strange unto him.

10. And thus he said, ze ask me quhat I mene be the crueltie contenit in my letter. It is of zow alone that will not accept my offeris and repentance. I confess that I have failit, bot not into that quhilk I ever denyit. And siclyke hes failit to sindrie of zour subjectis, quhilk ze have forgevin. I am zoung. Ze will say that ze have forgevin me oft tymes, and zit yat I returne to my faultis. May not ane man of my age, for lacke of counsell, fall twyse or thryse, or inlacke of his promeis, and at last repent himself, and be chastisit be experience? Gif I may obtene pardoun, I protest I sall never mak fault agane. And I crafit na uther thing, bot yat we may be at bed and buird togidder as husband and wyfe. And gif ze wil not consent heirunto, I sall never ryse out of yis bed. I pray zow, tell me your resolutioun. God knawis how I am punischit for making my God of zow, and for having na uther thocht but on zow. And gif at ony tyme I offend zow, ze ar the caus, becaus quhen ony offendis me, gif, for my refuge, I micht playne unto zow, I wald speik it unto na uther body, bot quhen I heir ony thing, not being familiar with zow, necessitie constranis me to keip it in my breist, and yat causes me to tyne my wit for verray anger.

11. I answerit ay unto him, but that wald be ovir lang to wryte at lenth. I askit quhy he wald pas

English shipp. He doth disavow it, and sweareth so, but confessith to have spoken to the men. Afterward I asked him of the inquisition of Hiegate. He denyed it, till I tolde him the very woordes, and then he said that Minto sent him word that it was said that some of the counsayle had brought me a lettre to signe to putt him in prison and to kill him if he did resiste, and that he asked this of Minto him selfe, who said unto him that he thought it was true. I will talke with him tomorrowe upon that poynte. The rest, as Willie Hiegate hath confessed, but it was the next daye that he cam hither.

12. In the end, he desyred much that I shuld lodge in his lodging; I have refused it. I have told him that he must be pourged, and that could not be don heere. He said unto me, I have hard saye that you have brought the lytter, but I wold rather have gon with your selfe. I told him that so I wolde myselfe bring him to Cragmillar that the phisicians and I also might cure him without being farre from my sonne. He said that he was ready when I wolde, so as I wolde assure him of his requeste.

13. He hath no desyre to be seene, and waxeth angry whan I speake to him of Wallcar, and sayeth that he will pluck his eares from his head and that he lyeth, for I asked him before of that, and what cause he had to complayne of . . . . the Lordes, and to threaten them. He

away in ye Inglis schip. He denyis it, and sweiris thairunto, but he grantis that he spak with the men. Efter this, I inquyrit him of the inquisitioun of Hiegait. He denyit the same quhill I schew him the verray wordis was spokin. At quhilk tyme he said that Mynto had advertisit him that it was said that sum of the counsell had brocht an letter to me to be subscrivit to put him in presoun, and to slay him gif he maid resistance. And he askit the same at Minto himself; quha answerit that he belevit ye same to be trew. The morne I wil speik to him upon this point. As to the rest of Willie Hiegaits, he confessit it, bot it was the morne efter my cumming or he did it.

12. He wald verray fane that I suld ludge in his ludgeing. I refusit it, and said to him that he behovit to be purgeit, and that culd not be done heir. He said to me, I heir say ze have brocht ane lytter with zow, but I had rather have passit with with zow. I trow he belevit that I wald have send him away presoner. I answerit that I wald tak him with me to Craigmillar quhair the mediciner and I micht help him and not be far from my sone. He answerit that he was reddy quhen I pleisit, sa I wald assure him of his requeist.

13. He desyris na body to se him. He is angrie quhen I speik of Walcar, and sayis that he sal pluk the eiris out of his head and that he leis, for I inquyrit him upon that, and yat he was angrie with sum of the Lordis and wald threittin thame. He denyis that,

denyeth it, and sayth that he had allready prayed them to think no such matter of him.

14. As for myself, he wold rather lose his lyfe than doo me the leaste displeasour. and then used so many kindes of flatteryes so coldly and so wysely as you wold marvayle at. I had forgotten that he sayde that he could not mistrust me for Hiegates wordes, for he could not beleve that his own flesh, which was myself, wold doo him any hurte, and in deede it was sayde that I refused to have him lett blud, but for the others, he wold at leaste sell his lyfe deere ynoughe, but that he did suspecte no body, nor wolde, but wolde love all that I did love.

15. He wold not lett me go, but wold have me to watche with him. I made as though I thought all to be true, and that I wold think upon it, and have excused my selfe from sytting up with him this night, for he sayth that he sleepith not. You never hard one speake better nor more humbly, and if I had not proofe of his hart to be as waxe and that myne weare not as a dyamant, no stroke but coming from your hand could make me but to have pitie of him. But feare not, for the place shall contynue till death. Remembre also in recompense therof not to suffer yours to be won by that fals race that wold doo no lesse to your selfe.

16. I think they have bene at schoole togither; he hath allwais the teare in the eye. He saluteth

and sayis he luifis thame all, and prayis me to give traist to nathing aganis him.

14. As to me, he wald rather give his lyfe or he did ony displesure to me. And efter yis he schew me of sa money lytil flattereis sa cauldly and sa wysely that ze will abasche thairat. I had almaist forzet that he said, he could not dout of me in yis purpois of Hiegaites, for he wald never beleif yat I, quha was his proper flesche, wald do him ony evil; alsweill it was schawin that I refusit to subscrive the same. But as to ony utheris that wald persew him, at leist he suld sell his lyfe deir aneuch, but he suspectit na body, nor zit wald not, but wald lufe all yat I lufit.

15. He wald not let me depart from him, but desyrit yat I suld walk with him. I mak it seme that I beleive that all is trew, and takis heid thairto, and excusit my self for this nicht that I culd not walk. He sayis that he sleipis not well. Ze saw him never better nor speik mair humbler. And gif I ha not ane prufe of his hart of waxe, and yat myne wer not of ane dyamont quhairintill na schot can mak brek but that quhilk cumis forth of zour hand, I wald have almaist had pietie of him. But feir not; the place sall hald unto the deith. Remember, in recompence thairof, that ye suffer not zouris to be wyn be that fals race that will travell na les with zow for the same.

16. I beleve they have bene at schuillis togidder. He hes ever the teir in his eye. He salutis every

every man, evin to the meanest, and makith much of them, that they may take pitie of him. His father hath bled this daye at the nose and at the mouth: gesse what token that is. I have not seene him, he is in his chambre. The King is so desyrous that I shuld give him meate with my own handes, but trust you no more there where you are than I doo here.

17. This is my first journay; I will end tomorrow. I write all, how little consequence so ever it be of, to the end that you may take of the wholle that that shall be best for you to judge (on margin, "your purpose"). I doo heere a work that I hate muche, but I had begon it this morning. Had you not lyst to laughe to see me so trymly make a lye, at the leaste, dissemble and to mingle truthe therwith? He hath almost told me all on the bishops behalfe and of Suderland, without touching any word unto him of that which you had told me, but only by muche flattering him and pr . . . . him to assure him selfe of me; and by my complayning of the r . . . . en the wormes out of his nose. (On the margin, "I have disclosed all, I have knowen that I wold"). You have hard the rest.

18. We are tyed to with two false races; the goodyeere untye us from them. God forgive me, and God knytt us togither for ever for the most faythfull couple that ever he did knitt together. This is my fayth; I will dye in it.

19. Excuse it yf I write yll, you must gesse the one halfe, I can not doo with all, for I am yll at ease,

body, zea, unto the leist, and makis piteous caressing unto thame, to mak thame have pietie on him. This day his father bled at the mouth and nose: ges quhat presage that is. I have not zit sene him, he keipis his chalmer. The King desyris that I suld give him meit with my awin handis, bot gif na mair traist quhair ze ar than I sall do heir.

17. This is my first jornay. I sall end ye same ye morne. I wryte all thingis, howbeit they be of lytill wecht, to the end that ze may tak the best of all to judge upon. I am in doing of ane work heir that I hait greitly. Have ze not desyre to lauch to se me lie sa weill, at ye leist to dissembill sa weill, and to tell him treuth betwix handis? He schawit me almaist all yat is in the name of the Bischop and Sudderland, and zit I have never twichit ane word of that ze schawit me but allanerly be force, flattering and to pray him to assure himselfe of me. And be pleinzeing on the Bischop, I have drawin it all out of him. Ye have hard the rest.

18. We ar couplit with twa fals races; the devil sinder us, and God knit us togidder for ever for the maist faithful coupill that ever be unitit. This is my faith; I will die in it.

19. Excuse I wryte evill, ye may ges ye half of it, bot I cannot mend it, because I am not weil at eis.

and glad to write unto you when other folkes be asleepe, seeing that I cannot doo as they doo, according to my desyre, that is, betwene your armes, my deere lyfe, whom I beseech God to preserve from all yll, and send you good rest, as I go to seeke myne till tomorrow in the morning, that I will end my bible. But it greevith me that it shuld lett me from wryting unto you of newes of myself, so much have I to write. Send me word what you have determinied heerupon, that we may know the one the others mynde, for marryng of any thing. I am weary and am asleepe, and yet I cannot forbeare scribling as long as ther is any paper. Cursed be this pocky fellow that troublith me thus muche, for I had a pleasanter matter to discourse unto you but for him.

20. He is not muche the worse, but he is yll arrayde. I thought I shuld have bene kylled with his breth, for it is worse than your uncles breth, and yet I was sett no neerer to him than in a chayre by his bolster, and he lyeth at the furder syd of the bed.
21. The message of the father by the waye.
The talke of Sir James Hamilton of the ambassade.
That that the Lard a Luss hathe tolde me of the delaye.
The questions that he asked of Jochim: of my state, of my company, and of the cause of my coming, and of Joseph.
The talke that he and I have had, and of his desyre to please me, of

And zit verray glaid to wryte unto zow quhen the rest are sleipand, sen I cannot sleip as they do, and as I wald desyre, that is in zour armes, my deir lufe, quhome I pray God to preserve from all evill, and send zow repois. I am gangand to seik myne till ye morne quhen I sall end my bybill. But I am faschit that it stoppis me to wryte newis of myself unto zow, because it is sa lang. Advertise me quhat ze have deliberat to do in the mater ze knaw upon this point, to ye end that we may understand utheris weill, that nathing thairthrow be spilt. I am irkit and ganging to sleip, and zit I ceis not to scrible all this paper in sa mekle as restis thairof. Waryit mot this pokische man be that causes me haif sa mekle pane, for without him I suld have an far plesander subject to discourse upon.
20. He is not over mekle deformit, zit he hes ressavit verray mekle. He has almaist slane me with his braith; it is worse than zour uncles, and zit I cum na neirer unto him bot in ane chyre at the bed-seit, and he being at the uther end thairof.
21. The message of the father in the gait.
The purpois of Schir James Hamilton.
Of that the Laird of Lusse schawit me of the delay.
Of the demandis that he askit at Joachim: of my estait, of my company, of the occasion of my cumming, and of Joseph. Item, The purpois that he and I had togidder.
Of the desyre that he hes to pleis

his repentance, and of th'interpretation of his lettre, of Will Hiegates doinges, and of his departure, and of the L. of Levinston.

22. I had forgotten of the L. of Levinston, that at supper he sayd softly to the Lady Rires that he dronk to the persons that I knew, I wold pledge them. And after supper he said softly . . . . I was leaning upon him and warming myselfe, You may well go and see sick folkes, yet can you not be so wellcom unto them as you have this daye left som body in payne who shall never be meary till he have seene you agayne. I asked him who it was: he tooke me about the body and said, One of his folkes that hath left you this daye: gesse you the rest.

23. This day I have wrought till two of the clock upon this bracelet to putt the keye in the clyfte of it, which is tyed with two laces. I have had so lyttle tyme that it is very yll, but I will make a fayrer, and in the meane tyme, take heed that none of those that be heere doo see it, for all the world wold know it, for I have made it in haste in theyr presence.

24. I go to my tedious talke. You make me dissemble so muche that I am afrayde thereof with horrour, and you make me almost to play the parte of a traytour. Remembre that, if it weere not for obeying you, I had rather be dead: my hart bleedith for yt. To be shorte, he will not com but with condition that I shall promise to be with him as heeretofore at bed and borde,

me, and of his repentance, of the interpretatioun of his letter, of Willie Hiegaites matter, of his departing,
of Monsiure de Levingstoun.

22. I had almaist forzet that Monsiure de Levingstoun said in the Lady Reres eir at supper that he wald drink to the folk yat I wist of gif I wald pledge thame. And efter supper he said to me, quhen I was lenand upon him warming me at the fyre, Ze have fair going to se seik folk, zit ze cannot be sa welcum to thame as ze left sum body this day in regrait that will never be blyth quhill he se zow agane. I askit at him quha that was. With that he thristit my body and said that sum of his folkis had sene you in fascherie, ze may ges at the rest.

23. I wrocht this day quhill it was twa houris upon this bracelet for to put ye key of it within the lock thairof, quhilk is couplit underneth with twa cordonnis. I have had sa lytill tyme that it is evill maid, bot I sall mak ane fairer. In the meane tyme, tak heid that nane that is heir se it, for all the warld will knaw it, becaus for haist it was maid in yair presence.

24. I am now passand to my fascheous purpois. Ze gar me dissemble sa far that I haif horring thairat, and you caus me do almaist the office of a traitores. Remember how, gif it wer not to obey zow, I had rather be deid or I did it: my hart bleidis at it. Summa, he will not cum with me except upon conditioun that I will promeis to him that I sall be at bed

and that I shall forsake him no more, and upon my worde he will doo whatsoever I will, and will com, but he hath prayed me to tarry till after tomorrow.

25. He hath spoken at the fyrst more stoutly, as this bearer shall tell you, upon the mater of his Englishmen, and of his departure, but in the end he commith to his gentlenes agayne.

26. He hath told me among other talk, that he knew well that my brother had told me at Sterling that which he had said there, whereof he denyed the halfe, and specially that he was in his chambre.

27. But now, to make him trust me, I must fayne somthing unto him, and therfore, when he desyred me to promise that when he shuld be wholle we shuld make but one bed, I told him, fayning to beleve his faire promesses ... did not change his mynde betwene this tyme and that, I was contented, so as he wold saye nothing therof, for, to tell it betwene us two, the Lordis wisshed no yll to him, but did feare leste, consydering the threateninges which he made in case we did agree togither, he wolde make them feele the small accompte they have maid of him, and that he wold persuade me to poursue som of them; and for this respecte shuld be in jelousy if at one instant ("by and by" written above) without their knowledge I did breake a game

and buird with him as of befoir, and that I sall leif him na ofter, and doing this upon my word, he will do all thingis that I pleis, and cum with me. Bot he hes prayit me to remane upon him quhil uther morne.

25. He spak verray braifly at ye beginning, as yis beirer will schaw zow, upon the purpois of the Inglishmen, and of his departing. Bot in ye end he returnit agane to his humilitie.

26. He schawit amangis uther purposis yat he knew weill aneuch that my brother had schawin me yat thing quhilk he had spoken in Striviling, of the quhilk he denyis ye ane half, and abone all yat ever he came in his chalmer.

27. For to mak him traist me, it behovit me to fenze in sum thingis with him; thairfoir, quhen he requeisted me to promeis unto him that quhen he was haill we suld have baith ane bed, I said to him fenzeingly, and making me to beleve his promisis, that gif he changeit not purpois betwix yis and that tyme, I wald be content thairwith, bot in the meane tyme I bad him heid that he leit na body wit thair of becaus, to speik amangis our selfis, the Lordis culd not be offendit nor will evill thairfoir, bot they wald feir in respect of the boisting he made of thame, that gif ever we aggreit togidder he suld mak thame knaw the lytill compt thay take of him, and that he counsallit me not to purchas sum of thame by him. Thay for this caus wald be in jelosy gif at

made to the contrary in their presence.

28. And he said unto me very pleasant and meary, think you that they doo the more esteeme you therefore? But I am glad that you talke to me of the lordis. I here that you desyre now that we shall lyve a happy lyfe, for if it weare otherwise it could not be but greater inconvenience shuld happen to us both than you think; but I will doo now whatsoever you will have me doo, and will love all those that you shall love, so as you make them to love me allso. For so as they seeke not my lyfe, I love them all egally.

29. Therupon I have willed this bearer to tell you many prety thinges, for I have to muche to write, and it is late, and I trust him upon your worde. To be short, he will goe any where upon my worde.

30. Alas, and I never deceavid any body, but I remitt myself wholly to your will, and send me word what I shall doe, and whatever happen to me, I will obey you. Think also yf you will not fynde som invention more secret by physick, for he is to take physick at Cragmillar, and the bathes also, and shall not com fourth of long tyme.

31. To be short, for that that I may learne, he hath greate suspicion, but yet nevertheless trustith upon my worde, but not to tell me as yet anything. Howbeit, if you will that I shall avowe him, I will know all of him; but I shall never

anis without thair knawledge I suld brek the play set up in the contrair in thair presence.

28. He said verray joyfully, and think zow thay will esteme zow the mair of that? Bot I am verray glaid that ze speik to me of the Lordis; for I beleve at this tyme ze desyre that we suld leif togidder in quyetnes, for gif it were utherwyse, greiter inconvenience micht come to us baith than we ar war of; bot now I will do quhatever ze will do, and will lufe all that ze lufe, and desyres zow to mak thame lufe in lyke maner. For sen thay seik not my lyfe, I lufe thame all equallie.

29. Opon yis point this beirer will schaw zow mony small thingis, becaus I have over mekle to wryte, and it is lait, I give traist unto him upon zour word. Summa, he will ga upon my word to all places.

30. Allace, I never dissavit ony body, bot I remit me altogidder to zour will. Send me advertisement quhat I sall do, and quhatsaever thing sall cum thairof, I sall obey zow. Advise to with zourself gif ze can find out ony mair secreit inventioun be medicine, for he suld tak medicine and the bath at Craigmillar. He may not cum furth of the house this lang tyme.

31. Summa, be all that I can leirne, he is in greit suspicioun, and zit notwithstanding, he gevis credit to my word, bot zit not sa far that he will schaw ony thing to me; bot nevirtheles, I sall draw it out of him, gif ze will that I avow

be willing to beguile one that puttith his trust in me. Neverthe-les, you may doo all, and doo not estyme me the lesse therfore, for you are the caus ther of, for, for my own revenge, I wold not doo it.

32. He givith me certain charges, and those strong, of that that I feare, evin to saye that his faultes be published, but there be that committ som secret faultes and feare not to have them spoken of so lowdely, and that there is speeche of greate and small. And evin touching the Lady Rires he saide, God graunte that she serve you to your honour; and that men may not think, nor he neyther, that myne owne powre was not in my selfe, seeing I did refuse his offres. To conclude, for a suerety he mistrusteth us of that that you know, and for his lyfe. But in the end, after I had spoken two or three good wordes to him, he was very meary and glad.

33. I have not seene him this night for ending your bracelet, but I can fynde no claspes for yt; it is ready therunto, and yet I feare least it shuld bring you yll happ, or that it shuld be knowen if you were hurte. Send me worde whither you will have it, and more money, and whan I shall returne, and how farre I may speake. Now as farre as I perceave I may do much with you (on margin, "Jay bien la vogue avec vous"). Gesse you whither I shall not be suspected.

all unto him; bot I will never rejoyce to deceive ony body that traistis in me. Zit notwithstanding ze may command me in all thingis. Have na evill opinioun of me for that caus, be ressoun ze ar the occasion of it zourself: becaus, for my awin particular revenge, I wald not do it to him.

32. He gevis me sum chekis of yat quhilk I feir, zea, evin in the quick. He sayis this far, yat his faultis wer publeist, bot yair is that committis faultis that belevis thay will never be spokin of, and zit thay will speik of greit and small. As towart the Lady Reres he said, I pray God that scho may serve zow for your honour; and said, it is thocht, and he belevis it to be trew, that I have not the power of myself into my-self, and that becaus of the refuse I maid of his offeris. Summa, for certanetie he suspectis of the thing ze knaw, and of his lyfe. Bot as to the last, how sone yat I spak twa or thre gude wordis unto him, he rejoysis and is out of dout.

33. I saw him not this evening for to end your bracelet, to the quhilk I can get na lokkis. It is reddy to thame, and zit I feir that it will bring sum malhure, and may be sene gif ze chance to be hurt. Advertise me gif ze will have it, and gif ze will have mair silver, and quhen I sall returne, and how far I may speik.

34. As for the rest, he is wood when he hearith of Ledinton, and of you, and my brother. Of your brother he sayth nothing, but of the Erle of Arguile he doth. I am afraide of him to heare him talke; at the leaste he assurith him selfe that he hath no yll opinion of him. He speakith nothing of those abrode, nether good nor yll, but avoydith speaking of them.

35. His father keepith his chamber; I have not seene him. All the Hamiltons be heere, who accompany me very honestly. All the frendes of the other doo com allwais when I goe to visitt him. He hath sent to me and prayeth me to see him ryse tomorrow in the morning early. To be short, this bearer shall declare unto you the rest, and if I shall learne any thing, I will make every night a memoriall thereof. He shall tell you the cause of my stay. Burne this lettre, for it is dangerous, neyther is ther anything well said in it, for I think upon nothing but upon greefe, if you be at Edinboroughe.

36. Now if to please you, my deere lyfe, I spare nether honour, conscience, nor hazard, nor greatnes, take it in good parte, and not according to the interpretacion of your false brother in lawe, to whom I pray you give no credit against the most fayhtfull lover that ever you had or shall have. See not also her whose faynid teares you ought not more to regarde than the true travails which I endure to deserve her place, for obtayning of which

34. He inragis when he heiris of Lethingtoun, or of zow, or of my brother. Of your brother he spiekis nathing. He speikis of the Erle of Argyle. I am in feir quhen I heir him speik, for he assuris himself yat he hes not an evill opinioun of him. He speikis nathing of thame that is out, nouther gude nor evill, bot fleis that point.

35. His father keipis his chalmer, I have not sene him. All the Hammiltounis ar heir, that accompanyis me verray honorabilly. All the freindis of the uther convoyis me quhen I gang to se him. He desyris me to come and se him ryse the morne betyme. For to mak schort, this beirer will tell zow the rest. And gif I leirne ony thing heir, I will mak zow memoriall at evin. He will tell zow the occasioun of my remaning. Burne this letter, for it is ovir dangerous and nathing weill said in it, for I am thinkand upon nathing but fascherie. Gif ze be in Edinburgh at the ressait of it, send me word sone.

36. Be not offendit for I gif not ovir greit credit. Now seing to obey zow, my deir lufe, I spair nouther honour, conscience, hasarde nor greitnes quhat sumevir, tak it, I pray zow, in gude part, and not efter the interpretatioun of zour false gude-brother, to quhome I pray zou gif na credite agains the maist faithful luifer that ever ze had or sall have. Se not hir, quhais fenzeit teiris suld not be sa mekle praisit nor estemit as the trew and faithful travellis quhilk I sustene

against my own nature, I doe be-
traye those that could lett me. God
forgive me, and give you, my only
frend, the good luck and prosperitie that your humble and
faythfull lover doth wisshe unto
you, who hopith shortly to be an
other thing unto you, for the
reward of my paynes. I have not
made one worde, and it is very
late, althoughe I shuld never be
weary in wryting to you, yet will I
end, after kyssing of your handes.
Excuse my evill wryting, and
reade it over twise; excuse also
that . . . . . . for I had yesternight
no paper, when I tooke the paper
of a memoria . . . . Remembre
your frende and wryte unto her
and often. Love me all . . . .

for to merite hir place, for obtening
of the quhilk aganis my naturall, I
betrayis thame that may impesche
me. God forgive me, and God give
zow, my only lufe, the hap and
prosperitie quhilk your humble
and faithful lufe desyris unto zow,
quha hopis to be schortly ane
uther thing to zow, for the reward
of my irksum travellis. It is lait; I
desyre never to ceis fra wryting
unto zou, zit now, efter the kissing
of your handis, I will end my
letter. Excuse my evill wryting
and reid it twyse over. Excuse that
thing that is scriblit, for I had na
paper zisterday quhen I wrait that
of ye memoriall. Remember upon
zour lufe, and wryte unto hir, and
that verray oft. Lufe me as I sall
do zow.

37. Remember zow of the purpois
of the Lady Reres,
    of the Inglismen.
    of his mother.
    of the Erle of Argyle.
    of the Erle Bothwell.
    of the ludgeing in Edinburgh.

The Bothwell or Earlier Letter (paras. 24—37)

The reasons for allocating these particular paragraphs to an earlier letter
than paragraphs 1 to 23 have already been mentioned (page 115). Since
paragraph 23 undoubtedly belongs to the later letter which contains a
detailed list (para. 21) of those contents which are all comprised in the
previous paragraphs, it seems reasonable to take the beginning of the
earlier letter at this point. The actual date of the letter is not exactly
ascertainable, since it depends on the date of Mary's arrival in Glasgow,
which is not definitely known, but was probably 22nd January, 1567;
this letter seems to have been written one or two days later.

(24) "I am now passing to my worrying talk"

It is difficult to believe that this is the actual beginning of the letter.
The saluation and address have been omitted, either because of a desire to
make the two letters appear as one, or perhaps because the first sheet contained some remarks which would have been inimical to the case which the
Lords presented against Mary. The sentence thus seems to mean, not that

the Queen is in the act of going to visit Darnley, but that, having dealt in the missing opening paragraphs of her letter with other matters, such as her arrival in Glasgow, she is now passing on to another subject, that of her tedious or worring conversations with her husband, which are, indeed the matters described immediately afterwards. It may be noted that the Scotch word, "purpois" means "conversation" or "subject of discussion".

"You make me dissemble so much that it horrifies me; you make me almost play the part of a traitor. Remember that, if it were not for (the necessity of) obeying you, I should rather die than do it; my heart bleeds at it".

This is straightforward enough, and, while it might perhaps be the attitude of mind of a murderess, it seems to chime much more closely with the circumstances which we have postulated, that the intention of arraigning Darnley at the forth-coming Parliament must have been considered, and one can see no reason why it should have been abandoned (page 46). It is clear from the emotion in the sentence, which, incidentally, is totally unlike the emotion in the letters of the "other woman", that Mary was much attached to Bothwell, even to the extent of carrying out a most unwelcome duty at his suggestion. It was essential that Darnley's schemes be prevented, and at once, before he fully recovered from his sickness. To have arrested him, or to have sought him with armed force would have precipitated civil war; but, if the King could be kept under control by his wife for another six weeks, by which time, if Bedford's embassage were to be trusted, an understanding could have been reached with Elizabeth, the situation would be different. Alliance with Elizabeth would mean quietness and support for Mary from her Protestant subjects; while the sudden and unexpected accusation of Darnley and his father in Parliament, with the immediate production of unequivocal evidence of their treachery, would place the escape of the King and Lennox out of the realm of practical possibility. It is possible that Mary would have allowed sentence of death to be carried out on her husband, and it is equally possible that she already contemplated this, but it seems more probable that she would have been content with banishment and divorce. She, who repeatedly forgave the treachery of her halfbrother Moray, and who refused to gain the Pope's approbation and assistance by executing half a dozen of her most ill-disposed subjects, was hardly likely to imbrue her hands in the blood of her husband. If, however, his death were what she sought, this would surely be the manner of it; less likely would have been an act of assassination, and least likely of all that such an assassination should be carried out as publicly as possible; that is, by gunpowder in the chief town of her realm.

Faced, then, with the task of acting as a not ill-disposed wife for the next six weeks, and contemplating the intended outcome of divorce and banishment, Mary would indeed feel "almost a traitor", yet there was no other way by which her country, her son and herself could be saved; and, if we be disposed to be condemnatory of her deception of her husband, we have only to recall that he thoroughly deserved to be punished for his own treasons and attempted murder.

"Summa, he will not come (back to Craigmillar) with me, except on condition that I promise that I shall be at bed and board with him as before, and that I shall not leave him again . . ."

If she really were contemplating divorce, she would naturally be hesitant to give such a promise. It is difficult to comprehend the last part of the sentence: Darnley had absented himself from Mary, but the reverse had not occurred. Perhaps the sentence should run, "and that I shall not leave him in the future".

". . . and, upon my word, he will do whatsoever I wish, but he has prayed me to wait for him until the day after tomorrow".

The delay in departure, be it noted, is caused by the King; Mary is apparently anxious to remove from Glasgow as soon as possible, as she very well might be. Darnley's reluctance to travel can hardly be due to his illness for, as we see from paragraph 35, he intends to rise early tomorrow morning. If, however, the gunpowder plot were of Darnley's making, he might be anxious to assure himself that all was in readiness before setting out for Edinburgh. In the event, Darnley was lodged in the Old Provost's House at Kirk o'Field, which abutted on the New Provost's House, now in the hands of the Balfours. The preparations for the explosion must have included the digging out of the cellar at the western end of the building, and the storing of the gunpowder in the Balfour's house: neither of these things could be done safely after the King had arrived at Kirk o'Field: there would be too many servants, guards and visitors for such preparations to be made. Darnley would not be so foolhardy as to wish the powder to be stored in his own cellars, but the house next door would provide an excellent cache, always assuming that Sir James Balfour, who had aided the King in the Riccio affair, was prepared to assist in this second attempt to murder the Queen. Darnley may have wished, therefore, to postpone his departure until he had received some message to the effect that all was in readiness.

(25) "He spoke with bravado at first, as this bearer will tell you, concerning the business of the Englishmen, and of his (own) departure (in the English ship), but, in the end, he became humble again".

The parenthesis concerning the ship is supplied from paragraph 11; that this subject is mentioned so briefly in both parts of the letter is one of the reasons for believing the two parts of Casket Letter II to have been addressed to different persons. The question of Darnley's departure to Flanders has already been dealt with at length (page 31), and we have seen that an English ship, perhaps Master Poule's, was lying in the Clyde three or four months earlier (page 37:) this may have been the same or another vessel. Since Darnley had now abandoned, at least for the time being, the project of leaving Scotland, he no doubt replied to Mary's questions on this point with the bravado of injured innocence.

(26) "He told me among other conversation that he well knew that my brother (Moray) had told me what he (Darnley) had said at Stirling, of which he (Darnley) denies half of it, and, above all, that he was in his (Moray's) chamber".

Unfortunately, we have no proof as to the nature of this matter: it seems (page 45), however, that there had been a quarrel between Moray and Darnley at Stirling in which the latter disclosed more of his intentions than a wiser man would have done, and Darnley was now anxious to deny that he had so spoken. Perhaps this incident is connected with the reduction in number of the King's servants and 'gentlemen' which was made shortly before the christening, and we may conclude that this was done on hearing the rumour, perhaps first from Darnley's own mouth, that he intended to kidnap the Prince and rule in his name.

(27) "To make him trust me, I had to feign some things, and, therefore, when he asked me to promise that, when he was healthy, we should both share one bed, I told him, pretending to believe his promises, that, if he did not change his mind between this time and that, I should be content to do so".

This agrees exactly with the argument of paragraph 24 above. It may be noted that this sentence provides evidence, which may also be seen elsewhere, of the haste with which the English translation was prepared, for the Scotch word "haill" has been rendered "wholle", although the original French must have been "gueri" or some other word which could not have given rise to this mistake. This, of course, is not an argument for saying that there never was a French version of this letter; the frequent French idioms translated almost literally are sufficient proof to the contrary.

"But, in the meantime, I bade him take heed to say nothing about it, for, between the two of us (i.e. Mary and Darnley), (although) the Lords could not be offended or take it ill, yet because of the threatenings which he had made to them, (namely), that, if ever we were in agreement, he would make them feel the small account which they had taken of him, they would be afraid lest he (Darnley) would persuade me to pursue some of them. For this reason, they (the Lords) would be suspicious ('in jealosy') if, suddenly and without their knowledge, I should go over to the opposite camp".

Mary got rather lost in this sentence by trying to say too much at once. It becomes more easily understood on displacing the verbal phrase, "they would be afraid", as has been done here: considerable liberties have been taken with the ultimate phrase, "if, at one instant, without their knowledge, I did break a game made to the contrary in their presence", but this is extremely difficult to render in modern English. The meaning, however, is plain. After the events of 29th and 30th September, 1566, when Darnley refused to give his reasons for discontent, and reiterated his intention of leaving the country, to Mary, the Privy Council and du Croc; the Lords sought to protect themselves by forming some sort of alliance among themselves, and Mary was obviously, and rightly, of their way of thinking. If she now consented to take him back, she would certainly "break the play set up to the contrary in their presence". Yet she must pretend to do so, or gone was her chance of controlling Darnley for the critical weeks that were to follow, and it would obviously be to her advantage that the news of this temporary agreement between them should not leak out until she was in a position to assure those of the Lords who would be most easily upset that they had nothing to fear. She would not announce, even to a few, her intention of "playing" Darnley until the time came for his arraignment, for she could trust none of her nobles, other than Bothwell, Seton and Livingstone, sufficiently to open so secret a matter to them.

(28) "He said very merrily, 'Do you think that they will esteen you any more for that?".

This is obscure; presumably, Darnley meant, "Do you think that they will think any more of you for remaining faithful to them?" or something of that sort, and he was probably right in his estimate.

" 'But I am glad that you speak to me of the Lords; for I now believe that you desire that we should live together in contentment (quietness). for, otherwise, greater inconvenience might come to us both than you (or we) think' ".

Mary's reason for asking him not to mention the proposed resumption of marital relations seems to have convinced Darnley that she was sincere: the "now" goes much more satisfactorily with "believe" (as in the Scotch version), than with "desire" (as in the English). The mistake in the English version is due to the incorrect translation of "J'entends", as "I hear", whereas it really means, "I understand" or "I believe". This error necessitated the "now" to the following phrases: "I now hear" was obviously incorrect in the context. The final phrase, "than you think" is the more logical, and, in that case, looks very like a threat; in effect, Darnley is saying, "Take me back and live with me in quietness, or there will be more trouble than you expect". If Darnley were to succeed with his project, he must return to Edinburgh as a free agent, and must appear to have reached some sort of agreement with his wife, for the manner in which the explosion was to be arranged was to be such that Darnley, escaping apparently in the nick of time, could accuse the Lords of an attempt to murder both himself and the Queen.

" 'But I shall do now whatsoever you will have me do, and will love all those that you love, provided that you make them love me also; for, as long as they seek not my life, I love them all equally' ".

This carries on the theme of the previous sentence. Mary's letter of early October, 1566, in which she told Darnley that, if he were to be loved, he must first make himself lovable, seems to have bitten fairly deeply.

(29) "Upon this point, the bearer will tell you many small things, because I have too much to write, and it is late; I give trust to him (the bearer) upon your word (advice). Summa, he (Darnley) will go anywhere, if I give my promise".

For a second time in this letter, the bearer is being trusted to add details (as in para. 25). "It is late", which bears out the suggestion that the opening phrase, "I am now passing to my worrying talk", applies to the subject matter of the letter, not to the actual process of going to visit Darnley. This proves, beyond all measure of doubt, that the opening portion of the letter is missing.

For a proper understanding of the next paragraph, it must be appreciated that paragraph 29 is really a parenthesis: perhaps it was added in the bottom margin after the letter had been completed. The sense carries straight on from paragraph 28 to paragraph 30, and Darnley's speech is still being reported.

(30) " 'Alas, I (Darnley) never deceived anybody, but I submit myself altogether to your will' ".

This is exactly the sense of paragraph 28, but amplifies it. ("I shall do now whatever you will have me do"). In the absence of punctuation, the translators failed to appreciate that the sentence beginning 'Alas' . . . should have been in quotation marks, and ascribed it to the author of the letter. Consequently, knowing that the recipient was (obviously) at a distance, they continued:

"Send me word . . ."

If, however, the French were "enseignez-moi", this was correct on their premise, that this was Mary's request to Bothwell, but, if the speaker were Darnley, and the request were made to Mary, the translation should have read

" 'Inform me . . .' "

which seems to fit the circumstances, for Darnley was anxious to justify himself, as we see from paragraph 10 of Casket Letter II, and Mary may well have complained of his deceiving her and others.

" 'Tell me what I (Darnley) should do, and, whatever happens, I shall obey you' ".

This is exactly the sentiment of Darnley's avowed speech of paragraph 28, but to apply it to a request by Mary that Bothwell should send her word what to do makes no sense at all; the Queen obviously knew perfectly well the answer to that question.

Darnley's speech continues,

" 'Consider, too, if you can find some more secret method without physic, for I should take medicine and the bath at Craigmillar; I may not go out of the house for a long time' ".

This reading requires considerable explanation: let us take the points in which it differs from the contemporary translations in order. First, 'secret invention'; the term 'secret' did not necessarily mean the same as it does to-day, and it was frequently applied to magical arts, which were 'secret arts'; while the word 'invention' means, roughly, 'contrivance' or 'method'. 'By physic' in the Scotch tongue, means 'without physic', and the proof that it had this connotation at the time lies in the Published French Translation of this very passage, which reads, 'quelque moyen plus couvert que par breuvage' (297), 'some means more secret than by a drink'. The age was one of superstition, and belief in magic was universal; the Lords themselves were to accuse Bothwell of bewitching Mary in order to make her his wife (85). A fair gloss on the phrase would thus be, "consider, too, if you can find some less public, or even magical, method without needing to take medicine". Secondly, "I" for "he"; Mary, in common with many other writers of her period, habitually used "i" for "j", and since, in the Italianate script which she employed, the loop of the 'l' was sometimes rather small, and that of the 'e' was occasionally rather large, confusion between 'il' and 'je' was very easy. Often, the true reading could only be ascertained by the inflexion of the verb, but in the present case, 'I or he should take', whether Mary wrote 'je dois prendre' or 'je prendrais', the verb would be phonetically the same as in the third person, and Mary was, like may of her compatriots, somewhat careless with her suffixes. Furthermore, if Mary wrote 'je dois prendre' or 'je prendrais', the translator, mistaking the 'je' for 'il', which was all the more likely since he was misled by the parenthetic paragraph 29, and honestly believed that the present paragraph was Mary's own thought, would have concluded that the Queen had written 's' in error for 't' at the end of the verb. A similar argument applies to the last phrase, "I (or he) may not come out of the house for a long time". The verb would be 'sortir', here translated 'come out', but which would be more correctly rendered in English, 'go out'.

If it be argued that the translator was likely to be correct, for he had the original French before him, it may be pointed out that there are numerous errors in the translations which we shall note from time to time, and, more important, that the passage loses all sense, if applied to Mary's own thought.

"Consider, too, if you can find some more secret invention without medicine, for he should take medicine and the bath at Cragimillar" is as near an approach to nonsense in the circumstances as could be contrived: if it means anything at all, it means that Mary is anxious to get her husband well again as soon as possible, and it is to be doubted if anyone will seriously pursue this argument further. "He may not come out of the house for a long time" merely inverts the previous sentence and exposes the falsity of the translation.

(31) 'Summa, . . ."

Mary uses this phrase, obviously, to sum up the conclusions which she has reached from her conversation with Darnley. It would be completely out of place if the preceding paragraph had been the expression of Mary's own thoughts, but, coming at the end of this long report of Darnley's conversation, it is a very natural expression. Its use here confirms that paragraph 30 is Darnley's own speech and should be in the first person throughout.

'Summa, by all that I can learn, he has great suspicion . . ." as, indeed, Darnley had shewn by his insistence on Mary's promise that he should be used as her husband.

". . . but yet, nevertheless, he trusts my word, but not enough to tell me anything as yet".

So far, Darnley has refused to confess what were his intentions with regard to the proposed visit to Flanders, but this sentence may also refer to the matter mentioned in the first, or later, part of Casket Letter II, paragraph 17, "He has told me almost all about the Bishop and Sutherland", another reason for believing that we are now dealing with the earlier of these two letters.

"However, I shall draw it all out of him, if you will that I avow (confess) (all to) him . . .".

The first part of this sentence is clear, and the correctness of Mary's estimate of Darnley's talkativeness is proved by the sentence in paragraph 17 which has just been quoted. The second part is less easy to understand. Mary could never have intended that Darnley would be persuaded to talk openly by telling him that Bothwell was her lover, that he and she were determined to murder him, or even that she was contemplating arraigning him before Parliament. The meaning probably is, "if you are willing that I promise everything that he asks"; Bothwell's advice on this point is required, for Mary is reluctantly, as we have seen, prepared to beguile Darnley into returning to Edinburgh, but there are limits beyond which she will not go without further persuasion. Must she promise still more than she has already done, simply to obtain the whole truth of Darnley's machinations from his own lips, or will what she has done suffice, and may the matter rest at that point? This is made plainer by the following sentence:

"But I shall never be glad to deceive anyone who puts his trust in me; nevertheless, you may command me in all things; do not think the worse of me for it, for you are the cause of it, because, for my own private revenge, I would not do it".

Having already seen that Mary is reluctant to deceive Darnley any further than is absolutely necessary, that reluctance is emphasized by this sentence. However, she continues, if Bothwell really thinks it necessary, she is prepared to be guided by him. She realizes, however, that it is not quite "playing the game", and places the blame squarely on his shoulders. She is unhappy about what she has already done in this matter of deceit: she would not have done so much unless he had persuaded her of the political necessity. She would never have led Darnley on for her own private (French, 'particulier') revenge. This could not have been written by a woman to that lover, to possess whom she was about to murder the husband in question; on the other hand, it also proves that Mary had some other intention contrary to Darnley's own interests, which coincides with the idea of an arraignment.

(32) "He shews strong signs of that which I fear . . ."

The contemporary translations are obscure, but this seems to be the sense of this phrase. Mary goes on to give instances, from which we may deduce that her fear was that he was not so humble as she hoped he might be, and that he might prove more difficult to control in the near future than had been expected: in other words, that his repentance was feigned.

". . . he goes so far as to say that his faults were published, but there are some that commit faults and believe that they will never be spoken of, and yet people will talk of great and small".

This would suggest that Darnley, in spite of his declaration to the contrary (para. 28), was far from loving the Lords.

"And concerning Lady Reres;, he said, 'I pray God that she may serve you to your honour' ".

This would again suggest that Darnley was not prepared to take his reconciliation with Mary in a completely submissive way, for Mary had thought well enough of Lady Reres to have her made wet-nurse to her son. There may be a connexion here between this occupation and Darnley's plan to kidnap the Prince: can it be that this spiteful remark was caused because he, or someone for him, had made overtures to Lady Reres for the handing over of the Prince, and had been repulsed? If so, Darnley would be anxious to discredit her, and that the Lennox faction had some deep dislike of her is shewn by the treatment she received at Buchanan's hands in his scurrilous description of the Exchequer House incident, for Buchanan was a Lennox retainer.

"And (he said) that it is thought, and he believes it to be true, that I have not power in my own hands, seeing I did refuse his offers".

Darnley is here reproaching Mary for being led by Bothwell and Moray. The letter, in which he offered repentance, is mentioned also in paragraph 10, and presumably was written when, having become ill, Darnley was in doubt what would happen, for he had taken an irrevocable step in leaving Stirling for Glasgow and had then, unexpectedly and disastrously, lost his power of action. That Mary then refused his offers, we also learn from paragraph 10. Once again, therefore, Darnley's dislike of the Lords is made apparent, and Mary is doubtful of the manner in which he will behave, even with the supervision which she will place over him until the sitting of Parliament.

"Summa, he certainly suspects of the thing you know, and for his life".

Darnley had committed treason, not once, but many times. His latest move in that direction had been so serious that he cannot have failed to suspect that he would be brought to trial, and that he might even come to the scaffold: much less than he had done would have sufficed for this. Even in this letter, however, the great secret of the trial dare not be mentioned, for letters may miscarry, and the arraignment is simply referred to as "the thing you know".

"But, in the end, as soon as I have spoken two or three good (kind) words to him, he is merry and out of doubt".

So Mary's deception was sufficient to hold him so far: of course, she did not know that Darnley's plan was so far advanced that the issue would be reached before Parliament had met in March or April, and that, although he suspected the truth, by apparently giving way to the Queen, he was in fact advancing his own plan to reach the throne.

(33) "I have not seen him this evening, because I was finishing your bracelet, for which I can get no locks (clasps): it is ready for them . . ."

Mary had put her head into the lion's mouth by visiting the Lennox stronghold to bring back her treacherous husband: is it possible that she could spend the time finishing a bracelet when she should have been advancing her affairs with all the powers of her persuasion? That could hardly be the case, and it is clear that this paragraph is an interpolation; there is a simple explanation how it came to be inserted at this point in the letter, for, as we shall see, the letter originally finished at the end of paragraph 35, paragraphs 34 and 35 were on one side of a sheet which was blank on the verso. Paragraph 33 was copied on to this blank side, and then the page was turned over, so as to bring this section into the body of the letter. If it be objected that this paragraph is so much shorter than the two paragraphs 34 and 35, the answer is that the remainder of the sheet was filled in with erasures, perhaps of the address, which would necessarily have been written on the blank outer leaf in those days before envelopes. This would account for the remark, "Excuse also that thing that is scribbled", which occurs in the spurious part of this letter, paragraph 36.

It will be noticed that, in the first or later part of this long letter, the last paragraph is devoted to this same bracelet, because, in this case, there was either no blank verso on which to copy it, or reversal of the page would have placed the interpolated paragraph in an impossible place.

If the Lords, who produced this letter, originally had both parts of it complete as separate letters, dated and addressed, they would, of course, know which was the earlier. Furthermore, if they were addressed to different people, the earlier to Bothwell and the later to Moray, and if they intended at first to produce them both as two separate letters to Bothwell, it would be necessary to introduce into each of them some unequivocal subject which would prove that the letters were really to the same person. The device of the bracelet served this purpose admirably. It was probably taken from two separate letters by the "other woman", and served, not only for continuity as between these letters, but also with Casket Letter III, where that lady's penchant for such presents is fully brought out.

In this letter, as would be expected in the circumstances described above, the bracelet is unfinished, for it lacks the locks: in paragraph 23 (the Moray letter), it is now complete.

". . . and yet I fear lest it bring you some misfortune, and may be seen if you should chance to be hurt. Send me word if you will have (accept) it, and if you will have more money, and when I shall return and how far I may speak. Now, as far as I can perceive, I am getting on well with you ("j'ai bien la vogue avec vous"). Guess whether I shall be suspected."

Concerning the "other woman", we shall have a good deal to say later on. At the moment, it will suffice to say that it is not difficult to imagine circumstances in which she might be staying, for the time at least, with people who were unaware of her liaison with Bothwell, and who would see the process of the making of the bracelet. This could hardly apply to Mary, who, if she were its maker, was not doing it in the presence of Darnley, for she had not seen him on account of it, but merely in her room and in the presence of her trusted servants, who, if she were in the throes of a violent love affair, would certainly know of it already. "Send me word if you will have it" also seems out of place, when such other important business was afoot; besides, as will be seen from paragraph 35, Mary was doubtful whether Bothwell was at Edinburgh at the time: he was, in fact, in Liddesdale. Since she was soon to return to Edinburgh herself, and since the bracelet was yet incomplete, why should he send her word, if he would have it? She could present it to him with her own hands in a week at most. "And if you will have more silver" also does not fit the case. There has been no suggestion of money passing between Mary and Bothwell, and this was not the time for her to be offering him any. She would hardly have taken with her more money than was needed for her expenses in Glasgow, and her "treasure" would be at Edinburgh. On the other hand. the "other woman" was also unlikely to be offering Bothwell cash, and the explanation may either be that she is prepared to add more silver ornamentation to the bracelet, or else that the sentence is inverted, "Send me word if you will have it, and (send me) more money if you have some", for the French in such a case would demand a verb in the future tense, "si vous en aurez", which, in translation would be rendered the same as "si vous voulez en avoir".

It is also difficult to understand why Mary should ask when she should return, for she has already said that she will remain at least until the day after tomorrow, and has (paras. 24 and 35) asked the bearer to explain the reason for the delay: Bothwell must have expected her back almost at once, and for her now to ask when she should set out is completely inconsistent. Furthermore, if the matter of Darnley's murder and the preparations for it were the cause of this question, the Earl was behaving most peculiarly in absenting himself from Edinburgh at this most critical time. Except in so far as the question of getting more information from Darnley was concerned, a matter dealt with sufficiently in paragraph 31, there was no need for her to ask how far she might speak. She knew the whole problem, and she knew the answer: it was merely a question of settling her conscience which had bothered her, and there was no need for her to refer to this point again, and out of context. On the other hand, the "other woman", perhaps staying at some house while Bothwell was at Edinburgh, might well want to know when she should return; while, how far she might speak could be taken to refer to the announcement to her hosts of the date of her departure and, perhaps, her destination.

The next sentence is quite inexplicable on the basis that Mary wrote it, "Now, as far as I can perceive I am getting on well with you", but it might be applicable in the stormy courtship of the "other woman" Mary has already said that Darnley "suspects the thing you know, and for his life": the final sentence of this paragraph, "guess whether I shall be suspected", is not only otiose, but in the wrong place.

Finally, the fact that this paragraph is entirely interpolated is shewn clearly by the first sentence of paragraph 34, which follows logically and intelligibly on paragraph 32, but is so inconsequential after paragraph 33, that the Scotch translation omits the two concluding sentences of paragraph 33 and the first phrase of paragraph 34.

(34) "As for the rest . . . . . "

As pointed out above, this phrase, which is omitted from the Scotch, is absurd, following as it does, on the paragraph about the bracelet; but it falls naturally into place after the preceding one (para. 32), which, like this, deals with Darnley's conversation.

"As for the rest, he is angry when he hears of Lethington (Maitland) and of you and of my brother (Moray). Of your brother (Huntly), he says nothing . . . . . "

Huntly was, of course, Bothwell's brother-in-law, but it was common parlance of the time to call a brother-in-law a brother. It should be noted that Mary refers to Huntly simply as 'your brother', and omits all epithet, unlike "the other woman", who, as we shall see, always refers to him as "your false brother". Mary, indeed, had no reason to consider Huntly false; he was always faithful to her, and had served her well, although he was later to surrender to *force majeure*.

The English translator, being fatigued, omitted the reference to 'my brother'; Mary had, in fact, three illegitimate half-brothers, but we can be sure that Moray is the one here intended: the other two, Lord John Stewart, Commendator of Coldingham, and Lord Robert Stewart, Commendator of Holyrood, played little part in the affairs of the time. The conjunction of the phrases, 'your brother' or 'my brother' can only be explained by assuming that this letter is actually written to Bothwell.

" . . . . . but of the Earl of Argyll, he speaks. I am afraid to hear him talk (thus). In the end, he assured me that he had no evil opinion of him (Argyll)".

The phrase, 'In the end', is rendered 'for' in the Scotch and 'at the least' in the English, neither of which makes sense. Probably the Scottish translator read 'afin' for 'enfin', while the English one wrote 'leaste' for 'last': this would make the sentence intelligible. The reflexive, 'he assures himself', can best be translated in this context as 'he assured me'.

"He says nothing of those who are 'out', neither good nor ill, but avoids that subject".

The Scotch 'out', English 'abroad', refers to the Earl of Morton and his seventy-six associates, banished since the Riccio murder, and recently pardoned. Darnley does not seem to have considered the restoration of these enemies of his as a threat to himself, or he would surely have complained on this point to the Queen. The explanation of his flight from Stirling, that he dreaded the return of Morton whom he had betrayed, therefore falls to the ground, and the reason for his conduct must be found in his own schemes.

(35) "His father keeps his room, I have not seen him".

This sentence is repeated in paragraph 16 of Casket Letter II, and thus supports the view that we are dealing with two letters to two different persons. We know from paragraph 2 that Lennox considered himself to be suspected, and we can be sure that he was participant in his son's plots.

"All the Hamiltons are here, (and they) accompany me very honourably, as do all (my) friends from roundabout, when I go to visit him (Darnley)".

The Hamiltons were close neighbours to Glasgow, and they were the hereditary enemies of the Lennox, each house claiming that, owing to the illegitimacy of the other, it was next in succession to the throne. Mary could not have chosen a better escort for her dangerous mission. "All the friends of the other" is unintelligible; probably 'autour' was misread as 'autre'.

"He (Darnley) desires me to come and see him rise tomorrow morning early".

"He hath sent to me" is omitted from the Scotch translation: it is probably inserted in the English version to agree with the interpolated paragraph 33. If Mary had not seen him that evening, she could only have learnt his wish by means of a messenger.

"To be short, this bearer will tell you the rest . . . . . "

Again, for the third time, as in paragraphs 25 and 29, the bearer is trusted to explain certain points more fully, and he must have been fairly deeply in the confidence of both Mary and the Earl. It was later alleged that Paris was the bearer of the letter, and this may be correct. From his depositions, we do not learn that he had any special knowledge of the events at Glasgow.

" . . . . . and, if I learn anything here, I shall make a note of it that evening".

In case it should be thought that Mary here indicates the second or later letter, and that it, too, was addressed to Bothwell, it should be observed that she does not say that she will write another letter, but only that she will "make every night a memorial thereof" (English), or "I will make you a memorial at evin" (Scotch), clearly meaning that she will make a note to remind her to tell Bothwell when she sees him of anything of importance which she may learn. This is all the more certain, when we remember that she expects to leave the day after tomorrow, which would make a letter the following evening pointless.

"He (the bearer) will tell you the reason for my staying (until the day after tomorrow)".

Another instance of the trust shewn to the bearer.

"Burn this letter, for it is dangerous, and nothing is well expressed in it, for I am thinking of nothing but troubles".

Even in its real form and unburdened by the mistranslations and interpolations of the Lords, there was enough material in this letter to put the Lennox faction on their guard, if it should be seen by one of their supporters. In the event, the letter was turned into ammunition to be used against her, and it would have been well for Mary had the Earl heeded her warning.

"If you be at Edinburgh when you receive it (i.e., when it arrives), send me word soon".

The English translation has blundered sadly here, omitting the greater part of the sentence, and producing a meaningles jumble. As we have seen, Bothwell left Edinburgh about 24th January, visited Liddesdale, and was back in the city by about 30th January. Mary clearly knows of this projected visit, which would be in connexion with his duties as Lieutenant of the Marches, but she does not know the exact date of his return. In the circumstances, the requests in paragraph 33, "Send me word if you will accept the bracelet, and if you will have more money, and when I shall return, and how far I may speak", become even more obviously out of keeping.

This letter ends here. It ought to have been dated and signed, but these formalities may have been omitted in view of Mary's belief that the letter was dangerous, although such a precaution would have been of little value, since, had the letter fallen into the wrong hands, it would have been quite obvious from whom it had emanated.

The remainder of the letter is spurious, and it will at once be obvious to the reader that the long paragraph 36 is lifted from one of the letters of the "other woman". Probably it was on the recto of single sheet, and was simply added to the Marian letter without the necessity of any manipulation, except of the address.

It begins with a statement so contrary to all that has gone before, that the English translator felt constrained to leave it out.

(36) "Be not offended if I give not over-great credit," which can only mean that the writer is giving little trust to the bearer. In the genuine Marian letter, we have seen four references to the credit which she gives to the carrier of her letter, and no less than two of them occur in the final paragraph.

"Now, seeking to obey you, My Dear Life (or Love), I spare no honour, conscience, hazard nor greatness whatever. Take it, I pray you, in good part, and not according to the interpretation of your false brother-in-law, to whom, I pray you, give no credence against the most faithful lover that ever you had or shall have".

When one considers this sentence dispassionately, it becomes at once obvious that it is completely inconsistent with all that has gone before. The change in idea is as great as the change in literary style, and Mary's faithful subject, the Earl of Huntly, is suddenly castigated as false. The resemblance in style and emotional tone to Casket Letter III, however, are so close that it is clear that this passage comes from a letter from that same lover of Bothwell, whose enmity to his brother-in-law, the advocate of the Bothwell-Gordon marriage, would be readily understandable. We may guess that Huntly had tried to get Bothwell to break off the liaison with this woman, and had even spread stories of her infidelty to him.

"See not her whose pretended tears should not be valued so highly as the true and faithful travails which I undergo to earn her place, for obtaining which, I betray, against my own nature, those who would prevent me".

This attack on Lady Jane Gordon would be extremely natural in the circumstances. It may be that we can discern here that the Earl's marriage, carried out for political reasons, has been promised to the author of this part of the letter to be but temporary, and that she will herself rise to the position of Countess of Bothwell as soon as that marriage can be terminated.

"God forgive me . . ."

She regrets the outburst of the previous sentence.

". . . and God give you, My Only Love, the good luck and prosperity which your humble and faithful lover wishes you, who hopes shortly to be another thing to you, for the reward of my troubles".

We are reminded here of the words in Casket Letter III, "the misfortune that my cruel destiny and continual misfortune have brought upon me", while the hope to become the Earl's wife bears out the idea suggested in the comment on the previous sentence.

"I have not made one word . . ."

This only occurs in the English version, and is unintelligible; probably it was inserted by an error caused by fatigue.

"It is late; I desire never to stop writing to you, yet I will end my letter now, after kissing your hands".

Casket Letter III, it will be recalled, concludes, "I finish after kissing your hands with as great affection, etc."

"Excuse my bad writing . . ."

It is unusual for a person of superior station to use this excuse when writing to an inferior, but it is not uncommon, however good the writing may be, in the reverse case. The author, as in Casket Letter III, evidently considers herself to be of lower rank than the Earl. Mary, herself, commonly used this formula when writing to her mother, but not when writing to any of her subjects.

". . . and read it over twice; excuse what has been scribbled, when I took a paper with some notes on it".

We now see why this particular leaf was chosen to complete the Marian letter: it provided an excuse for the erasures (of the address) which had necessarily to follow paragraph 33.

"Remember your lover, and write to her (me) very often. Love me as I shall love you".

(37) This paragraph is omitted from the English version and is another example of the effects of fatigue.

"Remember the speech about Lady Reres,
about the Englishmen,
about his mother,
about the Earl of Argyll,
about the Earl Bothwell,
about the Lodging in Edinburgh."

It has usually been concluded that these were instructions to remind the bearer of the letter of the points he was to explain at length. Another explanation is, however, possible. If it be agreed that paragraph 36 is the end of the letter by the "other woman" to Bothwell, this last sheet would be blank on the verso, the remainder of the letter being enfolded inside it, and the outer sheet being sealed or otherwise fastened, perhaps with tape. The address would then be written on the blank outside: in this case,

To the Earl of Bothwell   au M. le Comte de Boduel

at his lodgings in Edinburgh,   a son logis a Lislebourg,

and this inscription would occupy the central position on the sheet if, as is probable, the sheets were folded in three to facilitate sealing. On opening the letter, the address, of course, appeared on the back of the sheet containing paragraph 36. Inspired by paragraph 21 of Casket Letter II, the manipulator of the documents converted the "au' and 'a' to 'du' and 'de' respectively, and added above the words 'souvenez-vous', followed by four other headings to create the correct impression. This was done hastily; three obvious headings were chosen because they are among the few proper names which occur in this earlier letter: the manipulator, however, unaware of the background to the quarrel at Stirling, or, perhaps better informed about it than are we, or led simply by chance, also inserted 'de sa mére', a heading which seems to have no bearing on the matter whatsoever. Darnley's mother, if it were she that was intended, was in England, and seems never to have been mentioned in the whole Mary-Darnley imbroglio. Did Darnley, on the occasion of the quarrel at Stirling, taunt Moray with his illegitimacy? The truth of this explanation is borne out by the heading 'about the Earl of Argyll', for that gentleman is only mentioned in the letter to say that there is nothing to say about him (para. 34). The reference, 'about the Earl Bothwell', is quite inexplicable on any other grounds, and the utilisation of his address was a neat method of implicating Mary in the gunpowder plot at Kirk o'Field. The device was made necessary by the list given in paragraph 21, which is obviously a catalogue of the contents of that part of the letter, and required an addition when it was decided to combine the Bothwell and Moray epistles, to explain its greater length.

The conclusion is therefore inescapable that the Lords did not scruple to modify the evidence in their possession, and, furthermore, that the original of this letter would have supported no charge more serious than one of diplomatic deceit against the Queen. It does not support the contention that Mary was guilty of the murder of her husband, but it does imply that she intended to take steps to clip his wings. The main part of the letter is certainly genuine, and it can only have been written to Bothwell. The date was probably 23rd January, 1567; that is to say, the day after her arrival in Glasgow.

The Moray or Later Letter (paras. 1—23)

There is no address or salutation, as would naturally be the case if the original letter had been addressed unequivocally to Mary's brother, for such an address would have exposed the subterfuge.

(1) "Being gone from the place where I left my heart, it is easy to imagine what was my bearing (French 'contenance'), seeing that I was no more than a body without a heart, which was the reason that, until dinner time, I talked to no-one, nor did anyone dare to approach me, thinking that it would not be good to do so".

We may notice first of all, that this letter describes in detail the events of the first few days after Mary left Edinburgh on, probably, 20th January, 1567. If this letter had been addressed to Bothwell, it is improbable that this first paragraph would have found its place in it, for, although it would have been natural to insert such an emotional, but unimportant item in the earlier letter, it would have been out of place in the second letter to the same person.

Mary apparently reached Callendar House, the home of Lord Livingstone, father of one of the four Maries, and her faithful adherent, in time for dinner. Bothwell was in her company until the following day, when he returned to Edinburgh. Mary probably stayed two nights at Callendar, while the Hamiltons were being summoned to escort her, and would reach Glasgow on 22nd January. If the reference to her heart being left at a certain place were to the Earl and Callendar, the reference was inexact, for Bothwell had left the place before Mary. On the other hand, if the Queen had intended an allusion to her son, the matter becomes plain. Having left him at Edinburgh or Craigmillar, and being aware of Darnley's plot to kidnap him, she was naturally anxious, and it was not until she found herself in the friendly atmosphere of the Livingstone family that she recovered herself.

(2) "Four miles before (Scotch 'or' = 'before') I came to the town . . ."

There seems to be an hiatus between paragraphs 1 and 2, but that may merely be because nothing of sufficient importance happened at Callendar to merit reporting.

"Four miles before I came to the town (Glasgow), a gentleman (said to be Thomas Crawford) of the Earl of Lennox came and made his (Lennox's) commendations to me, making excuses because he (Lennox) did not come to meet me, the reason being that he dared not do so, because of the sharp words I had spoken to Cunningham".

This Cunningham was presumably the same as the Robert Cunningham, servant of the Earl of Lennox, who appeared on the latter's behalf at the trial of Bothwell on 12th April, 1567 (page 292). It may be suspected that he was one of the 'gentlemen' who were in attendance on Darnley at Stirling, when the quarrel arose between Moray and the King.

"And he desired that I should investigate the matter of which I suspected him (Lennox); this last was his (Crawford's) own remark, without orders (from Lennox)".

If the suggestion in the previous comment be correct, the matter which so worried Lennox was that, by sending an undue number of servants and gentlemen to attend on Darnley at Stirling, he had implicated himself, knowingly or not, in his son's plot to kidnap the Prince. Since Moray had quarrelled with Darnley, presumably on this very matter, there was no need for Mary to describe it in greater detail, and this supports the view that this letter was indeed to her half-brother.

(3) "I answered that there was no receipt against fear, and that he (Lennox) would not be afraid if he were not guilty; and also that I only answered sharply to the suspicions, expressed in his letter, that there was an intention to 'pursue' him".

Mary has pointed out that she had only answered sharply when Lennox had complained that she had intended to bring him to some sort of trial, i.e., to pursue him by process of law. This may mean that Lennox was expecting to be arraigned in the forthcoming Parliament, either because this would be the natural course for Mary to follow, or because he had somehow obtained information about her intentions.

(4) "Sir James Hamilton met me and told me that 'the other time', when he (Lennox) heard of my coming, he removed himself, and sent Houston to tell him (Hamilton) that he would never have believed that he (Hamilton) would have been opposed to him (Lennox), or would have joined with the Hamiltons. He (Hamilton) answered that he only came to see me, and would follow (pursue?) neither Stewart not Hamilton, but by my orders. He (Lennox) wanted him (Hamilton) to come and speak with him; he refused to do so".

This Sir James Hamilton seems to be otherwise unknown. The 'other time' seems to be a misreading, for Mary had not visited Glasgow since the Chase-about raid. Probably, the meaning is that, when Lennox heard of Mary's arrival at Callendar House and the summoning of the Hamilton escort, he withdrew to some nearby stronghold. When Hamilton, presumably accompanied by a body of his men, arrived in Glasgow, Lennox sent him a somewhat bitter message.

(5) "The Laird of Luss (a place on Loch Lomond in the Lennox country), Houston and Caldwell's son, with about 40 horsemen, came and met me. The Laird of Luss said that he was charged (summoned) to a 'day of law' (or court case) by the King's father, which should have been held on that day, as shewn by a warrant in his (Lennox's) own handwriting, which he (Luss) has; yet, in spite of this, (Lennox) knowing of my arrival, it (the court case) is postponed. He (Luss) was asked to come to him (Lennox), but he refused, and he (Luss) swears that he will not put up with (such treatment) at his (Lennox's) hands".

This seems to be introduced for two reasons, first as corroborating the unwillingness of Lennox to shew himself publicly, for fear of arrest by Mary and the Hamiltons; and secondly, that even his own supporters are not entirely at his devotion.

"Not one person from the town (Glasgow) has come to speak to me, which makes me think that they are his (i.e. at Lennox's devotion), yet nevertheless he (Lennox), at least his son (Darnley), speaks well of them (the townsfolk)".

This rendering is by no means certain, for the Scotch and English versions differ, and neither seems to make good sense. The meaning would seem to be that, although Darnley, speaking as representing his father, swears that the people of Glasgow are loyal subjects to Mary, nevertheless, she doubts this, for they have held aloof from her. As we see from paragraph 16, the Queen had not seen Lennox, who was probably not in Glasgow.

(6) "I see no other gentlemen but those of my company".

This sentence, absent in the English, serves to confirm the reading of paragraph 35, "all the friends of the other, etc."

(7) "The King sent for Joachim (one of Mary's servants) (last night?) and asked him why I did not lodge 'beside' him, for he would recover more quickly if I did . . ."

By 'beside', is probably meant, 'in the same house'. Mary, naturally mistrusting the Lennox faction, probably insisted on lodging at some distance from Darnley and in such a place that there would be plenty of accomodation close by for the Hamiltons. Traditionally, the house she stayed in was the Provand's Lordship, the only 16th century or earlier house yet standing in Glasgow.

". . . and why I came, was it to make a good arrangement with him?"

It should be noted that the Scotch version uses the correct "wherefore I came", which in English in rendered "why he came", an example of the ease with which, in Mary's writing, 'I' and 'he' ('ie'and 'il') could be confused.

"And if I had taken my inventory (made my state)?"

'Etat'in this sentence can have no other meaning. This question is not easy to understand. It is possible that Darnley, when he left Stirling, intending to proceed to Flanders, a venture for which considerable money would be required, had possessed himself of some of Mary's jewellery, of which she had a vaulable collection, and he was anxious to know whether the theft had been discovered. Alternatively, if he were at that time plotting her destruction, an up-to-date inventory of her possessions would be useful to him when the time came to lay claim to his deceased wife's belongings.

"And if I had brought (taken) Paris (Nicholas Hubert, alias French Paris) and Gilbert (Curle, one of Mary's *valets de chambre*) to write?', (perhaps, "to carry my letters").

It will be recalled that Paris was Bothwell's servant, who, according to his own untrustworthy deposition, "first entered into credit with the Queen at Callendar" on 21st or 22nd January, 1567, and who had accompanied her to Glasgow. He may well have taken the early letter (Casket Letter II, part 2) to Bothwell, but as we shall see, he did not carry this later letter.

"And that I had sent Joseph (Lutini) away".

The mystery of Joseph Lutini and his mission is one which has puzzled all who are interested in the events of these days. On 6th January, 1567, that is to say, when Darnley was in Glasgow, Bothwell on the borders waiting for Morton, and Mary in Stirling, a warrant was issued to this Joseph Lutini to proceed to France in the Queen's name and on her affairs (404), the nature of which are not stated. The warrant was apparently made out by Joseph Riccio, one of Mary's Secretaries, and brother of the murdered David. The two Josephs were close friends, and, being Roman Catholics, Lutini at least, and possibly Riccio, as we shall see, may have been in Darnley's confidence. It is probable that the safe-conduct was forged. At any rate, on 17th January, Mary addressed a letter to Drury at Berwick, asking for the arrest of the said Lutini (405), who "has lately left his charge and is departed forth of our realm", which proves that Mary had not signed the safe conduct, or this letter would have said so. "He has fraudulently taken with him the goods and money of divers his friends and companions". Curiously enough, Lutini was still in Berwick, and had not proceeded on his trip to France.

On 26th January, Joseph Riccio wrote a very curious letter to Lutini (738); he stated that he had told the Queen that Lutini had taken some of his (Riccio's) money, "and the reason why I said it and for whom, you will understand. . . . Then Bastian told the Queen that I asserted that you had gone on her affairs", which is exactly what the safe-conduct alleges, and is further proof that it, which is countersigned by Riccio, was a forgery. Presently, the Queen missed her bracelets, and Riccio at once stated that Lutini had taken them. Meanwhile, Moretta, the Ambassador from the King of Savoy, arrived in Edinburgh (24th January), (519) "who states that you told him at Berwick that I was the cause of your making this journey. Take care how you speak for if you mention on whose account you are going, we shall all get into trouble". He goes on, "For the love of God, say that you have taken the money, which I said that you took".

That Darnley should first ask of Mary's inventory and then speak concerning Joseph Lutini, suggests very strongly that Lutini and Riccio were associated with Darnley in his schemes. It seems that Darnley had taken various items, including Mary's bracelets and some sums of money Meanwhile, Lutini had been sent by Riccio to Berwick, perhaps to wait for Moretta, whose part in the proceedings we shall consider later. When Mary noticed that the bracelets and other items were missing, Riccio said that Lutini had taken them, and wrote to that person, whom he evidently expected to be still at Berwick, begging him to adhere to the same story "why and for whom", Lutini would understand.

"I am amazed who has told him so much, he spoke even of the marriage of Bastian".

Darnley certainly had some source of information at Mary's Court, and perhaps no-one better was to be found than Joseph Riccio, but one suspects that Sir James Balfour was also in touch with him. Bastian (Sebastian Pages) was to be married to Christina Hogg on Sunday, 9th February, and it was after their wedding masque that Darnley was murdered. The reference to this occasion has been held to mean that Mary had already decided to dispose of her husband on that night, but this can hardly be the case, for she is still of the intention to take Darnley to Cragmillar (para. 12), not to Kirk o'Field, and obviously the murder must in that case have been planned differently. However, the allusion may implicate Darnley: he may have already decided on Kirk o'Field and on the device of gunpowder, and furthermore may even then have reached the conclusion that the absence of the Queen at the masque would provide a suitable occasion for transferring the gunpowder to his own cellars from those of the New Provost's House.

"This bearer will tell you more about this".

This sentence is embodied in the course of the paragraph in the Scotch version, but comes at the end of it in the English translation. We may conclude that it was written in the margin opposite the middle of the paragraph. It may have been an afterthought, added just before sealing the letter. Probably it does not refer to any one specific question which Darnley raised, but to the whole subject of the "questions which he asked at Joachim". However, it does shew that the bearer was not Paris, for he is mentioned in the paragraph and would, presumably, have been named in the margin as the bearer, had he in fact been so. We may note that, whoever he was, he was certainly trusted, unlike the bearer mentioned in paragraph 36.

(8) "I asked him of his letters, in which he complained of the cruelty of someone; he said he was (then) in a maze, and that he was (now) so glad to see me that he thought he would die of happiness. He found great fault with me that I was pensive".

Mary might well be pensive after such an obvious evasion as the one just described.

(9) "I left for supper. This bearer will tell you of my arrival. He begged me to come back (after supper), which I did. He told me about his illness, and that (even when it was at its height?) he would not make a will, but would leave everything to me . . . "

It may be noted that such a statement on the part of Darnley is psychologically probable if he had recently robbed his wife and was now contemplating her murder.

". . . and that I was the cause of his illness, because of the sorrow he had that I was so strange to him".

As we see from this and the subsequent paragraph, Darnley is anxious to be taken back by his wife; it is he who is "making the running" and she who is the reluctant suitor. We can also see how hollow were his protestations: if Mary were "strange" to him, he had given her plenty of cause.

(10) "And he said, 'You ask me what I meant when I spoke of cruelty in my letter: it was of your cruelty, because you would not accept my offers and repentance. I confess that I have done wrong, but not in that thing which I have always denied".

This last sentence may be a reference to the Riccio murder, but it is rather more probable that it refers to the plot to kidnap the Prince.

" 'And many others of your subjects have done wrong too, and you have pardoned them' ".

This was true enough; Moray, Huntly, Morton, Maitland and many others had been pardoned, and Darnley himself had not been 'pursued' for the Riccio murder. It would be most surprising if one whose public acts had been so full of clemency should now turn to murder. On the other hand, Darnley had already shewn himself to be a murderer in intention, and even to have attempted the murder of his wife. There is no reason to think that he had suddenly changed his character. If, however, we are to ascribe Mary's sudden change of heart to her submission to the Earl of Bothwell, we are again at fault, for all the evidence shews that Bothwell was not a brutal man. During the short period in which he was in complete power, he carried out no act of terrorism and 'pursued' no one; after the Riccio murder, it was at his request that two of the convicted rebels were pardoned and escaped the gallows; and his treatment of the son of Cockburn of Ormiston, which we have mentioned before (page 53), was generous in the extreme.

" 'I am young; you will say that you have forgiven me many times, but that I return to my faults. May not a man of my age (nearly 21) fail twice or thrice for want of advice, or break his promise, and in the end repent, being chastened by experience? If I may be pardoned, I protest that I shall never do wrong again; and I ask nothing but that we may be together at bed and board as husband and wife. And if you will not consent, I shall never get up from this bed. I pray you, tell me your decision. God knows how much I am punished for making my God of you, and for thinking of nothing but you. And, if ever I have offended you, you are the cause, because, when anyone else wrongs me, if I might, for my refuge, discuss the matter with you, I should speak of it to no-one else. But, not being on good terms with you, when I hear anything, I must keep it to myself, and that makes me witless with anger' ".

Darnley's pleas are urgent; he has a great need to be allowed to return as a free agent to Edinburgh, and the hollowness of all his protestations is there for all to see.

(11) "I kept on answering him, but that would be too long to write in full. I asked why he wanted to sail in the English ship. He denies it, on oath, but he admits that he spoke to the men (crew). Afterwards, I asked him about Highgate's statement on examination".

The "inquisition of Highgate" is fully explained in Mary's letter of 20th January, 1567, the day she probably set out for Glasgow, to her ambassador in Paris, Archbishop Beaton (407):

"With this also, there is another matter that we must signify to you: lately, a servant of yours, named William Walker, came into our presence, being for the time at Stirling, and, in his communication, amongst other things, declared to us, how it was not only openly rumoured, but also he had heard by report of persons whom he esteemed (to be) lovers of us, that the King, by the asistance of some of our nobility, should (i.e., intended to) take the Prince, our son, and crown him; and, being crowned, as his father, should take upon him (self) the government, with sundry other attempts and purposes tending to this end. At the hearing whereof, you may well think we marvelled not a little; and, seeing the matter of such importance, could not but insist to have further knowledge of the speakers and authors, to the effect that we might better understand the ground and fountain whereof it proceeded. With the which he (Walker), being pressed, named William Highgate (Town Clerk) in Glasgow, also your servant, for his chief informer, who, he said, had communicated the matter to him, as appeared, of mind to gratify us; saying to Walker, 'If I had the mean and credit with the Queen's Majesty that you have, I would not omit to make her privy to such talk and rumours that pass in the country. Highgate said further, as Walker reported to us, that the King could not (be) content, nor bear with some of the noblemen that were attending in our court, but either he or they must leave the same;"

from which it appears that Highgate's conversation with Walker must have preceded Darnley's flight from Stirling on 24th December, and brings us back to the time of the quarrel between Moray and Darnley, and the reduction in number of Darnley's attendants. The letter continues,

"Whereupon, we took occasion, with diligence, to send for Highgate, who, being asked in (presence of) our Council of his communication had with Walker in this matter, he denied, both apart, as well as when confronted together (i.e. when confronted with Walker), that he ever talked with the said Walker upon any such subject. Only this far he confessed: that he heard of a rumour, how the King should be put in ward (made a prisoner), and for his informer on that point, named a servant of the Earl of Eglinton, called Cauldwell; who, being also sent for and examined, expressly denied that he ever spoke or entered in such terms with William Highgate. This story, of the rumour of the King's warding, was told by Highgate to the Laird of Minto, who again declared it to the Earl of Lennox, and, by him, the King was made aware thereof; by whose (i.e. the King's) desire and command, Highgate again, as he alleged, spoke (to) Cauldwell. But, in the end, amongst them all, we find no manner of agreement, everyone disagreeing on the whole matters spoken, which moved us to say to the two, whom we take to be your servants (i.e. Walker and Highgate), that we were certain that they had, by their proceedings and speeches, besides offending us, highly offended you, their master, whom we were assured to be so far ours, and affectionately inclined to our service and advancement, that you would be very ill content of their rash behaviour, and (would) repress and disallow such groundless talk, tending to our disquiet and disadvantage, and troubling the tranquillity of the country, which our study is to maintain and retain in such integrity as possibly may be.

And for the King, our husband, God knows always our part towards him; and his behaviour and thankfulness to us is similarly well known to God and the world, specially (to) our own impartial subjects (who) see it, and, in their hearts, we doubt not, condemn the same. Always, we perceive him occupied and busy enough to inquire of our doings, which, God willing, shall always be such as none report of us anyway but honourably, however (i.e. in what manner soever) he, his father and their faction (fautors) (may) speak, which we know want no good will to make us have ado (trouble), if their power were equal to their minds. But God moderates their forces well enough, and takes the means of (the) execution of their intentions from them; for, as we believe, they shall find none, or very few, approvers of their counsels and devices imagined (thought up) for our displeasure or misliking".

Thus, Mary, at the moment of her departure to Glasgow, wrote to the Archbishop. That she had reason to believe the accusation of Walker is shewn beyond doubt by the final paragraph of her letter; and, with this matter near the top of her mind, it is not surprising that she questioned Darnley about it.

"I asked him about the inquisition (statement on examination) of Highgate; he denied it until I told him the very words that were spoken, and then he said that Minto had warned him that some of the Council had brought a document to me to sign, to put him in prison and kill him if he resisted. And he asked about this of Minto himself, who answered that he thought it was true. To-morrow, I will speak with him (Minto?) upon this matter. As to the rest of Willie Highgate's (matter), he admitted it, but it was the day after my arrival before he did so".

This passage is very important, for it is clear that Darnley was implicated in the plot revealed by Walker, and that he was behaving in a singularly shifty manner: he denied it, until Mary told him the very words which he had said; then Darnley, no longer able to retreat by lies, brought out this new defence, that some of the Lords wanted Mary to order his arrest and, thus, give an opportunity for his killing, which could be explained on the ground that he had resisted capture. This story may well be true, and pos- possibly is to be dated to the Craigmillar "Conference", 20th November to 5th December, 1566. As we see from paragraph 14, however, Mary refused to sign the warrant. A woman wishing the death of her husband, and assured of the support of some of her chief Lords would surely have accepted this simple method, and not have chosen the cumbersome alternative of gunpowder.

The final sentence helps in dating this letter. If Mary arrived in Glasgow on 22nd January, this letter must have been written on 26th January at the earliest, for the day previously she would have referred, not to "the day after my arrival", but to "the day before yesterday". We receive confirma- tion of this date in paragraph 17, and we can therefore be fairly sure that Mary left Edinburgh on 20th, reached Glasgow on 22nd, and wrote this letter on 26th January, 1567.

(12) "Finally, he urged that I should stay in his lodging: I refused, and said that he must be purged and that could not be done here".

This does not make sense. Darnley could be purged as easily in Glasgow as Edinburgh. Probably the sentence should end "but that could not be done with me here", because, the lodging being small, Mary's presence would be awkward at a time of active medical intervention.

"He said to me, 'I have heard it said that you have brought a litter with you, but I should rather have gone with yourself (on horseback)', I believe he thought I would send him away prisoner (guarded in the litter)".

The importance of this thought of Mary's, not expressed by Darnley but only by herself, in proving the spurious nature of Thomas Crawford's evidence will be referred to again when we consider that gentleman's deposition to the Commission (page 163). The fact that Crawford said that Darnley thought he would be taken away as a prisoner proves con- clusively that his deposition, intended to support the statements in Casket Letter 11, was in fact composed from it.

"I told him that I would take him with me to Craigmillar where the apothecary and I might help him, and not be far from my son".

This sentence, undoubtedly from Mary's pen, shews that we have cor- rectly interpreted paragraph 30 in the Bothwell letter, which, attributed to Mary and not to Darnley, would bear a completely different construction.

It is to be noted that Mary is intending to take Darnley to Craigmillar, but it was to Kirk o'Field that he finally went. That the latter place was Darnley's own choice, we learn from the deposition of Thomas Nelson, Darnley's servant, who miraculously survived the explosion at Kirk o'Field (233): "The Deponer remembers it was devised in Glasgow that the King should have lain first at Craigmillar, but, because he had no will thereof, the purpose was altered, that he should lie beside the Kirk o'Field". This evidence from the Prosecution is conclusive: Kirk o'Field was Darnley's own choice.

"He said that he was ready whenever I wished, provided that I should promise what he asked".

The promise that Darnley had asked was that they should be together as husband and wife: in other words, that he should be pardoned and be left as a free agent; and it was exactly this promise which Mary had great difficulty in making, for she had determined to bring him to justice for his treasons.

(13) "He wants nobody to see him".

This has usually been ascribed to Darnley's sensitivity about his looks and the effect of smallpox on them, but, in that case, the remark is misplaced, and should have occurred in paragraph 20. It may be that there is an error in transalation, or that it is a reference to Darnley's lack of friendship for Mary's escort of Hamiltons. Taken, however, with the previous sentence, and remembering Mary's warning of silence in regard to this promise (para. 27 of the Bothwell letter), it seems that the translation is probably slightly at fault, and that the meaning is "He agrees that nobody should be aware of it".

"He is angry when I speak of Walker, and says that he will pull the ears from his head, and that he lies, for I asked him about that (para. 11), and what cause he had to be angry with some of the Lords and to threaten them. He denies that, and says that he loves them all, and prays me to (make them) trust nothing (on his part) against them".

This sentence is a little uncertain, owing to the difference between the English and Scotch versions, but the above rendering seems to be the meaning of it. The trend of the conversation, however, is clear, and it is obviously the same subject as that which is described at length in paragraph 28, another reason for believing that the two parts of this letter are to two different persons.

(14) "As for myself, he would rather die than do me the least displeasure; and after this, he said so many little flatteries to me, so coldly and so smoothly that you would have been amazed".

The reader should compare this with Casket Letter I, when it will become at once apparent that that letter is not written about Darnley, but about Mary's son.

"I had almost forgotten (to tell you) that he said that he could not mistrust me in the affair of which Highgate had spoken, for he would never believe that I, who was his own (French, 'propre') flesh, would do him any harm, and also he was told that I had refused to sign the warrant (to have him arrested and killed if he should resist)".

The English translation uses the nonsensical "refused to have him let blood", a mistake which was natural enough in a translator who was looking, consciously or not, for evidence of a bloodthirsty nature against the Queen. The importance of the error is, however, that the same mistake was almost certainly made by both the Scottish and English translators of Casket Letter I.

"But as to any others who would 'pursue' him, he would at least sell his life dearly enough, but he neither did nor would suspect anyone, but would love all whom I loved".

This is a repetition of the statement already made to Bothwell (para. 28), and again shews that this letter was to another person (Moray).

(15) "He would not let me go, but wanted me to stay awake (or up) with him (Scotch, 'walk' = 'wauk' = 'wake' or 'watch'). I pretended that I believed that all (which he said) was true, and that I would think about it, and excused myself from sitting up with him that night, because I was tired ('for I could not wake')".

No doubt Mary was tired after the events of 20th to 22nd January. "This night", French "ce soir", means, of course, in this context, "that night", the night which she is describing, not the one on which she is writing.

(16) "He says that he sleeps badly".

Darnley had enough on his conscience to interfere with an honest man's sleep, but the fear of retribution was more important: we have seen several signs that this fear was well to the front of the King's mind.

"Your never heard him speak better or more humbly, and, if I had not proof that his heart is of wax . . ."

Mary knows better than to trust to the hollow protestations of the husband who has so often deceived her.

". . . and were my (heart) not as a diamond in which no stroke can make a breach save that which comes from your hand . . ."

In view of Mary's erstwhile affection for her husband, and his protestations and humble speech, although she knew his heart to be of wax, nevertheless, her own must be made hard in these circumstances: no doubt it was difficult; "I am doing a work here which I hate greatly" she writes in paragraph 17, and this boasting of the hardness of her heart suggests that she was rather near the breaking point. The words, "save that which comes from your hand", at first sight, point strongly towards Bothwell and her love for him, but they would not be out of place towards Moray, her half-brother, whom she had always loved, who had almost always controlled her, who had agreed so well with her at St. Dizier in 1561, whom she had advanced in honours, legitimated and made her chief minister, and whom she had pardoned for rebellion and reinstated in all his honours and power, and to whom she was to offer her sisterly affection once again in Lochleven. Truly, it was the stroke which came from Moray's hand which made many an impression on Mary's affectionate heart, and such an interpretation does not seem out of place when we remember the state of tension in which she must have been in Glasgow, where she had now been for four days, and where her resolution to take steps against her husband must have been greatly shaken from time to time.

". . . would make me have pity on him. But fear not, the place will hold until death. Remember, in return, that you do not allow your (heart) to be won by those false people (French, 'gens') who will do their utmost to gain it".

So long as Moray continues to urge the policy of arraigning Darnley in Parliament, Mary will adhere to it, in spite of the blows to her heart or resolution. We may notice the happiness of the metaphor: her heart is likened to a besieged fortress, which will not surrender even until death, and the metaphor is continued in two separate sentences, unlike the changing purpose of the metaphors of the "other woman"; unlike them, too, it is simple and indirectly expressed: there is no excess of flowery expressions, and the whole emotional content is completely different from that person's effusions.

Mary asks, however, that, in return, Moray will continue to support her, and not allow himself to be drawn into an opposition party, as he had done once before. She need not have made such a request to Bothwell: there was no possibility that he would be lured into the extremist Protestant camp, whose members had been his enemies ever since the successful ambuscade on Cockburn of Ormiston. Mary seems, for a moment, to have had a glimmering of the truth, that Moray was using her to destroy the Roman Catholic party, and would then rise to the surface as supreme arbiter, with the aid of the fanatics of the Reformed Kirk. This seems to be a plea that Moray should continue to support Mary and the moderate Protestants, Bothwell and Huntly.

(16) "I think they have been at schools together".

"They" may mean Darnley and Lennox, but the sentence is obscure. The French, 'faire une école' means 'to blunder', and 'faire école', 'to set a fashion'; but perhaps this sentence simply means, "I think they are up to something".

"He has always a tear in his eye. He salutes everybody, even the lowest, and grovels to them, to make them have pity on him. To-day, his father bled at the nose and mouth; guess what that betokens".

This last sentence immediately brings to our mind a vision of a bloody death, not long to be delayed, in store for the Earl of Lennox; but a moment's reflection will remind us that, whatever in fact happened to Darnley, Lennox survived the incident unharmed, nor was he pursued by Mary or Bothwell during the two months that he remained in Scotland after his son's death. The answer is to be found in the meaning of the French proverbial expression: in the 16th century, to bleed at the nose was a common French expression simply indicating fear, and similar to the modern English expression 'cold feet'. Lennox had good reason for anxiety, even if he were not completely participant in his son's schemes.

This meaning for the phrase, 'saigner du nez', is given by Littré (Dictionnaire de la Langue Française, Paris, 1882), and examples of its use in this way are to be found in the works of Lanoue (1587), Amyot (1559), Carloix (1568), Pasquier (1619) and others; there cannot be the slightest doubt as to this interpretation, which removes even the semblance of bloodthirstiness from the passage, which merely comments on the appropriateness of Lennox's suffering from a nose-bleed at the time when he is shewing such marked signs of apprehension.

"I have not seen him; he keeps his chamber".

This is a repetition of the statement in paragraph 35, which again emphasizes the fact that we are here dealing with two separate letters.

"The King desires that I should give him meat with my own hands, but you give no more trust to him where you are, than I shall do here".

The sequence suggests that Darnley wishes Mary to serve Lennox with food, but it seems more likely that it is to himself that he refers, for Lennox was perhaps not even in Glasgow. Whichever is intended, the act would be symbolical of forgiveness, and Mary was loath to give such a demonstration at the moment.

(17) "This is my first 'journée': I shall finish it tomorrow".

Much ink has been spilt on this sentence; the meaning is by no means clear, but it will bear the construction, "This is a description of my first day's work here: I shall finish that work to-morrow". The first part of this statement is undoubtedly true: almost everything up to this point in the letter is an account of her conversation with Darnley, which seems to have taken place on that first day on which she reached Glasgow (22nd January). If she wrote this letter on 26th January, she would finish her work on 27th, either because she was returning to Edinburgh on that day, or because the 27th would be the last day of parleys, and the return was to take place on 28th January. This reconciles this sentence in the letter with the passage in paragraph 11, and avoids the conclusion that Mary wrote this letter on the day of her arrival, when she had spent a long time with her husband, even returning after supper (para. 9), and must, in that case, have stayed awake writing far into the night.

"I write everything, even things of little importance, so that you may take from it whatever seems best to make your judgment. I am doing a work here that I hate much, but I had begun it this morning".

If this letter were being written for the information of Moray, her chief minister, so meticulous a description of everything would be understandable, but it could have served little purpose if written to the lover who, with Mary's help, was to murder the young King within a fortnight. "I am doing a work here that I hate much" is clear, but the following phrase, "but I had begun it this morning", is completely unintelligible, and the suggestion that she is here referring to her letter does not fit the context. Probably Mary, weary from writing so much, made a simple slip of the pen and wrote "I began" for "I shall finish", and that she meant to say, "but I shall end it (the work which she so greatly hates) to-morrow".

"Do you not want to laugh to see me lie so well, at least, to dissemble so well, and tell him truth between times (French, 'entre main')?"

We can well imagine Moray finding something amusing in Darnley being cozened by the usually frank Mary, and the Queen knew her half-brother very well. Mary felt that the expression, 'to lie', was too strong, and softened it to 'dissemble', and there can be no doubt, from what she had said, that she felt she was playing false, although there was a good excuse for her actions, and her self-accusation peeps out in this sentence.

"He has told me almost all about the Bishop and Sutherland, and yet I never mentioned one word of what you told me, but only by much flattering and praying him to trust me; and by complaining about the Bishop, I have drawn it all out of him (French, 'Je l'ai tiré les vers du nez'). You have heard the rest".

Unfortunately, we lack the clue to the meaning of this paragraph. The 'Bishop' may be the papal nuncio, Bishop of Mondovi, with whom Mary had recently been negotiating and with whom Darnley may have been in contact. Alternatively, it may have been one of the Scottish Bishops. The Earl of Sutherland was closely related to the Gordons and had been banished after the battle of Corrichie (October, 1562), when the 4th Earl of Huntly had been defeated and died. Sutherland was recalled and reinstated during the Chase-about Raid, at the same time as the 5th Earl of Huntly was released from Dunbar and restored to favour. Sutherland was a Roman Catholic, and may have been implicated in Darnley's schemes, but he does not seem to have been seriously distrusted by Mary at this time, for he is mentioned without rancour in Casket Letter VIII. Moray must have given Mary some information which could, as a last resort, be used to draw Darnley on, but she has not needed to use it; perhaps some communication between the Bishop of Mondovi and Sutherland had been intercepted. This would coincide with Darnley's plot to seize the thrones of Scotland and England with the help of Phillip II. He may have named Sutherland as a staunch Catholic and, therefore, a likely supporter in such a cause, the more so, since he had been out of favour with the Queen and might be rankling under the effect of his banishment. We may notice that the ugle French phrase, 'I have drawn the worms out of his nose', is used

by Mary in one of her undoubted letters to the Bishop of Ross (5th October, 1568) (86).

On the margin of the English translation occur the words:
"I have disclosed all, I have known that I would".

This cannot be Mary speaking: she has just written that she has not
even mentioned 'one word of that which you told me', and, whether intending to deliver Darnley to justice or to the assassin, she could not have
'disclosed all'. Perhaps Darnley said it after he had told her about the
Bishop and Sutherland; the intention being that he had now told her
everything of the practices against her, and that he had not intentionally
kept anything back until this late disclosure. In this case, the original
sentence may have run "I, (Darnley) have told you all I know, as I intended (from the first)". It may be that Mary, on re-reading the letter,
also added this note in the margin, where the Scottish translator overlooked it, or, perhaps, it is altogether an interpolation.

We should notice that, in paragraph 31, Mary writes, "By all that I
can learn, he (Darnley) has great suspicion, but yet, nevertheless, he
trusts my word, but not enough to tell me anything as yet; however, I
shall draw it all out of him", another indication that this letter to Moray
is of later date than the Bothwell letter.

Paragraphs 18 and 19 are interpolations achieved by writing on the
blank verso which followed paragraphs 20, 21 and 22, which comprised the
original letter. By turning the sheet over, the interpolation was brought
into the body of the letter, exactly as in the case of paragraph 33. The letter
now required a new outer sheet, so paragraph 23, also an interpolation,
was written on the recto, and the letter enclosed within it. The reader will
at once recognise the style of the "other woman" in the two paragraphs
which follow:

(18) "We are joined to two false people (French, 'gens') . . ."

This refers to Bothwell's close union to Lady Jane Gordon and her
brother, whom the "other woman" always describes as false.

"The New Year (or 'the Devil') sunder us (from them), God forgive
me".

If the writer used the blasphemous appeal to the Devil, the phrase,
'God forgive me', is understandable. That the English gives 'Goodyear'
(French, 'bonne année') throws a good deal of doubt on the whole
sentence.

The Scotch version is quite different and is possibly more nearly correct.
Perhaps it should have been rendered:

"We are united to two false people, the Devil divided us whom God did
knit together for ever as the most faithful couple that he ever united:
this is my faith; I shall die believing it".

Since the "other woman" evidently considered herself married to Bothwell (see Casket Letter III), this is quite understandable, and is probably

the correct original version of the sentence. The contemporary translations are quite unintelligible as they stand.

(19) "Excuse it (me) for writing badly: you must guess half of it, but I cannot improve it (my writing), for I am not well at ease (i.e. 'I am worried'). And yet I am very glad to write to you when others are asleep, since I cannot sleep as they do, nor as I would desire, which is in your arms, My Dear Life (or 'Love'), whom I pray God to preserve from all evil, and to send you repose. I am going to seek my (rest) until the morning, ing, when I shall end (i.e. seal and forward, not necessarily complete the writing) my letter ('Bible' for 'billet' or 'bille'). But it grieves me that it (i.e., going to sleep) should prevent me from writing my news to you, because it is so long. Send me word what you have decided on this matter, so that we may understand each others wishes, and nothing thereby be spoilt".

This question is quite out of place in Mary's letter, and the recipient would have been completely at a loss as to its meaning. When this portion of the letter is restored to its proper context, as we shall see later, the meaning becomes more clear (page 176). Taken as a genuine part of Casket Letter II, the remark, "it grieves me that it should prevent me from writing my news to you", is surprising, seeing that the letter has already run to some 2,500 words, including some of the most detailed news ever written outside journalism.

"I am weary and going to sleep, yet I cannot stop scribbling so long as there is any paper. Cursed be this pocky fellow who troubles me so much, for without him I should have a far pleasanter subject to talk about".

We shall see later whence this fragment was lifted, but it is necessary to point out here that 'pocky' was a commonly used adjective expressing disgust and contempt, not necessarily, or even commonly, applied to a person suffering from some disease, and that the word 'fellow' could be used for either a man or a woman. The original French might well have been 'ce mauvais suject' or 'cet individu louche', which are both masculine (for without *him* I should have a far pleasanter subject'), but could be used for either sex. If the "other woman" had a man in mind, it was the Earl of Huntly, but she may have been thinking of his sister, as will be clear at a later place.

The original Marian letter now continues, the sense being carried on from paragraph 17, which dealt with Darnley's disclosures concerning the Bishop and Sutherland.

(20) "He is not much disfigured, yet he has had a very bad attack". The English 'arrayed' presumably arises from a misreading.

"He has almost killed me with his breath, for it is worse than your uncle's, and yet I sat no nearer to him than in a chair by his bedside, and he lay at the other side".

The importance of this in deciding on the nature of Darnley's malady will be referred to in Appendix A. It is worth noting that Bothwell had no uncle, although he had a great uncle, the Bishop of Moray. Mary had met the Bishop once, four and a half years before: if his breath lingered in her memory for so long, it is surprising that he had been such a lady killer. On the other hand, Moray's uncle, on his mother's side, was the Earl of Mar, extremely well known to Mary, and it seems much more likely that he was the person intended.

(21) "The message of the father in the road,
    The talk of Sir James Hamilton.
    Of what the Laird of Luss told me about the delay.
    Of the questions he asked Joachim: of my inventory, of my company, of the reason for my coming, and about Joseph (Lutini).
    The talk that he and I had together: of the desire he has to please me, of his repentance, of the interpretation of his letter, of Willie Highgate's affair, of his (Darnley's) departure.
    About Monsieur de Livingstone".

This is, quite clearly, a list of the headings of the letter we have just considered. It is written in the first person, and must therefore have been a memorandum for the compilation of the letter, which follows the same order as this list. It is not without interest that the English translation of the heading about Sir James runs thus, "the talke of Sir James Hamilton (erased) of the ambassade". This clearly indicates a writer who spelt the Scottish names phonetically in French, as Mary habitually did; she must here have written "Ambletoune", which misled the translator into reading 'ambassade'. Presumably the memorandum was made first: when the letter was written as far as paragraph 17, all the available paper had been used up. *Faute de mieux*, Mary continued the letter with paragraph 20 in the space above the list. On further examination, she found that she had omitted any reference to Lord Livingstone, and added a concluding paragraph on this subject. Since the verso had to remain blank for use as an envelope, there was now no room for signature, and the end of the letter was, perforce, informal. Perhaps no address was put on the verso; the completed letter being given to a messenger with directions to hand it to Moray; if an address were written, it was erased and was omitted by the translators or copyists.

(22) "I had almost forgotten that Lord Livingstone whispered to Lady Reres at supper . . ."

This presumably refers, therefore, to Mary's stay at Callendar House on the night of either 20th or 21st January.

'. . . that he would drink to the persons that I knew, if I would pledge them".

If this remark were whispered, how did Mary hear it?

"And after supper, when I was leaning upon his (shoulder) warming myself at the fire, he said to me, 'You have fair going to see sick folk, yet you will not be so welcome to them as you left somebody this day in unhappiness, who will never be merry until he sees you again'. I asked him, who it was. He nudged me and said 'one of those ('ces' often written 'ses') folk that left you to-day'. Guess you the rest".

It is just possible that the last four words are also part of Livingstone's speech, but it is more probable that they are Mary's comments.

The whole passage points at Bothwell, and that the Earl had already made it plain that he would be glad to be accepted as Mary's suitor in the event of Darnley's removal. It would follow that Moray and Mary had discussed this possibility, and it is not unlikely that they would have done so, for, with Darnley's arraignment in the air, a future husband would need to be found, and various eligible persons may have already been considered. This does not mean that Mary had made up her mind, nor that Moray was supporting the suitorship of Bothwell: it only means that both the Queen and her halfbrother had noticed his ambitions in this direction. Livingstone's readiness to drink to "the persons that I knew" need not necessarily have included Bothwell. Presumably, the toast was not drunk, and Lady Reres informed Mary of the whispered remark later in the evening.

(23) "I have worked to-day until 2 o'clock at this bracelet, to put the key in the lock, which is fastened underneath with two laces. I have had so little time that it is badly made, but I shall make a better (one). In the meantime, take care that no-one here sees it, for everybody would know it, because, for haste, it was made in their presence".

That Mary would spend her time at such a moment as this in making a bracelet which, apparently, was urgently required, seems most improbable. Nor was there any real reason why she should not have done so openly and then have given it to Bothwell; he was high in favour and deserved it, and such a present from a queen would not necessarily be compromising. However, the passage is certainly interpolated, as was paragraph 33 of the Bothwell letter, with the purpose of shewing that both letters were written to the same person and that a guilty love subsisted between Mary and the recipient; the place at the end of the letter is in itself suspicious from the point of view of forgery. This paragraph, like paragraph 33, may have been copied from one of the letters of the "other woman", or it may have been composed to accord with it.

As we have already seen (page 76), the Spanish Ambassador in London, de Silva, wrote to Philip II on 2nd August, 1567, and described a letter of which he had heard from Moray. That letter was certainly never produced. According to de Silva, it was on three sheets of paper, written and signed by Mary, and says,

". . . that he (Bothwell) is not to delay putting into execution that which had been ordered because her husband used such fair words to deceive her and bring her to his will that she might be moved by them, if the other thing were not done quickly. She said that she herself would go and fetch him (Darnley) and would stop at a house on the road, where she would try to give him a draught, but if this could not be done, she would put him in a house where the explosion was arranged for the night upon which one of her servants was to be married. He (Bothwell) was to try to get rid of his wife, either by putting her away or poisoning her, since he knew that she (Mary) had risked all for him, her honour, her kingdom, her wealth which she had in France, and her God, contenting herself with his person alone".

Lennox, also, it will be recalled, described a similar letter, and his information probably stemmed likewise from Moray. Now, there are negative reflexions, as one may say, of some of the statements in the 'de Silva' letter to be found in the 'Moray' part of Casket Letter II: for instance, Mary mentions Darnley's flattering, made so coldly and so wisely, and also that she will not be moved by his protestations ('the place will hold until death'), that the apothecary will help Darnley at Craigmillar, and she makes a reference to the marriage of Bastian, which did take place 'on the day for which the explosion was arranged', but the final remarks are not to be found in any of the Marian letters. A possible inference is that Moray based his description of what we may call the 'de Silva' letter on the letter which he had himself already received from Mary, part I of Casket Letter II, and this would account for the previous suggestion (page 77) that Moray had probably seen the 'de Silva' letter before he left Scotland. Of course the letter which Mary had written to him would not suffice as evidence, but, at the time at which de Silva wrote, there was no intention of producing any testimony against the Queen, and Moray's own word was all that was needed.

Finally, we must lay before the reader the text of the draft of Crawford's declaration, preserved amongst the Cambridge University manuscripts and printed by Henderson (313). The revised form was given as evidence before the Commission at Westminster on 9th December, 1568. The frequent corrections and alterations are an interesting reflection of the state of mind of the writer, and the comparison with the relevant sections of the 'Moray' part of Casket Letter II will shew that this deposition was composed with that letter as a guide. This spelling is modernised, and brackets indicate words erased.

"These are the words I remember were between the King and the Queen in Glasgow when she took him away to Edinburgh.

The King, for that my Lord his father was absent sick by reason whereof he could not speak with him himself, called me unto him, these words that had then passed between him and the Queen, he gave me in remembrance to report unto the said Lord his father.

After their meeting and short speaking together, she demanded of him his letters wherein he complained of the cruelty of some.

He answered that he complained not without cause, and, as he believed she would grant herself, when she was well advised.

She asked him of his sickness, he answered that she was the cause (of his sickness) and (this) further he said 'you asked (of) me what I meant by the cruelty contained in my letters; it is of you only, that will not accept my offers and repentance. I confess that I have failed in some things, and such like greater faults had been made to you sundry times, which you have forgiven. I am but young, and you will say you have forgiven me sundry times. May not a man of my age, for lack of counsel of which I am (altogether) very destitute fall twice or thrice, and yet repent himself, and be chastised by experience. If I have made any fail that you but think a fail howsoever it be, I crave your pardon and protest that I shall never fail again. I desire no other thing but that we may be together as husband and wife; and, if you will not consent hereto, I desire never to rise forth of this bed. Therefore, I pray you, give me an answer hereunto. God knoweth how I am punished for making my God of you, and for having no other thought but on you. And, if at any time I offend you, you are the cause (because) for it when any offendeth me, if for my refuge I might disclose my heart to you, I would speak it to no other, but when anything is spoken to me, and you and I not being as husband and wife ought to be, necessity compelleth me to keep it in my breast, and bringeth me in such melancholy as you see I am'.

She answered that it seemed him she was annoyed with his sickness, and she would find a remedy so soon as she might.

She asked him why he would have passed away with the English ship.

He answered that he had spoken with the Englishman, but not of mind to go away with him, and, if he had, it had not been without cause in respect of the manner how he was used, for he had neither to sustain himself nor his servants and need not to make further discourse thereof, for she knew it as well as he.

Then she asked him of the purpose of Highgate.

He answered that it was told him.

She required how and by whom it was told him.

He answered that the Lord of Wyate told him that there was a letter presented to her in Craigmillar, made by her own advice, and subscribed by certain others, who desired her to subscribe the same, which she refused to do. And he said to her that he would never trust that she who was his own proper flesh would do him any evil, and, if any other would do it, they should buy it dear, except they took him sleeping, albeit he suspected nobody. So he desired her effectuously that she would bear him company, for she found ever some ado to draw herself from him to her own lodging, and would never remain with him past two hours together at once.

She was very pensive, whereat he found fault. He said to her that he was advertised that she had brought a litter with her.

She answered that because she understood he was not able to ride on horseback, she brought a litter that he might be carried more softly.

He answered that it was not meet for a sick man to travel that could not sit on a horse, and especially in so cold weather.

She answered that she would take him to Craigmillar, where she might be with him and not far from her son.

He answered that upon condition he would go with her. That was, that he and she might be together at bed and board as husband and wife, and that she should leave him no more. And, if she would promise him it, upon her word, he would go with her where she pleased without respect of any danger of sickness wherein he was or otherwise. And if she would not grant to the same, he would not go with her in no wise.

She answered that it was for that effect that she was come, and, if she had not been minded thereto, she had not come so far to fetch him, and so she granted his desire, and promised him that it should be as he had spoken, and thereupon gave him her hand and faith of her body that she would love him and use him as her husband, (but) notwithstanding, before they could be together, he must be purged and cleansed of his sickness, which she trusted should be shortly, for she minded to give him the bath at Craigmillar (and then)

Then he said he would do whatsoever she would him to do, and would love all that she loved, but

She required him in especial whom he loved of the nobility and whom he hated.

He answered that he hated no man, and loved all alike well.

She asked him how he liked the Lady Reres, and if he were angry with her.

He answered that he had little mind of such as she was, and wished of God that she might serve her to her honour.

Then she desired him that he would keep to himself the promise between him and her and to declare it to nobody, for, peradventure, the Lords would not think it good of their sudden agreement, considering he and they were at some words before.

He answered that he knew no cause why they should mislike of it, and desired her that she would not (purchase some of) (them by her)

move any of them against him, like as he would (not do to you) persuade not against her, and that they would work both in one mind, otherwise it might turn to greater inconvenience to them both.

She answered that she never sought any way by him, but he was in the fault himself.

He answered again that his faults were published, and that there were that made greater faults than ever he made that believed were unknown, and yet they would speak of great and small.

(She asked of him if he might be ready to travel at that time).

(The words that the King spake unto me at his departing for the ol Glasgow)

farther, the King.   at that present time.

(at his departure out of Glasgow)

The King asked me what I thought of his voyage. I answered that I liked it not, because she took him to Craigmillar, for if she had desired him with herself or to have had his company, she would have taken him to his own house in Edinburgh, where she might more easily visit him than to travel two miles out of the town to a gentleman his house. Therefore, my opinion was that she took him away more like a prisoner than her husband.

He answered that he thought little less himself, and found himself indeed, save the confidence he had in her promise only, notwithstanding, he would go with her, and put himself in her hands, though she should cut his throat, and besought God to . . . mercy unto them both".

The reader should bear in mind that this narrative, which is supposed to corroborate Casket Letter II, is derived from Darnley's account of the interview. Meanwhile, Mary had written an account of the same interview in French. On translation of this account into Scotch, the same phrases and words appear to an extent which is quite impossible; and Mary's secret belief, that Darnley thought he was to be taken away prisoner, turns out, impossibly, to have been Crawford's own thought. It is highly significant that Crawford had great difficulty in phrasing the timing of the statement at the end of his deposition. First, he wrote, "The words that the King spoke unto me at his departing for the", and it seems obvious that the next words would have been "Kirk o'Field", but this would not agree with the Letter, so the words "for the" were deleted and "of Glasgow" substituted. Then, he tried again, deleting the whole sentence, he wrote, "Farther, the King at that present time", but not liking that, he substituted, "at his departure out of Glasgow", and finally gave up the whole question as insoluble, merely saying, "The King asked me, etc.". His difficulty, presumably, was the date on which the decision had been taken for Darnley to lie at Kirk o'Field. He knew Darnley had made this decision himself as soon as he agreed to return, but he did not know on what date Mary had been told of this, and here was his difficulty.

Crawford's second deposition (314) runs thus:

"The words between the Queen and Thomas Crawfo. (These are the words that were between) the Queen and me by the way as she came to Glasgow to fetch the King, when my Lord my master sent me to shew her cause, why he came not to meet her himself.

First, I made my Lord my master his humble commendations unto her Majesty, with the excuse that he came not to meet her, praying her Grace not to think that it was either for (proudness) stout stomach or yet for not knowing his duty towards her Highness, but only for want of health at that present and also that he would not presume to come in her presence why until he knew farther her mind, because of the (rude) sharp words that she had spoken of him to Robert Cunningham his servant in Stirling (by which he perceived) whereby he thought he was in her Majesty's displ . . . notwithstanding, he hath sent his servants and friends to wait upon her Majesty.

She answered that there was no receipt (against could serve) against fear.

I answered that my Lord had no fear for anything he knew in himself, but only of the cold and unkindly words she had spoken to his servant.

She answered and said that he would not be afraid in case he were not culpable.

I answered that I knew so far of his Lordship that there was nothing he desired more than the secrets of every creature's heart were written in their face.

She asked me if I had any farther commission.

I answered (that I had spoken the things I had in commission) 'no'.

Then she commanded me to hold my peace; and for and for that the better of whom".

Similar comments apply to this as to the other deposition of Crawford, and not one iota of reliance can be placed upon this piece of fabricated evidence, rendered still more dubious because there is some evidence that it was not Crawford who met Mary four miles outside Glasgow, for, according to Black, Crawford was himself Laird of Houston (92), and we see from the sequence of paragraphs 2 to 5 of Casket Letter II that Houston, whom Mary knew by name, met her in company with Luss and Caldwell's son after her meeting with the gentleman from the Earl of Lennox, whose name was apparently unknown to the Queen.

CHAPTER V

Casket Letter No. IV

The contemporary English translation of this letter is endorsed by a clerk "Letter concerning Holyrood House", but this is evidently an error for Kirk o'Field, for Mary had brought Darnley to Kirk o'Field on or about 31st January, 1567, and there he died at 2.0 a.m. on Monday, 10th February. The alleged background of this letter is described in Buchanan's 'Detection' thus (14):

> "About three days before that the King was slain, she practised to set her brother, Lord Robert (Commendator of Holyrood), and him at deadly feud, making reckoning that it should be gain to her, whichsoever of them both had perished. For matter to ground their dissention, she made rehearsal of the speech that the King had had with her concerning her brother; and when they both grew in talk, as the one seemed to charge the other with the lie, at last they were in a manner come from words to blows. But, while they were both laying their hands on their weapons, the Queen, feigning as though she had been perilously afraid of that which she earnestly desired, called the Earl of Moray, her other brother, to the parting (of them), to this intent, that she might either presently bring him in danger to be slain himself, or in time to come to bear the blame of such mischief as then might have happened".

This matter is also referred to in the second deposition of Paris (209):

> "Asked if he had heard anything of the affair of Saturday (8th February) morning? Replied, No, except that the Queen said, in the presence of those of her chamber, that there had been some quarrel between the King and my Lord of Holyrood (Lord Robert Stewart), which had been a good means of killing the King at that time, for there was no one in the room, other than herself, to separate them".

The intention, therefore, of this letter was to shew that Mary, who slept the night of 7th February at Kirk o'Field, had written late that night to Bothwell to apprise him of her intention of disposing of Darnley by this method. We may venture to point out that, since they were both in the same town, it was much more likely that Mary would send a messenger to ask Bothwell to come to her than that she should write a letter on such a dangerous topic. The copy of the original French runs thus (457):

"J'ay veille plus tard la hault que je n'eusse fait si ce neust esté pour tirer ce que ce porteur vous dira que Je treuve la plus belle commoditie pour excuser vostre affaire que se pourroit presenter. Je luy ay promise de le luy mener demain si vous le trouves bon mettes y ordre. Or monsieur j'ay ja rompu ma promesse car vous ne mavies rien commande de vous envoier ni escrire si ne le fais pour vous offencer et si vous scavies la craint que j'en ay vous nauries tant des subçons contrairs que toutesfois je cheris comme procedant de la chose du mond que je desire et cherche le plus c'est votre bonne grace de laquelle mes deportemens m'asseureront et je n'en disesperay Jamais tant que selon vostre promesse vous m'en dischargeres vostre coeur aultrement je penseras que mon malheur et le bien composer de ceux qui n'ont la troisiesme partie de la fidelité ni voluntair obéissance que je vous porte auront gaigné sur moi l'avantage de la seconde amye de Jason. Non que je vous compare a un si malheureuse ni moi a une si impitoiable. Combien que vous men fassiez un peu resentir en chose qui vous touschat ou pour vous preserver et garder a celle a qui seulle vous aporteins si lon se peult approprier ce que lon acquiert par bien et loyalment voire uniquement aymer comme je fais et fairay toute ma vie pour bein ou mal qui m'en puisse avenir. En recompense de quoy et des tous les maulx dont vous maves este cause, souvenes vous du lieu icy pres. Je ne demande que vous me tennes promesse de main mais que nous truvions et que nadjousties foy au subçons quaures sans nous en certifier, et Je ne demande a Dieu si non que coignoissies tout ce que je ay au coeur qui est vostre et quil vous preserve de tout mal au moyns durant ma vie qui ne me sera chere qu'autant qu'elle et moy vous serons agreables. Je m'en vois coucher et vous donner le bon soir mandes moy de main comme vous seres porté a bon heur. Car j'enseray en pein et faites bon guet si l'oseau sortira de sa cage ou sens son per comme la tourtre demeurera seulle a se lamenter de l'absence pour court quelle soit. Ce que je ne puis faire ma lettre de bon coeur si ce nestoit que je ay peur que soyes endormy. Car je nay ose escrire devant Joseph et bastienne et Joachim qui ne sont que partir quand J'ay commence".

Contemporary English (299)

"I have watched later there above than I wold have don, if it had not bene to draw out that that this bearer shall tell you, that I fynde the fayrest commoditie to

Contemporary Scotch (299)

"I have walkit laiter thair up then I wald have done, gif it had not bene to draw sum thing out of him, quhilk this beirer will schaw zow; quhilk is the fairest com-

excuse yor busynes that might be offred: I have promised him to bring him to morrowe. Yf you think it give ordre thereunto.

Now S^r I have not yet broken my promes w^t you for you had not commanded me to send you any thing or to write and I doo it not for offending of you. And if you knew the feare that I am in there-of, you wold not have so many contrary suspicions, wch nev^{r}the-less I cherishe as proceeding from the thing of this worlde that I desyre and seeke the moste, that is, yor favo^r, or good will, of wch my behaviour shall assure me, And I will nev^r dispayre thereof as long as according to yor promes you shall discharge yor harte to me, Otherwise I wold think that my yll luck, and the fayre behavio^r of those that have not the thirde parte of the faythfulnes and volun-tary obedience that I beare unto you, shall have wonne the advan-tage ov^r me of the second Loover of Jason. Not that I doo compare you so wicked, or myself to so unpitifull a person, Althoughe you make me feele some greefe in a matter that toucheth you, and to preserve & keepe you to her whom alone you belong, if a body may clayme to him selfe that wch is won by well, faythfully, yea entierly loving, as I doo & will doo all my lyfe for payne or hurt what soev^r may happen to me thereby.

moditie that can be offerit to excuse zour affairis. I have prom-ysit to bring him to him the morne. Put ordour to it, gif ze find it gude.

Now, schir, I have broken my promeis; becaus ze commandit me nouther to wryte nor send unto zow. Zit I have not done this to offend zow. And gif ze knew the feir yat I have presently, ze wold not have sa mony contrary sus-pisiounis in zour thocht; quhilk notwithstanding I treit and cher-eis, as proceeding from the thing in the world that I maist desyre, and seikis fastest to haif, quhilk is zour gude grace; of the quhilk my behaviour sall assure me. As to me, I sall never dispair of it, and prayis zow, according to zour promeis, to discharge zour hart unto me: Utherwayis I will think that my malhure, and the gude handling of hir that hes not ye third part of the faithfull nor willing obedience unto zow that I beir, hes wyn, aganis my will, yat advantage over me, quhilk the second lufe of Jason wan: not that I will compair zow unto ane so unhappy as he was, nor zit myself to ane so unpietifull ane woman as scho. Howbeit, ze caus me to be sumthing lyke unto hir in ony thing that tuichis zow, or yat may preserve and keip zow unto hir, to quhome only ze appertene; gif it be sa that I may appropriate that quhilk is wyn throch faithfull, zea, only luifing of zow, as I do, and sall do all the dayis of my lyfe, for pane or evill that can cum thairof.

In recompence whereof, and of all the evils that you bene cause of to me, Remember the place hereby. I desyre not that you keepe promes w^t me to morrowe, but that we may be togither, and that you give no credit to the suspicions that you shall have, wtout being assured thereof. And I ask no more of God but that you might know all that I have in my harte, wch is yours and that he preserve you from all evill, at the leist during my lyfe, wch shall not be deere unto me, but as long as yt & I shall please you. I go to bed, and give you good night.

Send me word tomorrow early in the morning how you have don for I shall thing long. And watche well if the byrde shall fly out of his cage or w^{t}out his ~~father~~ make as the turtle shall remayne alone to lament & morne for absence how short soev^r it be. That that I could not doo my letter shuld doo it w^t a good will, yf it weare not that I feare to wake you, for I durst not write before Joseph & Bastian and Joachim, who weare but now gon from I begon".

In recompense of the quhilk, and of all the evillis quhilk ze have bene caus of to me, remember zow upon the place heir besyde. I craif with that ze keip promeis to me the morne; but that we may meit togidder, and that ze gif na faith to suspiciounis without the certanetie of thame: And I craif na uther thing at God, but that ze may knaw that thing that is in my hart quhilk is zouris; and that he may preserve zow from all evill, at the leist sa lang as I have lyfe, quhilk I repute not precious unto me, except in sa far as it and I baith ar aggreabill unto zow. I am going to bed, and will bid zow gude nicht.

Advertise me tymely in the morning how ze have fairin; for I will be in pane unto I get worde. Mak gude watch, gif the burd eschaip out of the caige, or without his mate. As ye turtur I sall remane alone for to lament the absence, how schort yat sa ever it be. This letter will do with ane gude hart, that thing quhilk I cannot do myself, gif it be not that I have feir that ze ar in sleiping. I durst not wryte this befoir Joseph, Bastiane, and Joachim, that did bot depart evin quhen I began to wryte".

This letter is neither addressed nor signed, but the reader will have no difficulty in deciding that it is not a production of Mary's pen; that it is, in fact, a letter from the "other woman" to Bothwell. We see the same high-flown metaphors, the same tortuous style, and the same emotions as in Casket Letter III, and a glance at the contemporary translations will shew how the sense of the original was perverted in places, partly through ineptitude, and partly through a desire to provide evidence against the Queen.

Let us now consider the real meaning of this letter, sentence by sentence, and compare this modern translation with that of the prosecution.

"I have stayed awake longer up there than I should have done, if it had not been to prepare (French 'tirer'—'to draw up', 'prepare') what this bearer will tell you, which I find the best way of excusing your doings which can be presented".

The Scotch version emphatically changes the meaning of 'tirer', and reads "to draw something out of him", in order to support the idea, already suggested by 'up there', that Mary has sat up late in the upper room in which Darnley was lodged at Kirk o'Field, and was luring him on to give her some grounds for arranging the quarrel with Lord Robert, which is the matter about which the bearer will give details. The French, however, will not bear this construction. The writer has sat up late, worried by Bothwell's suspicions against her, and has prepared, or drawn up, some sort of excuse for his actions, and has suggested a meeting at which, if he be willing, they may reach some sort of agreement.

"I have promised him (the bearer) to bring it (that which she has pre-pared) to him (the bearer) to-morrow; if you find it good, act accordingly".

The suggestion, "I have promised him to bring him to him to-morrow", is intended to cover the bringing of Lord Robert into Darnley's presence, so that they might quarrel, but this is obviously absurd, since, in that case, the promise would have been made to Bothwell, not to the bearer, and the sentence would have run, "I promise you that I shall bring him to him to-morrow". If Bothwell agrees to the suggestion, he is to act accordingly. As may become rather more clear later, this letter was probably written to Bothwell shortly before his marriage to Lady Jane Gordon, in which case the matter which is worrying the writer is that event. It may be that Bothwell has partly used the excuse of political necessity for this marriage, and partly has accused this person of infidelity, stories of which seem to have been carried to him by Huntly, who would probably be desirous that this liaison should be concluded when Bothwell married his sister.

"Now, Monsieur, I have already broken my promise, for you have ordered me not to send or write anything; yet I do not do it to offend you, and, if you knew the fear which I have of doing so, you would not have so many contrary suspicions, which, however, I cherish as proceeding from the thing in the world that I most desire and seek: that is, your good grace, of which my behaviour will assure me, and I shall never despair of it (i.e., your good grace) so long as, according to your promise, you will open your heart to me about them (i.e., the suspicions)".

It is really quite impossible that this fawning paragraph could have been part of a letter which had just described a method of encompassing a murder. Nothing is more obvious than that the writer is extremely insecure in her attachment to the Earl, and she knows it. He has drifted away from her, and she is endeavouring to win him back. For Mary to have plotted the murder of Darnley with Bothwell, she must have known that he was completely on her side in the matter, as Casket Letters I and II shew that he was, and that state of affairs is not in evidence here. The suspicions were, presumably, those of her infidelity: what reason could Bothwell have for doubting Mary's love if, as is alleged, she had brought the King to Kirk o'Field for the purpose of his removal and Bothwell's elevation to the throne? And can we imagine any circumstances in which Bothwell would have commanded Mary not to write to him?

We may note that the word 'deportment' in modern French means 'bad behaviour', but, in the 16th Century, the word had no such connotation, and meant 'behaviour', whether good or bad, as does the English word 'deportment'.

"Otherwise, I shall think that my misfortune and the good management of those who have not the third part of the fidelity or voluntary obedience that I bear you . . . . ."

A reference to Lady Jane Gordon and Huntly. It may be noted that the Scotch version uses 'her' instead of 'those', presumably because it would have been unrealistic to suggest that Huntly would have stood in the way of Bothwell's marriage to the Queen; the blame is therefore cast on Lady Jane.

" . . . . . will have won over me the advantage of the second lover of Jason. Not that I compare you with one so unfortunate, nor myself with one so pitiless, although you make me feel a little so in anything which touches you, or to preserve and keep you for her to whom you alone belong; if one can own that which one has acquired by well and loyally, nay (French, 'voire'), solely loving, as I do and shall do all my life, in spite of any trouble or ill which can come to me from it".

This long and involved sentence is typical of the "other woman", and the reference to trouble and ill echoes the sentiments of the beginning of Casket Letter III. We may note that the English translator uses 'wicked' instead of 'unfortunate' as the epithet applied to Jason (Bothwell). According to Seneca's 'Medea', for it is more likely that our author had read this than the tragedy by Euripides, Jason divorced Medea in order to marry Glauce (Creusa), and Medea revenged herself on Jason by murdering their children. In this letter, the writer compares Lady Jane to Glauce and herself to Medea, but she is quick to point out that she is not so pitiless, although her love for Bothwell makes her "a little so". We may presume that the use of 'malheureuse' instead of 'malheureux' was an error on the part of the copyist.

"In return for which, and for all my ills of which you have been the cause, remember the place near here".

Up to 7th February, 1567, the alleged date of this letter, Bothwell had been the cause of no ills to Mary of which we have any knowledge. On the other hand, the author of this letter had obviously been deceived by him, and was about to be completely displaced by Bothwell's forthcoming marriage. He has not seen her for some time, and she asks that he may remember the place near here, which may have been some rendezvous of old, but cannot have been an allusion by Mary to Kirk o'Field.

"I do not ask that you keep your promise to-morrow (now?), but that we may meet ('nous nous trouvions', the copyist has omitted one 'nous'), and that you do not believe any suspicions which you will have without assuring yourself of them";

'De main' may mean to-morrow, but perhaps means 'now' ('de maintenant'); while 'nous en certifier' is surely a mistake for 'vous en certifier'; the 'v' and the 'n' not being dissimilar in Italianate script. This seems to mean that, in view of the reasons which Bothwell has sent her, she does not ask him to keep his promise to marry her *now*, but she wants to meet him, and, most important of all, he must not believe the stories of her infidelity which he has heard from Huntly. The reasons for the refusal of Bothwell to marry her now were, we may take it, at least in part, political, and she is prepared to accept the necessity for this, perhaps with promise of the reversion of his hand should it ever be politically convenient for him to divorce Lady Jane, but she is insistent that he must not believe her to be unfaithful.

"and I only ask of God that you may know what I have in my heart, which is yours, and that He preserve you from all evil, at least during my life, which will only be dear to me so long as both it and I are agreeable to you. I am going to bed, and wish you 'good-night'. Send word to me early ('a bon heur' for 'a bonne heure') to-morrow, how (comme = comment) you are (i.e., what you have decided) for I shall be worried".

'Comme vous seres porte' seems to mean 'how you will behave' in response to the suggestions which the bearer of this letter is to give him.

"And watch well: if the bird leave its cage, when, without its father (or 'mate'), like the turtle-dove, it will live alone to lament the absence for only a short time".

This sentence is very perplexing, but the above seems to be its meaning. The contemporary translators, and all who have followed, read 'per' as 'pair', 'mate' (particularly of a bird) and translate 'ou' ('where') as 'or'; the latter is a mistake, and the former is doubtful. The Scotch translation makes a number of unwarrantable changes, "Make good watch, if the bird escape out of the cage or without *her* mate; as the turtle, *I* shall remain alone for to lament the absence, how short that soever it be", while the English goes even farther, "Watch well if the bird shall fly out of *his* cage, or without *his* (father) mate as the turtle shall remain alone to lament and mourn for absence how short soever it be". There is no justification for the pronouns, and the intention of inserting them was to suggest that Mary was warning Bothwell that Darnley might escape from his cage (Kirk o'Field), where (not 'or') he would be without his mate (Mary), who would only lament his absence until Bothwell filled his place. Furthermore, the French 'demeurera' is definitely 3rd person, 'he, she or it will live', not 'I', as in the Scotch version.

However, the version "And watch well: if the bird leave its cage, where, without its mate, like the turtle-dove, it will live alone to lament the absence for only a short time" could well be a reference to the writer herself, meaning, "Take care that I do not leave my cage, when, without you, my mate, I shall only live a short time in sorrow, for I shall die of love, as did the turtle-dove in the adage". If, however, the reading 'father' be preferred to 'mate', the reference could be to Lady Jane, who was known to be in love with Ogilvie of Boyne before her marriage to Bothwell, and whom she later did marry; she was fatherless, for the 4th Earl of Huntly had died at Corrichie (1562). The meaning would then be, "Take care lest Lady Jane leave her cage before you marry her, where, without a father to guide her, she will not live alone long to lament her absence from you, for she will marry Ogilvie, and live with him like a turtle-dove". The reader may please him or her self in the matter: the clues are insufficient for a decisive conclusion.

"That which I cannot do, my letter (does) heartily (i.e., wishes you 'good-night'), if it were not that I fear you are asleep".

The writer, or the copyist, has gone astray here, but the meaning is clear.

"For I dared not write in front of Joseph and Bastienne and Joachim, who only left when I began".

The reader is asked to believe that this last sentence is an interpolation The end of a letter, or of a page of a letter, is the obvious place for such an addition, and this final remark is the only thing in this letter which points to Mary as the writer. It may be noted that the three named are all also named in paragraph 7 of Casket Letter II, which would have been the obvious way in which a forger would have underlined the common authorship of the two letters. But why 'Bastienne', apparently a female, for 'Bastiane'? Is this a copyist's mistake or did the forger err? One thing we can be sure of; Mary herself never wrote 'Bastienne'.

A better reason for believing that this last sentence is an interpolation is its incongruity. It should be compared with the opening sentence of the letter, "I have stayed awake longer up there than I should have done, if it had not been to prepare what this bearer will tell you". It cannot be believed that Mary prepared the plot for killing Darnley in the presence of the servants. But, if the presence of her servants prevented her from writing her letter, why did she not send them away; had the Queen no authority? And, finally, why should she make this remark at all, contradicting, as it does, the reason for her lateness in writing with which she began her letter?

Although the penultimate sentence looks as though it were the end of this letter, it was not. The letter continued, and the following portion was included in Casket Letter II, paragraphs 18 and 19, which we must now examine again in this new context.

"We are united to two false people; the Devil has divided us, whom God did knit together for ever as the most faithful couple that ever He united: this is my faith; I shall die believing it".

This underlines her own forthcoming separation from Bothwell, and his union, shortly to be concluded, with Lady Jane Gordon and her brother. If she used the words, 'the New Year will separate us', as is suggested by the contemporary English translation, that also would be appropriate, for the Bothwell-Gordon marriage took place in February, 1566.

"Excuse me for writing badly, but I cannot improve it, for I am not well at ease. And yet I am very glad to write to you when others are asleep since I cannot sleep as they do . . . . "

It is late, as it evidently was when Casket Letter IV was written, and the writer is 'ill at ease', as was also the author of that other letter.

" . . . . . nor as I desire, which is in your arms, My Dear Life, whom I pray God to preserve from all evil and to send you repose".

Here again is identity of feeling between the two letters.

"I am going to seek my rest until the morning, when I shall end my letter. But it grieves me that it should prevent me from writing my news to you, because it is so long. Send me word what you have decided on this matter, so that we may understand each other's wishes, and nothing thereby be spoilt".

This clearly refers to the question of the meeting between the author and Bothwell, and shews once again the same attitude as in the other letter; an attitude of readiness to agree, within certain broad limits, to his wishes and not to stand too much in his way.

"I am weary and going to sleep, yet I cannot stop scribbling so long as there is any paper".

Now we see why the letter failed to stop when it should have done, but has babbled on, saying nothing decisive, and repeating the sentiments and expressions of its earlier part.

"Cursed be this pocky fellow who troubles me so much, for, without him (her), I should have a far pleasanter subject to talk about".

Remembering that this was written in French, and that such masculine expressions as 'individu louche' or 'mauvais sujet' could well be translated 'pocky fellow', but might be applied to a woman, we can easily imagine that this post-postscript was written with Glauce, the Lady Jane, in mind, and, for a moment, the unfortunate woman becomes almost human as we see her throw down her pen with a curse: perhaps, we are wrong in this picture, and, true to her constant pattern, she wept as the pen fell from her fingers.

Did she finish the letter, or was it never sent? Perhaps Bothwell arrived the following morning and there was no need to send it, but whether it was kept by Bothwell or by her, it was an evil day for Mary when it fell into Maitland's hands.

CHAPTER VI

Casket Letter No. V

The contemporary copy of this letter in French is endorsed, in the hand of a clerk, "Anent the dispatch (i.e., dismissal) of Margaret Carwood; which (the dismissal) was before her (Carwood's) marriage: proves her (Mary's) affection". If it were not for this endorsement, we should be at a loss to know why this letter was included; but it emphasizes, perhaps more than any other of the Casket Documents, that these letters were not forged in the ordinary sense of the word, for no forger would waste his time on such a document as this.

Margaret Carwood was one of Mary's maids of the bed-chamber, and she seems to have been something of a favourite of the Queen. She married, on Tuesday, 11th February, 1567, the day after Darnley's death, John Stewart of Tullipowreis, and it is, perhaps, a little surprising that the ceremony was carried out at such a time. However, no doubt the arrangements had been made some time in advance, and there is at least some evidence to shew that Mary was so overcome by the events of the previous day that she had no control over the situation (see Appendix A). In the circumstances, if Margaret Carwood and John Stewart were much in love, and lacking a direct order to the contrary, for the Privy Council had other things to think about, it is not so very strange that the marriage was solemnized.

Now, if this letter and the previous one were really written by Mary, as the Lords alleged, and if the attribution as to its contents were correct, it must have been sent on 9th February, 1567, for Casket Letter IV must be the earlier: it distinctly alludes to the prohibition on writing and is obviously the first time that that prohibition was abrogated. This allows us to see that the attribution must be false, for it is unthinkable that, having proposed a plot for the murder of Darnley in the letter of the previous day, there should be no allusion to that plot or its failure in this present letter, and no allusion to the forthcoming explosion at Kirk o'Field. Furthermore, as with Casket Letter IV, there could be no reason for writing to Bothwell

178

when he and Mary were in the same town and a messenger could fetch him at any moment.

Nor is this all: from the letter, it is obvious that the servant, Margaret Carwood, according to the Lords, was in serious disgrace, but this does not fit the circumstances. As we see from Robertson's 'Inventories' (636), Mary not only paid for her bridal feast, but, on 8th February, the bride was granted a pension of 300 marks a year, and on 10th February, Mary paid £125, 6s. Scots (about £10, 9s. sterling) for Margaret Carwood's wedding dress. She would hardly have done this for a disgraced servant, and, in fact, although married, Margaret does not seem to have left Mary's service. It is true that her name is absent from a list of the Queen's household dated 13th February, 1567, but no doubt she was on her honeymoon: she was certainly in Mary's service on 23rd March, 1567, for, on that date, the Queen, in presenting her with 80 yards of fine linen, calls her "her servitrice".

In fact, the reader will have no difficulty in recognizing the typical style and emotions of the "other woman" in this letter, the contemporary French copy of which runs as follows (458):

"Mon cueur helas fault il que la follie d'une famme dont vous connoisses asses l'ingratitude vers moy soit cause de vous donner displesir veu que je neusse sceu y remedier sans le scavoir, et despuis que men suis apersue Je ne vous lay peu dire pour scavoir comment mi guovejernerois car en cela ni aultre chose je ne veulx entreprandre de rien fayre sans en scavoir votre volontay, laquelle je vous suplie me fayre entandre car la suivray toute ma vie plus volontiers que vous ne me la declareres, et si vous ne me mandes ce soir ce que volles que jen faise je men deferay au hazard de la fayre entreprandre ce qui pourroit nuire a ce a quoy nous tandons tous deus, et quant elle sera mariee je vous suplie donnes men vne ou ien prandray telles de quoy vous contanteres quant a leur condition mayes de leur langue ou fidelitie vers vous ie ne vous en respondray Je vous suplie qune opinion sur aultrui ne nuise en votre endroit a ma constance. Soupsonnes moi may quant je vous en veulx rendre hors de doubte et mesclersir ne le refeuses ma chere vie et permetes que je vous face preuue par mon obeissance de ma fidelite et constance et subjection volontaire, que je prands pour le plus agreable bien que je scaurois rescevoir si vous le voulles accepter, et men faytes la ceremonie car vous ne me scauriez davantage outrasger ou donner mortel ennuy".

Contemporary Scotch Translation (205)

"My hart, alace! must the foly of ane woman quhais unthankfulnes toward me ze do sufficiently knaw, be occasion of displesure unto zow, considering yat I culd not have remeidit thairunto without knawing it? And sen that I persavit it, I culd not tell it zow, for that I knew not how to governe myself thairin: For nouther in that, nor in ony uther thing, will I tak upon me to do ony thing without knawledge of zour will, quhilk I beseik zow let me understand; for I will follow **it** all my lyfe, mair willingly than zow sall declair it to me; and gif ze do not send me word this nicht quhat ze will that I sall do, I will red myself of it, and hasard to caus it to be interprysit and taken in hand, quhilk micht be hurtful to that quhairunto baith we do tend. And quhen scho sall be maryit, I beseik you give me ane, or ellis I will tak sic as sall content zow for thair conditiounis; bot as for thair toungis or faithfulnes towart zow, I will not answer. I beseik zow yat ane opinioun of other persoun be not hurtfull in zour mynde to my constancie. Mistrust me; bot quhen I will put zow out of dout, and cleir myselfe, refuse it not, my deir lufe, and suffer me to mak zow sum prufe be my obedience, my faithfulnes, constancie, and voluntarie subjectioun, quhilk I tak for the plesandest gude that I micht ressaif, gif ze will accept it; and mak na ceremonie at it, for ze could do me na greiter outrage, nor give mair mortall grief".

It will be clear that the translator was not up to his task, for he blundered considerably.

The letter is neither signed, nor addressed, but, while we may be sure that we have the opening paragraph, it is also obvious that the end of the letter is missing.

We must now proceed to an examination of a modern translation of this epistle, phrase by phrase.

"My Heart; Alas, must the folly of a woman, whose ingratitude to me you know well enough . . . . . "

This, even if it did not bear unmistakable signs of the style of the "other woman", could not be Mary speaking of Margaret Carwood, who received presents at the time of her marriage and was rewarded again soon after she returned to her mistress's service.

" . . . . . be cause to give you displeasure, seeing that I could not remedy it without knowing about it? And, when I did learn of it (the foolish act, whatever it was, of the servant), I could not tell you about it to find out how to act".

The translator has gone astray in this last sentence. It seems that, at the time that the writer discovered the foolish act of her servant, Bothwell was absent, for she was unable to apply to him for guidance, and this, again, does not fit the case of Mary and Margaret Carwood's marriage. As we shall see, there is some reason to suppose that the servant had been wagging her tongue too freely and, very probably, had reported some story of her mistress's infidelity to the Earl, which must, somehow or other, perhaps through the Earl of Huntly, have reached Bothwell's ears.

"For in that, nor in any other thing, would I undertake to do anything without learning your wish in the matter, which I beg you to tell me, for I shall follow it (your will) all my life more willingly than you will declare it to me".

Again we see the typical submission of the "other woman".

"And, if you do not send me word this evening what you want me to do, I shall get rid of her at the risk of making her undertake what could damage that at which we both aim."

The translator has blundered sadly here. It would seem that the servant is in possession of the facts about her mistress and Bothwell's relationship, which continues in spite of the Earl's marriage, and she knows that the "other woman's" intention is to marry Bothwell as soon as his present wife has been divorced. Nevertheless, although a full revelation of these details by a disgruntled and dismissed servant would interfere with her plans, the "other woman" is determined to be quit of her troublesome domestic.

"And, when she shall be married, I beg you, give me (another) one, or I shall take of them such as will content you as to their condition, but as to their tongues or fidelity to you, for those I shall not be answerable".

This suggests that it is the tattle of the servant which has caused the trouble. It also reveals that spark of self-respect which we saw for a moment at the very end of the continuation of Casket Letter IV, and which finally flares up in anger in Casket Letter VI, for these instances are merely a prelude to that outburst.

"I beg you not to allow your estimate of others to harm your opinion of my constancy. Suspect me; but when I want to put you out of doubt of them (i.e., of your suspicions) and to clear myself, do not refuse it, My Dear Life,"

We have seen this term of endearment before.

" . . and let me, by my obedience, prove my fidelity, constancy and voluntary submission, which I take to be the most agreeable thing that I can incur. If you wish to accept it (my obedience), make no ceremony about it, for you could not outrage me more, or cause me more mortal grief".

Here the document ends, abruptly and unexpectedly, but this is not the end of the letter, for that was removed from its setting and used to complete Casket Letter II, where it forms paragraph 36, which we have already seen.

"Be not offended if I give not over-great credit (to the bearer). Now, seeking to obey you, My Dear Life, I spare no honour, conscience, hazard, nor greatness whatever".

The theme of obedience continues, and the same term of endearment is repeated. From the list of her renunciations on Bothwell's behalf, we see that she is almost prepared to release him from his promise to marry her.

"Take it, I pray you, in good part, and not according to the interpretation of your false brother-in-law (Huntly), to whom, I pray you, give no credence against the most faithful lover that ever you had or shall have".

So Bothwell is, by now, married to Lady Jane, for Huntly is his brother-in-law, and the phrasing certainly suggests that Huntly has been spreading some sort of story to Bothwell about this person's infidelity to him which, perhaps, he has heard from the ungrateful servant.

"See not her (Lady Jane) whose pretended tears should not be valued so highly as the true and faithful travails which I undergo to earn her place, for obtaining which I betray, against my own nature, those who would prevent me".

The writer still harps on the possibility of her becoming Countess of Bothwell, but it is not quite clear in what way she has "betrayed" Huntly or anyone else, other than in deceiving the Lady Jane, and perhaps this is what she means. Probably she knew that Bothwell would not be pleased with this last outburst against his brother-in-law, and she is now trying to excuse herself for so acting. This idea is perpetuated in the following sentence:

"God forgive me; and God give you, My Only Life, the good luck and prosperity which your humble and faithful lover wishes you, who hopes shortly to be another thing to you for the reward of my troubles. (I have not made one word)

The words, here in parenthesis, occur only in the English version, and are probably inserted in error.

"It is late; I desire never to stop writing to you, yet I will end my letter now, after kissing your hands. Excuse my bad writing, and read it over twice. Excuse what has been scribbled when I took a paper with some notes on it".

Perhaps there were some memoranda on the paper on which this letter was written. As they were not in her handwriting, and were, probably struck through, they were not copied when the transcription was made.

"Remember your lover, and write to her very often, love me as I shall love you".

CHAPTER VII

Casket Letter VI

Darnley had died on 10th February, 1567: on 12th April, Bothwell was acquitted of the murder of the King and, on 19th April, he obtained the consent of the Lords to his marriage with the Queen. On 21st April, Mary set out from Edinburgh to Stirling to see her son who had been removed thither on 19th March and restored to the custody of the Earl and Countess of Mar. Most authors agree that she arrived at Stirling the same day, but Strickland (697) asserts, more in agreement with the length of the journey, that she spent one night *en route* and reached her destination on 22nd April. She certainly returned to Linlithgow on 23rd April, and, on the following day, was abducted to Dunbar, Bothwell bringing with her Huntly, Maitland and some others of her company. Little or no effort was made by the Lords to obtain the Queen's liberation, and it was at once assumed that the abduction was by her consent, in order to give Mary an excuse for marrying the Earl. Such a reason was, of course, as unnecessary as the other excuse of a pardon which we have already noticed (page 87), for, since the Lords had already consented, by signing the Bond at Ainsley's Supper on 19th April, no further reason or excuse was needed.

Bothwell's intention was certainly known at least to some of the Lords before he carried it into effect, for Lennox apparently told his wife by letter about the forthcoming seizure the day before it occurred, and on the day on which he himself left Scotland (441). Grange also knew about it, and his letter to Bedford (?) of 24th April reminds us that Lady Bothwell had already begun the action of divorce against her husband, in which the first move was taken on 20th March. Grange's letter runs (77),

> "This is to advertise you that Bothwell's wife is going to part with her husband; and great part of our Lords have subscribed the marriage between the Queen and him. The Queen rode to Stirling this last Monday (21st April), and returns this Thursday (24th April). I doubt not that you have heard Bothwell has gathered many of his friends, some say, to ride in Liddesdale, but I believe it not, for he is

minded to meet the Queen this day, called Thursday, and to take her by the way, and bring her to Dunbar. Judge you if it be with her will or not, but you will hear at more length on Friday or Saturday".

Mary remained at Dunbar until 6th May, 1567, when she returned with Bothwell to Edinburgh. Meanwhile, the process of divorce was carried on, Lady Bothwell's in the civil court on grounds of adultery, and Bothwell's in the Catholic Consistory Court on the grounds of consanguinity. Both petitioners had obtained judgment by 7th May, and Bothwell, created Duke of Orkney on 14th May, became Mary's husband on the day following.

In order to prove that the abduction, or "ravishment" as it was termed, was carried out by Mary's own consent and direction, the Lords produced three letters, Casket Letters VI, VII and VIII, all said to have been written by Mary to Bothwell in this short period of 21st to 23rd April, during which time she must also, if we are to believe them, have written the love-ballad. When we remember that Mary was only at Stirling for all or part of 22nd and the morning of 23rd April, we appreciate the remarkable fluency of Mary's pen.

The French copy of the letter with which we are now to deal is endorsed by a clerk "From Stirling before the ravishment—proves her mask of ravishing". It runs (458):

"Monsieur, helas pourquoy est vostre fiance mise en personne si indigne, pour subçonner ce que est entierement vostre. J'enrage. Vous m'avies promise que resouldries tout et que me manderies tous les jours ce que j'aurais a faire. Vous nen aves rien fait. Je vous advertise bien de vous garder de vostre faulx beau frere. Il est venu vers moy et sens me monstrer rien de vous me dist que luy mandies qu'il vous escrive ce qu'auries a dire, et ou, et quant vous me trouveres et ce que faires touchant luy et la dessubs m'a preschè que c'estoit une folle entreprinse, et qu'avecques mon honneur Je ne vous pourries Jamais espouser, veu qu'estant marie vous m'amenies et que ses gens ne l'endureroient pas et que les seigneurs se dediroient. Somme il est tout contrair. Je luy ay dist qu'estant venue si avant si vous ne vous en retiries de vous mesmes que persuassion ne la mort mesmes ne me fairoient faillir a ma promesse. Quant au lieu vous estes trop negligent (pardonnes moy) de vous en remettre a moy. Choisisses le vous mesmes et me le mandes. Et cependant je suis malade je differeray Quant au propose cest trop tard. Il n'a pas tins a moy que n'ayes pense a heure. Et si vous neussies non plus changé de pensee depuis mon absence que moy vous ne series a demander telle resolution. Or il ne manque rien de ma part et puis que vostre negligence vous met tous deux au danger d'un faux frere, s'il ne succede bien je ne me releveray Jamais. Il vous envoy ce porteur. Car je ne ose me fier a vostre frere de ces lettres ni de la diligence, il vous dira en quelle estat Je suis, et Juges quelle amendement m'a porte ce incertains Nouvelles. Je voudrois estre morte. Car Je vois tout aller mal. Vous prometties bien autre chose de vostre providence. Mais l'absence peult sur vous, qui aves deux cordes a vostre arc. Despesches la responce a fin que Je ne faille et ne vous fies de ceste entreprise a vostre frere. Car il la dist, et si y est tout contrair. Dieu vous doint le bon soir".

Contemporary English (300)	*Contemporary Scotch* (300)
Alas my Lorde, why is yor trust putt in a p'son so unworthy to mistrust that wch is wholly yours. I am wood. You had promised me that you wold resolve all, And that you wold send me worde every daye what I shuld do. You have don nothing thereof. I advertised you well to take heed of yor falce brother in lawe. He cam to me and w'out shewing me any thing from you told me that you had willed him to write to you that that I should saye, and where and whan you should com to me, and that that you shuld doo touching him. And thereupon hath preached unto me that it was a foolish enterprise and that w^t myn hono^r I could nev^r marry you seeing that being maryed you did carry me away. And that his folk wold not suffer yt. And that the Lords wold unsaye themselves and wold deny that they had said. To be shorte he is all contrary. I told him that seeing I was com so farre, if you did not w^tdrawe yor selfe of yo^rselfe that no psuasion nor death it selfe shuld make me fayle of my promesse. As touching the place you are to negligent (pdon me) to remitt yo^rself thereof unto me. Choose it yo^rselfe and send me word of it. And in the mean tyme I am sicke. I will differ as touching the matter it is to late. It was not long of me that you have not thought there-	Allace, my Lord, quhy is zour traist put in ane persoun sa unworthie, to mistraist that quhilk is haillely zouris? I am wod, Ze had promysit me, that ze wald resolve all, and yat ze wald send me word every day quhat I suld do. Ze haif done nathing yairof. I advertisit zow weill to tak heid of zour fals brother in law; He come to me, and without schawing me ony thing from zow, tald me that ze had willit him to wryte to zow that that I suld say, and quhair and quhen ze suld cum to me, and that that ze suld do tuiching him; and thairupon hes preichit unto me yat it was ane fuliche interpryse, and that with myne honour I culd never marry zow, seeing that being maryit ze did cary me away, and yat his folkis wald not suffer it, and that the Lordis wald unsay yameselfis, and wald deny that they had said. To be schort, he is all contrarie. I tald him, that seing, I was cum sa far, gif ze did not withdraw zour self of zour self, that na perswasioun, nor deith itself suld mak me fail of my promeis. As tuiching the place ze are to negligent, pardoun me, to remit zour self thair of unto me. Cheis it zour self, and send me word of it; And in the meanetyme I am seik, I will differ, as tuiching the mater it is to lait. It was not lang of me yat ze have not thocht

upon in tyme. And if you had not more changed yor mynde since myne absence than I have, you shuld not be now to aske such resolving. Well ther wantith nothing of my pte. And seeing that yor negligence doth putt us both in ye danger of a false brother, if it succeede not well, I will nev^r rise agayne. I send this bearer unto you for I dare not trust yor broth^r w^t these l^{res} nor wth the dilligence. He shall tell you in what state I am, and judge you what amendement these new ceremonies have brought unto me. I wold I weare dead. For I see all goith yll. You promised other manner of matter of your forseing, but absence hath powre ov^r you, who have 2 strings to yor bowe. Dispatche the annsweare that I fail you not. And put no trust in yor broth^r for this enterprise. For he hath told yt and is all against it. God give you good night".

thairupon in time. And gif ze had not mair changeit zour mynd, sen myne absence, then I have, ze suld not be now to ask sic resolving. Weill, thair wantis nathing of my part; and seing that zour negligence dois put us baith in the danger of ane fals brother, gif it succedet not weill, I will never ryse agane. I send this beirer unto zow, for I dar not traist zour brother with thir letteris, nor with the diligence. He sall tell zow in quhat stait I am, and judge ze quhat amendment yir new ceremonies have brocht unto me. I wald I wer deid, for I se all gais ill. Ze promysit uther manner of mater of zour foirseing, bot absence hes power over zow, quha haif twa stringis to zour bow. Dispatch the answer that I faill not, and put na traist in zour brother for this interpryse, for he has tald it, and is also all aganis it. God give zow gude nicht".

The reader will notice that the English version follows the Scotch translation slavishly, following the same turnings of phrase and falling into the same errors. That this letter is by the "other woman" cannot be doubted, but the style is more direct than in the previous letters, because anger has stripped her of her affectations: furthermore, the details do not coincide with three of Mary's visits to Stirling, and it is quite certain that this letter is not from her pen.

"Monsieur, Alas . . . . . "

Allowing for the state of annoyance in which the writer is, this opening is remarkably similar to that of Casket Letter V ("Mon coeur, Helas . . . . ")

"Alas, why is your trust put in a person (who is) so unworthy as to mistrust that which is entirely yours?"

In other words, "why do you place your trust in the unworthy Earl of Huntly who mistrusts me who am entirely yours?"

"I am angry. You promised me that you would arrange everything, and that you would send me word every day (i.e., as often as necessary) what I should have to do. You have done nothing about it, I warn you to be well on your guard with your false brother-in-law (Huntly)''.

As always in letters by the "other woman", Huntly is given the epithet 'false'; Mary had no reason to speak of him in this way, nor does she in those of her letters which we have. We may notice that this letter is obviously written after Bothwell's marriage to the Lady Jane.

"He (Huntly) has come to me, and, without shewing me anything (i.e. any letter) from you, has said that you sent word to him that he should write to you what I should have to say . . . . . ''

It seems certain that this is the meaning of the sentence, which, as it stands in the French copy, is unintelligible. The error has arisen through writing 'auries' ('you would have') for 'aurais' ('I should have'), which a more careful copyist could easily have done. We now see why the writer was so angry. Bothwell knows, only too well, for she has said it often enough, that she hates and mistrusts Huntly, yet now he sends this 'false brother-in-law', without even the courtesy of a note, but with instructions that she is to give him, Huntly, the details of the delicate arrangements which are being put in train, and that he, not she, is to put her words into writing and send an account to Bothwell. Perhaps he did this, in part hoping that she would break off the liaison, and in part because he was afraid that her discursive mode of writing would lead to some error of important detail. Furthermore, as we see from the second and third sentences of this letter ("You promised me that you would arrange everything . . . . . You have done nothing about it"), it was to have been Bothwell's business to make the arrangements, and now this is thrust upon her shoulders.

". . . . . and when and where you will find (meet) me, and what I will do about it",

'Lui' must mean 'it', not 'him' in this context: "what I shall do about this affair". Again, to make sense, it must be postulated that the copyist wrote 'faires' ('you will do') for 'fairai' ('I shall do'), for the writer could not say what the recipient of the letter 'will do', and the two words, 'faires' and 'fairai' are phonetically identical.

"and on this matter he lectured me, that it was a foolish undertaking, and that, with my honour, I could never marry you, seeing that, (you) being married, you were bringing me (thither) . . . . . ''

The word 'amenies' naturally means 'you were bringing', not 'you carried (me) away' as in the contemporary translations, but this reading is not quite so straightforward as might be imagined. Mary, herself, frequently wrote, as did many others of her day, 'an' or 'am' for 'en' or 'em', and this mirrored the pronunciation in French Court circles; furthermore it was common to omit the second 'm' or 'n' when this letter ought to have been doubled. We could, therefore, imagine Mary writing 'amenies' for 'emmenies', in which case the translation would be correct.

However, we have some evidence that this did not happen on this occasion. The use of 'am' or 'an' for 'em' or 'en' was, as mentioned above, common in Court circles, but, the "other woman" was, as we have seen, of inferior status to Bothwell, the copyist would certainly be of still lower rank; and it is likely that he used his own spelling. We see that in such words as 'amendement' and 'pensee' he used 'en', not 'an', and we can therefore be confident that his spelling of 'amenies' is in line with modern practice, and the phrase really does mean, " .... being married, you brought me", not "carried me away". The importance of this is obvious; the reading which has been accepted for nearly four hundred years connects this letter with Mary at Stirling urging on Bothwell to commit a pretended abduction in spite of the admonitions of the honest, but despised, Huntly. The present interpretation, which is the obvious reading, removes all connexion with Mary and the 'ravishment' from this letter.

On the other hand, the pattern of the "other woman's" affairs is being more clearly defined. Bothwell is now married, and she has become aware that his passion for her is cooler than of yore. However, she has managed to persuade him to take her to Crichton, or wherever he is now living, and where his wife is resident. It is known that Bothwell and Lady Jane were not in love and it is probable that they lived in separate apartments at Crichton. The continuation of the liaison would therefore do little harm, save in appearance, to the Countess. At the last moment, Bothwell has, however, recoiled from the arrangement: he has failed to send the expected instructions regarding this lady's move, and now, crowning insult, has sent his brother-in-law to negotiate the details, and, probably, to persuade her to give up the scheme.

" ..... and that his people would not endure it, and that the Lords would unsay themselves".

While, at first glance, this might appear to be a reference to the promise, given by the Protestant Lords at Ainsley's Supper to assist Bothwell to marry Mary, it does not really fit the case at all, for Huntly had no reason to think that the Lords would go back on their word, and, since he had long before that event given permission to his sister to divorce Bothwell, such a reference here is plainly impossible.

But the reference is quite compatible with such a situation as we have considered in regard to the "other woman". Her arrival at Crichton would naturally irritate Huntly's retainers in the Lady Jane's service: they "would not endure it", while the remark about the Lords strikes at the very root of the Bothwell-Huntly matrimonial alliance. This was not a reference to the Lords of the Congregation, but to the Lords in the Mary-Bothwell-Huntly faction, the intermediate party between the Catholic Reaction Party led by Darnley and Lennox, on the one hand, and the Reformed Kirk Party, led by Moray, on the other. Darnley's party was probably rather small, but drew great strength from his intrigues with Spain and the

Vatican; Moray's party had a strong following, although there were several divisions and factions within it; the Hamiltons, for example, siding with Moray partly for the sake of religion, but mainly for enmity to the Lennox, and playing always for their own stake in the reversion of the Crown

The Bothwell-Huntly party had few supporters, some Roman Catholic, some Protestant, but attached to it only out of loyalty to the Queen. They comprised such people as Lords Seton, Livingstone and Borthwick and some lesser folk. Bothwell and Huntly had only recently been relaxed from outlawry, and it must have been dubious to the pro-Marian Lords what would be their future line of conduct. Bothwell was powerful on the borders; he could raise several thousand men in the West Marches, and Huntly held great possessions in the North. Although both Lords were Protestant, many of Huntly's followers were Catholic. The pro-Marian Lords must have realised that either Lennox or Moray could crush them, should either Huntly or Bothwell break away; hence the importance of the Bothwell-Gordon marriage, the more so since Lady Jane was a Catholic, and hence, also, their disturbance at the realisation that that marriage was on the point of break-down. It may be taken that these pro-Marian Lords had promised their support to Bothwell and Huntly, provided that the marriage were accomplished: should Bothwell act so inconsiderately as to import his mistress into the same house as his wife, they would realize their insecurity, would "unsay themselves" and, perhaps, in a general *sauve-qui-peut*, ally themselves, some with Lennox and some with Moray. If this happened, and if friction grew between Bothwell and Huntly, either of the extremist parties would overwhelm the two Earls singly or together.

"Summa, he is all against it".

The phrase "summa" was frequently used by Mary, but it was also used by others, and its presence in this letter is not evidence of Mary's authorship.

"I told him that, (I) being come so far forward (in this affair), if you did not draw back yourself, then no persuasion, not even death itself, would make me break my promise. As to the place (of meeting in order to make the journey to Bothwell's house), you are too careless (pardon me) to leave it to me. Choose it yourself, and send me word of it. Meanwhile, I am ill: I shall put off as to that matter; it is too late. It is not because of me that you did not think about it sooner".

The phrase, 'il n'a pas tins à moi', may be a mistake for 'il n'a pas tenu à moi', or, even, perhaps, for 'il n'appartient pas à moi', but we can be certain that the error is the copyist's.

"And if you had not changed your mind more since my absence than I had, you would not need to ask (me to make) such a decision".

From this, it appears that the writer had been sent away, not left behind, by Bothwell, for she speaks of 'my absence'. Perhaps she had to evacuate her quarters at Crichton to make room for the new bride: as we have seen, Bothwell and Lady Jane removed thither in May, 1566, so this letter probably dates from June or July of that year.

"Now, nothing is lacking on my side, and since your carelessness puts us both at the mercy of a false brother, if it (our affair) does not succeed, I shall never get over it".

Once again, Huntly is termed 'false'. Had Bothwell kept the liaison secret, and not told Huntly about it, all would have been well, but Bothwell's carelessness of secrecy, and his cynical attitude to the marriage with Lady Jane, puts, not only her, but the Earl also in danger, an event which could result from the political implications which we have just described.

"I send you this bearer, for I dare not trust your brother (Huntly, strictly, brother-in-law) with this letter, nor with promptitude: he (the bearer) will tell you in what state I am, and you may judge what improvement this uncertain news (Huntly's message) has brought about in me".

The French reads, "He sends you this bearer", but it is quite certain that this is an example of misreading 'il' for 'je', which quite often happens with Mary's writing, and, presumably, would be an easy mistake with any Italianate script. As we shall see, this has some bearing on the preparation of the letters for production. We may notice that the French copy reads 'Ce incertains nouvelles', an error of grammar which may be ascribed to the copyist, and which both translations render 'these new ceremonies'.

The writer has already said that she is ill, and she here reiterates that this present treatment is not helping her to get over her indisposition. Mary, of course, was frequently ill, but there is no evidence that she was so at the time of her visit to Stirling in April, 1567, and it is more likely that we should have heard about it, either from Mary herself or from the Lords, if she had been: from the Lords, because, at first they alleged that the "ravishment" was genuine, in spite of Grange's letter to Bedford, and accused Bothwell of imposing on Mary; it would have been a nice addition to have claimed that she was ill at the time, and would have made Bothwell appear to have been even more inhuman. Furthermore, if Mary really did ride from Edinburgh to Stirling in one day, she must have been in tolerable health: that she was not ill at Stirling appears from the fact that she did not baulk at returning towards Edinburgh after such a short stay.

"I would I were dead, for I see all goes ill. You certainly promised that things would be different (i.e. "another thing of your providing"), but absence affects you, who have two strings to your bow. Hasten your answer, so that I do not fail; and do not trust your brother in this matter, for he has talked about it, and is certainly all against it. God give you good-night".

Perhaps Bothwell failed to reply, and the matter ended here, but we do not know, for no other letters from the "other woman" have been preserved. It is obvious that she was very near to the end of her tether when this was written, and it is also clear that the Earl had become a laggard suitor.

CHAPTER VIII

Casket Letter VIII

This, the second of the three letters alleged to have been written by Mary to Bothwell during her visit to Stirling of 22nd and 23rd April, 1567, and produced as evidence of her complicity in her own abduction, is only available to us in the Contemporary Scotch translation. It runs (460):

"My Lord, sen my letter writtin, zour brother in law yat was, come to me verray sad, and hes askit me my counsel, quhat he suld do efter to morne, becaus thair be mony folkis heir, and amang utheris the Erle of Sudderland, quha wald rather die, considdering the gude they have sa laitlie ressavit of me, then suffer me to be caryit away, thay conducting me; and that he feirit thair suld sum troubil happin of it: of the uther syde, that it suld be said that he wer unthankful to have betrayit me. I tald him, that he suld have resolvit with zow upon all that, and that he suld avoyde, gif he culd, thay that were maist mistrustit. He has resolvit to wryte to zow be my opinioun; for he hes abaschit me to se him sa unresolvit at the neid. I assure myself he will play the part of an honest man: But I have thocht gude to advertise zow of the feir he hes yat he suld be chargeit and accusit of tressoun, to ye end yat, without mistraisting him, ze may be the mair circumspect, and that ze may have ye mair power. For we had zisterday mair than 300 hors of his and of Levingstoun's. For the honour of God, be accompanyit rather with mair than les; for that is the principal of my cair. I go to write my dispatche, and pray God to send us ane happy enterview schortly. I wryte in haist, to the end ze may be advysit in tyme".

At the time of Mary's abduction, Bothwell was still legally married to Lady Jane Gordon. It has been accepted that Mary, anticipating the speedy division of the matrimonial bond, referred to Huntly as "your brother-in-law that was", but such an explanation lacks all probability. The letter does bear every stamp of Mary's authorship, and it will be noted that it differs in style completely from those which we have attributed to the "other woman". That Mary wrote this letter seems certain, but it is also inescapable that she wrote it after the divorce of Bothwell from his wife. This explanation has usually been rejected on the ground that Mary and Bothwell were continuously together from the date of the abduction (24th April, 1567) until the affair of Carberry (15th June, 1567), but this is untrue, for they were separated twice during this period, on each occasion for about two days. We must now briefly review the events of early June in order that the circumstances in which this letter was written may be understood.

As we have seen, Bothwell brought Mary back to Edinburgh from Dunbar on 6th May, 1567, they were married on 15th May, and we know, from the records of the Privy Council, that both Bothwell and Huntly remained in Edinburgh. Meanwhile, the Protestant Lords gathered their forces, Morton at Stirling or near-by, and Lord Home on the borders. Bothwell was not unaware of events, for, on 25th May, Drury reported (545) that all on whom the Earl (now Duke of Orkney) could rely had been sent warning to be ready for action, and that the Lords had contracted to punish the captors of the Queen and to set her at liberty.

On 28th May, the privy Council issued a call to arms (377), the pretext being a raid against the lawless inhabitants of Liddesdale, and the lieges were summoned to convene in warlike guise and with provisions for fifteen days at Melrose on 15th June. There can be little doubt that this proclamation was inspired by the activities of the Lords, rather than by affairs on the borders. On 1st June, Mary issued a further proclamation (378), denying that she intended any innovation in the laws, and repudiating the rumours that she was careless of her son's welfare.

Events moved rapidly: Edinburgh was the centre of the Protestant faith and, by 7th June, Mary and Bothwell vacated the city which was becoming dangerous to them, both from the threat from the Lords and from the alienated sympathies of the people. Since Bothwell never returned to Edinburgh, it must, if the Lord's story be true, have been prior to this date that the silver casket was deposited in Edinburgh Castle. This fortress would have been the natural refuge of Bothwell and Mary, for it was impregnable without a train of seige artillery such as did not exist in Scotland, and its guns commanded the city. There is some evidence that Bothwell did seek admittance (544), but was turned away by the Captain, Sir James Balfour, who had been insinuated into the command of this important stronghold on 8th May (543).

On the same day that Bothwell left Edinburgh, Maitland also departed (433) and joined the confederated Lords, one of whom, Athol, was Maitland's brother-in-law.

Bothwell took Mary to Borthwick Castle, twelve miles south of Edinburgh (201), and then proceeded to Melrose, whence he was said to have made a raid on Lord Home (379), but this is unlikely, since Home makes his appearance with his men a few days later, and we may imagine that Bothwell, finding that the Lord's preparations were more advanced than he had expected, and in apprehension of immediate attack, had gone to Melrose to pick up any of the lieges who should have already convened there in accordance with the proclamation of 28th May. Probably he returned to Borthwick on 9th or 10th June. Huntly had evidently remained in Edinburgh, for he was certainly there on 10th June. It was on 8th June that Mary wrote the Casket Letter which we are now considering and addressed it to Bothwell, then at Melrose, whose return with additional forces was urgently awaited. Probably, Bothwell found few recruits at Melrose, for it was a week before the proclaimed date. He returned to Borthwick and, there, on 10th June, knowing that the attack of the Lords was developing, he left Mary and moved to Dunbar. Hay Fleming casts an entirely unnecessary slur on Bothwell when he says (152), "Knowing that it (Borthwick Castle) could not stand a seige, he (Bothwell) slipped out and escaped". As a matter of fact, Borthwick was immeasurably strong, with walls thirteen feet thick (379), and Bothwell's confidence in the Lord's inability to take it was borne out in the sequel. It was obviously important for him at such a time to preserve his mobility and gather his forces.

On 10th June, the Lords advanced on Borthwick; their chiefs were Athol, Glencairn, Morton, Mar, Home, Lindsay, Semple, Ruthven, Sanquhar, Tullibardine, Grange, Ker of Cessford, Ker of Fawdonside and others (381). Finding Bothwell gone, they withdrew to Edinburgh, which they entered that night, in spite of some shew of defence organised by Huntly, the Archbishop of St. Andrews, and others, but which was defeated by the apathy of the townsfolk. Huntly and his colleagues obtained permission to enter the Castle, and were thus saved from capture by the Protestant faction.

The following evening (11th June), Mary departed from Borthwick and joined Bothwell, who took her to Dunbar. There, they gathered their forces, and, on 14th June, the Queen and Bothwell marched to Seton: on the following day the rival armies met at Carberry. No blow was struck, but, after protracted negotiations, Mary sealed her fate by surrendering to the Protestant Lords. Bothwell was permitted to withdraw to Dunbar, and the Queen was led into captivity. The details of the events at Borthwick and Edinburgh on 10th and 11th June are to be found in the letter of John Beaton, an eye-witness, of 17th June, 1567 (431), and the narrative of the Captain of Inchkeith (719).

We can now proceed to a consideration of the letter itself, which, like Casket Letter I, would seem to be an autograph postscript to an official letter, but which may have been a separate epistle.

"My Lord, since my letter written, ... "

This suggests that Mary wrote a letter to which this additional material was added, but it may be that this is merely a second letter by a separate bearer.

" . . . . . your brother-in-law that was . . . . . "

This description of Huntly, is to be compared with the invariable epithet 'false' of the "other woman". There is here no evidence that Huntly is distrusted: indeed, in what comes later, mistrust is expressly denied. As has already been stressed, the phrase "your brother-in-law that was", proves conclusively that this letter was written after 7th May, 1567.

" . . . . . came to me very sadly . . . . . "

Huntly was in Edinburgh when Mary and Bothwell left on 7th June. This letter cannot have been written on 11th June, when the Queen and her husband were separated once again, for Huntly was then in the Castle of Edinburgh. However, Borthwick is but twelve miles from thence. It would seem that, the day after the departure of Mary and Bothwell from Edinburgh, Huntly had obtained sufficient details of the meditated attack by the Lords to realise the great strength of the forces opposed to him and his party. Not unnaturally, he rode to Borthwick to discuss matters with the Queen.

" . . . . . and has asked my advice what he should do the day after tomorrow . . . . . "

This helps to date the letter. The Lords' attack was delivered on 10th June; and the expected date must have been known to Huntly who asked Mary what he should do "the day after tomorrow". It would seem likely that Mary and Bothwell had similar information, hence Bothwell's hurried visit to Melrose for recruits, and hence, also, the fact that Mary did not need to qualify her remark about "the day after to-morrow", for she knew that Bothwell would understand the allusion. This letter, therefore, was written on 8th June.

" . . . . . because there are many folks here (i.e. in the vicinity, including Edinburgh), and, among others, the Earl of Sutherland, who would rather die, considering the good they have so lately received from me, than suffer me to be carried away".

Sutherland and Huntly had both been restored to their lands and titles during the Chase-about Raid, but parliamentary ratification had only been obtained six weeks before, at the Parliament which ended its session on 19th April. These two Earls had good reason to be grateful to Mary, and she, also, to them. In the event of an over-powering descent upon Edinburgh by the Protestant Lords, they might find it difficult to avoid being drawn into the confederacy, for the sake of lands or life, and it was undoubtedly the intention of the Protestant Lords to carry Mary away from Bothwell and probably they had already decided on her imprisonment as soon as she should fall into their hands.

" . . . . . they conducting me; and that he (Huntly) feared that some trouble would come of it".

That is to say, Huntly protested that he and Sutherland would rather die than help to make Mary captive, but, with the slender forces at present at their disposal in Edinburgh, resistence would certainly lead to trouble for them.

"On the other hand, (he feared) that it would be said that he (Huntly) was ungrateful to have betrayed me".

As, indeed, it would have been; but there were only two courses open; to risk 'trouble' against overwhelming odds, or to join in the raid to capture Mary and, if possible, Bothwell, and so help to carry Mary away, thus shewing themselves to be thankless for her favours and to have betrayed her.

"I told him that he should have settled everything (resolved upon all that, his course of action) with you, and that he should avoid, if he could, (the company of) those who were most mistrusted (Morton, Home and the other Protestant rebels). He has decided to write to you by (or contrary to?) my advice, for it (not he) has disturbed me to find him so irresolute (in time) of need. I assure myself that he will play the part of an honest man".

Could this last sentence have been penned by the same person who so frequently had reviled the false Huntly?

"But I have thought good to warn you of the fear he has that he may be charged and accused of treason",

If the Protestant Lords gained Edinburgh, they would assuredly take the government into their hands and such of Mary's supporters as should fall into their power would be very likely to be charged with treason, either for complicity in the murder of Darnley, or for giving aid to Bothwell.

"so that, without mistrusting him, you may be more cautious and may bring larger forces. For we had yesterday more than three hundred horse of his (Huntly's) and Livingstone's".

But this important element could now be no longer assured to Mary and Bothwell, and the loss of such a company would, perhaps, influence very considerably the manner in which Bothwell would conduct the campaign: it was imperative that this news should be got to him as soon as possible.

"For the honour of God, be accompanied rather with more (men than you had intended) than with less, that is my chief worry. I go to write my dispatch".

"I go" or "I am going" (to write my dispatch) may simply mean to seal this letter and address it, adding the usual admonition to the bearer "to hasten (dispatch) for the life". Alternatively, it may be that she has other state documents to prepare, but, in that case, one wonders why Mary should mention them.

"God send us a happy meeting shortly".

This sentence, revealing that Mary was wholeheartedly on the side of Bothwell, is of great importance in understanding the nature of their relationship during their brief married life. Mary is, of course, in some fear of the Protestant Lords, and Bothwell is obviously the person whom she desires to gain the victory in the forthcoming struggle, but it is also to be noted that there is a complete lack of emotional outburst, such as we have seen in the "other woman's" letters, and which might have been justifiable at such a dangerous moment. It would be too much to claim that this sentence suggests a platonic relationship between the Queen and the Earl, but it at least goes some way to shew that their association was not one of lust alone.

"I write in haste, so that you may be advised in time".

If this letter were written on 8th June, and all the internal evidence supports this view, it is readily understandable why the concluding date, place and signature were deleted.

The attribution of this letter to Mary at Stirling on 22nd April cannot be maintained in face of the reference to Huntly as "your brother-in-law that was", nor would the fears of Huntly and Sutherland be explicable on this basis. Although we know that Huntly accompanied Mary to and from Stirling, and was abducted to Dunbar in the Queen's company, we have no evidence that either Sutherland or Livingstone were, and we do know that their presence at Dunbar is never mentioned, as it surely would have been had they been there. Furthermore, there would have been no risk of their being accused of treason if they had taken part in a "pretended ravishment", undertaken with the consent of the Queen.

A most important conclusion results from the dating of this letter to 8th June: it is that this letter cannot have been one of the documents within the silver casket alleged to have been opened by the Lords on 21st June, 1567, for it was written after Bothwell had left Edinburgh for the last time. This is but another example of the manipulations of the evidence by the prosecution, which, taken together, are evidence of the bad faith of Mary's rebellious opposition.

CHAPTER IX

Casket Letter VII

This, the third letter alleged to have been written by Mary at Stirling to Bothwell before the abduction, is, like the last letter, only available to us in the Scotch translation. It may be pertinent to state that, as soon as Mary left Edinburgh on 21st April, Bothwell began gathering forces which he used three days later to kidnap the Queen and her company. What need there could be for such letters as these three to urge him to the business must be doubtful. So far from lagging in the affair, the Earl was using every possible dispatch, and, it must be clear to all, that, had such an escapade been with the consent of the Queen, the details would all have been settled before she set out to visit her son.

On the other hand, if it were Bothwell who was pressing to marry Mary, and if she had either refused his offers or had been slow to accept them, the Earl, having obtained the consent of the Lords at Ainsley's Supper (19th April, 1567) might well have gone to the length of the abduction without the Queen's fore-knowledge. Indeed, if he knew that forces were rising which would sweep both him and her away unless he seized the government forthwith, this might be the only way to save the situation. In either case, since he and the Queen had been together daily for weeks, there was no need or reason for letters between them on this matter. As we have seen, Casket Letters VI and VIII have nothing to do with this affair, and we must now proceed to an examination of Letter VII, which is, in many ways, the most baffling of all this correspondence. The letter runs (459):

"Of the place and ye tyme I remit my self to zour brother and to zow. I will follow him, and will faill in nathing of my part. He findis mony difficulties. I think he dois advertise zow thairof, and quhat he desyris for the handling of himself. As for the handling of myself, I hard it ains weill devysit. Me thinks that zour services, and the lang amitie, having ze gude will of ye Lordis, do weill deserve ane pardoun, gif abone the dewtie of ane subject yow advance yourself, not to constrane me, bot to assure yourself of sic place neir unto me, that uther admonitiounis or forane perswasiounis may not let me from consenting to that that ye hope your service sall mak yow ane day to attene. And to be schort, to mak yourself sure of the Lordis, and fre to mary; and that ye are constraint for your suretie, and to be abill to serve me faithfully, to use ane humbil requeist joynit to ane importune actioun. And to be schort, excuse yourself, and perswade thame the maist ye can, yat ye ar constranit to mak persute aganis zour enemies. Ze sall say aneuch, gif the mater or ground do lyke yow; and mony fair wordis to Lethingtoun. Gif ye lyke not the deid, send me word, and leif not the blame of all unto me."

Superficially, this letter does seem to fit the circumstances of the intended 'ravishment' extremely well, but a moment's reflection will shew that the timing is awkward. It seems unlikely that it could have been written before 22nd April, and an immediate reply could not have been received before 23rd: the request for a reply, therefore, is possible, but depends on the writing of this letter very soon after the arrival at Stirling. If, of course, Mary spent the night at Linlithgow, she may have written this that same evening, but this neglects the fact that she either saw, or had opportunity to see, Bothwell on that very morning. Since Huntly was also in Edinburgh before Mary's departure, and accompanied her to Stirling, the reference to his telling Bothwell of the difficulties is hard to understand, since there must have been prior consultation at Edinburgh. In any case, how should there be many difficulties for Huntly? All he had to do was to allow himself to be kidnapped by superior force; a fairly easy part to play. Nor does the admonition to Bothwell to "make sure of the Lords" seem suitable when he had, ostensibly at least, done so at Ainsley's Supper two or three days previously. But the most impossible statement comes at the end, when Mary admonishes Bothwell to give many fair words to Maitland (Lethington). No one has ever suggested that he was a party to the abduction, yet this is certainly the implication here; but, if the phrase which contains his name have any other meaning, it is still impossible for it to be fitted into this context, for Maitland was at Stirling with Mary, and Bothwell at Edinburgh could not have given him any words at all, fair or foul.

The letter, however, is undeniably in Mary's style, but it has suffered from the incompetence or ill-faith of the translator. Since no manuscript version is extant, we cannot be sure that this published translation mirrors the original at all closely, but, in trying to find a solution to the mystery of its date, we must assume it to be more or less correct.

The letter is unaddressed and the only reason for identifying the recipient as Bothwell is that it speaks of 'your brother'; but Bothwell was not the only man known to Mary who had a brother, or who aspired to her hand. The date has always been assumed to be anterior to the opening of the Casket (21st June, 1567), but since it is abundantly clear that Casket Letter VIII was not one of the original documents therein, we do not need to bind ourselves by that particular date: this letter could have been written at any time up to the departure of Mary from Scotland on 16th May, 1568.

When Mary entered Lochleven Castle on 17th June, 1567, she found herself the captive of the Laird, Sir William Douglas, and his mother, relict of Sir Robert Douglas who had been killed at Pinkie in 1547. The dowager, formerly Margaret Erskine, had been James V's mistress, and was the mother of the Earl of Moray.

Certainly up to August, 1567, Mary refused to consent to a divorce from Bothwell; by the time she arrived in England (16th May, 1568), however, she was quite reconciled to this idea, and it was not long before she was negotiating a marriage with the Duke of Norfolk. We do not know when or why she altered her mind concerning her third husband. It seems not impossible that, coming to believe what was so frequently said, that Bothwell had devised the murder of Darnley, and noticing that, as week succeeded week, he still did nothing to liberate her, she, ignorant of the fate which had overmastered the Earl in Norway, gradually considered herself to be a woman wronged by an ambitious desperado. Probably her change of heart was gradual, certainly it was natural, and it appears to have been complete some time before she escaped from Lochleven.

Mary's first attempt at escape seems to have been a chance venture, when, in mid-July, 1567, she is said to have found an unattended boat (337), for the castle is set on an island in the middle of the loch. Thereafter, she set her mind to the project more seriously, and began by exercising her charm on her captors. On 5th August, 1567, Throckmorton in Edinburgh, wrote to Cecil (110): "She has won the favour and good-will of the house, men as well as women, and thereby she means to have great intelligence (news), and was in towardness to have escaped . . . . . They (the Lords) would have her relinquish Bothwell, whereof I do not now so much despair as heretofore"; by which we see that Bothwell's place in her affections was already beginning to fade.

On 28th October, 1567, Drury at Berwick, in a letter to Cecil, writes (111), "The suspicion of over-great familiarity between the Queen here and Mr. Douglas, brother of the Laird of Lochleven, increases more and more, and worse spoken of them than I may write". This 'Mr. Douglas' was George Douglas, youngest brother of the Laird and, like him, half-brother of the Earl of Moray, now Regent.

The question of Mary's marriage now came to the fore once again. On 19th March, 1568, Moray visited his sister at Lochleven (338). He apparently first suggested that she should marry Morton, whose wife was insane, and so could be disposed of; Mary repulsed the suggestion. The next suitor suggested was a kinsman of Moray's, Lord Methven; Mary again demurred, and then said that she wished to marry George Douglas. The Regent refused to agree to this, and, a few days later, Mary made her second attempt at escape. Drury, writing from Berwick to Cecil on 3rd April. 1568, (384), says,

"It may please your honour, since the dispatch of Nicholas Errington, I have understood of some more certainty of such matter as passed between the Queen and the Earl of Moray at his being with her now lastly at Lochleven, where at the first she burdened him of the rigour that was used unto her at this last Parliament. And he answered, that he and the rest of the nobility could do no less for their own surety, in respect they had enterprized to put her into captivity. From that she entered into another purpose, being marriage, praying she might have a husband, and named one to her liking, George Douglas, brother to the Laird of Lochleven. Unto which the Earl replied, That he was over mean a marriage for her Grace, and said further, that he, with the rest of the nobility, would take advice thereupon. This in substance was all that passed between the Queen and the Earl of Moray at that time; but after, upon 25th of the last (March, 1568) she enterprized an escape, and was the rather nearer effect, through her accustomed long lying in bed all the morning. The manner of it was thus: there cometh in to her the laundress early as other times before she was wonted, and the Queen (according to such a secret practice) putteth on her the weed of the laundress, and so with the fardel of clothes and her muffler upon her face, passeth out, and entereth the boat to pass the Loch; which after some space, one of them that rowed said merrily, let us see what manner of dame this is; and therewith offered to pull down her muffler, which to defend she put up her hands, which they spied to be very fair and white, wherewith they entered into suspicion who she was, beginning to wonder at her enterprise. Whereat she was little dismayed, but charged them, upon danger of their lives, to row her over to the shore; which they nothing regarded, but eftsoons rowed her back again, promising her that it should be secreted, and especially from the Lord of the house under whose guard she lyeth. It seemeth she knew her refuge, and where to have found it, if she had once landed; for there did, and yet do linger at a little villiage called Kinross, hard at the Loch-side, the same George Douglas, one Semple, and one Beaton, the which two were sometime her trusty servants, and, as yet appeareth, they mind her no less affection".

Semple was presumably John Semple of Belltrees, husband of Mary Livingstone, one of the Queen's four Maries; and Beaton was Sir John Beaton, brother of the Archbishop of Glasgow, Mary's ambassador at Paris.

Apparently after this escapade, George Douglas was forbidden the house (385), but he continued to keep in touch with Mary, who, with his assistance, finally escaped on 2nd May, 1568.

According to Tytler (741), the escape was engineered by one of the inmates of the Castle, the page, Willie Douglas, who abstracted the keys of the gate from under the Laird's nose when he sat at supper, by placing a napkin over the keys as they lay on the table beside him, and then removing the napkin and keys together. Mary was met when she reached the shore by George Douglas, Lord Seton, Sir John Beaton and others (386), and thus she began her fortnight's freedom which ended after the battle of Langside with her flight to England and her long captivity there.

It must at once occur to the mind of anyone who considers these events that Sir William Douglas, the Laird of Lochleven, was not so innocent of Mary's escape as he pretended: it might well be that both he and his mother would not object too strongly if his brother George should become Mary's fourth husband: he might prove more pliant than Moray as a kinsman in high position. Sir James Melville, for one, suspected that the dowager was not ignorant of the affair: "The old lady, his mother, was also thought to be upon the counsel" (647), and Henderson (312) was convinced that the Laird was implicated. The fact that he forwarded Mary's baggage to her three days after she escaped (191) is highly suggestive, and we know that he was not too strongly opposed to Mary, for, writing to Morton, then Regent, on 4th March, 1577, Sir William says (633).

" . . . . . and that there ran no vice in her, but that the same is as largely in you, except that your Grace condescended not to the destruction of your wife".

The most satisfactory assumption, then, is that this document, Casket Letter VII, was written by Mary to George Douglas, some time in April, 1568, shortly after he had been refused access to the Castle, an exclusion which may have been imposed by the order of the Regent, or may simply have been a subterfuge to suggest that the Laird, Sir William Douglas, was true to the Lords.

"Of the place and the time, I refer myself to your brother (the Laird) and to you (George Douglas)".

The 'place' is the rendezvous on the lake-side.

"I will follow him (i.e., the Laird's instructions), and will fail in nothing on my part. He (the Laird) finds many difficulties. I think he has told you about them, and what he desires for the handling (management) of himself".

The word 'follow' does not necessarily mean to follow in a physical sense. One can understand the Laird's difficulties. For his own protection, the escape must be managed in such a way as to make it appear that he was not implicated. Some such scheme as that which was eventually used, the purloining of the keys, was evidently insisted on by Sir William, whose intention was to play safe. If Mary's bid to recover her throne succeeded, he could count on favour, and, should it fail, he hoped to avoid suspicion of having betrayed his trust.

"As for the handling of myself, I understand ('entendre') it to be well devised".

The mistake of 'hear' for 'understand' is a natural one.

"Methinks that your services . . . . . "

George Douglas had already tried to arrange Mary's escape.

" . . . . . and the long friendship . . . . . "

Mary had now been in Lochleven for about ten months, which must have seemed a long time. George Douglas had evidently shewn his friend-liness towards her soon after her arrival.

"having the good-will of the Lords . . . . . "

This may mean, "if you have, etc.", but the accepted text is likely enough. The Douglas family were indeed in favour with their kinsmen Moray, Morton, and Mar; Morton had broken the entail of his Earldom, in favour of Sir William, who did in fact succeed to it.

"do well deserve a pardon, if you advance yourself above the duty of a servant . . . . . "

Perhaps, "if you have advanced yourself, etc.", but the need for the pardon, as one of Mary's keepers, is obvious enough.

"not to restrain me . . . . . "

In other words, "no longer to keep me captive, but, rather, to liberate me".

"but to assure yourself of such a place near to me that warnings and persuasions to the contrary may not (be able to) prevent me from consenting to that which you hope that your service (in liberating me) will one day obtain for you".

If George Douglas shews himself as a strong man, promises Mary, and insists on a place of importance at Court, he may succeed, with her help, in marrying her. Mary was older than George, by about five years; she had little to bribe him with, and she may have felt that such a reward as to allow him to marry her would have been a small price to pay for her liberty. Alternatively, she may have realised that he needed encourage-ment in his dangerous escapade, and thus held a bait before his eyes which the youth could scarcely refuse, but which was later to be snatched away. It may be noted that she did not definitely promise to marry him, but George must have assumed that she had done so. There is something a little Machiavellian in this, yet what else could she do? And, if he did prove himself a proper man, why, then, she might do worse than keep her half-promise.

"Summa, to make yourself sure of the Lords . . . . . "

George has already been said to have the good-will of the Lords, which previous phrase may, perhaps, be rendered "if you have, etc.", as we have seen. On the other hand, the Lords here mentioned may not be the same as the (Protestant) Lords referred to before. In such a letter, all names would be avoided for reasons of secrecy, should the letter fall into the wrong hands, and this reference may well be to the Hamilton Lords, who did, in fact, receive Mary and take part with her on her escape from Lochleven.

"and free to marry".

Since George Douglas was a minor, being under 21 years of age, consent to his marriage would be required, probably from the head of the family, presumably Sir William. We know, too, that George later married and his bride was a local lady: if he were already "handfasted", some legal process would be required before he would be free to take another bride, for 'handfasting' had almost the same significance as matrimony in Scotland at that period.

It is also possible that this phrase is completely mistranslated. If the verb were 's'allier', it might mean, either to marry, or to form an alliance with the (Hamilton) Lords, and this latter interpretation gains strength from the context, which both immediately before and afterwards, seems to deal with the negotiations with the Lords.

The next sentence is so badly translated as to be almost unintelligible; it runs,

"and that you are compelled for your safety, and to be able to serve me faithfully, to use a humble request, joined to an importunate action".

This seems to mean that George Douglas is to tell the Lords that he is compelled, by reasons of his own safety and by the wish to serve Mary faithfully, to make a humble request that they should join him in an importunate action. The 'importunate action' would, of course, be the release of the Queen, and Douglas's participation in a previous attempt to set her free might well be a matter which imperilled his safety.

"Summa, excuse yourself and persuade them the most you can that you are compelled (for your safety) to make pursuit against your (our?) enemies".

What there was to excuse himself for is not apparent. George Douglas was unlikely to have enemies at his age, so it is not impossible that, as in Casket letter IV, 'n' (of 'nos' in 'nos ennemis') has been read as 'v'. In passing, we may note that Bothwell, had he been the addressee, would have soothed no one's feelings by saying that he was gathering forces to make pursuit against his enemies.

"If the matter and ground (of this enterprise) are agreeable to you, you must say much, and (must give) many fair words to Maitland (Lethington)".

It is just possible that 'you shall say enough' is a fumbling translation of 'assez parlé', 'enough said', meaning, 'if you like the enterprize, I have said enough', but this is pure conjecture. There is at least some evidence that Mary had hopes that Maitland would assist in liberating her from

Lochleven: it seems that he had sent her a ring engraved with some words of the fable of the lion and the mouse to indicate his willingness to be of service to her, and this finds appropriate reference in the letter (635).

"If you do not like the deed, send me word, and do not leave the responsibility for everything to me".

The French, 'responsabilité' means either 'responsibility' or 'blame'.

If the above attribution of the letter be accepted, if follows that, like Casket Letter VIII, it, too, cannot have been one of the documents in the casket, for it was not written until ten months after that box had been opened.

CHAPTER X

The Love - Ballad

As with the previous two letters, the love-poem is only available to us in the Published French and Scotch Versions. It is a curious production, of little merit when considered as poetry and, for what this is worth, of considerably less poetic feeling than the poem written by Mary on the death of her first husband, Francis II.

Some phrases will be recognized immediately as duplicating passages from letters which were undoubtedly written by the "other woman"; notably "mon bien" (line 46), "Je vis en ceste foy" (line 55), "o mon seul bien" (line 86), "seul soubtein de ma vie" (line 125); and the whole emotional content of the poem is exactly similar to those affected epistles.

The poem is divided into twelve stanzas of unequal length. It runs (461)

I   "O dieux ayes de moi compassion
      E m'enseignes quelle preuue certane
      Je puis donner qui ne luy semble vain
      De mon amour et ferme affection
—   Las n'est il pas ia en possession
      Du corps, du cueur qui ne refuse peine
      Ny dishonneur, en la vie incertane,
      Offence de parents, ne pire affliction?
      Pour luy tous mes amys i'estime moins que rien,
10 Et de mes ennemis ie veulx esperere bien.
      I'ay hazardé pour luy & nom & conscience:
      Ie veulx pour luy au monde renoncer:
      Ie veux mourire pour luy auancer.
      Que reste il plus pour prouuer ma constance?

II — Entre ses mains & en son plein pouuoir
      Je metz mon filz, mon honneur, & ma vie,
      Mon pais, mes subjects mon ame assubiectie
      Et toute à luy, & n'ay autre vouloir
      Pour mon obiect que sens le disseuoir

206

20 Suiure ie veulx malgré toute l'enuie
Qu'issir en peult, car ie nay autre enuie
Que de ma foy, luy faire apparceuoir
Que pour tempest ou bonnace qui face
Iamois ne veux changer demeure ou place.
— Brief ie ferray de ma foy telle preuue,
Qu'il cognoistra sens feinte ma constance,
Non par mes pleurs ou feinte obeissance,
Come autres ont fait, mais par diuers espreuue.

III   Elle pour son honneur vous doibt obeissance
30 Moy vous obeissant i'en puys resseuoir blasme
N'estât, à mon regret, come elle vostre femme.
Et si n'aura pourtant en ce point préeminence
Pour son proffit elle vse de constance,
Car ce n'est peu d'honneur d'estre de voz biens dame
— Et moy pour vous aymer i'en puix resseuoir blasme
Et ne luy veux ceder en toute l'obseruance
Elle de vostre mal n'a l'apprehension
Moy ie n'ay nul repos tant ie crains l'apparence
Par l'aduis des parents, elle eut vostre acointance
40 Moy maugre tous les miens vous port affection
Et de sa loyauté prenes ferme asseurance.

IV   Par vous mon coeur & par vostre alliance
Elle a remis sa maison en honneur
Elle a jouy par vous de la grandeur
— Dont tous les siens n'auoyent nul asseurance
De vous mon bien elle à eu la constance,
Et a guagné pour vn temps vostre cueur,
Par vous elle a eu plaisir et bon heur,
Et pour vous a receu honneur & reuerence,
50 Et n'a perdu sinon la jouissance
D'vn fascheux sot qu'elle aymoit cherement.
Ie ne la plains d'aymer donc ardamment,
Celuy qui n'a en sens, ni en vaillance,
En beauté, en bonté, ni en constance
— Point de seconde. Ie vis en ceste foy.

V   Quant vous l'aymes, elle vsoit de froideur.
Sy vous souffriez, pour s'amour passion
Qui vient d'aymer de trop d'affection,
Son doil monstroit, la tristesse de coeur
60 N'ayant plesir de vostre grand ardeur
En ses habitz, mon estroit sens fiction

Qu'elle n'auoyt peur qu'imperfection
Peult l'affasser hors de ce loyal coeur.
De vostre mort ie ne vis la peur
— Que meritoit tel mary & seigneur.
Somme de vous elle a eu tout son bien
Et n'a prise ne iamais estimé
Vn si grand heur sinon puis qu'il n'est sien
Et maintenant dist l'auoyr tant aymé.

VI 70 Et maintenant elle commence a voire
Qu'elle estoit bien de mauuais iugement
De n'estimer l'amour d'vn tel amant
Et vouldroit bien mon amy desseuoir,
Par les escripts tout fardes de scauoir
— Qui pour tant n'est en son esprit croissant
Ayns emprunté de quelque auteur eluissant.
A feint tresbien vn enuoy sans l'avoyr
Et toutesfois ses parolles fardez,
Ses pleurs, ses plaints remplis de fictions.
80 Et ses hautes cris & lamentations
Ont tant guagné que par vous sont guardes.
Ses lettres escriptes ausquells vous donnez foy
Et si l'aymes & croyez plus que moy.

VII Vous la croyes las trop ie l'appercoy
— Et vous doutez de ma ferme constance,
O mon seul bien & mon seul esperance,
Et ne vous peux ie asseurer de ma foy
Vous m'estimes legier je le voy,
Et si n'auez en moy nul asseurance,
90 Et soubçonnes mon coeur sans apparence,
Vous deffiant à trop grande tort de moy.
Vous ignores l'amour que ie vous porte
Vous soubçonnez qu'autre amour me transporte,
Vous estimes mes parolles du vent,
— Vous depeignes de cire mon las coeur
Vous me penses femme sans iugement,
Et tout cela augmente mon ardeur.

VIII Mon amour croist & plus en plus croistra
Tant que je viuray, et tiendra ` grandeur,
100 Tant seulement d'auoir part en ce coeur
Vers qui en fin mon amour paroitra
Si tres à cler que iamais n'en doutra,
Pour luy ie veux recercher la grandeure,
Et faira tant qu'en vray connoistra,

— Que ie n'ay bien, heur, ni contentement,
Qu' a l'obeyr & servir loyamment.
Pour luy iattendz toute bon fortune.
Pour luy ie veux guarder santé & vie
Pour luy tout vertu de suiure i'ay enuie
110 Et sens changer me trouuera tout vne.

IX   Pour luy aussi ie jete mainte larme.
Premier quand il se fit de ce corps possesseur,
Du quel alors il n'auoyt pas le coeur.
Puis me donna vn autre dure alarme
— Quand il versa de son sang maint drasme
Dont de grief il me vint lesser doleur,
Qui me pensa oster la vie, & la frayeur
De perdre las la seule rempar qui m'arme.
Pour luy depuis iay mesprise l'honneur
120 Ce qui nous peut seul prouoir de bonheur.
Pour luy iay hasarde grandeur & conscience.
Pour luy tous mes parents i'ay quisté, & amys,
Et tous aultres respects sont a part mis.
Brief de vous seul ie cherche l'alliance.

X — De vous ie dis seul soubtein de ma vie
Tant seulement ie cherche m'asseurer,
Et si ose de moy tant presumer
De vous guagner maugré toute l'enuie.
Car c'est le seul desir de vostre chere amye,
130 De vous seruir & loyaument aymer,
Et tous malheurs moins que riens estimer,
Et vostre volunté de la mien suiure.
Vous conoistres avecques obeissance
De mon loyal deuoir n'omettant la science
— A quoy i'estudiray pour tousiours vous complaire
Sans aymer rien que vous, soubs la suiection
De qui ie veux sens nulle fiction
Viure & mourir & à ce j'obtempere.

XI   Mon coeur, mon sang, mon ame, & mon soussy,
140 Las, vous m'aues promes qu'aurois ce plaisir
De deuiser auecques vous à loysir,
Toute la nuit, ou ie languis icy
Ayant le coeur d'extreme peour transie,
Pour voir absent le but de mon desir
— Crainte d'oubly vn coup me vient a saisir:
Et l'autrefois ie crains que rendursi
Soit contre moy vostre amiable coeur

Par quelque dit d'un meschant rapporteur.
Un autrefoys ie crains quelque auenture
150 Qui par chemin deturne mon amant,
Par vn fascheux & nouueau accident
Dieu deturne toute malheureux augure.

XII   Ne vous voyant selon qu'aues promis
I'ay mis la main au papier pour escrire
—   D'vn different que ie voulou transcrire,
Ie ne scay pas quel sera vostre aduise
Mais ie scay bien qui mieux aymer sçaura
Vous diries bien qui plus y guagnera".

The meaning of this poem is much mutilated by incorrect transcription and misleading punctuation. The following rendering seems, however, to be correct.

(1) "O gods, have compassion on me
(2) And shew me what unquestionable proof
(4) Of my love and fixed affection
(3) I can give which does not seem unreal to him".

The attitude of the author is clearly similar to that which we have seen in Casket Letters III, IV, V and VI; indeed, these lines are a sort of pendant to Casket Letter V.

(5) "Alas, is he not already in possession
(6) Of the body (and) of the heart . . . .

This is to be compared with the words in Casket Letter III: " . . . and with the consent of the heart, in place of which, since I have already left it to you, I send you a sepulchre, etc." and " . . . in sign that you have made entire conquest of me, of my heart, etc.".

(6) "   . . . . . which does not refuse sorrow,
(7) Or the dishonour of (this) uncertain (way of) life,
(8) Offence to relations, or worse affliction?"

Line 7 is clearly a reference to her position as Bothwell's mistress. There is at least some evidence in Letter III that, at that time, she considered herself to be Bothwell's wife; after his marriage to Lady Jane, however, her position became more equivocal, and we can therefore date this poem as subsequent to the date of Bothwell's wedding (24th February, 1566). We may notice the reference to her relations which is mentioned later in the poem, when we shall return to this subject. The "worse affliction" may be compared with letter III, "the misfortunes and fears . . . of which you know", and with letter IV, "the ills of which you have been the cause".

(9) "For him, I value all my friends as less than nothing,
(10) And I (even) want to hope well for my enemies".

These rather absurd contrasts could hardly have been written by Mary at the time she was said to be plotting the death of her husband and the overthrow of his father.

(11) "I have risked for him both good name and conscience.

(12) I would for him renounce the world.

(13) I would die to advance him.

(14) What more remains to prove my constancy?"

Line 13 may be compared with letter IV, " . . . my life, which will only be dear to me, so long as it and I shall be agreeable to you" and letter III, " . . . for whom alone I wish to preserve (my life), and without which I only desire sudden death" Line 14 is reminiscent of letter V, "I beg you not to allow your opinion of others to harm your belief in my constancy".

(15) "Into his hands, and in his full power,

(16) I put my son, my honour and my life".

This sentence surely ends here, for, if we conclude that the full-stop should come after "subjects", we should have the awkward catalogue, "my son, my honour and my life, my country, my subjects", in which the "and" is completely misplaced. We can be quite certain that Mary never wrote these lines, for the statement that she put her son in Bothwell's full power was absolutely untrue; the Prince was kept by Mar, a relation of Moray, whose wife was a Lennox supporter, and Mar himself was one of the first to rise against Bothwell after Mary's marriage to him. On the other hand, Bothwell had at least one illegitimate son, William, who took his father's name of Hepburn, and who was sufficiently recognized by the family to become heir to Bothwell's mother. If this boy were the son of the author, his status in the family might be consonant with at least a partial recognition of his mother's matrimonial link with Bothwell, and in which she herself believed.

(17) "My country, my subjects, my submissive soul

(18) Is ('Et' for 'Est') all his".

We now see that the words "my country, my subjects", which did not fit in with the preceding sentence, do not find their place in this one either, for the verb is singular, and the plural, 'sont', would not have interfered with the scansion. It may also be doubted whether Mary would have described her kingdom as "mon pays", rather would she have called it "my realm", "mon royaume". Add to this that line 17 is the most uneven in the whole poem, and that the extra syllable is undoubtedly in the words, "mes subjects", and we begin to see that this line has been tampered with, the more so, because it is the only line, and this the only phrase, in the ballad which directly points to Mary as the author. In passing, we may compare "ame assujettie" with the words in letter III, "my thoughts are so willingly submissive (a subjectes = assujetties) to yours", and we may note that, in addition to the awkward scansion, the line shews the clumsy use of 'sujets' and 'assujettie' close together.

It is unfortunate indeed that the manuscript is missing: we may, however, be sure that this poem of 158 lines was not written without a number of erasures and corrections, and it is unlikely, labour apart, that a fair copy would be made, for paper was a comparatively scarce commodity in 16th century Scotland. One more erasure would therefore pass muster, especially if it were a small one. Suppose the original line 17 ran,

"Mon pais jecte (= jetté), mon ame assubiectie
E(s)t toute a luy".
"My country abandoned, my submissive soul
Is all his",

we should now have a line which was correct from the point of view of both grammar and scansion. It would also fit the context for there is good reason to suppose that the "other woman" was a foreigner. If that had been the correct reading, all that the manipulator needed to do was to insert 'sub' before 'jecte' (where accident may have left sufficient space) and to change the final 'e' to 's', at the same time inserting 'mes' above the line over a caret.

If the reader objects to the postulation of a manipulation of this sort, he is left with the certainty that not only this poem, but also letters III, IV, V and VI were all written by Mary, a position which is untenable, as has been abundantly made clear, by the difference in style and emotional tone between the real letters of Mary and these other writings.

(18) " . . . . and I have no other wish
(19) For my object than, without deceiving him,
(20) To follow (him; and this) I wish, despite every envy
(21) Which can come of it, for I have no other desire
(22) Than to make him aware of my faithfulness,
(23) Which, for storm or calm which may occur ('face' = 'fasse'),
(24) I never wish to change (or my) dwelling or position".

The final words of line 24, "demeure ou place" have been inserted as the object of "changer", the writer having forgotten that the object had already been expressed in "Que" in line 23. We may not be far wrong in thinking that "demeure ou place" refers back to "pays jetté": having abandoned her country, she is content not to change her present place of dwelling; she certainly can hardly have meant that she wished her present irregular position to have continued.

(25) "In short, I shall make such proof of my faithfulness
(26) That he will recognise my honest ('sans feinte') constancy;
(27) Not by my tears or pretended obedience,
(28) As others have done, but by various proofs".

Line 28 presumably refers to Lady Jane, and this idea is carried on in the next stanza.

(29) "She, for her honour, owes you obedience;
(30) I can be blamed for obeying you,

(31) Not being, to my regret, as she (is), your wife".

Again we see that the poem is subsequent to the Bothwell-Gordon marriage. The reader is asked to notice the emphasis on 'obeying', which as we have already seen is mentioned both explicitly and implicitly in letters III, IV and V.

(32) "What if, however, she shall not have precedence in that?"

"Et si" is probably best translated by the rhetorical question put here. It shews clearly that the writer was Bothwell's lover before his marriage, and no-one has ever suggested that this was the case with Mary.

(33) "For her profit, she makes use of constancy",

Although this mercenary attitude of Lady Bothwell is, in part, explained by the next line, that is not the whole explanation, for, as we presently see, Lady Jane was not at first inclined to be constant to the Earl. Perhaps the allusion is to the grant of the lands of Nether Hailes and others, made to her soon after Bothwell's act of adultery with the maid, Bessie Crawford, for which she afterwards divorced him.

(34) "For it is not a small honour to be mistress of your wealth".

Bothwell was, perhaps, the most impecunious of all the Scottish Lords: his estate was broken and was heavily mortgaged when he inherited it, and it must have suffered severely during the long period of his imprisonment, absence and outlawry (1562–1565). Nor did the Earl receive much in the way of grants from the Queen who was alleged to be his lover: only a woman of small means and inferior station could have referred to Bothwell's impoverished estate in such terms; Mary could never have done so.

(35) "And I, for loving you, can be blamed therefor;

(36) Yet I will not yield to her in every observance.

(37) She has no dread of (any) harm to you,

(38) But I have no rest, so much do I fear (even) the shadow (of it).

(39) By the advice of relations, she made your acquaintance;

(40) I, in spite of all mine, bear you affection;

(41) Yet, you are absolutely certain of her loyalty".

Once again, we see that the writer's relatives had counselled her to break off her intrigue with Bothwell. It is a little difficult to fit this into Mary's case: the only people who could strictly be called her 'parents' (blood relations) were in France and they apparently knew nothing of any intrigue with Bothwell.

We have no evidence that Mary's illegitimate half-brothers had any desire for her to break off relations with Bothwell, or had reproved her; on the contrary, Lord John Stewart was Bothwell's brother-in-law, and Moray had been reconciled with Bothwell after the Riccio affair, while her illegitimate half-sister, the Countess of Argyll, remained friendly to Mary to the end.

Line 41 returns to the doubts, mentioned in letters III, IV and V, which Bothwell had of the "other woman's" faithfulness. If the story of the

Prosecution be true, the Earl could have had no doubts of Mary's constancy of affection for him.

(42) "By you, My Heart, and by your marriage,
(43) She has restored her family to honour".

This was not true. Mary restored Huntly to his estates, which were far vaster than Bothwell's; but a foreign woman, who only saw as much as the Earls allowed her to see, and who knew of the political background to his marriage as much as he had told her, which was perhaps more than the truth, may be forgiven for getting the facts wrong. The only person who could not have made this mistake was the Queen.

(44) "She has enjoyed, through you, the importance
(45) Of which all of her (kindred) had no certainty".

Much the same comment applies to this as to lines 42 and 43.

(46) "From you, My Wealth, she has had constancy".

This particular epithet, 'Mon Bien', has also been seen in letter III ('Mon Seul Bien').

(47) "And she has won, for a time, your heart.
(48) By you, she has had pleasure and good fortune,
(49) And, because of you, she has received honour and reverence.
(50) Yet she did not even lose the enjoyment
(51) Of a boring dolt whom she used to love dearly".

The last two lines apparently refer to Alexander Ogilvy of Boyne, who, in 1599, became the Lady Jane's third husband. She was said to be in love with him before she married Bothwell, and three months after her marriage, he, apparently on the re-bound, married Mary Beaton, one of the Queen's Maries (May, 1566). At first sight, the tense of line 50 ('she has not even lost') suggests that the amour with Ogilvie still continues, but the use of the imperfect tense in line 51 shews that the tense in line 50 is dictated by scansion rather than syntax, and this poem is to be dated after that intrigue had ceased, that is to say, after the Ogilvy-Beaton marriage.

(52) "I do not complain of her loving thus ardently
(53) Him who has not, in judgment or in courage,
(54) In beauty, in kindness, or in constancy,
(55) Even an equal. I live in that faith".

In writing, 'point de seconde', the author was in error, she obviously meant 'second to none'. The phrase, 'I live in that faith', is familiar to us from the interpolated paragraph in the 'Moray', or later, part of Casket Letter II.

(56) "When you used to love her ('aymes' for 'aymies'), she was cold".

This line refers to the early days after Bothwell's marriage, when Lady Jane had not yet seen the value of 'profiting' by his love.

(57) "If you suffered from that patient love . . . . . "

'S'amour passion': presumably, since it was common to write 's' for 'c', this is in error for 'c'amour (= 'cet amour'; cf. 'ma mie', = 'm'amie' for 'mon amie') patient', for 'patient' and 'passion' are homonymous.

(57) "If you suffered from that patient love

(58) Which comes from loving with too much affection,

(59) Her mourning shewed the sadness of her heart",

The word 'deuil' is here used metaphorically, and the metaphor is taken up again in line 61.

(60) "Not gaining pleasure from your great ardour.

(61) In these (mourning) weeds, she shewed ('mon estroit' for 'monstroit) without pretence

(62) That she had no fear that (her) defect (of not loving you)

(63) Could efface it (your ardour) from that (your) loyal heart.

(64) Of your death, I did not see the fear

(65) Which such a husband and lord deserved".

At this date it was common to talk, at any rate in romantic prose and verse, of gallants dying of love. That is the meaning in this case: this is not a question of Bothwell having been wounded or otherwise in danger, which would have been quite out of context, but a continuation of the idea of Bothwell's suffering (line 57) from unrequited love, which his cruel wife did not appreciate might cause his death.

The words "I did not see" (line 64) suggest that the "other woman" was in residence at or near the place where the Earl and his Countess lived. This would fit in with the suggested date of letter VI, and makes one suspect that, after all, the lady was removed to the neighbourhood of Crichton soon after Bothwell went there with his bride in May, 1566.

(66) "Summa, ... "

This word, "somme" or "en somme", was, as we have seen a favourite of Mary, but it was in common use, and the "other woman" uses it, not only here but in letter VI also.

(66) "In short, from you, she has had all her wealth

(67) And (otherwise) she would not have won, nor ever valued,

(68) So great a fortune, since it is not hers (by right):

(69) And now she says that she has loved you well".

Line 68 harks back to the thoughts expressed in lines 42–45. "And *now* she says" (line 69) shews that this poem was written at a time when the Lady Jane was asserting her love for Bothwell, probably just after she had learned of his amour with Bessie Crawford, for which defection she extorted a considerable grant of land from her husband. This cannot be dated to the period of Mary's visit to Stirling (21st–24th April, 1567), for, as we have seen, Lady Bothwell had set the process of her divorce on foot as early as 20th March, 1567, and could not be claiming to love him then.

(70) "And, now, she begins to see

(71) That she has been of poor judgment

(72) In not valuing the love of such a lover,

(73) And she would indeed deceive my friend

(74) By letters all painted with learning,

(75) Which were, however, not the product of her own mind,

(76) Having ('ayns' for 'ayant') borrowed (them) from some
witty author:

(77) She has cleverly pretended an address without having it".

The writer here takes a disparaging view of Lady Bothwell's intellect:
she, with her knowledge of Greek mythology and her evident interest in
the Romantics, regards herself as a brilliant writer of letters and poems:
she certainly had some felicity of phrase, and was capable of expressing her
emotions on paper in a manner above mediocrity.

(78) "And, nevertheless, her painted words

(79) Her tears, her complaints full of inventions,

(80) And her loud cries and lamentations

(81 & 82) Have conquered so far that her written letters are kept by
you, and you credit them;

(83) And thus you love her and believe her more than me".

Here again there is some evidence that the writer was a witness of Lady
Jane's outbursts, and there is here further proof that this poem was
written before Bothwell's wife began the process of divorce in March, 1567.

(84) "You believe her, alas, too much, I perceive,

(85) And you doubt my steadfast constancy.

(86) O My Sole Wealth and My Hope,

(87) And can I not make you certain of my fidelity?"

We have already noticed that certain passages in the other letters by
this woman deal with her constancy of affection, and Bothwell's doubts
of her fidelity, for example, in letter IV, "you would not have so many
contrary suspicions". Letter III also uses the epithet, "My Sole Wealth".

(88) "I weigh little in your esteem, I see;

(89) And so you do not feel certain of me,

(90) And you suspect my heart without cause.

(91) Your mistrust does me too much wrong;

(92) You do not know the love which I bear you;

(93) You suspect that another love transports me;

(94) You value my words as wind;

(95) You depict my weary heart as (made) of wax;

(96) You think me a woman without judgment:

(97) And all this increases my ardour".

Line 95 bears a strong resemblance to a passage in the 'Moray' or
later part of Casket Letter II, "And, if I had not proof that his heart is
of wax, etc.?", but the resemblance is purely superficial. The phrase was a
common one, even as late as the Victorian Era, and it is to be noted that
this writer refers to her 'weary heart', while Mary, on that other occasion,
describes her heart as made of diamond; a completely different attitude to
her emotions. Line 97 bears a remarkable resemblance, in thought if not

in words, to a passage in letter IV, " . . . . . you would not have the contrary suspicions, which, nevertheless, I cherish as proceeding etc.". Both ideas are so extraordinary, and yet so similar, as to prove that these two writings are by the same person.

(98) "My love increases, and more and more will grow

(99) So long as I shall live, and it (my love) will hold to (its) greatness

(100) So much only as to obtain a share in that heart,

(101) To which, in the end, my love will appear

(102) So obvious that he will never doubt it.

(103) For whom I wish to search out the greatness (of my love),

(104) And it will do so much, that he in truth will know

(105) That I have no wealth, fortune nor contentment

(106) But in obeying and serving him loyally".

Line 106 may be compared with the "humble and obedient loyal wife" of letter III.

(107) "For him, I wait for every good fortune,

(108) For him, I wish to preserve health and life",

Line 108 brings to mind " . . . . . . of the sole support of my life, for whom alone I wish to preserve it". in letter III.

(109) "For him I desire to follow every good quality,

(110) Yet, without changing, he shall find me all one (i.e. the same)".

Line 109 finds its echo in letter III, " . . . . the most perfect person who ever was, and such as I desire to be, and shall take pains to imitate", and line 110 may be compared with " . . . . who ever vows to you completely her heart and body without any change", and "for death will not change (my heart)" in the same letter.

(111) "For him, also, I let fall many tears;

(112) First, when he made himself possessor of this body

(113) Of which, at that time, he did not have the heart".

The writer's "agreeable and willing loss" is mentioned in letter III, and while this reference is different, they are not incompatible with each other. More important, both the writer of letter III and of this poem were prepared to refer to an incident which not every woman would commit to paper.

(114) "Then (when) he gave me another harsh alarm,

(115) When he spilt a lot (literally, many teaspoonfuls!) of his blood,

(116) The grief of which left me miserable

(117) (And) which seemed to take away my life, and (gave me) the dread

(118) Of losing, alas, the only rampart which defends me".

It is usually assumed that these lines refer to the wounding of Bothwell

by Jock Elliot of the Park on 7th October, 1566, and this may, indeed, be
the correct explanation. In that case, since the event is obviously not in
the recent past, we must assume that the poem was written not earlier
than, say, December of that year. However, from the other indications
of date in the poem, it would seem to have been written about June, 1566.
We do not know of any other occasion on which Bothwell was wounded,
but on the other hand, we have very few details of his life. He had been
engaged in the Chase-about Raid, in which, it is true, there was no fighting,
although there may have been some skirmishing and sharpshooting, and
his duties on the border must have involved a good deal of raiding in which
he may well have received some flesh wound of which he and history said
nothing, but which made a deep impression on his emotional mistress.
This is pure hypothesis, but the poem was certainly written before Lady
Jane decided to divorce Bothwell, and the earlier date would agree with
the protestations by the Countess when she heard of his adultery with
Bessie Crawford. It is, even, not impossible that the whole story of the
maid was a disguise for the affair with the "other woman", and the grant
of the lands of Nether Hailes was a bribe to Lady Jane to keep the "other
woman's" name out of the business, in which case, one would have
expected the liaison to have ceased at that time.

(119) "For him, I have despised honour

(120) (That which alone can provide us with happiness);

(121) For him I have hazarded greatness and conscience",

This catalogue is to be compared with the words in the 'Bothwell' or
earlier part of Casket Letter II, the interpolated paragraph, "I spare
neither honour, conscience, hazard nor greatness".

(122) For him, I have abandoned all my relatives and friends

(123) And all other (trappings of) respectability have been put aside".

These two lines do not apply to Mary, and could not have been written
by her.

(124) "In short, with you alone I seek a wedding.

(125) Of you, I say, 'Sole Supporter of my Life' ";

This epithet will be found twice in letter III.

(126) "Of only so much as that, do I seek to make myself certain,

(127) And thus do I dare to put myself forward so far

(128) As to win you despite every envy.

(129) For it is the sole desire of your dear friend

(130) To serve and love you loyally",

This is to be compared with line 106 and the comment thereon.

(131) "And to value all misfortunes as less than nothing,

(132) And to follow your will by mine".

This last line reflects the same idea as that expressed in letter V, " . . . . .
for I will follow (your wish) all my life more willingly than you will declare
it to me".

(133) "You shall know with (what) obedience,

(134) Not omitting the knowledge of my loyal duty,

(135) How I shall study always to please you,

(136) Without loving anything but you, under the rule

(137) Of whom I wish, without any pretence,

(138) To live and die, and to this I swear".

Lines 136 and 137 echo the feeling of letter III in the passage, "to be worthily employed under your domination".

(139) "My Heart, My Blood, My Soul, and My Care,

(140) Alas; you promised me that I should have that pleasure

(141) Of talking with you at leisure".

This seems to be the end of the sentence. The words "all the night" would appear to go with the following sentence, which is the natural time for fears to be uppermost, and such an interpretation deletes what has always been regarded as a 'purple passage'.

(142) "All the night when I languish here,

(143) My heart being chilled with extreme dread

(144) Because I see (!) the aim of my desire absent,

(145) Fear of being forgotten seizes me with a shock".

From which we may conclude, perhaps, that the writer is no longer in residence, if she ever was, at Crichton. Perhaps "Toute la nuit" (line 142) is a copyist's error for "toutes les nuits", every night.

(146 & "At other times, I fear that your loving heart is hardened
147)   against me

(148) By some remark of a wretched tale-bearer".

Judging by letter VI, this refers to the Earl of Huntly, who had obviously spread tales of the writer's infidelity to Bothwell.

(149) "Yet another time, I fear some adventure

(150) Which deflects my lover on the road

(151) By another troublesome accident:

(152) God turn away every unhappy augury".

From line 151, we may guess that Bothwell had used some such excuse for failing to visit his mistress on at least one previous occasion.

(153) "Not seeing you according to your promise,

(154) I put my hand to paper in order to write

(155) Of a difference which I wished to set down";

'Different' can mean a 'disagreement', but probably has the more usual sense; that is to say, she wished to set down the differences between her unhappy self and the fortunate Lady Bothwell.

(156) "I do not know what will be your opinion,

(157) But I know well who (i.e., which of us two, Lady Jane and
                          the author) knows how best to love.

(158) You well may say who will win most from it".

CHAPTER XI

The Contracts of Marriage

The Lords produced two contracts or obligations of marriage between Mary and Bothwell, one in Scotch and one in French, which they claimed to have found in the Silver Casket. Neither of these was the actual marriage contract between Mary and Bothwell, drawn up and signed on 14th May, 1567, which is a long and prolix document in Scotch (329). The two contracts from the Casket were produced at Westminster on 7th December, 1568, and the minutes of that day's session refer to the Scotch Contract thus (327):

"They (Moray and his associates) also exhibited another writing in Scottish, which they avowed to be wholly written by the Earl of Huntly, dated 5th April, containing a form of a contract for marriage between the said Queen (Mary) and Earl Bothwell, subscribed 'Mary', which they avowed to be the proper hand of the said Queen, and, underneath it, 'James Earl Bothwell', which they also avowed to be the proper hand of the said Earl Bothwell. At which time he was commonly defamed, and not cleansed (as they termed it), which is, not acquitted (of the murder of Darnley) before 12th April following".

This contract was printed by Buchanan, and runs (328):

"At Seton, the 5th day of April, the year of God 1567; the right excellent, right high and mighty Princess, Mary, by the grace of God, Queen of Scots, considering the place and estate wherein Almighty God has constituted her Highness, and how, by the decease of the King her husband, her Majesty is now destitute of a husband, living solitary in the state of widowhood, in the which kind of life her Majesty most willingly would continue, if the weal of her realm and subjects would permit; but, on the other part, considering the inconveniences may follow, and the necessity which the realm has, that her Majesty be coupled with a husband, her Highness has inclined to marry. And seeing what incommodity may come to this realm, in case her Majesty should join in marriage with any foreign Prince of a strange nation, her Highness has thought rather better to yield unto one of her own subjects; amongst whom her Majesty finds none more able, nor indued with better qualities than the right noble and her dear cousin, James Earl Bothwell &c., of whose thankful and true service, her Highness, in all times bypast, has had large proof and infallible experience. And seeing not only the same good mind constantly persevering in him, but, with that, an inward affection and hearty love towards her Majesty, her Highness, amongst the rest, has made her choice of him; and therefore, in the presence of the eternal God, faithfully, and in the word of a Prince, by these presents, takes the said James Earl Bothwell as her lawful husband, and promises and obliges her Highness, that, how soon the process of divorce intended between the said Earl Bothwell and Dame Jane Gordon, now his pretended spouse, be ended by the order of the laws, her Majesty shall, God willing, thereafter shortly marry and take the said Earl to her husband, and complete the bond of matrimony with him in face of holy church, and shall never marry any other husband but he only, during his lifetime. And as her Majesty, of her gracious humanity and proper motive, without deserving of the said Earl, has thus inclined her favour and affection towards him, he humbly and reverently acknowledging the same, according to his bound duty, and being also free and able to make promise of marriage, in respect of the said process of divorce, intended for divers reasonable causes, and that his said pretended spouse has thereto consented, he presently takes her Majesty as his lawful spouse in the presence of God, and promises and obliges himself as he will answer to God, and upon his fidelity and honour that, in all diligence possible, he shall prosecute and set forward the said process of divorce already begun and intended between him and the said Dame Jane Gordon his pretended spouse, unto the final end of a decrete and declarator therein. And incontinent thereafter, at her Majesty's good will and pleasure, and when her Highness thinks convenient, shall complete and solemnize, in face of holy church, the said bond of matrimony with her Majesty, and love, honour and serve her Highness, according to the place and honour that it has pleased her Majesty to accept him unto, and never to have any other for his wife during her Majesty's lifetime; in faith and witnessing whereof, her Highness and the said Earl has subscribed this present faithful promise with their hands, as follows, day, year and place foresaid, before these witnesses: George Earl of Huntly and Master Thomas Hepburn, Parson of Auldhamstock, &c. Sic subscribitur

Marie R.

James Earl Bothwell."

It may be accepted that the body of this document is genuine, although less certainty attaches to the date and to the signatures. That it is genuine, follows from the unlikelihood of any forger bothering to produce such a document, which could have been written to include much more dangerous matter had it been the production of a pen controlled by the Lords of the Congregation. It is interesting to note that it is couched in fairly suitable law terms, but, when compared with the actual contract, signed 14th May, 1567, it will be found to be written in much less legal language than the latter. It may, perhaps, have served as a model for the actual contract, but, in that case, very considerable departures were made from it. There is only one phrase which is identical, 'living solitary in the state of widow-hood', in both contracts, and this was probably an accepted legal phrase. Whether it was actually signed or not, we cannot, or course, discover, since the original is lost, but the addition of the signatures would not have presented any insuperable difficulty. We may, however, proceed on the presumption that it was, in fact signed, and consider the question of the date.

First, it is certain that Mary was at Seton on 5th April, 1567, for a Privy Council was held there on that date (366), and Bothwell and Huntly, furthermore, would certainly have been of the sederunt. Since Lady Bothwell had actually begun proceedings for the divorce of her husband more than a fortnight earlier, there is nothing intrinsically impossible in such a contract being signed on that occasion, but the extrinsic factors are rather against this view. If Mary had already agreed to accept Bothwell, he, having on 19th April obtained the consent of the Lords, had no need to proceed to the extreme course of abducting her on 24th April, and, by all accounts, Mary required some persuasion on that occasion before she fell in with Bothwell's wishes. On the other hand, it is more than probable that the Earl had by 5th April made up his mind to marry the Queen, and he may well have had Huntly's support in this: together they may have drawn up such a contract to present to the Queen, and she may have refused to sign it. In such circumstances, Mary's signature might have been forged, either by Bothwell, to cover the treason of abducting the Queen, or by the Lords when the document fell into their hands.

Alternatively, since Mary arrived in Edinburgh after the abduction on 6th May, 1567, conducted thither from Dunbar by Bothwell, she may have spent the night of 5th May at Seton, and the contract could have been signed then. The clerk who made out the document might easily have erred as to the month, writing April for May, the more so since the month was yet young. Similar errors are by no means uncommon in state papers (page 287).

A third possibility remains. If the contract were signed at Dunbar as soon as Mary consented to Bothwell's forceful wooing, he may have presented her with a document which she had already rejected at Seton on

5th April and which yet bore that date. Alternatively, the contract could have been antedated to 5th April, in order to safeguard the Earl for the abduction, probably at his own insistence. On the whole, this last possibility seems slightly more likely than the others, but certainty is out of the question.

Even if the contract be accepted at its face-value, as signed on 5th April, there is nothing in it which need surprise us, still less is it evidence of Mary's complicity in the murder of her husband. We may at first be a little shocked that she should be prepared to marry a man who was still legally married, but such an event could be paralleled a score of times from the annals of royalty, who were then often a law unto themselves; and Mary was somewhat lax in matters of religion. We may also feel that she was precipitate in consenting to marry again so soon after the death of her husband, but two points must be taken into consideration: first, that all her love for Darnley must have died long before his death: and secondly, that she must have come to realise the precarious nature of her authority and her need for a stout staff on which to lean. During the previous two years, Mary had seen the Chase-about Raid, led by Moray; the murder of Riccio, led by Darnley and Morton; and finally, the murder of her husband by the Protestant Lords at a time when, as she was also aware, Darnley had been actively engaged in her own overthrow. She must have realised that the Lords would seize the first moment to complete the rebellion which had carried off her husband by destroying her or her authority. Marriage to a man capable of wielding power was therefore essential, and, in order to maintain the good relations which she believed to exist at last between herself and Elizabeth, the husband must be a Protestant and not a member of a foreign ruling house. To this must be added the fact that she had much in common with Bothwell, who, like herself had been brought up in France, and that he had shewn himself to be wholly loyal to the crown, despite the staunchness of his religious beliefs. When all these facts are taken into account, it is easy to understand, and not difficult to excuse, Mary's third marriage. It failed of its purpose, and the Queen was swept from her throne a short month later, but, had she not chosen as she did, the end could hardly have been longer delayed.

The French Contract was also produced at Westminster on 7th December, 1568 (327), and is described in the minutes of that session in these terms,

> "They (Moray and his associates) exhibited a writing written in a Roman hand in French, as they said, and would avow, by the Queen of Scots herself, being a promise of marriage to the Earl Bothwell; which writing, being without date, and although some words therein seem to the contrary, they did suppose so to have been made and written by her before the death of her husband; the tenor whereof thus followeth, 'Nous Marie par la Grace de Dieu, etc'."

This last suggestion by the Lords is quite without foundation, and, from the wording of the contract, we can be sure that it was in fact written after the death of Darnley, but on what occasion or for what reason we cannot say. The contract runs thus (90):

> "Nous Marie par la grace de Dieu Royne descosse Douaryer de France etc. prometons fidellemant et de bonne foy et sans contraynte a Jacques Hepburn conte de Boduel, de navoir jamays autre espoulx et mary que lui, et de le prandre pour tel toute et quante fois quil men requirira, quoy que parante amye ou aultres y soient contrerayres: et puis que Dieu a pris mon feu mary henry stuart dit darnelay, et que par se moien je suis libre, nestant soubs obeisance de pere ni de mere des mayntenant je proteste que, lui estant en mesme liberte, je seray prest et decomplir les ceremonies requises au mariage, que je lui promets devant Dieu que jenprante ce tesmoignasge et la presante. Signée de ma mayn ecrit ce
>
> Marie R. "

> "We, Mary, by the grace of God, Queen of Scotland, Dowager of France, etc., promise, faithfully and in good faith and without constraint, to James Hepburn, Earl of Bothwell, never to have any other spouse and husband than him, and to take him for such each and every time that he shall require it of me, although (any) relative, friend or others be contrary to it; and since God has taken my deceased husband, Henry Stewart, called Darnley, and since, for this reason, I am free, not owing obedience to either father or mother at this present time, I protest that, he being equally free, I shall be ready to accomplish the requisite ceremony of marriage, which I promise him before God, whom I take as witness, and this present. Signed by my hand; written this . . . . "

If this document were signed by Mary, as seems likely, much the same remarks apply to it as to the Scotch contract, and, since we know no more of its date than that it was subsequent to Darnley's death, it provides no serious proof against the Queen. However, if Mary did put her signature to it, it is certainly curious that the space for the date was left blank, and we may even suspect that it may have been erased as being so close to the date of the marriage as to make it valueless as evidence of Mary's intention to marry Bothwell so long before. The Lords certainly made a valiant effort to make bricks without straw, when they protested that, "although some words therein seem to the contrary, they did suppose" it to have been written by Mary before the death of her husband, and it speaks volumes as to the biassed attitude of the English Commissioners that this bare-faced supposition could have been included in the minutes, despite the reference in the contract to "God having taken the deceased Henry Stewart".

If the contract had been written by Mary, it would presumably have concluded with the words, "Ecrite et signee de ma main ce . . . . . ". The termination, "Signee de ma main. Ecrit ce . . . . " implies that the Lords were wrong in ascribing the penmanship to Mary, but, whether her hand held the pen or no, this document was never composed by her. It was certainly either written, and this seems the more likely, or dictated word for word by Bothwell, and, since he wrote a Roman (Italianate) hand, this might well be mistaken, in good or bad faith, for Mary's, especially among people who habitually used a Gothic script. That Bothwell composed the contract is to be concluded from the words, "quoique parent(s), ami(s) ou autres y soient contraires"; words which echo the love-ballad, which Bothwell had by now received. Mary herself could never have referred to her late husband as "Henry Stewart called Darnley"; to her, he was always "the King", and he was, besides, Duke of Albany. If she had wished to delete these signs of her royal favour, he would still have been called, "Henry Stewart, Lord Darnley".

The words "without constraint" seem to protest too much, and one is led to the conclusion that this document was signed by Mary at Dunbar soon after the abduction, when, Mary being completely in his power, Bothwell would certainly have insisted on adding such words as these. At no other time would the question of constraint have come to the mind of the author. This conclusion does not necessarily invalidate the previous suggestion that the Scotch contract was also signed at Dunbar. The French obligation of marriage is obviously the composition of someone who has had little or no legal training: its shortcomings were so obvious that it could well be that, on the advice of Huntly, and with the help of Thomas Hepburn, a more legal document was drawn up immediately after the signature to the French Contract had been obtained, and which it replaced. However, that this contract was signed by Mary is reasonably certain, for who would preserve such a worthless document if it lacked a signature? In this context, we may notice that the words, "lui étant en même liberté", do not indicate that Bothwell either was, or that Mary considered him to be, at that time free to marry her. The sentence continues, "je serai prête, etc.", employing the future tense, and the meaning is undoubtedly, "when he is in the same liberty, I shall be ready, etc.".

The manuscript copy of the contract has been believed by some to be the genuine original produced by Moray, and if that were the case, it could easily be shewn to be a forgery; first, because the body of the document is not, as the Lords declared, in Mary's handwriting, and secondly, because the signature, superficially very similar to Mary's, differs from it in the important particular that the initial letter is larger than the rest, while Mary invariably wrote her name with all the letters the same size. However, the argument that this contract is an original lacks cogency. It depends on the fact that Morton's receipt of January, 1571, mentions twenty-one documents, while those produced were twenty-two (eight letters, two contracts nd twelve sonnets); consequently, one document was missing and, for some reason not obvious, this must be it. However, no one could seriously describe a poem in twelve verses as twelve documents, and the number 'twenty-one' must have been otherwise reached; the evidence that one document had been abstracted between the end of the Commission (January, 1569) and Morton's receipt two years later therefore falls to the ground.

CHAPTER XII

Conclusions

We have now considered in some detail the discovery of the Silver Casket, the first mention of its contents, and the production of the documents, and we have examined exhaustively the text of those which have come down to us; it is now time to draw the strands together and to present an account of how the letters were assembled and made ready for production. First, however, we must dispose of the question of the "other woman", so far as that is possible. Until the factual content and style of the letters had been considered, it had always been possible for those who believed in the Queen's complicity in the murder of her husband to entrench themselves by pronouncing that she had, in fact, written all the letters and the ballad in the circumstances which the Lords had alleged. The examination which has just been made destroys this position, and it must be obvious to the reader that it is quite impossible that all the letters were written by the same person. At the same time, it is also undeniable that the documents were not forged within the ordinary sense of that word. No forger, desirous of proving a guilty liaison between the Queen and her lover and of demonstrating their combined guilt in the murder of the King would have produced such lengthy, indefinite and inconsistent compositions. We are therefore forced to accept the solution of a combination of the letters of at least two persons, with a few rather small additions on the part of a forger.

Bothwell was certainly something of a ladies' man. We have seen that he was "handfasted", or at least reputed to be so, to Lady Scott and to Anna Throndssen, daughter of a Norwegian admiral. He was married to Lady Jane Gordon and to Mary Queen of Scots. Buchanan alleges that Lady Reres, sister to Lady Scott, had been his mistress; his wife cited the maid, Bessie Crawford, as co-respondent; and Randolph alleged that he had taken "another wife" in France shortly before his return to Scotland in 1565.

Of the "other woman" we can be certain of very few facts. We know that she had a son, perhaps William Hepburn, the only known offspring

227

of the Earl: unfortunately, history does not relate when this boy was born, and the fact of his existence does not carry us much further. More important, it seems rather more than a probability that the "other woman" was French. The style of her letters, especially of Casket Letter III, is so typical of the French spirit of that date, that she must either have been French or have been brought up in France, and we also see that she was someone in a walk of life sufficiently below the Earl's for her to regard his embarrassed estate as something very fine indeed.

It has been suggested (262) that some of the Casket Letters were written by Anna Throndssen, but there are good reasons for doubting, albeit reluctantly, this ascription. It is true that, during the 16th century, an educated Danish-Norwegian (the countries were then united) would have spoken French, probably fluently. It was said that they used French to each other, Danish to the servants and German to the dog, but it is very much to be doubted whether a Norwegian who had not been educated in France would have so thoroughly captured French emotion and style as is displayed in Casket Letters III and IV. It is possible that Anna was educated in France, but we may guess that she was not, for she had six sisters and the cost of sending them all abroad would have been considerable, even for an admiral. Furthermore, even four hundred years ago, an admiral's daughter, especially one who was cousin to the Vice-Regent of Norway, would hardly have been quite so overcome by the estate and position of the impecunious Bothwell, to whom she had lent money and for which debt she had him detained on his arrival in Norway. Anna's story, however, does illustrate one important point: she was in Scotland in 1563 and had presumably lived there since 1561, yet her presence was completely unnoticed by all the spies, gossip-writers and scandal-mongers. What could be done once, could be done again, and Bothwell was fortunate that, for such a purpose, he possessed the isolated castle of Hermitage. Anna received her safe-conduct to return to Norway in 1563 (91), and she was certainly there when Bothwell arrived within the jurisdiction of her cousin in 1567. It is not unreasonable to assume that she had been there during the whole intervening period, in which case she could not have written letters understandable only in the context of Bothwell's marriage to Lady Jane Gordon.

There is yet another reason for dissociating Anna from the Casket Letters; it is the question of hand-writing. It seems more than likely that those of the "other woman's" letters which were produced were, at least in part, originals. If that be so, her handwriting must have been similar to Mary's, and Anna's was not. With her Scandinavian up-bringing, she naturally wrote a somewhat Gothic script, and, although there are certain Italianate features in her hand, it could never have been confused with the Queens's. Once again, it must be emphasized that, to the Scottish Lords and the English Commissioners, who almost all wrote a Gothic hand, any Italianate writings would appear somewhat similar, and the suggestion is made that, when the "other woman's" letters first came into their hands, the Lords genuinely believed, until they examined them more closely at a later date, that they were written by the Queen, a mistake which would be all the more probable if she bore the extremely common French name of Marie.

The list which we have of Bothwell's amours may not be inclusive, but the "other wife" mentioned by Randolph in 1565 could well fit the picture. A girl of moderate station, she would have come with her lover to Scotland in March, 1565. Tricked by a promise of marriage, or even something more legal, she soon began to realise the insecurity of her position. Bothwell seldom visited her at the Hermitage, and it was now, say November, 1565, that Casket Letter III was written. Soon after this, two things seem to have occurred: the political necessity of the Gordon alliance was borne in upon the Earl, and, at the same time he became tired of his lover's possessiveness. Probably he told Huntly of his dilemma, and, in an attempt to cause her to break off the affair, Bothwell pretended that Huntly had told him of something which caused him to doubt her fidelity. That this was an invention can scarcely be doubted: the author of those letters and of the ballad could only love one person at one time, and her devotion to Bothwell is apparent. At the same time, she was informed of the political nature of the Bothwell-Gordon marriage, and that it would only prove temporary. It was in these circumstances that Casket Letter IV was written, perhaps in December, 1565, or January, 1566. The marriage took place, but the liaison continued, Bothwell at times seeking to cause a rupture, but never sufficiently purposefully to achieve his object. He now returned to the story of an infidelity, this time naming one of his mistress's servants as his informant; Casket Letter V was the reply, and the date would be March or April, 1566. In May, Bothwell removed to Crichton, and the idea of importing his mistress into the castle or some nearby dwelling seems to have been raised, only to be postponed, and this led to the writing of Casket Letter VI. Probably the woman gained her end: she came to Crichton and was there or thereabout at the time when Lady Jane discovered Bothwell's infidelity: but Bessie Crawford was blamed, although, in this, Lady Jane may have been wrong. Lady Jane's behaviour on this occasion is mentioned in the love-ballad which was presumably written about July, 1566. After this, there is silence; we hear no more from the "other woman": perhaps she died, for she was ill when Casket Letter VI was written; perhaps Bothwell eventually got rid of her, and sent her back to her native land.

All this, of course, is purely hypothetical, but it seems to fit the facts, and it is rather natural to assume that all these letters were written in the space of a few months. In the above recital, we may have wronged Bothwell. It is possible that he did not invent the stories of his lover's infidelity, but that

Huntly, in the interests of policy and his sister, invented them, and convinced the Earl of their truth. This, at least, is what the "other woman" herself believed.

It is not impossible that the ballad was written much later, after Bothwell had been wounded, for one passage may refer to that incident. In that case, the liason dragged on longer than one would have expected when the principals were so ill assorted, he so reluctant and she so temperamental. Did it last until after Bothwell's marriage to Mary? Probably not, for we may discount Hay Fleming's (152), "yet it was alleged that he (Bothwell) passed several days a week with his divorced wife, regarding her still as his lawful spouse and the Queen as his concubine". Now, Fleming must be wrong in this, for there is no evidence of any affection for the Lady Jane on the part of the Earl, and it was she who instituted the first process of divorce. Hay Fleming may be referring to Bothwell's continued maintenance of a mistress, but, if so, he not only fails to disclose his authority for the first part of his statement, that he passed several days a week with his divorced wife (mistress?), but the reference which he gives to the second part of his allegation, shews that he completely inverted du Croc's remark. The French Ambassador, speaking of the ease with which divorce was obtainable in Scotland, wrote to Charles IX on 27th May, 1567, as follows (718):

"Aultant en a faict le conte Boduel de sa femme, laquelle il laissa disant qu'il ne l'avoit jamais espousée, et l'avoit toujours tenue pour concubine, et, elle vivant, espousa la royne Marie d'Escosse"; which may be translated, "The Earl Bothwell has done as much with his wife, whom he left, saying that he had never married her, and that he had always regarded her as a concubine, and, she living, he married Queen Mary of Scotland". The only other reference to the rather unlikely state of affairs of Bothwell continuing to support another woman after his marriage to Mary comes from the answer of the Scottish Lords to Throckmorton on 20th July, 1567, when the Lords were justifying their action in imprisoning Mary to the Ambassador sent by Elizabeth, although they had not yet reached the point of accusing their Queen of anything more than a refusal to abandon her husband, and were concentrating their attack on the Earl. In their answer, they state (660),

> "What remained to finish the work begun, and to accomplish the whole desire of his (Bothwell's) ambitious heart, but to send the son (Prince James) after the father (Darnley), and, as might be suspected, seeing him (Bothwell) keep another wife in store, to make the Queen also drink of the same cup, to the end he might invest himself with the crown of the realm?"

The evidence, therefore, seems to be inadequate to support the hypothesis that Bothwell and the "other woman" continued their affair so long, and, the two partners being such as they were shewn in the letters to be, an early end was to have been expected to it. Here we must leave the subject of the identity of this unfortunate woman: had Bothwell's tastes been less French, he might not have preserved those fatal letters which, entwined irrevocably with those of the Queen, became, in the hands of the Lords of the Congregation, fetters to bind Mary Stewart in perpetual imprisonment.

We have already noted in detail the points which assist in dating the genuine Marian letters which were produced from the Silver Casket, but it is well to recapitulate the conclusions which have been reached in the previous ten chapters. Casket Letter I was written to Bothwell from Stirling on or about 11th January, 1567. By adding the words "from Glasgow this Saturday", an innocent letter referring to her son was converted into a guilty one referring to her husband. Casket Letter II was originally two letters, the second, earlier part being to Bothwell soon after Mary's arrival at Glasgow in January, 1567, and the first part, written two or three days later, being to Moray. Both parts were diluted with additions from the "other woman's" letters, each being given one paragraph referring to a bracelet in order to shew that they were to the same person. Finally, the two letters were run together and presented as a single letter, perhaps when it was realised that the movements of Mary and Bothwell were such as to render the sending of more than one letter almost impossible. The genuine parts of Mary's letter reveal nothing more sinister than a probable decision to bring Darnley to justice and Mary's distaste at acting the necessary deception. Casket Letter VIII was written to Bothwell from Borthwick on 8th June, 1567, and contains no sinister matter; written on this date, it could not have been discovered in the Silver Casket. Casket Letter VII, probably written from Lochleven to George Douglas, presumably dates from April, 1568, and it, too, cannot have been an original "Casket" document. The two contracts of marriage were probably both signed by Mary, under duress at Dunbar between 25th April and 5th May. The French contract was signed first, for Mary did not read Scotch with ease, and then, because this document was insufficiently legalistic, a second contract in Scotch which had perhaps been previously prepared, was subsequently signed. The genuine Marian documents therefore provide no evidence of the Queen's guilt of the murder of her husband; they shew that she was grateful to Bothwell, and treated him with confidence and affection, but they shew no signs of inordinate or improper intimacy. On the other hand, the whole series produces abundant proof of the ill-faith and perjury of Moray and the rest who were associated with him in the Commissions at York and Westminster.

We must now turn our attention to the first appearances of the Casket and of the letters. These two items are deliberately separated in this manner, because, as we have already seen, and as shall again be demonstrated, they were not at first associated.

The first mention of the Casket occurs in a letter from Drury at Berwick to Cecil, dated 25th June, 1567, eight days after Mary's incarceration in Lochleven and four after the date on which the casket was later alleged to have been found. Drury writes (108), "There is here that the Queen had a box wherein are the practices between her and France, wherein is little good meant to England", and, four days later, Drury again mentions a box and the manuscripts in it "part in cipher deciphered". Curiously enough, although Mary's letters to Bothwell are spoken of from time to time, the casket itself is never mentioned again until Moray gave a receipt for it and its contents to Morton on 16th September, 1568, when the Regent was setting out for the first sessions of the Commission at York. Nor must we forget that, on 15th October, 1570, Randolph wrote to Cecil concerning the alleged bond for the murder of Darnley (291), "This bond was kept in the Castle (of Edinburgh) in a little box covered with green cloth, and, after the apprehension of the Scottish Queen (15th June, 1567) at Carberry Hill, was taken out of the place where it lay by (Maitland), in presence of James Balfour, the Clerk of the Register and keeper of the keys where the registers are". Balfour was, at that time, keeper of Edinburgh Castle. If Randolph's story were true, there was a strange collection of boxes at the Castle, and Maitland had at least access to one of them. If it were not true, then there was a readiness to invent stories about documents in boxes. It may be worth mentioning that it was by no means unusual, as it is to-day, for silver or jewelled boxes to be provided with a cloth cover. The point is that there is some evidence that, on or about 21st June, 1567, a box was found, and in it were discovered diplomatic documents belonging to Mary, not Bothwell. How it was discovered, we do not know, but the Castle and Holyrood House were in the hands of the rebels, and its discovery is not surprising. There was no immediate contemporary connexion between this discovery and the murder of Darnley, a fact which is surprising if the circumstances had been as described in Morton's declaration in which it was alleged that no less than eleven persons, some of whom were in English pay, were present at the opening of the casket and the 'sighting' of its contents. We have already shewn (page 71) that, from internal evidence, that declaration is not to be trusted, and the first hints we get about the finding of the box lend additional support to that belief.

We may conclude, therefore, that, soon after Mary's imprisonment, the Lords discovered a box which belonged to the Queen and which contained some papers of no great importance. Later, when the question of a tribunal in England was raised, a decision was taken to put the incriminating letters into this box, and the story of its discovery and opening was concocted. This decision was a shrewd move, for it served three purposes: by its lustre, the box focussed attention on its contents; by its value, it shewed the importance which Bothwell accorded to these letters; and by its previous ownership, it shewed the unseemly behaviour of the Queen. For this Casket was "garnished in many places with the Roman letter 'F' set under a royal crown" (326), and had therefore belonged to Mary's first husband, Francis II of France; that she could give the possessions of her first husband to such a paramour as the 'infamous' Bothwell was to confirm that she was capable of trampling on the whole decalogue.

Now we must turn from the Casket to its contents. While the discovery of the casket was first reported from the Scottish borders, the first account of the letters or a letter appeared in London, which seems to be a curious site of origin, but which is understandable if we imagine that the inventor of a letter was the Earl of Moray. This nobleman was undoubtedly implicated in the murder of Darnley, not by his own hands, for he left Edinburgh on the afternoon before the murder, but by his share in the conspiracy. The paths of the various plotters converged on Kirk o'Field, and their different ramifications were such as to have confused inquirers ever since. In effect, there were three plots on foot. First, there was the scheme of Mary and Bothwell, probably encouraged by Moray, of separating Darnley from the Lennox faction, preventing his departure to Flanders, and of bringing him and his father to justice at the forthcoming session of Parliament; in the intervening period, Darnley would be kept under supervision, but it was probably not intended to arrest him until his actual denunciation before the three estates.

Secondly, there was Darnley's scheme, in which he was assisted by Sir James Balfour. This plot involved the storing of gunpowder in the house next to his lodging at Kirk o'Field. On the evening of 9th February, Mary would attend the masque at 'Bastian's' marriage festivities, returning to Kirk o'Field for the night. During her absence, the gunpowder was to be conveyed into the cellars of Darnley's lodging, the fuse laid, and all would be ready for Mary's return with such of her Lords as were in Edinburgh, all of whom were Darnley's enemies. As soon as the cavalcade was seen, Darnley would light the fuse and escape from the house into the South Garden, which was separated from Kirk o'Field by the Flodden Wall, itself pierced by the gable-window of Darnley's room, thus providing a ready means of escape (523). Since the cavalcade would approach the house from within the wall, this escape would be unnoticed both by those approaching and by such servants and guards as were on duty outside the door of the house. Meanwhile, Mary and her retinue would have entered the house and would all have been destroyed in the imminent explosion. Darnley's escape would be ascribed to chance, and his way to the throne would be clear. Evidence could be produced to shew that the explosion had been arranged by the Protestant Lords with intent to destroy the Queen and Darnley together, and no doubt that evidence had not been neglected in arranging the details. The unnecessary powderbarrel (page 271) seems to have been one such clue (528).

Thirdly, there was the plot of Moray, Morton and their associates. Informed of the details of Darnley's plot, presumably by Sir James Balfour, for he certainly acquired a hold over them at this time (546), if they had been honest men, they would have arrested Darnley and informed the Queen, but Moray had aimed at the throne for at least six years, as is shewn by a remark of Cecil's in 1561 (303) and by Moray's conduct during the Chase-about and Riccio rebellions, and he now saw that his chance had come. His plan was simple: it was to allow everything to proceed, but to set an ambuscade in some cottages beside the South Garden. When Darnley had lighted the fuse, climbed out of the window, crossed the road outside and entered the garden, in order to shelter behind the garden wall during the forthcoming explosion, he was to be promptly strangled by the emissaries of the Lords. In the event, their job was the easier because Darnley, in order to simulate the almost miraculous nature of his escape from the explosion, was unarmed and almost naked. His servant, carrying a few clothes behind him was likewise strangled. Thomas Nelson, the third servant, perceiving what had happened in the garden hesitated—and was saved, for the explosion did not harm him and, when the house fell, he was left perched on the town-wall, the cat-walk of which formed the floor of the little gallery whose gable-window opened through the rampart. Two other servants, less lucky, were killed in the explosion (538). Had Moray's plot gone aright, Mary and his worst enemies, Bothwell and Huntly, would have died in the explosion by the hand of Darnley, and, as uncle of the infant Prince, he would certainly have become Regent. Perhaps this would have satisfied him, as it later did, but, should the sickly boy die, the throne would indubitably be his.

Moray's plot failed, because the cavalcade which Darnley saw did not include Mary and did not enter the house. The reason was that Bothwell had got wind of both plots; how he heard of the Lords' scheme, we do not know, but, in all probability, Darnley's gunpowder plot was told to him by the King's servant, 'Sandy' Durham: this assumption is made from the treatment meted out to him in Wilson's 'Oration' (17), which makes it plain that Durham was suspected "of spying of his (Darnley's) secrets and carrying news to the Queen"; we know, too, that Durham obtained permission to be absent from Kirk o'Field that evening (538). There is some reason to believe that Sir James Balfour betrayed Darnley, for Bothwell permitted him to be made Captain of Edinburgh Castle, and must thus have considered him his friend.

After the masque at Holyrood, Mary "was in long talk with Bothwell, none being present but the Captain of her Guard (Stewart of Traquair)", as Buchanan's 'Detection' puts it (15). If the story of the prosecution were true, that Mary had remained at Kirk o'Field until the gunpowder was safely placed in her bedroom beneath Darnley's, and all that now remained was for the fuse to be ignited, why the delay, and what need was there for long talk between her, Bothwell and Stewart of Traquair? The presence of the latter points directly to Mary's security as the subject of conversation, for he, as Captain of the Guard, was responsible for her safety. We may therefore conclude that Bothwell explained, more or less, the situation to Mary, probably omitting any reference to the Lords and their additional plot. From the fact that the talk was long, we may deduce that Mary was not easily convinced. At length, however, she consented to remain at Holyrood and not to return, as planned, to Kirk o'Field, and to allow Bothwell to reconnoitre the neighbourhood of the King's lodging. It was Bothwell and his men whom Darnley saw, and, believing it to be his wife returning after the masque, he set in motion the events which so quickly led to his own death.

It has usually been assumed that Bothwell left Holyrood, joined the emissaries of the Protestant Lords and assisted in the murder of Darnley, but we have good evidence that this was not the case. Holyrood was outside the town-wall, being at the extremity of the suburb of Canongate. The wall itself was ruinous, and we know, both from the depositions of some of those convicted for the murder and from the town records that there was a gap in it beside the deserted Blackfriars' monastery, some 200 yards East of Kirk o'Field (524). Lennox, in his 'Supplication', mentions that Mary was wont to visit Darnley by means of a 'privy way' (512), by passing round the back of the Canongate, and, by avoiding all streets and gates, and by entering the city through this gap close to her husband's lodging, she thus avoided all publicity for her visits. Now, the Lords, knowing that Darnley would emerge from the one window which pierced the town-wall, economically placed their ambush on that side only; not having to enter the city at all, they therefore ensured added secrecy in the setting of their trap. Bothwell, if he had had murder in his heart, and with nothing to fear from his allies outside the wall, would certainly have used this privy route, not only for his approach to Kirk o'Field, but for his retreat to Holyrood after the deed was done, had he been participant with the Lords in the assassination. Now, little faith can be given to the depositions of Powrie, Dalgleish, Hay and Hepburn of Bolton, all of whom were executed for the murder of Darnley, but although there are notable discrepancies between them, there is one point on which they are all agreed, which is, the route taken by Bothwell, with themselves in attendance, both when he went to Kirk o'Field and when he returned to Holyrood after the explosion (18). They entered the city through the Netherbow Port, and, it now being after midnight, they had to wake the porter to gain admittance, and to him they gave Bothwell's name. They struck South across the city and entered Mary's 'privy way' hard by the Blackfriars but from inside the town, not from without, and, passing along the inner side of the town-wall, came to Kirk o'Field. When the unbelievably noisy explosion had wakened the townsfolk, instead of joining their friends

outside by way of the gap at the Blackfriars, which they could so easily
have reached, they cut through various wynds or closes, crossed the two
main streets of the city, and came to the city wall at its farthest point from
Kirk o'Field, intending to leap over into Leith Walk, but, finding the wall
too high, they returned to the Netherbow, again gave Bothwell's name to
the porter, and so were allowed to pass out into the Canongate to Holyrood.
If Bothwell were a murderer, his movements are quite inexplicable; in fact,
they can only be understood on the basis that the Earl did not dare to come
into contact with the Lords' emissaries round the South Garden, for he had
seriously interfered with their plans by preventing Mary's return to Kirk
o'Field, and he may have feared lest his scheme might have leaked out
when he was seen to be closetted with Mary after the masque, and when he
left the Palace alone; some watcher in the Palace might have reached the
members of the ambush before the explosion had occurred, and Bothwell's
life would not then have been safe had he ventured within striking distance
of those who lay in wait.

Bothwell probably considered himself completely innocent of the murder
of Darnley, but morally he must bear some guilt, and so Mary came to
believe in Lochleven where she learnt more of the story, for then it was
that she began to think of a divorce, and, in all her subsequent statements,
she names Bothwell as one of the murderers. Probably she refused to believe
that he was not in league with Moray and the rest, for she would not know,
or, if she had known, she would not have realised, the significance of the
route which he took to and from Kirk o'Field. Bothwell was morally guilty,
for he knew that his approach, simulating that of Mary, would set in train
the events which must lead to Darnley's death. If he had made a demonstration in force outside the South Wall, or if he had done nothing at all,
Darnley would not have died that night. Nevertheless, the murder was not
his act, and he only saw that chance had placed in his way the means for
others to remove a traitor to his Queen and the obstacle to his own
ambition. That the Lords should fail in half of their object and forward
his own progress to the throne would have seemed something of a joke to
this veteran of border warfare.

When the result of the explosion was fully known, there must have been
consternation in the ranks of the Lords. How much did Bothwell and Mary
know and what would be their course of action? It is significant that
Moray slipped away from Scotland before the opening of Parliament in
April 1567, suggesting that he feared that he might be arraigned, even as it
had apparently been the intention to arraign Darnley.

Moray left Scotland on 10th April, 1567 (189), and reached France at
the end of the month. As early as 8th May, Grange wrote to warn him to
be ready for a return (444), for the combination which was to overthrow
Mary and Bothwell was gaining ground, and an association had been
formed against the Government by 1st May (188).

Yet Moray was in a quandary. He knew the background of Darnley's plotting, he knew that Philip II was the murdered man's supporter, and that the King of Spain had thereby lost his only chance of regaining his superiority over any part of the British Isles. Moray must have known that Philip was bound to suspect the Protestant party of Darnley's murder, and if Bothwell, now head of the Government, took that line, Moray might find it difficult to prevent his associates and even himself from coming to disrepute or even condign punishment. Furthermore, lest Moray should accuse the King of Spain of participation in Darnley's plot, it was likely that that monarch, slow of decision though he was, would, sooner or later, accuse Moray of the murder in order to prevent Moray from striking the first blow: any subsequent disclosure on his part would then lose much of its force, if it were the mere repartee to such an accusation. It was then, it seems, that the idea occurred to Moray of assuring Philip that he held actual proof of Mary's complicity in the murder of Darnley. There would be no need to produce the proof; it did not need to exist; the mere assurance of its ex stence would serve, for Philip would understand the hint, "If you w ll agree to join me in accusing, or assenting to the accusation, of the Queen, I shall say nothing about your part in Darnley's affairs". It was then, having reached this conclusion, that he decided to invent a letter, written by Mary at Glasgow to Bothwell, and based on the one which he had himself received from her at that time. The next question which arose was the manner in which the assurance was to be conveyed to Philip. It was quite out of the question to visit the Spanish Ambassador in Paris, because to be seen with that person would create a considerable stir, a report would be bound to reach Scotland, and besides, Moray wished to remain near the Normandy coast, so that he could hasten to Scotland at once if necessary. Equally, to send a messenger direct to Spain was impossible, not only because of the publicity of such a move, but also because he had with him few people whom he could trust, perhaps only one, and they (or he) would be needed should he return to Scotland. The situation, however, was different in England, for the Government there was at one with Moray's schemes, it had helped him repeatedly in the past, and had recently, as we have seen, given its support to a plot to destroy Mary and Darnley, as was shewn by the instructions of Bedford when he attended the christening (page 44). If this seems to be too strong a conclusion, the reader is asked to remember that Bedford's written instructions would certainly be strengthened by a verbal communication which would never be put on paper. That his written instructions are so suspicious is as much proof as we could hope to obtain.

Mary was arrested on 15th June, 1567, at Carberry. It would take a fortnight at least for the news to reach Moray, and we see that he acted at once, for his secretary, Nicholas Elphinstone, probably the only trusty messenger he had at his disposal, reached London by 8th July (732), *en route* for Scotland, where he arrived about 14th July (734). It was on 12th July that de Silva, the Spanish Ambassador in London, wrote to Philip II (520), "The Queen's adversaries assert positively that they know that she had been concerned in the murder of her husband, which was proved by letters under her own hand, copies of which were in 'his' possession". This is the first reference to the Casket Documents, and we may remind the reader that the use of the plural does not necessarily imply more than one letter. It has generally been assumed that de Silva's information came from du Croc, who had left Edinburgh on 29th June, and would therefore be in London about 4th July, at least a week before this letter was written. If, on the other hand, Elphinstone had been the informant, the letter was not so long delayed, and, in that case, the 'his' of de Silva's letter would mean Moray.

The second reference to the Casket Letters occurs in de Silva's letter to Philip II of 21st July (443), "I mentioned to the Queen (Elizabeth) that I had been told that the Lords held certain letters proving that the Queen (Mary) had been cognizant of the murder of her husband. She told me that it was not true, although (Maitland) had acted badly in the matter, and, if she saw him, she would say something that would not be at all to his taste". Now, Elizabeth may have heard something from Robert Melville, who left Edinburgh on 21st June, from du Croc, or even from another messenger who left Scotland on 9th July, but it may well be that de Silva and the Queen were at cross purposes, he speaking of Moray's invented letter, she speaking of something which had come to her from Scotland. It is even possible that, knowing nothing whatsoever about the subject which de Silva had raised, she invented some sop to put off the inquisitive Spaniard. That de Silva's first informant was indeed Elphinstone is confirmed by the fact that the third reference to the Casket letters occurs in his letter to Philip II of 2nd August, 1567. Moray, following his secretary to Scotland, arrived in London on 23rd July (316). He stayed some time there, for there was no need to hurry and it was important to assure himself of the attitude of Elizabeth and Cecil, and to pave the way for his own elevation to the Regency. Moray saw de Silva on 31st July, and this is the latter's account of what Moray told him (447), Mary's complicity in the murder of Darnley, said Moray, was

> "proved beyond doubt by a letter which the Queen had written to Bothwell containing more than three sheets of paper, written with her own hand and signed with her name; in which she says in substance that he is not to delay putting into execution that which he had been ordered, because her husband used such fair words to deceive her, and bring her to his will, that she might be moved by them if the other thing were not done quickly. She said that she herself would go and fetch him (Darnley), and would stop at a house on the road where she would try to give him a draught; but if this could not be

done, she would put him in the house where the explosion was arranged for the night upon which one of her servants was to be married. He, Bothwell, was to try to get rid of his wife, either by putting her away or poisoning her, since he knew that she (the Queen) had risked all for him; her honour, her kingdom, her wealth which she had in France, and her God; contenting herself with his person alone".

Moray added that he had heard of this letter from a man who had read it.

Moray arrived in Edinburgh on 11th August. The whole question of the Casket Letter or Letters was now shelved for there was no need for them. Moray's invention had served to prevent Philip II from making things difficult for him, and the matter was allowed to drop.

We must now return to events in Scotland after the imprisonment of the Queen and prior to the arrival of Moray from France. From the first, the Lords took the line that they were fully prepared to obey Mary as their rightful sovereign, provided that she would separate herself from the "tyrant", Bothwell, and they justified their continued restraint of their Queen by her refusal to give up the husband of whom they had originally approved. The discovery of the "box", which was first reported on 25th June, made no difference to their attitude, and no mention of any proof of Mary's guilt appears in any of the official documents which have come down to us as emanating from Scotland during this period, which is good evidence that no incriminating letters had yet been discovered. The French Ambassador, du Croc, left Edinburgh on 29th June; that he had no copies of any letters may be assumed from the complete silence of French diplomatic circles on this point, not only then, but at a later date when the question of Mary's letters was being publicised in books produced by the English Government in both England and France, and this confirms that it was from Elphinstone and France, and not from Scotland, that de Silva obtained the information which inspired his first reference to "letters" on 12th July.

On 9th July, someone, who may have been John Wood, left Edinburgh with letters for Moray (445). He would reach London about 14th July. He certainly carried letters from Maitland and from Robert Melville, and it is not impossible that it was from him that Elizabeth obtained the information which de Silva communicated to Philip II on 21st July: "I mentioned to the Queen (Elizabeth) that I had been told that the Lords held certain letters proving that the Queen (Mary) had been cognizant of the murder of her husband. She told me that it was not true, although (Maitland) had acted badly in the matter". Now, Elizabeth's information, if she had any and was not improvising in order to cover her ignorance, cannot have come from Elphinstone, for she denied that such letters existed. If she had heard anything from Wood, what he had said could not have been to the effect that the Lords had discovered letters in Mary's handwriting proving her guilt, for she said that "it was not true"; rather, it seems that Wood, if it were he, had told her that Maitland had secured letters which, although not Mary's, could be passed off as hers. It is surprising that any emissary of the Lords should be so outspoken, but we must remember that there were factions within the Congregation, and that Maitland was by no means popular. If we imagine that the Secretary had obtained Bothwell's papers, in Edinburgh Castle, Holyrood House or elsewhere, and had discovered the "other woman's" letters, he would at once have appreciated that the writing was sufficiently like Mary's for the letters to be used. The other Lords, however, must have regarded this scheme as too dangerous; they refused to be stampeded into accusing their Queen of murder, and Wood, who, it will be recalled, was later one of Moray's Commissioners at York and Westminster, and was therefore high in the Lord's councils, incautiously told Cecil or Elizabeth more on this subject than he should have done. This would explain the facts, and it would also account for the official attitude of the Lords towards their Queen remaining unchanged.

Elizabeth dispatched an ambassador, Nicholas Throckmorton, to Scotland, ostensibly to protect Mary's interests and to secure her liberation. Throckmorton arrived in Edinburgh on 12th July, and, two days later, he wrote to Elizabeth, and stated expressly (83),

> "The Lords guarding her (Mary) keep her very straitly, and their rigour proceeds by order of these men, because she will by no means lend her authority to prosecute the murder (of Darnley) nor consent by any persuasion to abandon Bothwell for her husband, but avoweth constantly that she will live and die with him . . . . . The principal cause of her detention is, these Lords seeing her fervent affection to him, fear if put at liberty, she would so maintain him that they should be compelled to be in continual arms against him. They also mean a divorce between them . . . . . but they do not intend to touch her in surety or honour, for they speak of her with respect and reverence, and affirm that, the conditions aforesaid accomplished, they will restore her to her estate".

Elphinstone arrived in Edinburgh soon after this letter was written. Presumably he brought with him the account of the letter which he had mentioned to the Spanish Ambassador and which Moray, soon after, was to describe to de Silva. If the explanation given above of Maitland having "acted badly in the matter" be correct, a good deal of discussion would be required before Moray's story would be adopted, for the Lords had evidently already refused to adopt a somewhat similar scheme at Maitland's suggestion. Eventually, however, the device was decided upon, perhaps because this letter had already been mentioned to de Silva by Elphinstone, and this decision led to two results, first, to the redundancy of the spurious letters which we have imagined Maitland to possess, and secondly, to an alteration in the attitude which the Lords adopted to Mary. Their first action was to force the Queen to abdicate in favour of her son, and it is probable that they threatened to charge her with the murder of her husband should she refuse. Next, they, informed Throckmorton of Mary's guilt and of their proof of it, for, on 25th July, 1567, the English Ambassador wrote to Cecil (289), that the Lords intended to charge Mary with the murder of her husband "from the testimony of her own handwriting", which is the first definite mention of the Casket Letters emanating from Scotland.

Moray arrived in Edinburgh on 11th August; he accepted the Regency on 22nd, having, meanwhile, visited Mary at Lochleven and having left her thoroughly cowed. The situation was well under control; the Queen was captive, neither France, England nor Spain would intervene, and there was no need to produce proof of Mary's criminality. The Lords must now have held all the so-called Casket Documents, save Casket Letter VII, which had not been written, but it is to be presumed, from subsequent developments, that no decision had yet been taken on how to manipulate them. Parliament met in December, 1567, and in the minutes of the preliminary Council meeting, the letters are mentioned, but are in no way described: they are simply referred to as "divers her privy letters written and subscribed with her own hand, and sent by her to James Earl Bothwell, Chief executor of the said horrible murder, as well before the committing thereof as thereafter"; similar phraseology was used in the Act of Parliament of 15th December, save that the letters were now said to be "written wholly with her own hand". The minutes of Council are certainly suspect, for the original does not exist, and the present copy is taken from a subsequent one sent to Cecil, and which Hosack thought was a fabrication (323). From the attestation of the pro-Marian Lords of 12th September 1568 (251), it would appear that only one document was produced in the Parliament, for they stated,

"And, if it be alleged that her Majesty's writing (singular), produced in Parliament, should prove her Grace culpable, it may be answered that there is in no place mention made in it (singular) by the which her Highness may be convicted, albeit it (singular) were her own handwriting, as it (singular) is not. And also the same is (singular) devised by themselves in some principal and substantial clauses".

The statement continues by enunciating a legal generalisation which, in contrast, is put into the plural:

"And such alleged privy writings can make no probation in criminal causes, which will be clearer than the light of day".

A return is now made from the general to the particular,

"And so by the said writing (singular) nothing can be inferred against her Majesty".

In Scottish Parliamentary procedure, it was usual for the forthcoming business to be considered by a special committee called the Lords of the Articles. This body, composed of representatives from the three estates, made all the decisions, and, at the subsequent meeting of the full Parliament, the members signified their assent or negation with little or no discussion. In this Parliament, the place of the Lords of the Articles was taken by "the Lords of Secret Council and others, Barons and men of jugment". According to the minute sent later to Cecil, there were 28 members, of whom only two could be thought to be at all fair-minded. The names were Moray, Morton, Glencairn, Errol, Buchan, Gray, Graham, Ochiltree, Innermeith, the Bishop of Orkney, the Commendators of Dunfermline and Culross, Sir James Balfour, Home, Ruthven, Semple, Glamis, Lindsay, Macgill, Balnaves, Maitland, Drumlanrig, Cuninghamhead, Erskine of Dun, Grange, Pitarrow, Haliburton and Craigmillar. The Bishop of Orkney had been under a heavy cloud for his part in conducting the marriage service of Mary and Bothwell and was anxious to win his way back into favour. Erskine of Dun was a noted Minister of the Kirk, and Mary had once agreed to hear him preach, while the Laird of Craigmillar had certainly received favours from Mary. The remainder were all of the strong anti-Marian party. Whatever documents were produced, no one of that assembly would have been disposed to examine them carefully, if at all. Their avowed intention was to find some formula by which they could place the law on their side and justify to the public their own rebellious actions, and they would accept without question and without inspection the description of any of Mary's letters which Moray was prepared to give, while the subsequent Parliamentary session would probably vote without discussion and ratify without demur whatever this body had decided. Some letter at least was produced, but it would not have been available for inspection, and those of the three estates who were favourably disposed towards the Queen would be in such a minority that they would not dare to intervene.

So far, the only 'manipulation' of letters which had yet taken place was the invention of that one which Moray had described to de Silva, and which may well have been based on his own letter from Mary when she was at Glasgow. Subsequent events suggest strongly that no forgery had so far been committed; the description of an imaginary letter was all that had been required, and it is particularly remarkable that there is as yet no hint that this, or any other, epistle had been found in a silver casket. Since the situation was now completely under control, no further action was needed. Moray had told Lennox about the imaginary letter when they met in London, and he, and the Lords in Scotland, continued to regard this as the official story.

Suddenly, however, the whole aspect was changed. On 2nd May, 1568, Mary escaped from Lochleven, was defeated at Langside, and, after exactly a fortnight of freedom, crossed the Solway and arrived in England and renewed captivity. It was, of course, unthinkable that Elizabeth would retain Mary as her prisoner without at least some shew of an enquiry, if only for the purpose of silencing the comments of other governments which might be glad to make use of such an opportunity to revile the Queen of England. The attitude of the English Government hitherto had shewn that the Protestant rebels need not be too careful in the preparation of their evidence; they could be certain that any tribunal erected by Elizabeth would be biassed in their favour; nevertheless, the case for the prosecution must be prepared and whatever supporting evidence there was must be produced.

As soon as news of Mary's arrival in England became known to him, Lennox, then at Chiswick, prepared his 'Supplication', which, as we have seen, was written between 22nd and 28th May, on which latter date it was presented by him to Elizabeth (503). Since there had been no change in the official story, or, at least, no such change had been notified to him, Lennox described, in his 'Supplication', that letter of which he had heard from Moray ten months before, and, naturally enough, since he was dependent on his memory, this description varies slightly from de Silva's account of 2nd August, 1567.

Meanwhile, Moray, doubtful of how matters would proceed, promptly sent John Wood to the English Court, as soon as he knew that Mary had retreated into that country. Wood set out on 21st May, and would reach London about 27th May (493). On that same day, Moray received a communication from Cecil, the contents of which we do not know, although we may guess at their nature (499), and, immediately the Regent sent instructions to Buchanan to prepare a brief for the prosecution (494), which ultimately appeared as the 'Book of Articles' and was the basis of the 'Detection'.

The first version of the 'Book of Articles' was in Latin, and was completed early in June. As we have seen (page 82), this has only one short reference to what is undoubtedly the same letter as that described by Lennox and de Silva: "She prepared herself from Edinburgh to ride to Glasgow", wrote Buchanan, "of mind, as well appears from her letter (or letters), to bring him (Darnley) to Edinburgh". It therefore appears that, as late as 27th May, 1568, the Casket Documents as we know them had not yet been assembled and reliance was still being placed on the imaginary letter of Moray.

On 22nd June, 1568, Moray wrote to the English government (207) mentioning the letters, the Scotch translations of which, he says, have already been sent by John Wood, and we know that a packet was in fact forwarded by Drury at Berwick on 6th June. Wood was with Lennox near London by the time this packet arrived (10th June) (448), and, on the following day, the latter wrote to Moray, saying (448), "There is sufficiency in her own handwriting by the faith of her (Mary's) letters to condemn her". This is conclusive that, by 6th June, 1568, the Casket Documents, not in existence on 27th May, were now available, almost certainly in their final form, and we may conclude that the manipulation and translation of the letters was decided upon and carried out in the short space of less than ten days before the packet was dispatched.

A short summary will suffice for the remaining details; in September, Buchanan prepared his English version of the Book of Articles and added a postscript which undoubtedly refers to the letters in their final form (page 83). The Scotch translations were produced at York on 10th or 11th October (214), and the original French at Westminster on 7th, 8th and 14th December, 1568. The Commissioners of the Queen of Scots were not allowed to see the documents, and their contents were never disclosed to them.

Let us return to the ten critical days, 27th May to 6th June, 1568. Everything had happened rather suddenly. On 27th May, Moray heard from Cecil, and it seems likely that the nature of the communication was that Elizabeth was shewing herself as Mary's partisan, and that the Regent would do well to produce a corrective as quickly as possible (499). The immediate response, as we have seen, was for instructions to be sent to Buchanan at St. Andrews (500) and for the preparation of an indictment of the Queen to be set on foot. We may guess, however, that Moray and the more important of his Privy Council would continue to discuss this extremely important business for some time, and it may be taken for granted that Maitland, undoubtedly the possessor of the most subtle genius in Scotland, would be of the sederunt. If it be true that Maitland had already, before Moray's return to Scotland in August, 1567, suggested the use of some letters found among Bothwell's effects, not written by Mary, but in writing not dissimilar from her own, it would not be surprising if he were to broach that subject again, and, indeed, the subject must necessarily have been mentioned, for Moray must have lamented that the letter which had stood him in such good stead with de Silva and in the Parliament was purely imaginary, although based on the letter which he had received from Mary when she was at Glasgow.

There is, of course, no reason to believe that any of the Casket Documents was a forgery in the usually accepted sense of that word; indeed, all the evidence is to the contrary. The discussion concerning the manipulation of the letters must have taken some time, for we have shewn that Casket Letter II certainly passed through two separate stages, being first prepared as two separate letters, each receiving some additional matter from the letters of the "other woman", and, later, being condensed into one epistle. The work of reading and assimilating the contents of the letters alone would take some time; in the few days at their disposal there was no time for much forgery; nor was much required. A few words had to be inserted, such as the date of Casket Letter I and the alteration of the address of the Bothwell part of Casket Letter II: the supreme simplicity and effectiveness of these touches guarantees the authorship of Maitland, and we have another clue that his was the guiding spirit, for it must have been now that the story of the discovery of the letters in the Silver Casket was concocted. This device was also Maitland's offspring, and the proof of this lies in Randolph's letter of 15th October, 1570, to Cecil (291). Speaking of the alleged bond for the murder of Darnley, he wrote, "This bond was kept in the Castle (of Edinburgh) in a little box covered with green cloth, and, after the apprehension of the Scottish Queen at Carberry Hill, was taken out of the place where it lay by (Maitland), in presence of James Balfour"; and this statement itself receives confirmation from the letter of Drury to Cecil of 28th November, 1567 (290), in which the same incident is described thus, "The writings which did comprehend the names and consents of the chiefs for the murdering of the King are turned to ashes, the same that concerns the Queen's part kept to be shewn". We now see why Dalgleish was never questioned concerning the discovery of the Casket, for the whole story was not concocted until long after the death of that unfortunate man.

We have seen that when, in 1571, Morton gave a receipt for the Casket and its contents to Lennox, the then Regent, he specified twenty-one documents. Two explanations present themselves to account for this number which so much exceeds the actual number of documents produced (eleven). Either there were twenty-one sheets of paper which together comprised the eight letters, the love-ballad and the two contracts, or the casket contained some ten additional documents, a reserve of ammunition which was never expended because the eleven which were produced were accepted without reserve by the English Commissioners and these ten, obviously less conclusive documents, seemed unnecessary.

The re-shuffling of the sheets of Mary's letters with those of the "other woman" and the alteration and addition of a few phrases were not, however, all that was necessary. In at least one place, part of one letter had to be copied on to the blank verso of another, and it may be that other sheets had to be copied out in order to omit irrelevant material such as addresses, signatures, dates or unacceptable phrases. It is possible that a professional forger was pressed to this service, or even that Maitland undertook it himself, but another, and less pleasing solution presents itself: it is that the copying was done by someone whose own handwriting was so similar to Mary's that it is difficult to tell them apart, and who was devotedly attached to Maitland and wholly at his bidding; that person was Maitland's wife, Mary Fleming, one of the Queen's four Maries.

First, as to Mary Fleming's ability to copy the one page of the "other woman's" letter on to the blank verso of Mary's own letter, there can be no doubt. She, like the other three Maries, had been brought up in France and had been taught by the same writing-master as the Queen herself. Her signature is almost identical with the Queen's, and there would have been no necessity for her to attempt a conscious imitation. That she was deeply in love with Maitland we know from her behaviour after his death. It is possible that she would do his bidding, and copy a letter of which she knew nothing on to a sheet of another letter of which she knew as little, but this may be doubted. She must surely have seen and recognised the writing on the recto, and she must have suspected that she was betraying her mistress, although she may not have known to what extent.

If this idea seems shocking, that Mary could have been thus abused by one of her own four Maries, the reader is asked to consider the circumstances dispassionately. Five girls of equal age are brought up together, away from their parents. The mother of one of them, Lady Fleming, is forced to retire from her post of governess to them in disgrace. Four of the girls are equals in birth and fortune, but the fifth is a Queen, and the future bride of a future King. In this atmosphere, can it be doubted that there must have been jealousies innumerable springing up among them? It would be difficult to imagine circumstances in which the seeds of hate were more likely to have been sown; only the very noblest young woman could have retained her affection for the undoubtedly spoilt and favoured Queen. That one of the four should have done so is as much as we have any right to expect; this Mary Seton did: she was the only one of the four Maries who followed her Queen into exile and remained with her until the bitter end. On the other hand, Mary Beaton thought little enough of the Queen to flirt outrageously with Mary's most vicious enemy, Randolph, the English Ambassador, and it has even been suggested that she was the source of some of that minister's information concerning the Queen's secrets. No one need be surprised if Mary Fleming loved her husband enough to betray the Queen to whom she had been linked in such an unsatisfactory relationship.

In concluding the story of the appearance, manipulation and production of the Casket Letters, it has been necessary to resort to hypothesis, yet the explanation which has been offered is consistent with all the known facts, and, more important still, consistent with itself, for the principal actors in the drama are seen to bear each his own character, unchanging from first appearance to final curtain, and the evidence of the Casket Letters has been shewn not only to exculpate Mary Stewart from the crime of murder, but also to spread the guilt where it deserves to lie. Her story is inextricably entwined with that of Bothwell's unknown mistress, whose fate can hardly have been less miserable than that of the Queen herself. This unfortunate woman spun a thread which, woven by Moray, Maitland and the rest, became, in due course a shroud for Mary's authority. Unconsciously, the bitter lampoonist hit the mark when, in mocking song, he asked,

"Mary, Mary, quite contrary,
How does your garden grow,
With silver bells and cockle-shells
And pretty maids all in a row?"

BOOK III

"How the Garden Grew"

CHAPTER I

From the Christening to Kirk o'Field

1566

17th December, Tuesday.   The baptism of Prince James was solemnized by the rites of the Catholic faith in the Chapel Royal at Stirling at four o'clock in the afternoon. The Prince was carried by de Brienne, representing Charles IX as godfather; du Croc stood proxy for the other godfather, the King of Savoy, whose ambassador Moretta, had not yet arrived in Scotland. Mary's illegitimate half-sister, the Countess of Argyll, represented Elizabeth as godmother. Athol carried the taper, Eglinton the salt, Semple the chrism and the Bishop of Ross the laver. The ceremony was conducted by the Archbishop of St. Andrews, John Hamilton, assisted by the Bishops of Dunkeld and Dunblane. The ceremony was followed by a banquet at which presents and compliments were exchanged, and after which there was dancing and a masque (664). Darnley, although in Stirling, absented himself from all the ceremonies.

18th December, Wednesday.   This day "they had in the park the hunting of the wild bull, at which the Queen was present" (664).

19th December, Thursday.   In the evening, there was a great banquet for the Ambassadors, which was followed by a masque, for which the Latin verses had been written by Buchanan. There was also a great display of fire-works (146).

20th December, Friday.   On this day the Queen made an assignation for £10,000 and 400 chalders of victual to augment the stipends of the ministry (389). This, and the ratification of it on the following day, are signed by Mary, but not by Darnley, thus shewing that the King, although in Stirling, was standing aloof from all business. This absence from the council-board could not have been because he feared to be insulted by the English Ambassador (Bedford); and we must therefore conclude that it was to further his own designs that he remained away from the christening festivities also.

251

This same day, Maitland wrote a short and friendly note to Cecil, chiefly concerning the events at the christening (64).

21st December, Saturday.   The Lords of Secret Council ratified the Act augmenting the stipends of the ministers (389).

This Act, like that on the former day, is not signed by the King.

23rd December, Monday.   Du Croc, the French Ambassador in Scotland, wrote to Mary's Ambassador in Paris, the Archbishop of Glasgow (340),

"The baptism of the Prince was performed on Tuesday last. It was the Queen's pleasure that he should bear the name James, together with that of Charles (the King of France's name), because, said she, all the good Kings of Scotland his predecessors, who have been most devoted to the crown of France, were called by the name of James. Everything at this solemnity was done according to the form of the holy Roman Catholic Church. The King had still given out that he would depart two days before the baptism, but, when the time came, he made no sign of removing at all, only he still kept close within his apartment. The very day of the baptism, he sent three several times desiring me either to come and see him, or to appoint him an hour that he might come to me in my lodgings; so that I found myself obliged at last to signify to him that, seeing he was in no good correspondence with the Queen, I had it in charge from the most Christian King to have no conference with him, and I caused tell him likewise that, as it would not be very proper for him to come to my lodgings, because there was such a crowd of company there, so he might know that there were two passages to it, and if he should enter by the one, I should be constrained to go out by the other. His bad deportment is incurable, nor can there ever by any good expected of him, for several reasons which I might tell you, was I present with you. I cannot pretend to foretell how all may turn; but I will say that matters cannot subsist long as they are without being accompanied with sundry bad consequences . . . . The Queen behaved herself admirably well all the time of the baptism, and shewed so much earnestness to entertain all the goodly company in the best manner that this made her forget in a good measure her former ailments. But I am of the mind, however, that she will give us some trouble yet, nor can I be brought to think otherwise so long as she continues to be so pensive and melancholy. She sent for me yesterday, and I found her laid on the bed weeping sore, and she complained of a grievous pain in her side. And, for a surcharge of evils, it chanced that, the day her Majesty set out from Edinburgh for this place (10th December, 1566), she hurt one of her breasts on the horse, which she told me is now swelled. I am much grieved for the many troubles and vexations she meets with. From Stirling, this 23rd December, 1566".

This letter was carried to France by de Brienne who departed the same day.

On this day, the Queen restored the Archbishop of St. Andrews to his consistorial jurisdiction (422), an act in favour of the Roman Catholic Church which she was to reverse on 7th January, 1567.

24th December, Tuesday. Perhaps moved by Christian charity, although other less pure motives have been suggested, Mary pardoned Morton and 76 of the fugitives who had been concerned in the murder of Riccio (147). We know from a letter of Bedford to Cecil of 9th January, 1567, (65) that the pardon was granted through the insistence of the English Government, and that Bothwell, Moray, Athol and others helped to persuade the Queen to this act of leniency. Bedford's activity in this direction does not conflict with the view that Cecil expected the imminent destruction of Mary's authority, which, as we have seen, (page 44), is at least a possible explanation for Bedford's instructions regarding the Treaty of Edinburgh, and Moray and Bedford had ample opportunity to discuss this matter, for they departed, apparently on this day (336), to St. Andrews where the English Ambassador was Moray's guest for some days. Having performed this act of grace, Mary and Bothwell, presumably attended by various Lords and Ladies in waiting, set out for Drymen, some 20 miles from Stirling, where, according to Buchanan, their behaviour was 'lascivious' (179).

This same day, the pardon of Andrew Ker of Fawdonside also passed under the signet (192). It is notable that this pardon is separate from that of Morton and the rest, and, furthermore, we know that Mary never forgave this participant in the murder of Riccio, who had threatened her with a dag (pistol) on that occasion: as long after as 1568 she was still at enmity with him (537). It therefore follows that the pardon was granted by Darnley, presumably after the departure of the Queen to Lord Drummond's house.

Later the same day, Darnley departed to Glasgow, where he presently became sick. We know that, at Glasgow, he visited the English ship in the Clyde (Casket Letter II); we may conclude that this was before he fell ill, and that he was then contemplating putting into action his plan to withdraw to Flanders, and, with the aid of Philip II, mount an invasion of Britain, which, including the seizure of Scarborough Castle and the Scilly Isles, would lead to his ascent to the throne of a united Britain.

25th December, Wednesday. The Thirteenth General Assembly of the Church of Scotland met on this and the three subsequent days (390). Apparently, the Countess of Argyll was ordered to do penance for the part she had played at the baptism of the Prince (360), for her participation in a Roman Catholic ceremony gave offence to the godly, and all the proceedings of the Assembly were bitterly anti-Catholic.

26th December, Thursday.   The Bishop of Mondovi, papal nuncio to Scotland, awaiting developments at Paris, wrote to
the Cardinal-Secretary (611). He mentioned that Moretta, the Ambassador from Savoy to the baptism, had not arrived in time for the ceremony.
Moretta, like Andrew Ker, had a part to play in the events at Kirk o'Field.

27th December, Friday.   The General Assembly of the Church of Scotland
resolved on a supplication to the Queen to ask for
the quashing of the consistorial powers of the Archbishop of St. Andrews,
granted four days before (391).

29th December, Sunday.   Mary and Bothwell returned to Stirling from
Drymen (361), and their journey may have been
prompted by learning the news that Darnley had absented himself and
was no doubt preparing to execute one or other of his plots.

30th December, Monday.   Mary and Bothwell visited Tullibardine, some 18
miles north of Stirling, where they only remained
one night. The Laird, Sir William Murray, was the brother of the Countess
of Mar, and he had been knighted by Darnley, whose man he was (361).
We may see in this an attempt to open negotiations with the Lennox
faction, and possibly an attempt also to discover to what extent Darnley's
plot to seize the Prince had proceeded, for Murray's brother-in-law, the
Earl of Mar, was the Prince's keeper. Buchanan alleges (179) impropriety
as the motive of the journey, but it hardly seems likely that Mary would
have gone to the house of one of her husband's adherents for such a purpose. As Mahon points out (497), it is certainly strange that she should
travel from Drymen to Stirling, passing Tullibardine, and then return
thither the following day. We can only assume that Darnley's evasion was
causing considerable confusion and indecision in the ranks of Mary's
followers.

Further light on the pardon of Andrew Ker is thrown by Bedford's
letter to Cecil of this date (64):

> "I have been six or eight days at St. Andrews and other places in
> Fife, where Moray and his friends have used me with much honour;
> so now I draw homeward as fast as I can. The Queen (Mary) has
> granted to Morton, Ruthven and Lindsay their relaxation and dress,
> wherein Moray has done very friendlily for them to the Queen, as I
> have by your advice. Bothwell, Athol, etc. helped therein, or it would
> not have been so soon have got. George Douglas (Darnley's illegiti-
> mate uncle) and Andrew Ker are specially excepted".

This whole letter bears out the hypothesis that the English Government
was involved, with Moray and Morton, in some device, which, as the
instructions to Bedford at his setting out suggest, was definitely adverse to
the Queen.

The Bishop of Mondovi at Paris has now heard of the baptism, although he errs as to its date, and he has also learnt that Mary has recovered from her illness (612).

31st December, Tuesday.   Mary returned to Stirling with Bothwell (361).
                            Labanoff is at fault in ascribing a letter (418) to Elizabeth to this date; the letter is dated "at our Palace of Holyrood house, the last day of December, and of our regime the 24th year", which clearly puts it in 1565.

1567

1st January, Wednesday.   Moretta, the laggard Savoyard Ambassador, arrived in Paris about now, and he seems to have seen Alava, the Spanish Ambassador, and the Bishop of Mondovi there (572); they would have been able to give him full details of the state of Darnley's affairs.

2nd January, Thursday.   At a meeting of the Privy Council at Stirling, the sederunt included Huntly, Argyll, Moray, Maitland and others, but Bothwell was not present (507), and we may conclude that, on this or the previous day, he had set out for the borders to meet Morton, whose return from banishment would be hourly expected, in circumstances which we have considered in connexion with Casket Letter I.

3rd January, Friday.   Mary wrote to Elizabeth (64), to thank her "dearest sister" for her good intentions with regard to the succession. She will proceed in this matter forthwith, and will send some of her Council to treat with Elizabeth.

5th January, Sunday.   Bedford left Stirling, carrying the above letter (361), and also Mary's answers and requests concerning the negotiations which the English Queen had opened with her. These are embodied in a memorial (66), of which only item No. 3 need detain us here; this item runs, "Her approval that Archduke Charles marry the Queen's majesty". Now, this may mean that Mary agrees to Elizabeth marrying that princely *pis aller* of high-born ladies, but that would hardly fit the circumstances, and Bedford's instructions from Elizabeth (355) make no mention of the possibility of the latter's marriage, although, it is true that Robert Melville, writing to the Archbishop of Glasgow, on 13th November, 1566, mentions such a possibility (656). On the other hand, negotiations concerning Mary's marriage to the Archduke had gone on almost continuously from the death of Francis II until her marriage with Darnley, and it seems possible that Mary asked for the sanction of the Queen of England to the union of the Archduke and herself. This could only mean that a divorce from Darnley was in consideration and must, in the nature of things, have been discussed with Bedford. Now, Mary cannot have discussed the question of Darnley's assassination with the English Ambassador, and, if she had, in fact, been contemplating such a deed, she would certainly have avoided any reference to her future marriage. The conclusion is, therefore, that Mary discussed with Bedford the intended divorce, perhaps even informing him of her husband's treachery and her intention of arraigning him, and opened the question of a foreign match, to which, in the past, Elizabeth had always been opposed, although less inimical to the Archduke than to the rest of Mary's foreign suitors.

6th January, Monday.   Maitland, Mary's Secretary of State, married Mary Fleming at Stirling (634). The bride was the daughter of Malcolm, 3rd Lord Fleming (123), and one of the Queen's 'Four Maries'. She was Maitland's second wife, for he was a widower, and the courtship had lasted nearly two and a half years.

On this same day, Bedford, who had left Stirling the day before, departed from Edinburgh. Such surprising haste indicates that he was carrying important messages.

We have seen (page 148) that the behaviour of Joseph Riccio and Joseph Lutini gives rise to the suspicion that they were participant in Darnley's plot. It was now that the latter received a passport to proceed to France "for some of our affairs". The document is signed "Marie R" and counter-signed "Riccio"; it is printed in Labanoff (404), where it is stated to be a contemporary copy. If the passport had been written by Riccio, who had forged the Queen's signature somewhat ineptly, this might account for the belief that it is a copy and not the original. Lutini probably left Stirling at once, but he proceeded no farther than Berwick, where he later met Moretta.

7th January, Tuesday.   On this day, Mary transferred the nomination of the Commissaries to the Court of Session (372), thus reversing her decision of 23rd December, by which she had restored the Archbishop of St. Andrews to his consistorial jurisdiction (178).

9th January, Thursday.   Darnley's illness receives its first notice in a letter written this day by Bedford at Berwick to Cecil (65). He writes,

> "I am now returned, having been well used in Fife by divers: and then took leave of the Queen, whose letters to her Majesty I bring myself, and also her hand to that agreed on for the matters I proposed to her. She says she will send some express messenger of honour and credit. I have long letters to you from the Secretary, and shall set out within these few days, as fast as I can on my own horses. The agreement between the Queen and her husband nothing amended . . .
> The King is now at Glasgow with his father, and there lieth full of the smallpox, to whom the Queen hath sent her physician. The jurisdiction in divers cases according to the canon laws, lately obtained from the Queen by the Bishop of St. Andrews, who meant to erect his court in Edinburgh, being found contrary to religion and not liked of the townsmen, has been revoked by her at the suit of Moray . . . . . Mor-

ton, having obtained his dress, is much beholden to you. Though some let (hindered) it all they could, his friends stuck to it and prevailed; wherein Bothwell, like a very friend, joined Moray, as did Athol and others".

10th January, Friday.   Morton, now at Berwick, and, as he himself says, on the point of entering Scotland, sent a letter of thanks to Cecil for his friendly offices (66). It may be expected that he arrived at Whittinghame on this or the succeeding day.

11th January, Saturday.   It was either on this day or a few days earlier that Mary at Stirling wrote to Bothwell on the borders the letter which we know as Casket Letter I. We learn from it that Mary intended to leave Stirling on Monday, 13th January, and would arrive at Craigmillar with her son two days later. Her health was still poor, and she was suffering from that same pain on which du Croc had commented a fortnight before. She was anxious to know how Bothwell had fared with the returned Morton, as well she might be, for, at such a critical juncture, a great deal would depend on the attitude of that powerful Earl. One may guess that Morton's pardon was one of the conditions which Elizabeth had stipulated for the promise of nomination of Mary to the succession of the English throne. Morton, betrayed by Darnley a year earlier, and a protégé of Elizabeth, now owing Mary gratitude for his 'relaxation and dress', might be expected to join with Bothwell and the Queen in thwarting Darnley's schemes, but his precise Protestantism might make an alliance with him difficult, and he was generally thought to be a shifty and treacherous character. Bothwell, therefore, was delegated to meet Morton and persuade him to assist the Government. Fourteen years later, Morton declared that the object of Bothwell's mission was to draw him into a plot for the murder of Darnley, in which he refused to be implicated, but since he said nothing of this at the sessions of the Commission, we can be sure that this is not true. Unfortunately, we do not know when Bothwell, who was apparently joined at Whittinghame by Maitland, returned to Edinburgh, but it may be assumed to have been a day or two before Mary set out for Glasgow, which she did on 20th January.

13th January, Monday.   Mary left Stirling with Prince James on this day, *en route* for Edinburgh. She spent the night at Callendar House (362), the home of Lord Livingstone, a short distance from Glasgow, which may account for the allusion in Casket Letter II, "Sir James Hamilton came to meet me, and told me that *the other time* when he (Lennox) heard of my coming, he departed away". Hay Fleming prints a warrant signed by the Queen and dated at Callendar on 16th January, but this is probably an error for 14th, confusion between xvi and xiv being very easy.

14th January, Tuesday.   Mary arrived in Edinburgh on this day, but whether she left her son at Craigmillar, or kept him at Holyrood (362), is unknown. Her object in bringing her son to Edinburgh or nearby is obvious: she knew that a plot was on foot to kidnap the Prince, and that this scheme emanated from Darnley and the Lennox faction. The Countess of Mar, wife of James' guardian at Stirling, was a member of a family devoted to the Lennox, while Edinburgh was strongly anti-Catholic in feeling. It could hardly have been wise for her to depart to the seat of government, leaving her son in such doubtful hands.

Maitland was still in Stirling at this date (358); it therefore seems likely that he joined Bothwell at Whitinghame on 15th or 16th, and that they would both have returned to Edinburgh by 17th or 18th, where Maitland certainly was on 17th (518). Bothwell's failure to reach an agreement with Morton and his inability, therefore, to send Mary the news which she so urgently awaited, may be regarded as the cause for the dispatch of her secretary to assist in the deliberations.

17th January, Friday.   Mary, at Edinburgh, wrote to Drury, the Marshal of Berwick, praying him to apprehend an Italian named Joseph (Lutini), her servant, who had lately left her charge and had fraudulently taken the goods and money of divers friends and companions (67). This suggests very strongly that the passport of 6th January in Lutini's favour was a forgery. It has already been suggested that it was Darnley who had appropriated the goods and monies, and that Joseph Riccio, in blaming Lutini, was trying to shield the King.

18th January, Saturday.   Moretta, the Savoyard Ambassador, reached London about now (572).

De Silva, the Spanish Ambassador in London, wrote to Philip II that Mary had been approached by some persons who wanted to induce her to allow a plot to be formed against Darnley (309). This sounds like a version of the Craigmillar incident of early December, but it may refer to the plan to arraign the King which we have postulated as the natural course of the Scottish Government at this time. It is to be noted that de Silva's information was that Mary had refused to allow such a plot to be carried out (278). If Moretta was de Silva's informant, this would fit in with that person's subsequent part in affairs at the time of Darnley's death, and the coincidence of his presence in London with de Silva's letter is not to be overlooked.

20th January, Monday.   On this date, Mary wrote to her Ambassador in Paris, Archbishop Beaton. We have already seen the contents of this letter (page 151), which is largely about the Walker-Highgate affair, mentioned in Casket Letter II. The great importance of the letter to Beaton is that it was signed by Mary at the moment of her departure to Glasgow, when her mind must have been full of Darnley's treachery and her own efforts to thwart him. Indeed, her indignation is apparent in the outburst with which the letter concludes (408):

"And for the King our husband, God knows always our part towards him, and his behaviour and thankfulness to us is similarly well known to God and the world, specially our own indifferent (i.e. unprejudiced) subjects sees it, and, in their hearts we doubt not, condemns the same. Always we perceive him occupied and busy enough to have inquisition of our doings which, God willing, shall always be such as none shall have occasion to be offended with them, or to report us in any ways but honourably; howsoever, he, his father and their fautors (part-takers) speak, which we know want no good will to make us have ado, if their power were equivalent to their minds. But God moderates their forces well enough, and takes the mean of execution of their pretences from them, for, as we believe, they shall find none, or very few, approvers of their counsels and devices imagined to our displeasure or misliking".

Soon after this letter was written, Mary proceeded to Callendar House, where she probably remained two nights, while her escort of Hamiltons gathered to accompany her into Glasgow. Bothwell was with her on the journey to Callendar. It was here that, according to his deposition, Bothwell's servant, French Paris, first entered into credit with the Queen.

21st January, Tuesday. Bothwell left Callendar House, and returned to Edinburgh (452).

22nd January, Wednesday. Mary arrived in Glasgow, having met various persons outside the town, as described in Casket Letter II. The date of her arrival is vouched for by Drury, writing from Berwick (451).

On the same day, du Croc left Edinburgh for Paris; and Pius V wrote a congratulatory letter to Mary for having her son baptised with the rites of the Catholic Church (613).

23rd January, Thursday. Mary wrote to Bothwell, as we have seen, the second or earlier part of Casket Letter II, in which she described her conversation with Darnley. Drury's letter of this date to Cecil confirms many of the events which we have been discussing. It runs (736),

"Right Honourable; As this bearer, Mr. Throckmorton, hath, by some necessary business of his own, occasion to repair to the court, so I have something not unmeet to advertise, which is that, at my arrival here, my Lord of Bedford being departed, I found here one Joseph (Lutini), an Italian, and a gentleman who had served the Queen of Scots, and dispatched with her good favour and licence towards France about certain of her Grace's affairs, as by the copy of his passport, accompanied herewith, may appear; who, taking this town in his way, through weak constitution of health made his stay here for his better recovery; in which meantime, I received a letter from the Queen of Scots, purporting a request to apprehend and stay him for that he had, against the laws, taken goods and monies from some of his fellows, as by the copy of the letter sent herewith your honour may be informed at length, which since, as appeareth by one that pursueth him, the Queen's tailor, is but some old reckoning between them; and therefore giveth me to think by that I can gather as well of the matter as of the gentleman, that it is not it that the Queen seeketh so much as to recover his person. For, as I have learned, the man had credit there, and now the Queen mistrusteth lest he should offer his service here in England, and thereby might, with better occasion, utter something either prejudicial to her or that she would be loath should be disclosed but to those she pleaseth. Whereupon I have thought good to stay the man till such time as the Queen's Majesty's (Elizabeth's) pleasure, or my Lords of the Council, be signified unto me, which the sooner it be, the more shall the poor stranger be eased.

The occurrents are: the Lord Darnley lieth sick at Glasgow of the smallpox, unto whom the Queen came yesterday; that disease beginneth to spread there. The Lord Morton lieth at the Lord of Whittinghame's, where the Lord Bothwell and (Maitland) came of late to visit. He standeth in good terms for his peace. Here we look for (Maitland) or Melville very shortly to repair. This evening arrived here the Ambassador of Savoy, Monsieur de Moretta. The return this way of Monsieur du Croc is also looked for here. Thus, having nothing farther to trouble your honour, I humbly take my leave. From Berwick, this 23rd January, 1567".

24th January, Friday. Du Croc met Moretta some twelve miles North of Berwick, and turned back to accompany the latter as far as Dunbar (522).

On this day, also, Bothwell departed from Edinburgh on a visit to Liddesdale (450).

25th January, Saturday. Du Croc and Moretta separated at Dunbar, the former proceeding South "by easy stages", the latter going to Edinburgh (573).

26th January, Sunday. As we have seen, this is the probable date of the first or later part of Casket Letter II from Mary to Moray, in which the events at her arrival in Glasgow are described.

Drury wrote that Mary would return from Glasgow, if no danger to Darnley's health would arise from cold weather, on 27th January (529).

Moretta had arrived in Edinburgh the day previously. He had seen Lutini in Berwick, and he now saw Riccio, with the result that the latter wrote a frantic letter to Joseph Lutini (738),

"I have told the Queen and Timothy that you have taken my money, and the reason why I said it and for whom, you will understand. When we had returned from Stirling (14th January), Timothy asked where were your horses and clothes. I told him that your clothes were in your box, and Lorenzo Cagnoli told him that you had taken everything with you, together with your horses, and that you had told him, 'I have properly tricked the secretary (Joseph Riccio) because he thinks that my clothes are in my box, but there is nothing there'. When Timothy heard this, he began to say, 'Thus have you tricked me, Mr Secretary; the Queen shall do me right in this matter'. And so he found Bastian and made him tell the Queen that I had assured him that you were gone for her affairs, and, on that, he had lent me a hundred scudi, and everyone began to say that there was some knavery afoot, and that I knew of it, and that you had put your hand among the Queen's papers; and I, who did not wish to be so suspected, began to say that you had carried away six Portuguese (pieces) and five nobles, and that you had promised to leave me your horses; and the Queen immediately asked me, 'Where are my bracelets?', and I said that you had taken them away with you, and that they were in your purse with my money; and Bastian began to say that you owed him sixty francs; and everyone began to say, 'It is necessary to send after him', and they did so much that the Queen commanded (Maitland) to send a letter to have you stopped on the road.

Meanwhile, Monsieur de Moretta arrived here, who says that you told him that I was the cause that you took this journey. Take heed of what you say, for if you say for whom you have gone, we shall both be in real trouble. I have always said that you had gone because you had taken money, and to let the anger which the Queen had against you die down, and that I had advised you to do so, and that I had lent you money to make this journey, the sum of sixty scudi and two Portuguese (pieces), so that you can still say the same; and I said that, the money which you have taken from me, you would give back when you were returned from France, and thus shall you and I both be excused. And if you do otherwise, you will be the cause of my ruin, and I think that you would not wish to see me ruined. For the love of God, act as if I were your son, and I pray you for the love of God and of the good friendship which you have borne me, and I, you, to say as I tell you, which is that you are making this journey to bring back your money; and to let the Queen's anger subside, and the suspicion which she has of you; and the money which I said you have taken from me, that you have taken it, for fear that you should happen to lack in your journey, and that you would restore it when you were returned, and that it was not necessary that I should have made so much trouble; and that you are a man of wealth, and that you would not have taken it without returning it to me, because I was always your friend, and you would never have thought that I would have made such a fuss of it. And I pray you not to want to be the cause of my ruin, and if you say as I tell you, you shall be excused, and I also.

The Queen sent to you by word of mouth to take them (the bracelets?) with you; take care of yourself that you remember it, take care that she does not rattle you with her speech, as you know well; and she has told me that she wants to speak to you in private, and take care to speak as I have written and not otherwise, so that our words, if she confront the one with the other (may be the same), and neither you nor I shall be in any trouble whatever, and I beg you to do as I have written and not otherwise. Let me know before you come here what you wish, and I pray you to have pity on me and not to be the cause of my death; and by doing as I send you word, you shall be in no trouble, nor I as well, and I shall be evermore obliged to you, and you will find that I shall recognise it in such a manner as will content you for it of me, and I pray you to want to write to me by express messenger before you arrive here what you wish to say, so that I may not be in more trouble than I am.

I am not going to write anything more now, because I shall tell you it when you are here, and I pray you to have pity on me and on yourself, because if you say otherwise than that which I have written, you will be in trouble as well as I.

Praying God that He give you happiness. From Edinburgh this Sunday,

Your all-but brother
Joseph Riccio

I beg you to burn this letter as soon as you have read it".

From the disjointed and repetitive style of this letter, we see that Joseph Riccio was a very worried man; something Moretta had said therefore caused him great disquiet. We may guess the sequence of events to have been after this fashion: Darnley took money and horses and such jewellery as he could lay his hands on before departing from Stirling, for money was scarce in sixteenth century Scotland and, whichever plan he put into operation for the seizure of the throne, he would need all the money he could get. Lutini was his confederate in this and he probably also had some message to give to Moretta from Darnley and, in any case, it would be as well to be out of the way: he therefore persuaded Riccio to forge a passport and he then proceeded to Berwick, where he awaited the arrival of Moretta, pleading ill-health as the excuse for not continuing his journey. Meanwhile, Mary discovered the thefts, and Riccio, who had a guilty conscience and suspected more perhaps than he knew, tried to cover up, blaming Lutini, and putting his defalcation in as good light as possible. Mary, however, sent to Berwick to cause Lutini's arrest, which was carried out; she then proceeded to Glasgow with yet another trouble to carry in her mind, although she may not have realised its full implications. Drury, suspecting that there was more in the matter than appeared on the surface, did not return the servant as requested, but retained him until he had received instructions from London. It is possible that Lutini never received Riccio's letter, but that it was intercepted by Drury. Moretta saw Lutini in Berwick and, on arriving in Edinburgh, the Queen still being absent at Glasgow, put the fear of death into Riccio. From this it may be concluded that Moretta knew of the device intended by Darnley against the Queen. Was it for his arrival in Scotland that the King was waiting when he refused to leave Glasgow "until after to-morrow?"

27th January, Monday. Mary and Darnley perhaps began the return journey to Edinburgh on this day, although they may have remained at Glasgow another night. They seem to have passed the first night at Kilsyth, twelve miles from Glasgow (513). Since Darnley was travelling in a litter, the journey had to be made in easy stages.

On this day, Archbishop Beaton in Paris wrote a letter of warning to the Queen (341). After writing about several other matters, he continues,

"For none of the heads preceding thought I to have dispatched expressly towards your Majesty, if by the Ambassador of Spain I had not been required thereto, and specially to advertise you to take heed of yourself. I have heard some murmuring in likewise by others, that there be some surprise to be trafficked in your contrary, but he would never let me know of no particular, only assured me he had written to his master to know if by that way he can try any farther, and that he was advertised and counselled to cause me haste towards you herewith. Further in this instance, and at his desire partly, I spoke earnestly to know at the Queen-Mother (Catherine dei Medici) if she had heard any discourse or advertisement lately, tending to your hurt or disadvantage, but I came no speed, nor would she confess that she had got nor heard any such appearance, and that both the Comte de Brienne, and, since then, the Ambassador la Forrest, have assured (me) that your affairs were at very good point. In like manner that Robert Stewart had shewn her that you had forgiven my Lords of Morton, Ruthven and Lindsay, so she thought there was nothing to be feared, and approved greatly the ruth and pity you had of your own (people), and appeared to be very content that you had so graciously treated them, which she esteemed the right way to hold you at ease, and saw nothing that might stop it, except if it were the variance between you and the King, which she desired God to appease among the rest of your traverses and cumbers; for it would be a great mean to compass more easily all your designs and enterprises, and in special it would occasion that Madame of Lennox, whom she knew well favoured by a great part of the nobility of England, would concur with you . . . . . finally, I would beseech your Majesty, right humbly to cause the Captains of your Guard be diligent in their office, for, notwithstanding that I have no particular occasion whereon I desire it, yet can I not be out of fear until I hear of your news. I desire with all my heart, if it shall be your pleasure, it must be with the same bearer (Robert Dury). And so I pray the eternal Lord God to preserve your Majesty from all dangers, with long life and good health. At Paris, the 27th day of January, 1567".

The Archbishop of Glasgow, therefore, knew that some device was being prepared to the Queen's disadvantage, and his knowledge came from the Spanish Ambassador and "by others". He hastened to dispatch a warning, but it came too late, for Mary did not receive his letter until the day after the explosion at Kirk o'Field.

These circumstances support the view that the Spanish Ambassador, Alava, knew of Darnley's projected attempt to murder the Queen. His information to Beaton was too late to be of service to Mary and was, in any case, so tenuous as to have been of little or no value had it arrived in time, but it served his turn, for, as we see from Beaton's letter, rumours were already spreading in Paris, and, by taking the bull by the horns, Alava was disarming any subsequent suspicion of the part played by Spain.

28th January, Tuesday. Mary and Darnley seem to have reached Callendar House, some nine or ten miles beyond Kilsyth (513).

Evidence of Bothwell's visit to Liddesdale appears in a letter from Scrope to Cecil of this date (509), "Yesterday the Earl of Bothwell on the sudden did make a journey from Jedburgh into Liddesdale and did apprehend a dozen persons or thereabouts . . . . ". They were counterattacked by a gang of Elliots and "if good hap had not chanced, the Earl himself had been in great peril" (279). Bothwell's behaviour in carrying out a normal border raid against the moss-troopers is hardly consonant with the theory that he was involved in a plot for the imminent destruction of Darnley.

29th January, Wednesday. Mary and Darnley probably reached Linlithgow, about 10 miles beyond Callendar and sixteen from Edinburgh, and here they stayed one or two nights (513).

31st January, Friday. By this date, Mary, Darnley and Bothwell had all reached Edinburgh (180). We know that Darnley had himself made choice of Kirk o'Field for his lodging until the doctors would pronounce him free from contagion and he could return to Holyrood, for his servant, Thomas Nelson, later deposed (20):

"The deponer remembers it was devised in Glasgow that the King should have lain at Craigmillar, but, because he had no will thereof, the purpose was altered, and conclusion taken that he should lie beside the Kirk o'Field, at which time this deponer believed ever that he should have had the Duke's house, and knew no other house until the

King alighted, at which time he passed directly to the said Duke's house, thinking it to be the lodging prepared for him. But the contrary was shewn him by the Queen, who conveyed him to the other house (the Old Provost's Lodging), and, at his coming thereto, the chamber was hung, and a new bed of black figured velvet standing therein.".

The Duke of Châtelherault's house was on the northern side of the church; the two Provost's lodgings, the Old and the New, lay to the East. Darnley must have been familiar with Hamilton House, but he cannot have believed that he was to be lodged in the home of his hereditary enemies, and one may see, in his pretending to go to it, a subterfuge, an attempt to impress on bystanders his own ignorance of the lodging to which he was going. Furthermore, the preparations for receiving the royal lodger can only have been completed on 31st January at earliest, for Servais de Condé, Mary's Major-Domo, said, on 20th May, 1567 (641), that the furniture was delivered there in February; a mistake on his part of one day is permissible, but he would not have been much further out in his reckoning.

Darnley was now lodged in the Old Provost's House at Kirk o'Field. Before his arrival there two things had happened: Moretta, the Ambassador of the King of Savoy, and also representing the King of Spain, had arrived in Edinburgh, and Sir James Balfour had made preparations for the *coup d'état*. The New Provost's House, which abutted on the western end of Darnley's lodging, was in the possession of Balfour's brother, and he had laid in an adequate supply of gunpowder. We have evidence of this in a letter of Drury to Cecil of 28th February, 1567 (739); in it, he writes, "There is one of Edinburgh who affirms how Mr. James Balfour bought of him powder as much as he should have paid three score pounds Scottish." Presumably, in order to avoid suspicion, the powder would have been obtained in fairly small quantities (£60 Scots was equivalent to about £5 sterling) from different sources. As we shall see, certain preparations for the disposal of the gunpowder in the cellar of Darnley's lodging had also to be carried out, and this would necessarily have been done before the King's arrival with his servants and guards. Since the choice of Kirk o'Field was Darnley's, and was not made known by him until after 25th January (see Casket Letter II), Mary, and Bothwell who was by then on his way to Liddesdale, can have had nothing to do with these preparations.

Darnley, was to have his bath and be free to mix with the world on Sunday, 9th February, yet he was not to return to Holyrood until the following day. It is difficult to explain this prolongation of his sequestration other than by his own desire. On Sunday, Bastian and Christina Hogg were to be married, and Darnley knew that Mary would attend the masque at the Palace that evening. She would certainly return and stay the night with him, for she had promised to "be at bed and board with him as before", and this was the first night on which he would be free from all infection. Her absence, at the masque, would provide an excellent opportunity to remove the powder from the adjacent house to his own cellars: Darnley had ten days to wait before he would be King indeed.

CHAPTER II

Kirk o'Field

The details of the buildings at Kirk o'Field are taken from the extremely careful and accurate reconstruction of them which Mahon has described in his "Tragedy of Kirk o'Field", to which work the reader is referred for further information. There can be no doubt as to the correctness of Mahon's reconstruction, verified as it is by a number of confirmatory facts.

The Collegiate Church of St. Mary in the Fields lay immediately inside the southern portion of the Flodden Wall, as the town wall of Edinburgh was called. A short distance to the North lay Hamilton House, the "Duke's Lodging", whilst opposite the eastern end of the church was a complex of buildings, also within the Flodden Wall, set aside for the Church dignitaries. These buildings formed a square, surrounding a courtyard, the southern side of which was occupied by the two houses with which this story is concerned. The most westerly, which faced towards the church, was the New Provost's House, owned at this date by Robert Balfour, brother of Sir James Balfour, the King's henchman. It was here that the gunpowder was stored until the evening of 9th February. The remainder of the southern side of the quadrangle was formed by the Old Provost's Lodging, a somewhat rambling, L-shaped building, in which Darnley lived from the time of his arrival in Edinburgh on 31st January until his death ten days later.

This house had originally looked on to a considerable garden on its southern side, but the building of the Flodden Wall had closed its aspect on this side and the garden was now separated from the house, not only by the town-wall and the clear space outside it which was necessitated by military considerations, but also by the northern wall of the garden which the building of the town wall had rendered necessary. It was in this garden that the bodies of Darnley and his servant, William Taylor, were discovered after the explosion which completely destroyed the Old Provost's Lodging.

The ground fell steeply from West to East, and the King's lodging stood upon vaults which necessarily increased in height, being tallest under the short leg of the 'L', the long leg of which abutted on the back of the New

267

Provost's House and ran parallel to the Flodden Wall. This part of the building consisted of a single large room (the Salle) which was nearly fifty feet long, and, during Darnley's visit, would be used as a reception room. The vaults below were about 6 feet deep at the eastern and only 2 feet deep at the western ends respectively. Probably the eastern end was used as a store room.

Since it was here that the gunpowder was to be placed, the preparations must have included the excavation of a considerable amount of soil and the opening of a doorway between the vault at its western end and the New Provost's House.

The Salle was separated from the remainder of the building by a passage-way at its eastern end, under the landing which joined the two parts of the house. The vaults on both sides could be entered only from this passage-way, that on the East, under the short leg of the 'L' being used as a kitchen. This passage-way led from the courtyard, under the house, to a door or postern in the Flodden Wall by which access was gained to the South Garden. The main entrance to the house was from the courtyard, where a door, immediately to the East of this passage-way, gave on to a 'turnpike' stair. The short leg of the 'L' consisted of three floors: the basement kitchen (entered only from the passage-way above-mentioned) and, on the first storey, the Queen's bedroom, with, above it, the King's bedroom. Each of these rooms was entered through a small closet or garderobe, and seems to have been 16 or 17 feet in length by about 10 feet in width, internal dimensions. A side door, presumably reached by a flight of steps outside, faced eastwards immediately behind the turnpike stair, between it and the Queen's bedroom, and gave on to a small landing which joined the stairway to the Queen's bedroom and the Salle.

The King's bedroom had a small projecting gallery on its southern side. The Flodden Wall skirted this part of the building so closely that the window of the gallery was incorporated in the rampart and the floor at this point must actually have rested on the "battling plane", or footway, behind the rampart. It was to this fact that Thomas Nelson owed his life, for, when the house disintegrated in the explosion, he was left standing on the "battling plane" of the wall, where, of course, he would be invisible to the ambush in the South Garden. The "battling plane" at this point was probably not more than 13 feet above ground level.

Eastward of the Old Provost's lodging, at a distance of about 200 yards, lay the deserted Blackfriars' monastery, and, at this point, the Flodden Wall had not been completed. It was through this gap that Mary was wont to come to Kirk o'Field, thus avoiding traversing the city, approaching the King's lodging from the East along the track which accompanied the town wall. There must have been a small window in the eastern end of Darnley's bedroom which would render this path visible to those within the house.

That the gunpowder was actually placed below the Salle and not in the Queen's bedroom is conclusively shewn by Mahon. The main points of the argument are that the vaults themselves were destroyed, which can only have occurred if the powder were beneath them, for the crushing of vaults downward is quite incredible; that the 'Picture', sent by an anonymous spy to Cecil and which yet remains in the Record Office, shews the eastern gable as the only part of the house left standing; and that, at the trial of the Earl of Morton in 1581, the indictment bears that, "Powder had been a little of before, placed and put in under the ground and angular stones and within the vaults, low and dern (hidden) parts and places of the lodging" (526). To this we may add that, when Mary visited Darnley on the evening of 9th February, she must have been attended by several ladies-in-waiting. At this time of the year, Edinburgh is distinctly cold, and, when they left, late in the evening, to attend the masque at Holyrood, they must have collected their wraps from the Queen's bedroom, for there was nowhere else that these could have been left. The gunpowder, therefore, could not have been introduced into the Queen's bedroom during the time of her visit, as was later to be claimed.

When Darnley arrived at Kirk o'Field, his plot for the destruction of the Queen and such nobles as should attend her on her return from Holyrood after the masque must have been complete to the last detail, the house must already have been prepared and the gunpowder stored in the adjacent New Provost's House. We cannot say at what point the Lords of the Congregation became aware of the plot. They had, however, already shewn signs of forming a confederation against Darnley and they apparently had the support of the English Government in a general conspiracy for the overthrow of both the King and the Queen, although the *modus operandi* of this plot cannot have been decided. They probably obtained the details which enabled their subsequent action from Sir James Balfour shortly before or very soon after the King's arrival at Kirk o'Field. They knew that Darnley would light the fuse at the moment of the Queen's return, as soon, in fact, as he saw her entourage approaching from the Blackfriars, and that he would then escape from the house through the gallery window of his room, using a chair, shewn in the 'Picture', to assist in lowering himself from the sill. There were two or three small cottages beside the South Garden, and here the Lords decided, to place their ambush. Mary and, presumably, Bothwell, Huntly and some others would perish in the explosion, but Darnley would also die by their hands and the regency would automatically pass to Moray.

1567

31st January, Friday.   Mary, Darnley and Bothwell had all returned to Edinburgh, and Darnley had taken up residence at Kirk o'Field, being still infected. His convalescence was to end on 9th February and the event would be signalised by a bath.

5th February, Wednesday.	Mary apparently slept at Kirk o'Field on this night, as she may also have done on other occasions (439).

7th February, Friday.	Mary apparently wrote to Drury to repeat her demand for the return of Lutini (696). On receipt of this letter, Drury wrote to Cecil for instructions: Lutini had told him that "He doubteth much danger, and so affirmeth unto me, that if he return (to Scotland), he utterly despaireth of any better speed than a prepared death" (737).

Darnley also wrote to his father at Glasgow; we may discredit Lennox's account of this letter (514): it is probable that he wrote to confirm the part which Lennox was to play on the night of 9th–10th February. His presence in the neighbourhood would be required to provide timely assistance to the King.

Mary again slept at Kirk o'Field (439), and it was during this night that she was alleged to have written Casket Letter IV concerning the plan to cause a quarrel between Darnley and Lord Robert Stewart on the following day. She was also presumed to have written Casket Letter V at about this date, concerning the approaching marriage of Margaret Carwood.

8th February, Saturday.	Mary dispatched Sir Robert Melville to London to continue the negotiations begun by Bedford; unfortunately his instructions have not been preserved. He carried a short letter from Mary and another from Maitland (68). The Queen also busied herself in charitable matters: Bastian (Sebastian Pages) and Christina Hogg, who were to be married on the following day, received material for a wedding dress; and Margaret Carwood, who was to marry John Stewart on 12th February, received a similar gift (694), and also a pension of 300 marks a year (638).

It was also on this day that the quarrel occurred between Mary's half-brother, the Lord Robert Stewart, and her husband (454). Moray was either present, or was called in by Mary to separate the quarrellers; a fact which proves conclusively that Mary did not organise the dispute in order that Darnley might be killed, as Buchanan alleges (14).

9th February, Sunday.	There can be no certainty on which day Darnley had his bath. The probability is that the ceremonial cleansing took place on this day, because, otherwise, it would have been difficult to rationalise his continued stay at Kirk o'Field until the time of the masque of Bastian's wedding. According to Lennox (514), Mary took "such pains about him that, being in his bath, would suffer none to handle him but herself."

The marriage of Sebastian Pages and Christina Hogg took place in the morning and was followed by a dinner at midday, at which the Queen was present (639). In the course of the morning (432), Moray sought and

obtained permission to leave Edinburgh, alleging that his wife was ill at
St. Andrews and that he wished to go to her.

At 4 o'clock in the afternoon, Mary accompanied by Argyll, Bothwell,
Huntly and Cassillis, supped in the Canongate at the house of the Bishop
of the Isles (639); it was a farewell dinner for Moretta, the Savoyard
Ambassador, who was to leave on the following day. The entertainment
over, Mary and her retinue repaired to Kirk o'Field, where they arrived
probably between 7 and 8 o'clock (530). There they remained until about
10 or 11 o'clock, when they left Darnley in order that the Queen might
attend the masque at Holyrood. It was subsequently alleged that it was
during this period that the gunpowder was placed in Mary's room, but
this would clearly have been difficult because the attendant lords and
ladies would have had servants and bodyguards who would have so
cluttered up the courtyard, doorways and passages that such an intrusion
by six or seven men each carrying a bag containing perhaps 40 lb. of
powder, to say nothing of a barrel so large as to stick in the doorway, is
quite incredible. The barrel was abandoned in the garden, where it was
later found, and it is by no means impossible that the 'marks' on it were
intended as a clue to point suspicion in the required direction: in other
words, that it was a 'plant'. Bothwell himself records (331) that the "Lords
of the Council . . . found a barrel or cask in which the powder had been,
which we preserved, having taken note of the mark upon it". That Mary's
decision to return to Holyrood was not suddenly remembered or announced is made quite clear by Mahon (531), to whom the reader is
referred for the arguments on this point, of which the most important is
that, had it been understood that she was to stay all night, her horses
would have been taken away to the stables, of which there were apparently
none at Kirk o'Field, and she would have had no means of conveyance.
That she would have walked to Holyrood a mile away at that time of night
is quite unthinkable. That she would return to Kirk o'Field after the masque
is stated by the Venetian Ambassador in Paris, whose informant was
Moretta (505).

Mary apparently only stayed a short time at the masque (69), and then,
according to Buchanan (15),

"After that she was come into her chamber, she was in long talk with
Bothwell, none being present but the Captain of her Guard (John
Stewart of Traquair). And when he also withdrew himself, Bothwell
was then left alone, without other company, and shortly after retired
into his own chamber. He changed his apparel, because he would be
unknown to such as met him, and put on a loose cloak such as
'Swartrytters' wear, and so went forward through the Watch".

We can only guess what happened at this meeting, but it is at least
certain that no one ever accused Traquair of complicity in the murder of
Darnley, and, in any case, if Mary and Bothwell were the guilty parties,

what need was there for this 'long talk'? All the arrangements had been made and, if the servants of Bothwell alleged to be sitting beside the pile of gunpowder in the Queen's bedroom at Kirk o'Field had had any sense, they would have lit the fuse and escaped long before: the King was above them and there was no need to tarry. We may guess that Bothwell, who had, no doubt, received his information from Sir James Balfour or Sandy Durham, disclosed Darnley's plot and, after long argument, Traquair was despatched to increase the guard on the infant Prince, for Darnley's *coup d'état* must have included a plan for the seizure of this important pawn (539). Finally, Bothwell himself received permission to proceed to Kirk o'Field, arrest the King, and produce evidence of his culpability.

Presumably, as soon as Mary and her retinue withdrew from the King's lodging, his servants began to carry the gunpowder from the New Provost's House to the cellar under the 'Salle' and prepare the fuse, for it would be in the room above that Mary would take leave of her noble escort on her return. When all was ready, Darnley would take up his station at the eastern window of his bedroom, watching for the torches which would betoken the arrival of his wife by the 'privy' way from the gap in the wall at Blackfriars, at the sight of which he would give the signal to light the fuse, and he and his servants, of whom he had six (538), would have escaped from the window which pierced the town-wall. Help was at hand, for Andrew Kerr was in the neighbourhood (317), and it may be he who is shewn in the 'Picture' with several horses not far from the South Garden.

Meanwhile, the Lords of the Congregation quietly installed their ambush in the cottages beside the South Garden. The great Lords, no doubt, were absent and had left the deed to their servants, some of whom, such as Archibald Douglas, who was undoubtedly present, were men of position.

10th February, Monday.   Bothwell, having left the Queen at about 1 o'clock, gathered some of his servants, and left Holyrood. Had he obeyed the instructions which we have imagined the Queen to have given, he would have surrounded the house and waited to arrest the King as soon as he should emerge; had he been in league with those who set the ambush in the South Garden, he would have approached the house at Kirk o'Field by way of the gap in the wall at the Blackfriars; had he been merely reconnoitring he would have gone by the least expected route, approaching from the North by way of the Horse Wynd. From the agreement in the depositions of four of his servants who were executed for the murder, we know that he entered the city by the Netherbow Port, waking the porter for the purpose, and giving his name to him, passed to the Blackfriars and struck into Mary's 'privy way' from inside the town wall. Approaching in this way, he avoided contact with those in ambush and, since he would not be one of those who slew the King, indeed he had saved the Queen's life, his conscience was clear, and he had no hesitation in announcing his name both to the guard at Holyrood and to the porter at the Netherbow. Nevertheless he must have known that, in passing to Kirk o'Field by way of the Blackfriars, Darnley would mistake him and his servants for Mary and her entourage, and would set in motion the train of events which would inevitably end in his own death.

So it fell out; Darnley ordered the fuse to be lit, escaped from the house, and he and his servant, William Taylor, were strangled in the garden; Nelson escaped, as we have described: the remaining servants perished in the explosion (318), and Bothwell's main obstacle in his path to the throne had been removed. It was said (419) that some women who lived near the garden, perhaps even in one of the cottages where the ambush was set, heard the King cry out, "Have pity, kinsmen, for the love of Him who had pity on all the world". Archibald Douglas was a relation of Darnley's mother.

From the depositions of Hay, Powrie, Dalgleish and Hepburn, we know that Bothwell was with them close to Kirk o'Field at the time of the explosion, upon which they made their way with all speed to the north-eastern corner of the city, intending to jump the wall but, finding it too high, they returned to the Netherbow, woke the porter, and passed down the Canongate to Holyrood where, giving Bothwell's name to the guard once again, they entered. Bothwell then proceeded to have a drink, undressed and went to bed where he feigned sleep until the arrival of the news of the explosion and the King's death. The latter part of this statement is quite incredible, for the news of the explosion, which must have roused the town, for Clernault reported (on 16th February) that it was equal to a volley of twenty-five or thirty canon (665), cannot have taken long in being brought to the Palace. Bothwell may have reached Holyrood before the exact site of the explosion was known there, but he cannot have had time to 'call for a draught', undress and get into bed before the place would have been in a furore.

According to Bothwell's own account (331), he

"being in my bed with my first princess, the sister of Earl Huntly, her brothers came in the morning to inform me of the King's death, at which I was highly distressed, as also many other noblemen with me. The said Earl of Huntly was of opinion that a Council should be held immediately, to deliberate about the means of apprehending the traitors who had committed the said deed. Then we were ordered by the Queen, who was greatly distressed and afflicted, with the Lords of the Council aforesaid, to gather together some soldiers, in order to make a diligent search for the said traitors, and apprehend them. This we did, and, coming to the house where the King lay a corpse, we first put his body under a guard of honour . . . . In our fury we apprehended some persons suspected of the deed, and put them under arrest, until they should render to us a sure account of the place they had been when the murder was committed. Nor did I ever cease making strict search that I might get at the bottom of the whole; for I could not imagine that I could ever be suspected. Some Lords of the Council, fearing lest the Queen and myself should make inquires respecting them, united themselves and manoeuvred against the Queen and the rest of us, in order to prevent our arriving at any certainty".

Apart from the announcement of the King's death, this story is probably more or less correct. Certainly the Council met, and directed a letter to Catherine dei Medici, which is important as the first account of the murder (344).

"Madam, the strange event which occurred in this town last night constrains us to be bold to write briefly to you, in order to give you and yours to understand the miserable deed which has been perpetrated on the person of the King, in such a strange manner that one has never heard tell of a similar affair. At about two hours after midnight, he being in his bed, his lodging was blown into the air by force of powder, as one might judge by the noise and the terrible and sudden event, which was so vehement that, of a 'salle', two bedrooms, cabinet and garderobe, nothing remains which was not carried far away and reduced to powder, not only the roof and floors, but also the walls to the foundation, so that not one stone rests on another. And those, that are the authors of this evil, only just failed in destroying the Queen by the same means, with a great part of the nobles and Lords who are for the present in her suite, who were there with the King in his room until nearly midnight. And her Majesty only just failed to remain in order to lodge there all the night, but God has been so kind to us, that these assassins were frustrated in half their attempt, He having reserved her Majesty to take vengeance such a barbarous and inhuman deed deserves. We are engaged in an enquiry, and we doubt not that shortly we shall arrive at a knowledge of those who did it. For God will never permit such a mischief to remain hidden, and, having once uncovered the matter, your Majesty and all the world shall know that Scotland will not long endure that such a cause for shame should rest upon her shoulders and which would be enough to render her hateful to all Christianity, if similar wickednesses should lie hidden or unpunished. We did not wish to miss making this advertisement to the King's Majesty and yourself by this gentleman, present bearer, the Seigneur de Clernault, who will relate to you all the details, since he is well informed to this end. His sufficience is such that we leave the rest to him, so as not, with a longer letter, to importune your Majesty, whose hands we kiss, and we pray God, Madam to have you in His holy keeping. From Edinburgh this 10th February, 1567. (signed)

Archbishop of Saint Andrews, Argyll, Huntly, Athol, Cassillis, Bothwell, Caithness, Sutherland, Alexander Bishop of Galloway, John Bishop of Ross, Robertson Treasurer, Livingstone, Fleming, Bellenden, Secretary Maitland".

As a matter of fact, Clernault did not leave Edinburgh until the following day. Presumably, the letter was written rather late, after Moretta had already departed. We may imagine that, had Darnley's plot succeeded, the Savoyard would have remained to give comfort and counsel to the new ruler.

We do not know what other steps the Council took, but we can imagine that the day was too full of bustle for much to be done in the way of examining witnesses and those who had been apprehended. As for Mary herself, it is highly significant that she did not sign the letter to her mother-in-law: a few days later she described herself as "grevious and tormented" and it may well be thought that this latest event produced such a nervous shock as to render her at least temporarily incapable of transacting business. The fact that Margaret Carwood this day received payment for her wedding dress (607) does not contradict this point of view, for the gift had been made, as we have seen, on 8th February.

CHAPTER III

After Kirk o'Field

1567

11th February, Shrove Tuesday. Archbishop Beaton's warning letter of 27th January had arrived the previous day, so when Clernault set out, he carried not only the letter from the Lords of the Council to the Queen-Mother, but also a letter from the Queen to her Ambassador in Paris. That this letter was not drafted by Mary appears from the manner in which it so closely parallels the letter of the Lords to Catherine dei Medici, and from the fact that it is in Scotch, which Mary never wrote. It runs (689):

"Most Reverent Father in God and trusty counsellor, we greet you well. We have received this morning your letters of 27th January, by your servant, Robert Dury, containing in one part such advertisement as we find by effect overtrue, albeit the success has not altogether been such as the authors of that mischievous fact had preconceived and had put it in execution, and if God in His mercy had not preserved us, as we trust, to the end we may take a vigorous vengeance of that mischievous deed, which, before it should remain unpunished, we had rather lose life and all. The matter is horrible and so strange, as we believe the like was never heard of in any country. This night past, being 9th February, a little after two hours after midnight, the house wherein the King was lodged was in an instant blown in the air, he lying sleeping in his bed, with such a vehemency that, of the whole lodging, walls and other, there is nothing remained, no, not a stone above another, but all either carried far away or dung in dross to the very ground-stone. It must be done by force of powder, and appears to have been a mine; by whom it has been done or in what manner, it appears not as yet. We doubt not but, according to the diligence our Council has begun already to use, the certainty of all shall be used shortly; and the same being discovered which we wot God will never suffer to lie hid, we hope to punish the same with such rigour as shall serve for example of this cruelty to all ages to come. Always, whoever

276

has taken this wicked enterprise in hand, we assure ourselves it was dressed as well for us as for the King; for we lay the most part of all the last week in that same lodging, and was there accompanied with the most part of the Lords that are in this town that same night at midnight, and, of very chance, tarried not all night by reason of some masque in the Abbey (Holyrood); but we believe it was not chance, but God, to put it in our head. We dispatched this bearer upon the sudden, and therefore write to you the more shortly. The rest of your letter we shall answer at more leisure within four or five days by your own servant. And so for the present commits you to Almighty God. At Edinburgh, 11th February, 1567".

The document known as 'Cecil's Diary' states that Mary "wrote to the Earl of Lennox, promising to take trial", but this letter is unfortunately lost. It seems also that Mary or her Council were alarmed for her safety, and on this day she retired to the Castle of Edinburgh (364). This probably facilitated the marriage of Margaret Carwood to John Stewart of Tully-powreis, which now took place, the Queen providing the bridal feast (636). We can assume that all the arrangements had been made some days before and that no active intervention on the part of the Queen was required.

News of the assassination had reached Drury, who wrote twice to Cecil (534). In the earlier letter he wrote, "Even at this present there be advertisements come unto me and sent from Dunbar that the Lord Darnley was upon Sunday at night slain . . . It is also reported that some evil act is set or was meant at that present to his father". In the later letter he added, "I have now farther knowledge that he lies slain. His body was found in a field and strangled as it would seem . . . His father is also slain".

Meanwhile the Council was pursuing its enquiries. Unfortunately the only record of its activity on this day is a copy of some depositions (68):

"In the presence of the Earls of Huntly, Cassillis, Caithness, Sutherland, Bishops of Galloway, Ross, Comptroller, Justice-Clerk, etc.

Barbara Mertine, sworn, etc. deposes that, before the crack raise, she passed to the window of her house in the Friar Wynd, opposite the Masters of Maxwell's lodging, and heard 13 men come forth of the Friar Gate and pass to the Cowgate and up the Friar Wynd. Then the crack raise and 11 came forth, 2 of whom had clear things on them, and passed down the passage that comes from the Friars and so to the town. She cried on them as they passed, called them traitors and said they had been at some evil turn.

May Crokat, spouse of John Stirling, servant to the Bishop of St. Andrew's, dwelling under the Master of Maxwell's lodging, deposes she was lying in her house between her two twins when the crack raise . . . thought it was the house above and came running to the door in her sark alone, and even as she came forth . . . there came out of the Friar Gate 11 men, and she caught one by his . . . which was of silk, and asked where the crack was. But they made no answer, and 4 went up the wynd, and other 7 down to the Cowgate port etc.

John Petcarne, surgeon, dwelling in said wynd . . . archers of the guard, deposes that he neither heard nor knew anything till about four hours . . . of Signor Francis (de Busso), who is a little lean fellow, came and cried on the deponent to come to his master, which he did and remained with him till about six hours."

The persons seen by Mertine and Ctokat were undoubtedly Bothwell and his party as they passed to and from Kirk o'Field.

The explosion had apparently done some damage to the New Provost's House, on which the 'Salle' abutted, for the Treasurer was ordered "to take away the hewn work of the back door of the (New) Provost's Lodging of the Kirk o'Field and to build up the same door with lime and sand" (438). This again suggests that the powder lay at the western end of Darnley's lodging, and not in that part in which he and the Queen had their rooms.

12th February, Wednesday. On this day, Darnley's body, which had been embalmed, was placed in the Chapel at Holyrood. The apothecary was paid the sum of £42. 6s. Scots for his services (363).

The Council continued its deliberations, which must have been sorely hampered by the guilt or guilty fore-knowledge of so many of its members. It must be remembered that, in those days, the art of criminal detection was non-existent, reliance being placed almost solely on informers. The Council therefore offered a reward of £2,000 and a pension to anyone who would reveal the authors of the crime. The wording of the proclamation describes the murder in similar terms to the letters to the Queen-Mother and Archbishop Beaton, but refers also to the servants thus (2): "The bodies of his Grace and a servant (William Taylor) found dead within short space of the same lodging, besides some others that, through the ruin of the house, were oppressed, and some (one—Thomas Nelson), at God's pleasure preserved".

Clernault passed through Berwick on his journey South.

14th February, Friday. Moretta, apparently with Father Edmund Hay in his company, passed through Berwick (569); the latter was an emissary from the papal numcio, who was still at Paris, and had arrived in Scotland shortly before the christening.

15th February, Saturday. Darnley's body was this day interred in the Royal Vault in the Chapel (the old Abbey Church) at Holyrood. There seems to be no contemporary account of the ceremony, and later descriptions are conflicting.

Darnley's servant, Sandy Durham, who Buchanan says was a spy, but who could hardly have betrayed his master unless the latter had been guilty, was rewarded with a Court post and pension of £100 Scots per annum (423). He may have been associated with Balfour in warning Bothwell or the Lords of the King's plot. Bothwell also received the empty reward of the reversion of the superiority of Leith (629); since this had been previously mortagaged to the citizens of Edinburgh, it brought him no financial benefit.

Du Croc, whom we last saw at Dunbar with Moretta on 25th January, had now reached Dover, where he was overtaken by a secret courier, who was probably an emissary of Ker of Fawdonside, and who informed him, as we shall presently see, of the death of both Darnley and Lennox (533).

16th February, Sunday. Mary left Edinburgh to stay at Seton. According to the Bishop of Ross (1), Mary had, until now, shut herself up in a darkened room, as the French custom was, and she would have

"a longer time in this lamentable wise continued, had she not been most earnestly dehorted by the vehement exhortations and persuasions of her Council, who were moved thereto by her physicians' informations, declaring to them the great and imminent dangers of her health and life, if she did not, in all speed, break up and leave that kind of close and solitary life, and repair to some good, open and wholesome air; which she did, being thus advised and earnestly thereto solicited by her said Council".

James Melville wrote to his brother Robert, then on embassy in London, that "Lennox was at Linlithgow, but had returned to Glasgow" (536). This suggests that Lennox was near Edinburgh about the time of the murder, and his withdrawal, without visiting the corpse of his son, may have been due to a guilty conscience. If Lennox had been participant in Darnley's plot, he would have been at hand on the night of the explosion, and the persistent reports of his death with his son indicate that some people, at least, expected him to be in the vicinity. Clernault arrived in London on this day (525), reported the death of Darnley, and added, "It is clearly seen that this proceeds from a mine".

17th February, Monday. The first of a number of defamatory placards was set up in Edinburgh during the previous night (730). Bothwell and three others were named as the "doers" of the murder the Queen assenting thereto.

Sir James Balfour, evidently realising his equivocal position, departed from Edinburgh about now (280).

De Silva, reporting to Philip II a conversation with Sir Robert Melville, wrote that it had been Darnley who had selected Kirk o'Field as his residence in Edinburgh (535).

The Pope, having by now given up all hope of the success of Mondovi's nunciature, recalled Laureo from Paris (614).

18th February, Tuesday.   Mary at Seton wrote to the Archbishop of Glasgow (410). The letter is in Scotch, which is suggestive that it was composed, not by her, but by her Council. She says that when she last wrote, immediately after Darnley's death, she was "so grievous and tormented" that she could not answer the "particular heads" of his letter. The letter deals with sundry matters and she thanks him for his warning:

> "We thank you heartily for your advertisement made to us, of it which the Ambassador of Spain shewed you, as also of your communication with the Queen-Mother. But, alas, your message came too late, and there was over-good cause to have given us such warning".

19th February, Wednesday.   A second placard had been set up in Edinburgh during the previous night (424); it denounced three of Mary's foreign servants as the murderers.

News of Darnley's death reached Paris. The nuncio wrote (three days later) (615),

> "On the 19th of the present month, M. du Croc, the French Ambassador in Scotland arrived here. He had left Edinburgh on 22nd of last month and, while at Dover, received an express messenger sent him by the French Ambassador with the Queen of England, with an urgent commission to use all speed to reach this court, and be the first to communicate the news of the death of the King of Scotland and of the Earl of Lennox, his father . . . Outside the house, on the morning of the last Sunday of Carnival time, at an early hour, he and his father were found dead in the public street, both of them stripped".

Mahon's suggestion (535) is that Andrew Ker had sent the messenger to London, where he had been directed to Dover. Since Ker had come upon the bodies of Darnley and his servant in the dark, he had taken the second body for that of Lennox. Ker was near Kirk o'Field to assist his master the King, and he must therefore have expected Lennox, whom the world believed to be at Glasgow, to have been at hand.

20th February, Thursday.   The Earl of Lennox wrote to the Queen, answering her reply to his earlier letter, and asking that, since the murderers of his son were "yet not known" she should call a Parliament "to take such good order for the perfect trial of the matter as I doubt not . . . (that) the bloody and cruel actors of this deed shall be manifestly known" (4).

21st February, Friday.   Mary at Seton, replied to Lennox, thanking him for his letter and advice, telling him that she had already proclaimed a Parliament for this purpose (5).

Correr, the Venetian Ambassador in Paris, whose informant must have been du Croc, wrote, (94) "Until further advices are received, this assassination is considered to be the work of the heretics, who desire to do the same by the Queen, in order to bring up the Prince in their doctrines, and thus more firmly to establish their own religion to the total exclusion of ours", which seems to be a remarkably accurate account of events.

23rd February, Sunday. Clernault arrived at Paris either on this day or soon after (570). The message which he brought was that "some scoundrels fired a mine, which they had already laid under the foundation of the said lodging. The house was reduced to ruins in an instant" (616).

24th February, Monday. Moretta arrived in London from Scotland, and remained there until 6th March (569). On this same day, Elizabeth wrote to Mary to the following effect (70).

"Madam, My ears have been so astounded and my heart so frightened to hear of the horrible and abominable murder of your deceased husband and my dead cousin, that I have scarcely spirit to write; yet I cannot conceal that I grieve more for you than for him. I should not do the office of a faithful cousin and friend, if I did not urge you to preserve your honour, rather than look through your fingers at revenge on those who have done you such pleasure, as most people say. I counsel you so to take this matter to heart, that you may shew the world what a noble princess and loyal wife you are. I write thus vehemently not that I doubt, but for affection. As for the three matters communicated by (Robert) Melville, I understand your wish to please me, and that you will grant the request of Lord Bedford in my name to ratify the treaty made six or seven years past. On other things, I will not trouble you at length, referring you to the report of this gentleman (Killigrew)".

The bearer, however, did not set off until 27th February.

Mahon points out (547) that, at the time Elizabeth wrote, she had received no evidence, unless from Moretta, that the murder was for Mary's pleasure, and that the Savoyard had left Edinburgh too soon after the crime to know how diligently the assassins would be pursued. On the other hand, if the English Government had been trafficking with Moray and his associates for the overthrow of the Queen and her husband, the failure of the main part of the plot might well produce such a spiteful outburst.

26th February, Wednesday. Sir James Balfour returned to Edinburgh. Two days later, Drury wrote (740) that Balfour "came to Edinburgh on Wednesday at night accompanied to the town with thirty horsemen; when he was near unto the town, he lighted and came in a secret way . . . he is hateful to the people". It is not unlikely that he had some secret understanding with the Lords, yet he obviously did not consider himself entirely secure.

Lennox again wrote to the Queen (6); he had now changed his mind, and considered the time until the session of Parliament too long. He therefore asked that all those who had been named in the placards should be "apprehended and put in sure keeping". If the writers of the placards should fail to appear, the accused might be released, otherwise they should face a trial. This suggestion was surely an outrage to justice, that people should be arrested on anonymous evidence, and it is obvious that Lennox's advice had a political motive.

On this day, Mary granted a precept of remission to Huntly for the rebellion of 1562 (162). This sudden legalisation of a state of affairs which had been recognised for nearly eighteen months was probably Bothwell's doing.

Robert Melville, in London, wrote to Cecil (70):

"The Queen's Treasurer (of her French dowry, Dolu by name) is come, and Bastian, one of the valets of her chamber with him, who has a letter to your Sovereign... I have no letter from my Sovereign: my brother has written that her Grace went to Seton to repose there and take some purgations . . . Athol and the Comptroller (Murray of Tullibardine) have departed, but sent for to come again under pain of rebellion. Lennox was at Linlithgow, but went back to Glasgow, where he is presently . . . A Parliament is proclaimed for 14th April. The Prince is in the Abbey of Holyrood House".

That Mary was evidently ill, as the Bishop of Ross later said, appears from the fact that she was taking physic.

27th February, Thursday.   Drury, at Berwick, was informed of a placard set up the night before (308), "where were these letters written in Roman hand, very great, M.R., with a sword in a hand near the same letters; then an L.B. (for Lord Bothwell?) with a mallet near them".

The nuncio at Paris, who now had the benefit of Clernault's information, described the assassination of Darnley in a manner which is, in some parts,, correct (617). He makes the lodging much smaller than it actually was and speaks of a mine.

"From the fact that the King was found dead in the garden by the side of the house, and with him the servant who slept in his room, without any apparent injury to their bodies, the conjecture has been made that he got up from bed because of the smell of powder (!) before the mine exploded, and was, along with his servant, after-wards (!) suffocated by the smoke".

Killigrew left London on this or the following day, bearing Elizabeth's letter of 24th February (547).

28th February, Friday.   Drury, at Berwick, wrote to Cecil (739), "There hath been other bills bestowed upon the church doors, as upon a tree called the Tron, wherein they speak of a smith who should make the key (i.e. who made duplicate keys so that the assassins might enter the King's lodging in order to strangle him), and offers he and others will with their bodies approve these to be the devisers, and upon the same venture their lives".

After much gossip, he continues,

"The Earl of Bothwell was on Thursday at Edinburgh, where he openly declared, affirming the same by his oath, that, if he knew who were the setters-up of the bills and writings, he would wash his hands in their blood. His followers, who are to the number of fifty, follow him very near. Their gesture, as his, is of the people much noted. They seem to go near and about him, as though there were who would harm him; and his hand, as he talks with any that is not assured unto him, upon his dagger, with a strange countenance, as the beholders of him thinks . . .

I send your Lordship the copy of some of the bills set up . . . The Lady Bothwell is, I am by divers means informed, extremely sick and not likely to live. They will say there she is marvellously swollen . . .

The Queen . . . upon Wednesday . . . dined by the way at a place called Tranent belonging to the Lord Seton, where he and the Earl of Huntly paid for the dinner, the Queen and the Earl Bothwell having, at a match of shooting, won the same of them".

No other writer informs us of the gay outing to Tranent, which is probably as apocryphal as the alleged poisoning of Lady Bothwell.

Drury also states that Moray has not yet returned to Court, although Mary has sent for him.

1st March, Saturday. Bothwell now received the casualties of the sheriffdom of Edinburgh and of the bailliary of Lauderdale; we have no knowledge of the value of this gift (182).

Mary, still at Seton, replied to Lennox's letter of 26th February, denying that there was any intention of deferring the trial of any who should be apprehended until the forthcoming Parliament. She, or her Council for her, continues (7).

"And where ye desire that we should cause the names, contained in some tickets affixed on the Tolbooth door of Edinburgh, to be apprehended and put in sure keeping: there is so many of the said tickets, and there withal so different and contrary to others in accounting of the names, that we know not upon what ticket to proceed, but, if there be any names mentioned in them that ye think worthy to suffer a trial, upon your advertisement, we shall so proceed to the cognition taking as may stand with the laws of this realm, and, being found culpable, shall see the punishment as rigorously executed as the weight of the crime deserves".

De Silva, in London, writing to Philip II, has seen Moretta, "who gives signs that he knows more than he likes to say" (571), and that Darnley had tried to see the Savoyard while he was at Kirk o'Field, but Mary had prevented the meeting (574).

5th March, Wednesday.   Killigrew probably arrived in Edinburgh about
           now: he had left London on 27th February.

6th March, Thursday.   Alava, the Spanish Ambassador in Paris, wrote to
           Philip II, saying that it was the opinion of many
that it was the Queen of Scots who had got rid of Darnley, who would
otherwise have killed her, and who had spoken in damaging terms against
both God and his wife. Furthermore, the Archbishop of Glasgow affirmed
that the assassination was controlled from England, where the intention
had been to kill the Queen as well (721).

7th March, Friday.   Mary had now returned to Edinburgh (195), presum-
           ably in order to meet Killigrew, who was, however,
kept waiting until the following day.

8th March, Saturday.   Killigrew wrote to Cecil (71). He has this day dined
           with Moray, who has therefore returned to Edin-
burgh; Huntly, Argyll, Bothwell and Maitland were in the company,
Killigrew had then had audience of the Queen "in a dark chamber and
could not see her face, but by her words she seemed very doleful, and
accepted my Sovereign's letters and message in very thankful manner. I
hope for her answer in two days, which I think will gratify the Queen's
Majesty (Elizabeth) . . . I find great suspicions and no proof nor appearance of apprehension (arrest) yet". Killigrew finally mentions that
Darnley's servants, Standen, Nelson and Gwynne intend to return to
England when they can get passports. It has been suggested that Mary was
too ill to receive the English Ambassador, and that her place was taken by
an impersonator (549), and this seems a not impossible explanation of the
darkened room.

The Spanish Ambassador in London had joined with Beaton in warning
Mary of a plot against her life, and he, on this day, expressed his surprise
that she had not acknowledged his message (552).

Lennox now wrote to Cecil (71) "touching this late unnatural and most
cruel murder of the King, my son", asking Cecil to "be a means and re-
membrancer to her Majesty (Elizabeth) to revenge the shedding of her
Highness's own innocent blood".

The Bishop of Mondovi, still at Paris, wrote to the Cardinal-Secretary
(618),

> "There arrived here four days ago a young Frenchman (Sebastian
> Pages: he had left Scotland about 19th February), valet of the Queen
> of Scotland, from whom I received a letter from her Majesty of the
> 16th., written in (French) with her own hand . . . One rib in the King's
> body was found broken by the distance of the 'jump of the fall' . . . "

So Mary was well enough to write a letter on 16th February, but it is
notable that this is the only letter in her own hand for a considerable
period.

11th March, Tuesday. Archbishop Beaton, Mary's Ambassador at Paris, has received the Queen's letter of 11th February. He replied at length (657). He excused himself for the misdeeds of Walker and Highgate, denying that he knew anything of their proceedings, and then continued,

" . . . the discourse shortly of the horrible, mischievous and strange enterprise and execution done contrary to the King's Majesty, who, by craft of men, has so violently been shortened of his days. Of this deed, if I would write all that is spoken here, namely of the miserable estate of that realm and also in England by the dishonour of the nobility, mistrust and treason of your whole subjects, yea, than that yourself is greatly and wrongously calumniated to be the motive principal of the whole of all, and all done by your command, I can conclude nothing (i.e. I cannot reach any conclusion) by (i.e. except) that (which) your Majesty writes to me yourself, that, since it has pleased God to preserve you to take a rigorous vengeance thereof, that, rather than that it be not actually taken, it appears to me better in this world that you had lost life and all".

This was to quote Mary's own letter back to her, for these were the very words which she (or her Council) had used in the letter of 11th February. He continues,

"Here, it is needful that you forth-shew, now rather than ever of before, the great virtue, magnanimity and constancy that God has granted you, by Whose grace I hope you shall overcome this most heavy envy and displeasure of the committing thereof, and preserve that reputation in all godliness you have gained of long, which can appear no ways more clearly than that you do such justice as to the whole world may declare your innocence, and give testimony for ever of their treason that has committed, without fear of God or man, so cruel and ungodly a murder, whereof there is so much evil spoken that I am constrained to ask you mercy that neither can I nor will I make the rehearsal thereof, which is over odious. But, alas, Madam, this day over all Europe, there is no subject in head so frequent as of your Majesty and of the present estate of your realm, which is for the most part interpreted sinisterly".

Further on, Beaton wrote,

"I did thank the Ambassador of Spain on your behalf of the advertisement he had made you, suppose it came too late, who yet has desired you to remember your Majesty that yet he is informed and advertised by the same means he was of before, there is yet some notable enterprise against you, wherewith he wishes you to beware in time; I write this far with great regret, by reason I can come no ways to the knowledge of any particular from his master".

12th March, Wednesday. The Bishop of Mondovi wrote to the Cardinal-Secretary (620), "Most people impute the crime to the Earl of Moray, who, being the Queen's brother, has always had the throne in view, although he is a bastard. He is persuaded by the contrary sect (i.e. the Protestants) that it is his by right, especially as he maintains that his mother was secretly espoused by the King, his father". We may recall here that, in August, 1559, Cecil had instructed Sadler "to explore the very truth whether the Lord James (later, Earl of Moray) do mean any enterprise towards the crown of Scotland for himself or no, and, if he do, . . . it shall not be amiss to let the Lord James follow his own device therein" (619).

13th March, Thursday. On this day, Moray, who was always careful to commit as little as possible to paper, wrote an extremely ambiguous letter to Cecil (72). It runs,

"However these last accidents have altered many men's judgments, yet, being assured that constant men will mean constantly, I would not pretermit (miss) this occasion to signify the constancy of one thankful heart for the many and large benefits I have from time to time received by your means. And as I am touched myself, so do I judge of you and all men that feareth God and embraced the life of Christianity and honour, as concerning this late accident so odious and so detestable; yet am I persuaded discreet personages will not rashly judge in so horrible crimes, but, of honest personages, mean honestly, until truth declare and convince the contrary—neither for particular men's enterprises so ungodly, withdraw their good will from so great a multitude as, I am sure, detests this wild attempt, even from their hearts".

Maitland wrote an equally equivocal letter, in reply to letters of Cecil's which have unfortunately not been preserved (72).

"By Mr. Killigrew and Mr. Melville, I received your letters of 25th and 26th February, and thank you heartily for your frank speech. For my own part, I like your intention, so I know it does not offend such here as have most interest to wish the matter to be earnestly recommended to such as you be; for they mean to demand nothing but right, and that in due time and orderly. For the third mark you wish I should shoot at, to wit, that her Majesty (Mary) would allow of your estate in religion (i.e. become a Protestant), it is one of the things in earth I most desire: I dare be bold enough to utter my fancy in it to her Majesty, trusting that she will not like me the worse for uttering my opinion and knowledge in that (which) is profitable for her every way. And I do not despair, but although she will not yield at the first, yet, with progress of time, that point shall be obtained".

These two letters suggest that there was a very close association between the Protestants of the two countries, and we may guess that much more was said by the bearer of these letters (Killigrew) than the letters themselves contained, for Moray commissioned him to speak to both Cecil and Throckmorton, for, "he hath heard and seen more nor I can write" (425).

14th March, Friday. Killigrew set out for London carrying the foregoing letters.

The Privy Council consisting of Huntly, Argyll, Moray, Bothwell and others, issued a proclamation denouncing James Murray of Purdovis, brother to Murray of Tullibardine, of treason, in that he had "set up certain printed papers upon the Tolbooth door of Edinburgh, tending to her Majesty's slander and defamation" (3). It will be recalled that this same Murray had slandered Bothwell in 1565, alleging that the Earl intended to murder Moray (page 54).

15th March, Saturday. The Bishop of Ross went to Stirling to arrange for the transfer thither, to the care of the Earl of Mar, of Prince James (526).

Mary, or her Council, wrote to Robert Melville in London in favour of Anthony Standen, one of Darnley's servants, who had returned to England (409). The letter was incorrectly dated 15th February (453).

The Justice-Clerk, Bellenden, a fervid Protestant, wrote to Sir John Foster at Berwick (102) that he should "never give him trust in time coming if the Earl Bothwell and his complices gave not their lives ere midsummer for the King's death".

Moretta, with the Jesuit Edmund Hay in company, arrived in Paris (593). The Savoyard told the Venetian Ambassador that Darnley had been assassinated outside the house (621).

16th March, Sunday. The Bishop of Mondovi reported the arrival of Moretta and Hay to the Cardinal-Secretary (621); he wrote

"From both one and the other, we have been able to understand fully the state of affairs in Scotland. At this moment, they are in such confusion owing to the death of the King that there is fear of a very extensive insurrection, for the Earls of Moray, Athol and Morton and other lords have joined with the Earl of Lennox, the King's father, under pretext of avenging his death. The Earls of Bothwell, Huntly and many other men of importance are with the Queen for the same purpose . . . Hence it is thought that (Moray), aiming at the succession to the throne, desires upon this occasion, to murder the Earl of Bothwell, a courageous man, much trusted and confided in by the Queen, with the intention of being afterwards able to lay snares for the life of her Majesty with greater ease, especially as he can hope, through the slothfulness of the Earl of Lennox, to obtain, by his permission and consent, the governorship of the Prince, and, by consequence, of the whole realm. If he should gain this, which may God avert, he may be able to accomplish the wicked end he has set before himself, and herein the favour of England will not be wanting. The English Queen is jealous of the Prince, as the legitimate heir of both those realms, and will not omit to favour the said Moray, her dependant, bound to her by many obligations as well as by religion".

He continues by stating that Hay has told him that Mary is very anxious that he, the nuncio, should go to Scotland, but both Hay and Moretta think that he should not go. Finally, he gives an inaccurate account of the murder.

17th March, Monday.   Lennox replied to a letter of Mary's, unfortunately lost, in which she had evidently offered to make him guardian of the Prince. Lennox now asked her to come to a final decision on this point, and then, somewhat belatedly, replied to Mary's letter of 1st March. He asked for the arrest of all those mentioned in the first and second placards, mentioning Bothwell, James Balfour, David Chalmers, John Spens, Signor Francis, Bastiane, John of Bordeaux and Joseph Riccio, whom he "greatly suspects".

19th March, Wednesday.   Mar, having agreed to take custody of the Prince at Stirling, gave up his command of the Castle of Edinburgh (183), retaining only the Castle of Stirling in his keeping. Cockburn of Skirling was made Captain of the Castle of Edinburgh (311).

Another Cockburn (Captain Cockburn) wrote to Cecil (532), "Bastian . . . shewed the great hazard that our Queen's Grace escaped that night, for were (it) not for Secretary (Maitland) and Bastian that was married that day, her Grace would not fail to have lain in that same house and been utterly destroyed".

20th March, Thursday.   The Prince was given into the custody of Mar at Stirling (184). Presumably he had left Edinburgh on the day before; his mother did not accompany him.

Lady Bothwell made the first move in her suit to divorce her husband, for the procuratory was signed on this day (186).

Correr, the Venetian Ambassador at Paris, having seen Moretta, reported (95) that Moray was suspected above all, having sought Darnley's death on account of a quarrel, in which the King had behaved very badly. On the night of the assassination, Darnley had heard a great disturbance, so certain women who live in the neighbourhood declared, and, from a window, perceived many armed men were round the house. So he, suspecting what might befall him, let himself down from another window looking on the garden. But he had not proceeded far before he was surrounded by certain persons, who strangled him with the sleeves of his own shirt, under the very window from which he had descended.

22nd March, Saturday.   Adam Gordon, Huntly's brother, was awarded the estate of Findlater which had caused the tumult between Ogilvie and John Gordon and precipitated the affair of Corrichie in 1562.

23rd March, Sunday. "There was a solemn soul-mass with a dirge sung after noon, and done in the Chapel Royal of Holyroodhouse, for the said Henry Stewart and his soul, by the papists at her Majesty's command" (181). It was the first Sunday after the customary forty days of mourning.

The Queen replied to Lennox's letter of 17th March; the nobility have been summoned to meet next week "when the persons nominated in your letter shall abide and underlie such trial as by the laws of this realm is accustomed"; Lennox himself was therefore also requested to attend in order that he may "declare those things which you know may further the same (365).

25th March, Monday. Elizabeth saw de Silva, whom she told (440) that grave suspicions existed against Bothwell and others who were with the Queen, who did not dare to proceed against them in consequence of the influence and strength of Bothwell, who was Admiral and Captain of the Guard.

28th March, Good Friday. It was some time during this week that Bothwell received the royal gift of some costly Church vestments, perhaps those which had been captured at Strathbogie in 1562 (183).

The Council met on this day, Bothwell being of the sederunt. It was enacted that the trial of the Earl and all other persons suspected as principals or accessories to the murder of the King, should take place on 12th April following, and warning be given to the Earl of Lennox, and all others that would accuse Bothwell, to appear in the Court of Justiciary on that day (365). A letter, signed by the Queen, was forthwith directed to Lennox in appropriate terms (8).

Mary then, or on the following day, repaired to Seton (498), where she seems to have remained until early April.

29th March, Saturday. Drury at Berwick, presumably having heard that Lady Bothwell was intending to divorce her husband, informed Cecil (103) that "the judgment of the people is that the Queen will marry Bothwell". Of Mary's health, he wrote, "She has been for the most part either melancholy or sickly ever since (the murder?), in especial this week upon Tuesday and Wednesday often swooned . . . the Queen breaketh very much, upon Sunday last divers were witnesses, for there was a mass of requiem and dirge for the King's soul."

The English Ambassador in Paris is now reported as having announced that Lady Bothwell had died of poison, and that the marriage of the Earl to the Queen would follow (96).

30th March, Easter Day. According to Drury, (310) "The Earl of Huntly has now condescended to the divorce of his sister from the Earl Bothwell".

Alava made the curious suggestion that Mary and Catherine dei Medici had together concerted the murder of Darnley (722).

3rd April, Thursday.   Moray's will is dated on this day (321). He made the Queen chief guardian of his only child, a dauthter, which certainly suggests that, at that time, he did not believe Mary to be a murderess.

4th April, Friday.   Mary seems to have returned to Edinburgh from Seton on this day (194), but, if so, she probably went back to Seton again, for a Privy Council was held there on the following day (366).

5th April, Saturday.   This is the apparent date of the Scotch contract of marriage between Mary and Bothwell.

Sir Henry Norris, the English Ambassador at Paris, wrote to Cecil (506), "As at first I thought thereof, I remain not to be removed, which was that the origin of the fact (the death of Darnley) came from hence, for, besides that their desire is (as I am advertised) to have the Prince hither, so do I see that all they that are suspected for the same fact make this their chief refuge and sure anchor".

Now Norris is surely wrong in attributing the murder to French counsel, although, as we have seen, rumours to this effect were in circulation. However, he may have been correct in attributing the centre of the plot to Paris, for the nuncio had been there for a long time, and it would certainly seem that he was at least implicated in Darnley's activities.

7th April, Monday.   Moray left Edinburgh on this day, and departed from Scotland on the 9th or 10th. He was in France by the end of the month (189).

8th April, Tuesday.   Elizabeth now wrote to Mary (632),

"Madam, you having been so much troubled by M. Du Croc (who had arrived in Scotland from France a few days before (497)), I would not have had so little consideration as to bother you with this letter, if the bonds of charity towards the ruined and the prayers of unfortunates had not constrained me. I understand that an edict has been promulgated by you, Madam, that every one who wishes to do justice on those who murdered your late husband, and my late cousin, must come to do so on the 12th of this month. Which thing, as it is the most honourable and necessary thing which can be done in such a case, nothing of mystery or cunning being concealed therein; so, the father and friends of the dead gentleman have humbly requested that I should pray you to postpone the date, for they know that the wicked have combined to do by force that which by justice they could not do; therefore, I can, only for the love of yourself, whom it touches the nearest, and for the consolation of the innocent, exhort you to concede to their request, which, if it be denied to them, would make you greatly suspected, more, I hope, than you think or than you would willingly allow. For the love of God, Madam, use such sincerity and prudence in this case which touches you so closely, that all the world shall have reason to pronounce you innocent of a crime of such enormity, a thing which, if you do it not, you would deserve to fall from the ranks of Princesses, and, not without cause, become opprobrious to the people; and rather than that should happen to you, I would wish you an honourable burial, than a soiled life. You see, Madam, that I treat you like my daughter, and promise you that, if I had one, I should not wish better for her than I desire for you, as the Lord God will bear me witness, Whom I heartily pray to inspire you to do that which will be most to your honour and to the consolation of your friends; with my very cordial recommendations, as to her to whom I wish the most good that can come to you in the world for the future. From Westminster, this 8th April, in haste".

It is amazing that Elizabeth should have dared to write such an offensive letter to her "sister and cousin". It shews, only too clearly, the manner in which she was interfering in the affairs of Scotland. There was, of course, no substance in her complaint; Lennox had been urging the trial of Bothwell and others, hoping that they might be imprisoned and rendered helpless before the trial came on. Now that the trial was approaching, and the Earl still had liberty to defend himself in the time-honoured way of Scottish nobles brought to trial, that is to say, by surrounding the Courts of Justice with their armed retainers (just as Moray had done when Bothwell was to be tried in 1565 for breaking ward), Lennox sought Elizabeth's assisstance. He, who recently had urged an early trial, now asked for a postponement, and the English Government, as was to be expected, came down heavily on the side opposed to Bothwell, who had been odious to them ever since the ambuscade on Cockburn of Ormiston in 1559. Elizabeth's letter, however, did not reach Edinburgh until the very morning of the trial, and the proceedings were not stayed.

The English Government did not stick at words only, but began to foment disorder in Scotland. Bedford at Berwick was given orders (281) "to stand fast for the maintenance of God's honour and for the punishment of the late murder", and to circularise all the Border notables "who seem to mislike Bothwell's greatness".

10th April, Thursday. The Bishop of Mondovi now gave up his mission and left Paris for Italy (594).

11th April, Friday. Lennox, at Stirling, wrote to Mary (319). He alleged that he was ill and unable to travel, and requested her, meanwhile, to imprison the suspected parties and to postpone the trial, that he might have "sufflcient time" to seek "for manifestations of this most odious crime". Finally, he asked the Queen to grant him her commission for apprehending such persons as he should be informed were present at the murder of his son. As Hosack wrote, "the unreasonable nature of these fresh demands is sufflciently apparent".

12th April, Saturday. Elizabeth's letter of 8th April arrived in Edinburgh at 6 o'clock in the morning, but the beareer was told that the Queen must not be distrubed at that early hour. He returned again between 9 and 10, when Bothwell was about to proceed to the trial. At length, Maitland and Bothwell made their appearance, at which, writes Drury (322),

> "all the Lords and gentlemen mounted on horseback, till that (Maitland) came to him (the bearer, who was Provost-Marshall of Berwick), demanding him the letter, which he delivered. The Earl Bothwell and he (Matland) returned to the Queen, and stayed there within half an hour, the whole troop of Lords and gentlemen still on horseback attending for his coming. (Matland) seemed willing to have passed by the Provost-Marshall without any speech, but he pressed towards him and asked him if the Queen's Majesty had perused the letter, and what service it would please her Majesty to command him back again. He answered that, as yet, the Queen was sleeping, and therefore he had not delivered the letter, and that there would not be any meet time for it till after the assize, wherefore he willed him to attend (wait). So, giving place to the throng of people that passed, which was great, and, by the estimation of men of good judgment, above four thousand gentlemen besides others, the Earl Bothwell passed with a merry and lusty cheer, attended on with all the soldiers, being two hundred, all harquebusiers, to the Tolbooth".

Elizabeth's letter could not possibly have arrived sooner, and it must have been obvious that it would not lead to a postponement of the trial; its purpose, therefore, must have been to unsettle the Government and give encouragement to the opposition.

The record of Bothwell's trial no longer remains in the books of Adjournal, but a copy, signed by the Justice-Clerk, runs as follows (73):

> "In the Justiciary Court of our Sovereign Lady the Queen, held in the pretorium of Edinburgh by Archibald, Earl of Argyll, &c., her Justice-General.

The Queen's advocates, Masters John Spens of Condy and Robert Crichton of Eliok, produced her letters dated 28th March and executions of service, etc. (The dittay, or indictment, against Bothwell follows) Bothwell's procurators, chosen by him in Court; Master David Borthwick of Lochthill, and Master Edmund Hay. After a protest by Henry Kinross as procurator for Andrew Master of Errol, Constable of Scotland, that his rights should not be prejudiced, Matthew Earl of Lennox, being often times called, appeared by his servant, Robert Cunningham, protesting against the shortness of time; that his absence was through fear of his life; and that any judgment by the assize would be in error; producing copies of Lennox's letters to the Queen on 26th February and 17th March; in which last he names Bothwell; Master James

Balfour; Gilbert Balfour, his brother; David Chalmets; black Master John Spens; Signor Francis; Bastian; John de Bordeaux; and Joseph, David's brother, as suspected murderers of the late King. The assize (jury), Andrew Earl of Rothes; George Earl of Caithness; Gilbert Earl of Cassillis; Lord John Hamilton, Commendator of Arbroath, son to the Lord Duke (Châtelherault); James Lord Ros; Robert Lord Semple; John Maxwell Lord Herries; Laurence Lord Oliphant; John Master of Forbes; John Gordon of Lochinvar; Robert Lord Boyd; James Cockburn of Langton; John Somerville of Cambusenethan; Mowbray of Barnbougle; Ogilvie of Boyne; removed out of court and, after long reasoning had by them upon the said dittay and points thereof, they voted and acquitted the said James Earl of Bothwell of art and part of the said slaughter of the King and points of the said dittay, and by their Chancellor (Foreman), George Earl of Caithness, protested that no evidence in its support had been brought by the pursuer (prosecutor)".

13th April, Sunday. Bothwell now posted up a challenge, offering to fight hand to hand with any person of good repute who should dare to maintain that he was guilty of the murder (426). This challenge received three answers, all anonymous and similar to the earlier placards (74). The first was a promise to fight Bothwell, accusing him of the murder; the second names seven persons (three Balfours, John Spens, Barton, Borthwick and Sandy Durham) as the devisers of the murder, and 12 others as murderers with the hands (Ormiston, Branston, Hepburn of Bolton, Talla, two Blackadders, two Edmonstons, Lauder, James Cullen, Patrick Wilson, 'wanton' Sim Armstrong); the third placard ran, "There is none that professes Christ and his Evangel that can with upright conscience part Bothwell and his wife, albeit she prove him an abominable adulterer and worse, as he has murdered the husband of her he intends to marry, whose promise he had long before the murder".

14th April, Monday. Parliament began; the Queen was not present, and nothing further was done than the calling of the names of the members (367).

15th April, Tuesday. Foster, at Alnwick, alleged that, when Lennox was going to the trial of Bothwell, surrounded by a large force of his friends, he received an order not to enter the town with more than six in his company (731). Hosack explains how Foster's misconception arose, for the law prohibited an accuser in any criminal case from appearing at the bar with more than four attendants, while six were allowed to the accused (320).

16th April, Wednesday. Mary rode to Parliament for the choosing of the Lords of the Articles, whose duty it was to prepare the business of Parliament; they included Morton, Argyll, Marischal, Huntly and Bothwell, with eleven others, of whom seven were clergy.

Bothwell rode before her (368); it was his duty, as Great Admiral, to carry the sceptre: Argyll carried the crown and Crawford the sword (282).

19th April, Saturday. Parliament was closed on this day. The business transacted was an act ratifying the establishment of the Protestant faith; the ratification of certain lands to Mar, Maitland's father, David Chalmers, Bothwell, Huntly and several others; an act of oblivion, concerning a previous act of 1563; an act against the up-setters of placards; the ratification of Moray in his Earldom and to Lord John Stewart of a pension; the ratification of the Earls of Crawford, Rothes, Morton and Angus; and the reduction of the forfeiture of several persons, including Huntly, Sutherland and four other Gordons.

There was also a petition made by (76) "The professors of the Evangile of Jesus Christ, even so many as has refused that Roman Antichrist, unto their Sovereign, the Queen's Majesty", wherein they desired the establishment of Christ's religion, "with the abolishment of the contrary religion (or, rather, superstition) which is papistry"; that vacant benefices be disposed in their favour; that schools and the poor be attended to; and that other measures be taken for the support of the Reformed faith; and, finally, that the murderers of the King should be punished.

The Earl of Moray, meanwhile saw de Silva in London, and told him that Darnley's lodging had been "completely undermined" (280), a fact which is strongly against the later story that the gunpowder had been placed in Mary's bedroom.

Drury, writing to Cecil from Berwick (542), says that Balfour, who had returned secretly to Edinburgh nearly two months before, "for some fear he conceives, he keeps his house, especially in the night, with great watch and guard". This fear of Balfour's could be understood if he had first betrayed Darnley to the Protestant Lords, and had then informed Bothwell, not only of the King's plot, but also of the Lords' countermeasure.

On the evening of this day, Bothwell apparently invited certain Lords to supper at Ainsley's tavern. He managed to persuade his guests to sign a document to the effect that they believed in his innocence of the murder of the King, and would take his part in any quarrel arising from this cause, and further, that, if the Queen should be willing to take the Earl as her husband, they would do their utmost to advance the marriage; to this they bound themselves with most solemn promises. Later, they were to declare that their signatures had been extorted by a warrant from the Queen ordering them to sign, and for fear of the hackbutters by whom the tavern was surrounded, but both these excuses were probably untrue.

The copy of the bond, attested by James Balfour, purports to be signed by the Archbishop of St. Andrews and six other bishops, including Ross, by the Earls of Huntly, Argyll, Morton, Cassillis, Sutherland, Errol, Crawford, Caithness and Rothes, and by Lords Boyd, Glamis, Ruthven,

Semple, Herries, Ogilvie and Fleming (371). The list given by Buchanan's amanuensis differs considerably (370).

20th April, Sunday.   Grange wrote to Bedford; the letter is so important that it must be given in full (75):

"It may please you to let me understand what will be your sovereign's part concerning the late murder among us. Albeit her Majesty was slow in our last troubles, and lost favour, we bore to her yet; if she will pursue revenge for the murder, she will win the hearts of all honest Scotsmen again. And, if we understand she would favour us, we shall not be long in revenging it. You shall receive the articles presented by the Kirk, and a protestation made by Parliament. The Queen has granted to abolish all laws made by her predecessors for religion that may hurt us in lives, lands or goods. The Act of Oblivion shall be ratified. Parliament dissolved this day. There is none other but Huntly and Sutherland's restitution, an Act of Council for the Minister's stipends, and a part of things assured to them in such places as they shall not get payment thereof. I pray your lordship cause copy all their other writings and send them to Robert Stewart (in France). The last articles concerning the King's death were refused, and the Queen very angry that we desired them. Edinburgh. G.

Farther, the Queen caused ratify in Parliament the cleansing (acquittal) of Bothwell. (Ker of) Cessford is put in Edinburgh Castle, but (Ker of) Fernihurst, Buccleuch and Bedrule has disobeyed and ridden home. She intends to take the Prince out of Mar's hands, and put him in Bothwell's keeping, who murdered his father. The night Parliament was dissolved, Bothwell called most of the noblemen to supper, to desire their promise in writing and consent to the Queen's marriage, which he will obtain; for she has said she cares not to lose France, England and her own country for him, and shall go with him to the world's end in a white petticoat before she leaves him. Yea, she is so far past all shame that she has caused make an act of Parliament against all that set up any writing that speaks anything of him. Whatever is unhonest reigns presently in our court.

Albeit Bothwell set a writing offering to fight any gentleman that charged him with the murder, now, when an answer is made, an act of Parliament is set out under pain of treason that none shall answer or set up any writing; yea, he that takes them down or reads them shall die the death. Therefore, please your lordship to print these two answers and write to Robert Stewart to do the like and send them some"

The whole character of Grange as a dishonest, treacherous spy and mendacious schemer is apparent from this letter. The opening sentences undoubtedly ask for assistance in an insurrection. It was not true that

Bothwell's acquittal was ratified in Parliament, and there is no evidence that Mary ever intended to hand the Prince over to Bothwell, nor did she ever do so. It is to be noted that he makes no mention of either the hackbutters or the Queen's warrant when mentioning "Ainsley's supper", and Mary's outspoken remarks about her attachment to Bothwell were apparently heard by no other than Grange. It would, of course, have been impossible to permit, even tacitly, the continued slander of a high official by anonymous placards, and action against the up-setters was well merited.

21st April, Monday.   Mary set out for Stirling (202) on what was to prove the last occasion on which she was to see her son. She may have completed the jounry (36 miles) in one day, but the probability is that she spent the night at Linlithgow.

According to Moray and his associates, it was during the three days between now and Wednesday that Mary wrote Casket Letters Nos. VI, VII, VIII and the Love-Ballad.

22nd April, Tuesday.   Mary probably arrived at Stirling on this day. She wrote to the nuncio, explaining that she could not trust her written letters to pass through England safely, and begging him to keep her in his Holiness's good grace, promising to live and die in the Catholic faith (622). It seems likely that, with the Government in the hands of Bothwell and a largely Protestant Council, who had forced through an act against the Roman Church, Mary feared that the Pope would blame her for permitting the final suppression of Catholicism, which she was powerless to prevent. She was so nearly a prisoner in the hands of her Council at Edinburgh, that she did not dare to write to the Bishop of Mondovi from thence, but waited until she reached the comparative seclusion and freedom of Stirling before she composed her letter.

23rd April, Wednesday.   Lennox, already on shipboard and about to leave Scotland for England, wrote to Drury, enclosing a letter for his wife, in which he told her that Bothwell was about to kidnap the Queen (441). It is by no means impossible that the abduction had been decided at Ainsley's supper, for Lennox was not the only person who had knowledge of it.

Mary, accompanied by Huntly, Maitland, Sir James Melville and some thirty horsemen, rode from Stirling to Linlithgow (427). Meanwhile, Bothwell departed from Edinburgh and concentrated a force of some 800 horse at Calder (283).

24th April, Thursday.   Grange wrote to Bedford (77),

"This is to advertise you that Bothwell's wife is going to part with her husband, and great part of our Lords have subscribed the marriage between the Queen and him. The Queen rode to Stirling this last Monday, and returns this Thursday. I doubt not but you have heard Bothwell has gathered many of his friends, some say to ride in Liddesdale, but I believe it not, for he is minded to meet the Queen this day, called Thursday, and to take her by the way and bring her to Dunbar. Judge you if it be with her will or no; but you will hear at more length on Friday and Saturday, if you will find it good that I continue in writing as occasion serves".

The excuse of riding in Liddesdale for gathering forces was a good one, for the moss-troopers had just 'despoiled' Biggar (441); however Bothwell used his force to intercept Mary and her escort at the bridge over the Almond, some six miles East of Edinburgh. She and her attendants were conducted to Dunbar.

25th April, Friday. Presumably it was during the twelve days which she spent at Dunbar that Mary was forced to sign the French Contract of Marriage, and, possibly the Scotch one, dated 5th April, also. Sir James Melville says that he was permitted to leave Dunbar on this day (646), but his account is not to be trusted.

What was the reason for the abduction? There is some evidence that Bothwell had proposed marriage to Mary and had been repulsed (670); this event is dated by Nau about 20th April. It may be that it had occurred earlier, on 5th April, and that the Contract in Scotch of that date had been prepared in the hope that the Queen would sign it, but this she had refused to do. It seems likely that Bothwell, although he had the Lords consent to his marriage to the Queen, did not trust the opposition. He knew that, if he could not stabilise his position as head of the Government, the Lords of the Congregation would speedily bring about his fall. For an ambitious man, this might have been sufficient cause, but Bothwell had hitherto always been loyal to the Queen, and he must have known that his fall would leave her at the mercy of the Protestant faction, whose actions had repeatedly shewn that they meant to remove all power from Mary's hands. Bothwell, therefore, was following the dictates of his ambition, but he was also trying to do the only thing which, he believed, could save Mary from actual or virtual deposition from the throne. He must, therefore, have depended upon his powers of persuasion to force the Queen to marry him and entrust the Government to his hands, and it is incredible that, in these circumstances, he would, as Melville says, have (646) "ravished her and lain with her against her will". We may note, in passing, that Melville at least does not accuse the Queen of having consented to the 'ravishment'. Eventually, Mary gave in, probably against her better judgment, and Bothwell was now in a position, as he thought, to deal with the opposition.

On this day, Elizabeth gave instructions to Lord Grey of Wilton to proceed to Scotland (77). The memorandum is a strong indictment of Bothwell and Mary, and speaks of the "contempt or neglect in the burial of the King's body". The mission was countermanded, and Grey did not leave London.

26th April, Saturday. Grange wrote, as he had promised, to Bedford (78), "The Queen will never cease until she has wrecked all the honest men of this realm. She was minded to cause Bothwell ravish her, to the end that she may sooner end the marriage, which she promised before she caused murder her husband. Many would revenge it, but they fear your mistress"

Meanwhile, an anonymous writer informed Cecil that (78) "it is bruited by the Scottish Ambassador (in Paris) that the Lord James was the author of the King's death, and Lord Lennox is deluded and mocked by him, as the Hamiltons in time past were".

Lady Bothwell's suit for divorce was this day begun before the Commissary Court of Edinburgh, Bessie Crawford being cited as co-respondent (703).

27th April, Sunday. The Archbishop of St. Andrews was granted a commission, at Bothwell's instance, to try the validity of the Earl's marriage (704).

The lieges of Aberdeen, hearing of the abduction, sent a message desiring to know what they should do 'towards the reparation of the matter' (666), but no other move was made to aid the Queen's release. Drury at Berwick stated that the kidnapping was known to be with Mary's consent (105).

29th April, Tuesday. The process of divorce at Lady Bothwell's instance began its hearing. The case was defended (708).

30th April, Wednesday. Witnesses on behalf of Lady Bothwell were called and examined (708) on this and the subsequent day.

1st May, Thursday. Some of the nobles convened at Stirling, and bound themselves to strive to the utmost of their power to defend the Queen, the Prince and his keepers (188). This was the first overt move of the opposition against Bothwell, which was to gain sufficient strength by mid-June to crush the Earl and overthrow the Queen.

De Silva wrote to Philip II, describing the abduction of Mary in the following terms (333), "They (Bothwell's men) shewed an intention of taking her with them, whereupon some of those who were with her were about to defend her, but the Queen stopped them, saying she was ready to go with the Earl of Bothwell wherever he wished, rather than bloodshed and death should result". When we remember that she and her band numbered some 35 persons, while Bothwell had brought 800 men to the field, the pertinence of this as evidence that the Queen was willing to be abducted loses its sting.

3rd May, Saturday. The Commissary Court gave sentence in favour of the Countess of Bothwell (709). On the same day, the Consistory Court began the hearing of Bothwell's suit for annulment of the same marriage on the grounds of consanguinity (709).

Alava, in Paris, reported to Philip II that the English ambassadors alleged that Mary had arranged the assassination of her husband in order that she might marry Bothwell (722). It is interesting that this, the first outspoken denunciation of the Queen, is made by a Spaniard and emanated, not from Scotland, but from England.

5th May, Monday. Witnesses in Bothwell's suit were called and examined
(710).

6th May, Tuesday. Lady Bothwell's procurator appeared in her behalf
(710).

On this day, Bothwell escorted Mary back to Edinburgh, Huntly and
Maitland being in her company (150). Craig was asked to proclaim the
banns of marriage between the Queen and Bothwell, but refused to do so
without her written authority (373).

7th May, Wednesday. Judgment was given in Bothwell's suit (711),
"declaring the marriage to be, and to have been,
null from the beginning in respect of their contingence in blood, which
hindered their lawful marriage without a dispensation obtained of before".
We know, of course, that a dispensation had been obtained, and that the
judgment was only obtained by collusion

Craig received a written order, signed by Mary, ordering him to proclaim the banns, which he later reluctantly did (373).

Robert Melville wrote an interesting letter to Cecil (79). There is no
doubt that he considers the Queen's abduction to have been against her
own will. Argyll, Athol, Morton, Mar, Tullibardine and others have convened at Stirling and have signed a band to 'purge the realm of the detestable murder of our King', of which Bothwell is the principal author.
"These Lords will nowise think her (Mary) at liberty so long as she is in
the said Earl's company, albeit he may persuade her Majesty to say otherwise". The nobility want Elizabeth's assistance, which France has already
offered. Bothwell is expected to go to Stirling to seize the Prince, but Mar
is victualling the Castle and will not surrender. We thus see that insurrection is on the point of breaking out, an insurrection which uses Bothwell
instead of religion as its pretext, but which is otherwise similar in object
to the Chase-about Raid and the murder of Riccio; that is, to subvert the
Government and place power in the hands of the Lords of the Congregation.

8th May, Thursday. James Balfour replaced Skirling as Captain of the
Castle of Edinburgh. For him to have obtained such
an important post, Bothwell must have believed him to be his friend, which
might well be the case had he been the source of the Earl's information
concerning either Darnley's or the Lords' plot at Kirk o'Field.

Grange wrote to Bedford (80): he describes the intentions of the Lords
to overthrow Bothwell, and asks for Elizabeth's assistance; the "cruel
murderer" and "barbarous tyrant" Bothwell has tried to poison the Prince.
Du Croc has now returned to Scotland and offers the King of France's aid
to suppress Bothwell: he has offered, also, to join openly with the rebellious
Lords, who are about to be joined by many persons of substance, whom he
names. Mary, he alleges, has melted the font presented by Elizabeth in

order to raise money (this was untrue: the font was not melted down until after Mary was in Lochleven). He continues, "It will please you to haste these other letters to my Lord of Moray, and write to him to come back into Normandy to be in readiness when my Lords write". The rebellion against the Government was obviously gathering momentum.

9th May, Friday. The banns of marriage between Bothwell and the Queen were published on this day. At a Council meeting, Craig who was called to justify his insolence, spoke out very forthrightly: it says much for Bothwell's tolerance that he escaped punishment (373).

10th May, Saturday. Robert Melville wrote to Throckmorton (81), alleging that Bothwell had overawed the assize at his trial, and enclosing a letter for Moray, which was probably similar to Grange's letter of two days before.

Randolph wrote to Leicester (376) that Elizabeth was greatly incensed by Grange's writings, but this did not lead the English Queen to alter her course of persecution or to offer any assistance to Mary.

De Silva informed Philip II that the insurgent Lords "considered the raising of the child to the throne, the government being carried on by them in his name" (285).

11th May, Sunday. Mary, who had lodged at the Castle since her return to Edinburgh from Dunbar, now removed to Holyrood (200).

12th May, Monday. The Queen now appeared in proper person before the Lords of Session, and declared herself to be free and under no constraint (374). She announced that,

> "although, at first, commoved against Bothwell, yet, from his good behaviour towards her, from her knowledge of his past, and for a reward of his future services, she freely forgave him for the imprisonment of her person, and being now at full liberty, she intended to promote him to further honours" (628).

Drury, describing events at Kirk o'Field, mentions the presence of Andrew Ker of Fawdonside on horseback near the place (106).

14th May, Wednesday. The marriage contract between Mary and Bothwell was concluded, and the Earl was created Duke of Orkney (411). The Queen gave a certificate ratifying the action of the Lords in signing the bond made at Ainsley's Supper (11).

15th May, Thursday. The marriage of Bothwell (now Orkney) to Mary took place in the Chapel in Holyrood, the ceremony being performed according to the rites of the Protestant faith by the Bishop of Orkney (157). Du Croc, who was whole-heartedly on the side of the dissident Lords, Bothwell being much hated by the French Government, refused to attend (630).

The Bishop of Dunblane and Robert Melville were forthwith dispatched with copious instructions, the former to the Court of France (414) and the latter to England (412), to give information of the marriage and to secure, if possible, the consent of both governments to the *fait accompli*.

18th May, Sunday. Du Croc wrote to Catherine dei Medici (420),

"The letters which I have written to your Majesty by the Bishop of Dunblane are merely delusive; you can suppose that I did not entrust to him what I would write to you. Your Majesties cannot do better than to make him very bad cheer, and find all amiss in this marriage, for it is very wretched, and it is already repented of. On Friday, her Majesty sent to seek for me; when I came, I perceived an estranged demeanour between her and her husband, for this she wished me to excuse her, saying that, if I saw her sad, it was because she could not rejoice, for she did nothing but wish for death. Yesterday, being shut up in her cabinet with Bothwell, she cried aloud, and then sought for a knife to stab herself; those who were in the chamber adjoining the cabinet heard her. They think that, if God does not aid her, she will become desperate. I have counselled and comforted her the best I could, these three times I have seen her. Her husband will not remain so long, for he is too much hated in this realm, as he is always considered guilty of the death of the King".

20th May, Tuesday. Drury wrote of Mary (553): "The opinion of divers is that she is the most changed woman of face that in so little time, without extremity of sickness, they have seen . . . It is thought the Queen has long had a spice of the falling sickness (epilepsy) and has, of late, been troubled therewith".

23th May, Friday. A proclamation of the Privy Council reinforced the Act (of 19th April, 1567) anent the maintenance of the Reformed faith.

25th May, Sunday. Bothwell does not seem to have been oblivious to the storm which was brewing in Scotland, for Drury reported to Cecil that all on whom he could rely had had secret warning to be ready for action (545).

27th May, Tuesday. Bothwell (658) and Mary (659) both wrote to the Archbishop of Glasgow, explaining the reasons which had led to the marriage, and Bothwell also wrote to Charles IX (717).

28th May, Wednesday. The Queen, through her Privy Council, now called the lieges to arms, bidding them to convene fully armed, with provisions for fifteen days, at Melrose on 15th June following, and giving the reason as a raid into Liddesdale (377), but it is certain that the summons was dictated by the increase in strength of the opposition, rather than by the lawless state of the borders.

1st June, Sunday. The Queen issued a proclamation denying that she intended to subvert the laws, change the state of religion, or neglect or harm her son (378).

2nd June, Monday.   It was not until now that Philip II made any acknow-
                       ledgment that he had heard of the death of Darnley,
and his statement on this occasion was as brief of possible: "It has given
me much sorrow on account of my friendship with the Queen" (575).
Mahon thinks that the delay and the brevity of the utterance suggest that
Philip was touched very near by the collapse of his plans for obtaining
control of Scotland, which the death of Darnley had rendered futile (548).

5th June, Thursday.   Maitland now withdrew from Court and joined his
                         brother-in-law, Athol (648).

Robert Melville at last left on his embassy to England, to which Court
he had been accredited at least a fortnight before. His reluctance to leave
may be connected with the obvious sympathy, which he had shewn in
his letters, with the rebellious Lords. Bothwell took the opportunity to
write to Elizabeth, expressing his desire for her friendship in manly,
but respectful, terms (82).

6th June, Friday.   The Lords assembled at Stirling issued a proclamation,
                       in which they declared that, since the Queen's Majesty's
most noble person is, and has been for a long space, detained in captivity
and thraldom, the nobility have assembled to deliver her from captivity
and bondage (649).

It was probably on this day that Mary and Bothwell sought admittance
to the impregnable Castle of Edinburgh, but were turned away by the
keeper, Sir James Balfour.

7th June, Saturday.   Mary and Bothwell left Edinburgh, and following the
                         course which we have already described (page 193),
were finally overthrown, largely by the machinations of du Croc and the
treachery of Grange at Carberry on 15th June. Bothwell never saw Edinburgh again, and Mary entered the city for the last time as a captive. The
rebellion had at last succeeded, and that success which divested Mary and
Bothwell of the dominion and government of Scotland, clothed the rebels
with the robes of righteousness; and that infamy which, with failure, would
have been theirs, henceforth enshrouded a couple who, if not without
faults, at least merit as kindly treatment at the hands of posterity as do
those who, by force and by fraud, usurped their place. It is a tale to cleanse
the heart with pity and horror, one such as Chaucer dreamt of when he
wrote;

> "And there I saw the dark imaginings
> Of felony, the stratagems of kings,
> And cruel wrath that glowed an ember-red,
> The pick-purse and the coward pale with dread,
> The smiler with the knife beneath his cloak,
> The out-houses that burnt with blackened smoke;
> Treason was there, a murder on a bed,
> And open war, with wounds that gaped and bled".

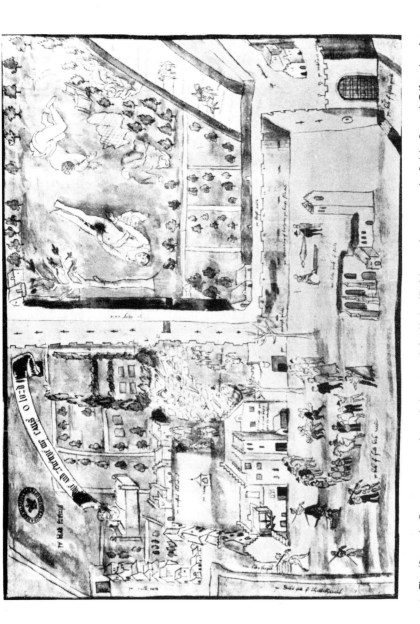

1. The 'Picture'. Contemporary coloured drawing of the Kirk o'Field tragedy, now in the Public Record Office, London, England. (From "Lord Bothwell" by R. Gore-Browne; London, Collins, 1937)

2. A View of Edinburgh from the North, made in 1544.
    1) Kirk o'Field Church.   6) St. Giles' Church.
    2) Holyrood.   7) Cowgate.
    3) Canongate.   8) Wynd leading to Kirk o'Field.
    4) Netherbow Port.   9) Castle.
    5) Netherbow.   10) Calton Hill.
(From "The Mystery of Mary Stuart" by Andrew Lang; London, Longmans, Green & Co., 1901)

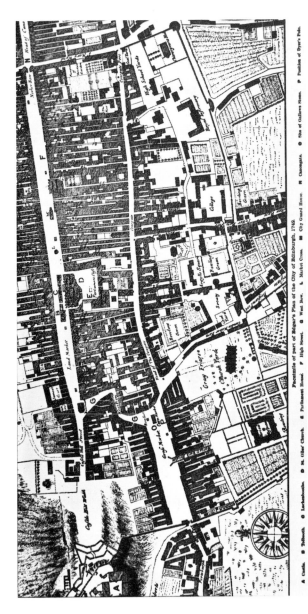

3. Part of Edgar's Plan of the City of Edinburgh, 1742. The rectangular building below the word 'College' lies almost exactly on the site of Kirk o'Fields Church (see Fig. 4). (From "The Trial of Captain Porteous" edited by William Roughead; Glasgow, Hodge & Co., 1909)

Facsimile of part of Edgar's Plan of the City of Edinburgh, 1742.

A Castle. B Tolbooth. C Luckenbooths. D St. Giles' Church. E Parliament House. F High Street. G West Bow. L Market Cross. G City Guard House. H Canongate. O Site of Gallows Stone. P Position of Dyer's Path.

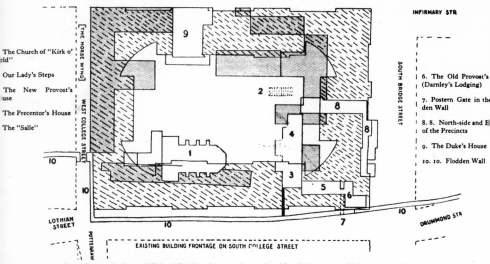

CHAMBERS STREET

INFIRMARY STR

The Church of "Kirk o' ld"

Our Lady's Steps

The New Provost's use

The Precentor's House

The "Salle"

9

2

8

4

8

1

3

5

6

10

10

10

10

7

10

LOTHIAN STREET

POTTERRAW

DRUMMOND STR

SOUTH BRIDGE STREET

[THE HORSE WYND]

WEST COLLEGE STREET

6. The Old Provost's (Darnley's Lodging)

7. Postern Gate in the den Wall

8. 8. North-side and E of the Precincts

9. The Duke's House

10. 10. Flodden Wall

EXISTING BUILDING FRONTAGE ON SOUTH COLLEGE STREET

Superimposed plans of Kirk o' Field and its precincts, the old and the present University buildings.
Unshaded buildings are those which existed in 1567. Buildings dotted are those of the old University buildings.
Buildings hatched are those of the present University.

4. Plan of Kirk o'Field. (From "The Tragedy of Kirk o'Field" by R. H. Mahon; Cambridge University Press, 1930)

5. Mahon's Model. A bird's-eye view of Kirk o'Field before the building of the Town Wall in 1513. (From "The Tragedy of Kirk o'Field" by R. H. Mahon; Cambridge University Press, 1930)

6. Mahon's Model. View from the South-East, as it appeared in 1558, after the building of the Town Wall and damage to the Church. (From "The Tragedy of Kirk o'Field" by R. H. Mahon; Cambridge University Press, 1930)

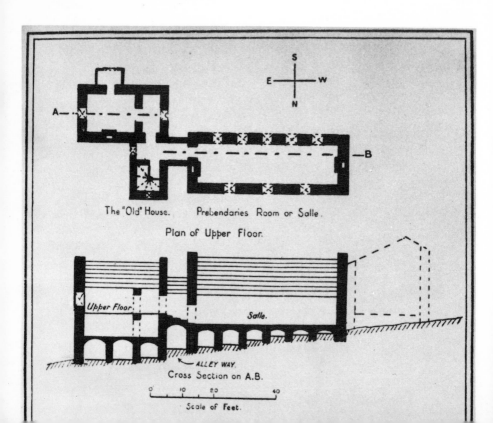

The "Old" House.   Prebendaries Room or Salle.

Plan of Upper Floor.

Upper Floor.   Salle.

← ALLEY WAY.

Cross Section on A.B.

0   10   20   40

Scale of Feet.

9. The Silver Casket in the Lennoxlove Museum. (From "The Stuarts" by J. J. Foster; London, Dickinson's, 1902)

7. Mahon's Model. View from the South-East, after the explosion in 1567. (From "The Tragedy of Kirk o'Field" by R. H. Mahon; Cambridge University Press, 1930)

8. Plan and Section of Darnley's Lodging, the Old Provost's House at Kirk o'Field. (From "The Tragedy of Kirk o'Field" by R. H. Mahon; Cambridge University Press, 1930)

Madame ma bonne sœur ayant entendu par me lord bysel
que tant sen fault que mes rebelles cessent a vobr
commandemant lu pour iute de mes subiects quau cantrere
ils leur ont ise & pretendent vser dauantaurge
de rigueur en toute haste ie vous ay voulla fayrece
mot pour prier de donner credit a monsseur de nowe
& priene expedition pour la grand nesesite ay en
quoy iay layssay tomber mes affayres pour vous
complayre ne scheischant plus secours ailleurs ie
voy les deleys demora parquoy ie vous suplie on
promytemant me resouleire de votre ayde ou
moy referer car datendre e plures a trayter
auegues mora & ce pendant qui lse fussemayn
du tout ce ne serort mon bien ni grandhuneur
avons que vous enestant mesler ils en fussoth si
pende compte ayant emoye les discours anlong
a mlord Ress iene vous in porteneray plus pour
le presant siron vous baysant les meins priendien
vous annogrense sernte gardo de bonne felle ce
au sasme de feullet votre trescffedumne bonne
sœur et cousine marie R

A la Royne dangleterre
madame ma bonne sœur

10. Letter from Mary Queen of Scots to Queen Elizabeth. Original in the British Museum.
(From "Mary Queen of Scots" by T. F. Henderson; London, Hutchinson & Co., 1905)

11. Inventory of Mary Queen of Scots' Jewels. Her testamentary dispositions of June 1566 are written in the margin in her own hand. (From "Inventaires de la Royne Descosse" edited by J. Robertson; Edinburgh, 1863)

12. Inventory of Mary Queen of Scots' Jewels. Her concluding disposition and signature (June, 1566). (From "Inventaires de la Royne Descosse" edited by J. Robertson; Edinburgh, 1863)

13. Handwriting of Anna Throndssen, kindly supplied by Dr. Palle Birkelund, Librarian

Zours :L:
humble and obedient Syster at Command
MARIC DE BCThunC

3d I hublr and
obedient forbant

N. Kyrkcaldy

yprig. at Comanddment
maitland

marie flemy
S.S

14. Signatures of Mary Beaton, William Kirkcaldy of Grange, William Maitland younger
of Lethington and Mary Fleming. (From "The Mystery of Mary Stuart" by Andrew Lang;
London, Longman's, Green & Co., 1901)

15. Signatures of the Earl of Bothwell, Sir Richard Maitland of Lethington and Sir Walter Ker of Cessford. (From "The State Papers and Letters of Sir Ralph Sadler" edited by A. Clifford; Edinburgh, Archibald Constable & Co., 1809)

The Maladies of Mary Queen of Scots and Her Husbands

(The contents of this appendix are taken, with modification, from a paper by the author published in the Proceedings of the Scottish Society of the History of Medicine, 1955–56)

Mary was born at Linlithgow Palace on 8th December, 1542 (124). There were contradictory reports about her birth: that she was premature, that she was a boy, that she was sickly, and so on. There was no truth in any of these stories, but her heredity was poor. Her mother, Mary of Lorraine, after whom she took to a considerable degree, was to die of dropsy, probably the result of heart disease, at the age of 44. She had already borne Mary's father two sons, one of whom had died at about one year of age, while the other had succumbed when only eight weeks old. James V, Mary's father, died a week after her birth, being only 31. He had always been somewhat eccentric (650), and it is said that the rout of Solway Moss turned his head. He became melancholic, and, in a short space, he "turned him upon his back, and looked and beheld all his nobles and lords about him, and gave a little smile of laughter, thereafter held up his hands to God and yielded up his spitit".

The first reliable account which we have of Mary as a baby comes from Sadler, the English Ambassador, who saw her when she was three months old. Mary of Lorraine said to him, "The Governor (i.e., the Earl of Arran, later Duke of Châtelherault) said that the child was not like to live, but you shall see whether he saith truth or not", and, "therewith she caused me to go with her to the chamber where the child was, and shewed her unto me, and also caused the nurse to unwrap her out of the clothes, that I might see her naked. I assure your Majesty, it is as goodly a child as I have seen of her age, and as like to live, with the grace of God". Thus Sadler wrote to Henry VIII on 23rd March, 1543 (99). On 2nd July, he wrote that she could not be removed from Linlithgow to Stirling, as she was "breeding of teeth" (22), but, on 26th July, she was taken to the latter place for safety's sake, and Sadler saw her again on 10th August. He wrote that Mary of Lorraine had siàd that "her daughter did grow apace, and soon would be a woman if she took of her mother, who is of the largest stature of women" (100). It was said that Mary had had smallpox, and was now perfectly well; but in view of her subsequent story, it is more likely that she had had chicken-pox. There can, of course, be no certainty about the diagnoses made at that date, when it was not yet fully realised that such diseases as smallpox, measles and chickenpox were different entities.

A month later, the infant Mary was crowned at Stirling. The ravaging of the borders and the sack of Edinburgh followed in the succeeding years, being Henry VIII's 'rough wooing' of the baby Queen for his son, Edward (later Edward VI). Mary was kept mainly at Stirling, where she was safe from Henry's troopers, and her case-history remains a blank for five years.

In March, 1548, when she was 5 ¼, she was ill at Dumbarton, and was even rumoured to be dead: Huntly heard that she had smallpox, but La Chapelle, who was in Edinburgh, said that it was measles, and this seems the more likely.

Later the same year, Mary was sent to France. She set sail from Dumbarton towards the end of July, 1548. 'Lack of weather' kept the flotilla in the Clyde, and de Bréz´, who accompanied her, was able to write to her mother from time to time, before they sailed to the North and West of Ireland, to land ultimately at Roscoff, near Brest, on 13th August, 1548. Thus, on 31st July, de Bréz´ wrote (673), "The Queen, thank God, fares exceedingly well and has not yet been sick on the sea". She arrived in good health, and, on 18th August, he wrote (674), "She has been less ill on the sea than anyone in her company, so that she made fun of those that were"

On arrival in France, Mary was lodged with the royal children at Saint Germain. We learn that instructions were given that no workman or other stranger was to be allowed to enter Saint Germain, expecially the palace, if he had come from any place where infectious disease had broken out; later, this order was also enforced at Poissy (675).

On 26th December, 1548, Ferreri at Paris wrote to the then Bishop of Orkney a letter which runs in part (624).

"Inquiries are being made here about a medical adviser, who may pay attention to her (Mary's) health, according to the custom of courts. There are many French who desire the office . . . The greater part of them either do not appreciate the importance of their art, or are not the persons to comprehend a Scottish temperament . . . Only one is of Scottish race, William Bog, Doctor of Medicine. He is so learned that he will bear comparison with any Frenchman, and is by far the best in diagnosing Scottish temperaments . . . A very important point is that Lady Fleming (Mary's guardian) would not be able to explain in her own language, except to a Scot, what the little Queen's ailments were".

At this date the old Pythagorean doctrine of the 'four humours' dominated medical theory. Since an excess or lack of one or more of these humours (blood, phlegm, choler and black-bile) was thought to be the cause of all disease, a diagnosis of the temperament was important in discovering the cause, and therefore the treatment, of any ailment. Whether the Bishop approached Mary of Lorraine or not, is unknown, but Dr. Bog does not seem to have secured the appointment.

In March, 1549, Mary, first rumoured in Scotland to be dead, was said to have had measles; perhaps this was rubella. When she was nearly 8, in September, 1550, the English Ambassador wrote, "For the last ten or twelve days, the Queen of Scots has been so dangerously ill of the prevailing flux that her recovery was doubted, but within the last two she is considered to be out of danger". Otherwise, apart from a plot to poison her in 1551, nothing appears in the record. In 1553, the Cardinal of Lorraine writes to her mother in Scotland that Mary is in good health. In February, 1554, he writes again to say that she has toothache and her cheek is swollen (679). He unconsciously lets us see what he thinks of doctors, for he adds, "I am amazed to hear that some have written to you that she is sickly. *Even* the doctors say that her constitution gives promise that she will live as long as any of her relatives".

In April, 1554, Mary now being in her twelfth year, the Cardinal writes again, saying that she was "troubled with a faintness at the heart, when, to satisfy her good appetite, she sometimes eats too much" (125). Now, for the first time, we begin to step out of the realm of childish illnesses, and see here the beginning of Mary's unhappy mental state, for these symptoms are undoubtedly functional; it may be that her age is of some relevance.

Later the same year, Mary herself records in one of her Latin themes that she has toothache (677), and then there is again a blank in the case history. The summer of 1556, however, was the hottest in the memory of man, 'in consequence there have been upon us an infinite number of diseases'. Mary took ill, apparently after eating melon (678). The Cardinal writes, on 19th August, of a "persistent fever, wonderfully severe and sharp" (625). Mary took medicine on the second day, was bled on the third day, and was better on the fourth. However, she had a number of relapses, and the doctors prognosticated seven attacks. Although the Venetian ambassador had thought her to be over the worst by 14th August (126), on 23rd September he says that she has not yet recovered her health. On 2nd October, the Cardinal is still concerned for her (626), and writes of a remittant fever, which sounds very much like malaria. She went to the Cardinal's Château of Meudon for a change of air. In November, she was still said to have a quartan ague (126) (an attack of fever recurring every third day, typical of malaria), but, on 30th November, Wotton wrote to Mary Tudor that she was "meetly well amended" (126). Probably in the following year, 1557, she had smallpox, but the date is not ascertainable (680); she was attended by the great French physician, Fernel, who saved her beauty, as Mary wrote to Queen Elizabeth, when the latter had the same disease in 1562 (33).

The year 1558 was inportant for two events; on 24th April, Mary married Francis the Dauphin, and, on 17th November, Elizabeth succeeded her halfsister, Mary Tudor, on the throne of England. Mary Stewart was not yet sixteen.

Be the cause what it may, Mary soon became ill. On 18th March, 1559, Sir John Mason wrote to Cecil (126), "The Queen of Scots is very sick, and these men fear she will not long continue. God take her to Him as soon as it may please Him". On 24th May, Throckmorton wrote (126), "Assuredly, the Scottish Queen, in mine opinion, looketh very ill on it; very pale and green, and therewith all short-breathed; and it is whispered here amongst them that she cannot long live". This is a typical description of adolescent anaemia, commonly called 'green-sickness' (chlorosis), which is believed to have resulted from tight-lacing, but which might also follow malaria. On 18th June, she swooned in church, and had to be given wine from the altar (126), and, three days later, she swooned again. At this time, the Spanish Ambassador wrote that she was "suffering from a certain incurable malady" (126).

Soon after this, on 10th July, 1559, Henry II of France died from a lance thrust in the eye while jousting, and Francis and Mary became King and Queen of France. Mary's ill-health continued: in August, her weakness and sickness were increasing daily; she was ill after meals, swooned, and had to be revived with *acqua composita* (spirits) (681). She believed herself to be pregnant, and even wore the 'floating tunic' in use as a maternity gown in those days. Chantonnay said she "looked very evil and in dangerous case". In September, she "felt herself well, contrary to her wont" (127), but, on receiving unwelcome news from Scotland, she again fell sick. On 28th, "she being at evensong, was for faintness constrained to be led to her chamber where she swooned twice or thrice" (682). In November, she felt ill, looked very pale, and kept her chamber all day. However, by December, she was well enough to suffer an accident while out hunting (127), being winded and knocked from her horse by a blow from the branch of a tree.

On 25th April, 1560, when Mary was in her eighteenth year, she heard of her mother's illness, and, with much emotion, she took to her bed (127). Mary of Lorraine died in Edinburgh on the night of 10th/11th June, and Mary heard the bad news on 28th. The Venetian Ambassador wrote that (127) "she loved her mother incredibly, much more than daughters usually do, and shewed such signs of grief that she passed from one agony to another".

This was not all, however, for, on 5th December of the same year, the boy King, Francis II, died. A fortnight later, Mary "still will not receive any consolation, but, brooding over her disasters with constant tears and passionate and doleful lamentations, she universally inspires great pity" (685); and, more than a month after his death, she is still said to be overwhelmed with grief (686).

Let us now pause and recapitulate the story thus far. Mary's early youth is healthy, in spite of her poor heredity. She suffers from the usual diseases of her age and times: chickenpox, smallpox, measles, dysentery and malaria; she may also have had chlorosis. Her father had died when she was a week old, and she was separated from her mother at the age of 5½ only to see her once more for a short time when she was seven, and Mary of Lorraine visited France. Even before she left Scotland, her residence was frequently secluded, and her mother saw little of her. In France, she was brought up in luxury, and she was probably grossly spoiled: after all, she was a Queen, and the destined bride of a future King. Soon after puberty she developed indigestion; after her marriage, she believed herself to be pregnant, and she began to shew signs of emotional instability. She fainted in public places, especially church, and became ill when she received bad news. The deaths of her mother and husband threw her into excessive transports of anguish, especially considering that her memory of her mother must, of necessity, have been slight.

Intellectually, she does not seem to have shone; she was bad at languages, having little facility with Latin, and none with Scotch and English. She was an indifferent horsewoman; and Queen Elizabeth was admittedly her superior in both dancing and, appropriately, in playing on the virginals. Mary had some musical ability, however, and she composed some verses which are not without merit.

Francis II, Mary's husband, was borne on 18th January, 1544. His health was so poor that he was spoken of as 'un roi pourri'. He was continually in the hands of the physicians, and the astrologers optimistically predicted that he would die at the age of eighteen. Although he was frequently ill, we have few details of his illnesses. In 1547, he had smallpox; in 1549, he was seriously ill; in September, 1556, he had a 'quartan ague' which lasted with remissions for five months.

In connexion with the disease from which he died, it is interesitng that there exists a letter from de Montmorency to d'Humières, the governor of the royal children, in which he tells him to see that the Dauphin uses his pocket handkerchief more frequently (676). Evidently, he suffered from a chronic respiratory infection, probably associated with enlargement of the adenoids.

Mary was married to Francis on 24th April, 1558, when he was only fourteen. He succeeded to the throne of France in July, 1559. On 15th November of that year, Killigrew wrote to Elizabeth (683), "it is very secretly reported that the French King has become a leper, and, for fear of his coming to Châtelherault, the people have removed their children, and of late certain of them are wanting about Tours, which cannot be heard of; and commandment shall be given that there shall be no seeking for the same". The explanation for this horrible insinuation is that one of cures recommended for leprosy was bathing in the blood of young children.

In mid-November, 1560, the weather was warm and spring-like, but suddenly became very cold. Francis was out hunting on 16th, and caught a chill. On 24th November, the Venetian Ambassador wrote (684), "He had a sudden attack of extreme cold accompanied with some fever. It is caused by a flow of catarrh which exudes from the right ear, and, if the discharge be stopped, he suffers great pain in the teeth and jaws, with an inflammation behind the ear, like a large nut". Francis suffered so much pain that he became delirious. On 2nd December he improved, but the next day he became unconscious, and he died two days later, on 5th December, 1560 (128). After his death, it was found that his brain was much destroyed by an abscess.

This story is quite typical of a chronic inflammation of the middle ear (otitis media), with gradual extension of the disease into the air cells of the mastoid process. The disease causes a perforation of the ear-drum which allows the pus to drain out of the ear. If the process extends sufficiently far, all the cells in the mastoid process are destroyed, and the inflammation may extend to tissues behind or below it, hence the swelling behind the ear, which would increase in size when the flow of pus became obstructed. As frequently happened in the days before adequate surgical treatment, the inflammation also extended upwards, through the bone of the skull into that part of the brain which immediately overlies the middle ear (the temporal lobe). The sudden break-through releases the tension in the ear, and there is, at that moment, an apparent improvement in the patient's condition. However, as the inflammation extends in the brain, forming an abscess within it, the pressure in the skull rises, consciousness is lost, and death ensues in one or two days. All the features of this disease are mentioned by the Venetian Ambassador, and there can be no doubt as to the cause of death. It is probable that the 'leprosy' was really an eczema caused by the continuous irritation of the purulent discharge from the ear.

The death of Francis was summed up by Calvin in these words (157), "Did you ever hear anything more timely than the death of the little King? There was no remedy for the worst evils, when God suddenly revealed himself from Heaven, and He, Who had pierced the father's eye, smote the ear of his son"; and John Knox added his epitaph (399), "Lo, the potent hand of our God from above sent unto us a wonderful and most joyful deliverance; for unhappy Francis, husband to our Sovereign, suddenly perished of a rotten ear". He continues (400), "As the said King was at mass, he was suddenly stricken with an aposthume (abscess) in that deaf ear that never would hear the truth of God". To this we may add that Francis was not yet seventeen when he died; but it must also be remembered that his death, by diminishing the power of the Guises and by making Catherine dei Medici ruler of France, saved the life of the Protestant leader Condé, who was then lying in prison under sentence of death: it also eased the path of the Reformers in Scotland.

The year 1561 found Mary a widow in a land ruled by her unfriend, Catherine, and in which her erstwhile all-powerful uncles, the Duke of Guise and the Cardinal of Lorraine, were reduced to small account. Her brother-in-law, Charles IX, was now King. She set her heart on marrying Don Carlos, son of Philip II of Spain by his first wife. When news arrived that these negotiations had broken down, and when the coronation of Charles was imminent, she became ill again. She was at Nancy, and was said to have a 'tertian ague' (129). She missed the coronation on 15th May and, a few days later, Throckmorton wrote (159) that she had "somewhat amended, but was keeping her bed for the most part, no man but physicians being allowed to speak to her", which suggests more a mental breakdown than an ague. By 28th May, she was at Rheims, apparently well (304). In July, she was still ill, and Throckmorton writes (130) that "it hath somewhat impaired her cheer, though she makes no great matter of it, the worst being passed".

Soon afterwards, as was to be expected when her presence was so obviously unwanted in France, she embarked for Scotland. She never lacked physical courage, and she needed it on this occasion, for she knew that Elizabeth would intercept her voyage if she could. She arrived at Leith on 19th August, 1561, where she was so disappointed at the sorry welcome and poor arrangements, that she broke into tears.

In September, 1561, Mary made her first 'progress'. At Stirling, her bed-curtains caught fire, and she was nearly suffocated (131). Soon the cavalcade reached Perth, the first town to throw off the old religion, and still displaying its despoiled church and ruined monasteries. The pageant which welcomed her was uncompromisingly Protestant, and, although the burgesses presented her with a golden heart filled with gold, the reception was cool. Perhaps as a result, she became ill, "As she rode through the street, she fell sick, and was borne from her horse into her lodging, not being far off, with such sudden passions as she is often troubled with after any great unkindness or grief of mind" (132).

About this time, Mary came under the complete dominance of her half-brother, Lord James Stewart, later Earl of Moray. It is to be noted that, throughout her free life, she was always completely dominated by the nearest man. In France, it was the Cardinal of Lorraine; in Scotland, first Moray, then Riccio, then Darnley and, finally, Bothwell. The immediate result of the dominance of her Protestant half-brother was the overthrow of the 4th Earl of Huntly at Corrichie in 1562.

Earlier that year, she had had a riding accident, when her horse fell with her at Falkland. In July, when she heard that the meeting with Elizabeth, on which she had set her heart, had been postponed, she took to her bed (305), while in August she is reported to have had bouts of fainting. Randolph wrote (32), "For displeasure of this, the next day when she heard of this, she fell sick, and is grieved at heart (that) he (Captain Hepburn who had grossly insulted her) is fled her country, not doubting but he will be apprehended, if possible. Yesterday, being Sunday, she fell very sick at her mass, but recovered in half an hour and is now very well; the like has chanced to her divers times at her chief devotion. We hope, if it chance again, it will drive her altogether from her mass". On her return to Edinburgh after Corrichie, in late November, she caught influenza, then masquerading under the name of the "New Acquaintance" (306).

During 1563, various marriage projects were set on foot, and, expecially, the Don Carlos match was re-opened; all came to nought. There were troubles in Scotland, Catherine dei Medici was shewing herself to be in opposition to Mary's plans, and Elizabeth's policy was patently adverse. In December, Mary took to her bed with pain in her side, afterwards frequently referred to as 'spleen', but which was, almost certainly, caused by a gastric ulcer (37). Randolph said that the pain was on the right side, but we can be sure that he is in error (a very common error, by the way, in describing a part of another's anatomy), because, whenever the pain is subsequently mentioned, as it often is, it is said to be on the left (the same side as the spleen). Randolph said she had danced overmuch on her birthday, but she herself spoke of a chill caught in chapel.

Randolph gives us another vignette of her at this time (38): "For two months, she has divers times been in great melancholy; her grief is marvellous secret, and she often weeps when there is little apparent occasion". Probably he hit the mark when he wrote, "Some think the Queen's sickness is caused by her utterly despairing of the marriage of any of those she looked for".

There is a blank in Mary's medical history until May, 1565. In February of that year, Darnley came to Scotland, and, in May, Randolph writes (44), "I know not how to utter what I conceive of the pitiful and lamentable estate of this poor Queen, whom ever before I esteemed so worthy, so honourable in all her doings, and, at this present, find so altered with affection towards Darnley", and, in another letter, "she is now so much altered from what she was that who now beholds her does not think her the same. Her majesty is laid aside, her wits not what they were, her beauty another than it was, her cheer and countenance changed into I know not what. A woman more to be pitied than ever I saw" (45).

Less than two months later, Mary married Darnley, thus strengthening her claim to the throne of England. Immediately her husband dominated her, so that Randolph wrote, "She has given over to him her whole will, to be ruled and guided as himself best liketh".

By November of this year, Mary was understood to be pregnant; she fell ill with the pain in her side once more (434), and she was still complaining of it on 1st December (49).

By now, Darnley had shewn the cloven hoof. His demand for the Crown Matrimonial, and Mary's refusal to grant it, was followed, on 9th March, 1566, by the murder of Riccio, at which time the Queen was six months pregnant. The desire to bring about a miscarriage, which would lead to Mary's death, was an integral part of the Riccio plot.

When the rebellion had been overcome, Mary retired to Edinburgh Castle, where her son was born between 10 and 11 of the forenoon on 19th June, 1566, "albeit dear bought with the peril of her life, she being so sore handled that she wished she had never been married" (644). Five days later, she was still weak and had a hollow cough (101). Before the end of July, however, she was well enough to go to Alloa, and, in August, she, Darnley and others went hunting in the 'Meggotland'.

On 8th October, 1566, Mary left Edinburgh to hold Justice Eyres at Jedburgh and, these being concluded, she rode to Liddesdale on 16th October to see Bothwell, who had been wounded a week before. She stayed at the Hermitage for two hours and then returned to Jedburgh. On the following day she was taken ill. Mary had had an attack of the 'spleen' a few days before her ride to Hermitage (175). The day after her return, she vomited blood frequently, the pain in her side was very sharp, and she lost consciousness several times. It was thought that she had been poisoned, but, in fact, all these symptoms are to be expected from gastric ulcer, which the exercise of the long ride and the worry associated with public and private affairs would undoubtedly have exacerbated. On 19th October, she had lost the power of speech and had convulsions, and, on 20th, she lost her sight. By 24th, she had improved, but she became very ill again on 25th: she seemed dead, "her eyes closed, her mouth fast, and her feet and arms stiff and cold" (397). However, she was restored to life by her surgeon, Arnault, who was said to be 'a perfect man of his craft'. Certainly, it is difficult to imagine better treatment for a case of haemorrhagic shock than that which he employed, remembering that blood transfusion was, at that time, unknown: he bandaged very tightly her great toes, her legs from the ankle upwards, and her arms, then he poured some wine into her mouth, which he caused to be opened by force". He also gave a clyster (enema); later, she vomited a great quantity of corrupt (old) blood. The whole story could well be accounted for by

haemorrhage from an ulcer alone, but some symptoms, such as the stiffness
of her arms, suggest an hysterical overlay.

On 28th October, Darnley, who was amusing himself at Peebles, paid
her a short and tardy visit. Her convalescence was interrupted on 30th
by a fire which drove her to fresh lodgings (144). In November, she was
able to resume her progress of the borders, and suffered a riding accident
before the town of Berwick, when Sir John Foster's "courser raise up with
his fore-legs to take the Queen's horse by the neck with his teeth, but
his fore-feet hurt her Majesty's thigh very evil" (645).

By 20th November, Mary was at Craigmillar, still in the hands of her
physicians. Du Croc said that her disease was "principally a deep grief
and sorrow" (339).

The baptism of James took place at Stirling on 17th December, 1566;
Darnley was proving difficult, and du Croc describes on 23rd how he saw
Mary lying on a bed, weeping sore, and complaining of a violent pain in
her side. She had had yet another riding accident a week before. On 24th
December, Darnley removed himself from Stirling and went to Glasgow,
where he fell ill, and he was still convalescent, and officially contagious,
when he returned to Edinburgh with Mary at the end of January. He was
lodged at Kirk o'Field, and there he died in the early morning of 10th
February, 1567.

If we look back at Mary's life in Scotland, we see very clearly her habit
of becoming ill whenever things went wrong, but, when the danger was so
pressing as to threaten her very life, she rose above her emotions, and
shewed commendable courage, resolution and promptitude. We see the
domination of herself which she continually permitted to men near her;
and we see her tolerance in religious matters. Finally, we see an illness,
gastric ulcer, which, if not caused by worry, is at least aggravated by it.

Henry Stewart, Lord Darnley, later Earl of Ross, Duke of Albany
and King Henry of Scots, was born in 1546, and was thus not yet 21 at the
time of his death. He was the great-grandson of Henry VII, and his
father, the Earl of Lennox, afterwards Regent, was presumptive heir to
the throne of Scotland, if the illegitimacy of the Hamiltons could be proved.

Little is known of Darnley's life in England; he seems to have been
athletic, skilled in languages, and musical. He followed his father to
Scotland in February, 1565, and, in April, was ill with what was called
measles, being lodged in Stirling Castle, where he was visited by the
Queen, who, it was said, often stayed with him until midnight; "Her care
was marvellous great and tender over him" (43). On 23rd April, he was
said to be "doubtfully sick, sometimes well, other times taken with sharp
pangs, his pains holding him in his stomach and head" (42). He had not
fully recovered until the end of May; he was married to Mary on 29th
July, 1565.

Darnley was extremely tall. His reputed skull and thigh bone are preserved in the museum of the Royal College of Surgeons of England (583); unfortunately, the attribution, although probable, is not certain. The femur, however, is 536 mm. in overall length, which corresponds to a height of between 6 ft. 1 in. and 6 ft. 3 in. (628) According to Melville, Elizabeth referred to Darnley as a "long lad" (643) We have seen that Mary was also tall, for she took after her mother ("who is of the largest stature", wrote Sadler), and it is worthy of remark that in the two well known engravings of Mary and Darnley together, they are shewn as being of equal height: this, however, may be a convention.

Darnley's constitution seems to have been moody and irritable; he was addicted to alcohol and women, and one seeks almost in vain for a decent trait in his character. Drury wrote in February, 1566, that "All people say that Darnley is too much addicted to drinking. The Queen having remonstrated on one occasion, he used such language and behaviour that she left the place in tears".

On 24th December, 1566, a week after the baptism of James, Darnley left Stirling unobtrusively for Glasgow. His plans were interrupted by an illness, which has usually been said to be smallpox, but which was almost certainly syphilis. According to the story of the Lords of the Congregation against Mary, he had been poisoned (179). This "appeared from the breaking out of the body"; "He became exceeding sick, so as his whole body broke out in evil favoured pustules", but he recovered, "by force of the young age that potently expelled the poison, which was supposed to have been given him to end his troubled days". A contemporary diarist says that he had smallpox, "but some said poison", while Nau, Mary's secretary after her imprisonment in England, also says smallpox. The author of the 'Oration' argued that, since Mary was an adulteress, she was therefore also a poisoner (16), which is perhaps an overstatement.

There is an interesting statement in the manuscript entitled "Le^S Affaires du Comte de Boduell", written by Bothwell when he was in prison at Copenhagen. "Some time after", he wrote, (330), "the King fell sick of the smallpox". The manuscript is in French, and the term used for 'smallpox' is 'petite vérole'; however, the word 'vérole' has been deleted, and 'roniole' substituted in Bothwell's writing. As it now reads, the disease is thus called the 'little itch' ('roniole' = 'rognole'). It seems likely that the word 'petite' was accidentally omitted from the deletion; 'rognole' is still a slang term for syphilis. Further, the reader is referred to those words, written by Mary, in Casket Letter II, "I thought I should have been killed by his breath, for it is worse than your uncle's; and yet I sat no nearer to him than in a chair by his bed, and he lieth at the further side of it". It seems, therefore, that Darnley's breath was fouler than usual.

The disease, syphilis, began to ravage Europe at the very end of the fifteenth century, and at that time it was much more virulent and fulminating than to-day. By at latest 1530, it had been discovered that the disease could be controlled by the administration of large doses of preparations of mercury, either by mouth or by the inunction of a preparation applied to the skin. When administered in the necessarily toxic dose, the mercury caused death (necrosis) of the gum (alveolar) margin, with loosening of the teeth, and the patient's breath became peculiarly malodorous. Such a course of treatment came to be known as a 'salivation of mercury'. The conclusion is obvious that Darnley had undergone such a 'salivation', and that he, and his physicians, therefore believed him to be suffering from syphilis. His disease was certainly considered to be contagious, hence the importance of finishing the treatment with a medicated bath; but it was not thought to be infectious, for he was not kept in quarantine.

The conclusion that Darnley suffered from syphilis throws doubt on his attack of so-called measles in April, 1565, 21 months before the Glasgow illness, which is first mentioned by Drury, as we have seen, in January, 1567. This doubt is strengthened by the quotation above (page 312), which shews that the illness, with pains in the head and stomach, which lasted for almost two months, is by no means typical of measles, and the presumption is that this was an early manifestation of syphilis.

Darnley's reputed skull and femur have been described at length by Professor Karl Pearson (582); they undoubtedly both shew signs of syphilitic osteo-myelitis, and, although the provenance is somewhat doubtful, there is a likelihood that they are, in fact, the remains of the wretched King. The only question which arises is whether such advanced bone changes could have occurred in so short a time: as the disease now manifests itself, such changes would not be expected for a good many years, and Darnley died six weeks after his illness at Glasgow had begun. Dr. W. V. Macfarlane, Venereologist at the Newcastle General Hospital, writes as follows (576),

"With reference to your query about Darnley's skin eruptions, I think it safe to say that either or both (i e., those of April, 1565, and January, 1567) could easily have been due to secondary syphilis. We have to bear in mind that, in those days, it was a much more virulent disease than in the present century, and that, while the morbiliform eruption (measles-like rash) was succeeded by a small-pox type of eruption several (twenty-one) months later, this was by no means rare. Towards the end of the last century and in the first decade or two of the present century, relapses of secondary eruptions are recorded several years after the initial stage of the disease.

As to the skull condition being due to syphilis, I think this is quite feasible, even although the bone changes would appear to have followed so soon after the secondary eruption. We are too inclined to think that bone changes of an osteo-myelitic nature may not occur for several years after the secondary stage: this is quite wrong, and, while in the secondary stage of the disease, although periostitic changes are the commonest variety, gummatous osteo-myelitic processes can occur in cases undergoing the changes of precocious tertiarism. Various authorities, including Wassermann himself, believed that destructive bone changes were not uncommon in early syphilis; cranial osteo-periostitis, when it does occur in syphilis, usually occurs in the early stages".

The conclusion seems certain that Darnley had syphilis, and the probability is that he had contracted this disease before he met the Queen. He was slain on 10th February, 1567; tradition says that he was suffocated by means of a towel steeped in vinegar by his kinsman, Archibald Douglas.

Mary, now aged a little over 24, was once more a widow. She has often been accused of criminal negligence in her failure to pursue the slayers of her husband, but the details which we have of her health at this time suggest that she had given way to her emotions and was in no condition to conduct affairs of state. All the letters, save one written on 16th February, sent to England and France at this time are in Scotch, which Mary could not write, and were probably drafted by the Council. While we have little direct evidence of Mary's health after the death of Darnley, indications of her break-down are not wanting. Thus, Darnley died on 10th February; on 11th, Mary received an important letter from Archbishop Beaton, warning her of an attempt to be made against her: she did not reply to that letter, and in a letter later sent in her name, it is said that she was "so grievous and tormented" that she could not. Robert Melville, who was on an embassy to Elizabeth, had received no word from her a fornight after Darnley's death. In spite of her strong family affection, she did not write to her uncles or to her grandmother, although she was usually a good correspondent. On 15th February, Darnley was buried: Mary did not attend the funeral. On 16th February, she removed to Seton. According to the Bishop of Ross, "she would have continued using none other than candle-light, had not the Privy Council, moved by the advice of her physicians, pressed her to leave that kind of solitary life, and repair to some good, open and wholesome air". On 8th March, Killigrew, who brought an autograph letter from Elizabeth, which naturally called for an autograph reply, had an audience in a dark room. Mary hardly spoke, and it has been suggested that she was impersonated by one of her Maries. She does not seem to have replied to Elizabeth's letter. Clernault arrived from Paris on 25th March, and some weeks later wrote to Archbishop Beaton, "She has as yet neither listened to or looked at anything that I brought from you or others". On 29th March, Drury, the Marshall of Berwick, records that she is ill: "This Queen breaketh much", and also that she is subject to frequent fainting fits. In the middle of March, the infant James was removed to Stirling Castle, but Mary did not accompany him on the journey.

Later, in April, Mary visited her son in Stirling; on her return, she was kidnapped by Bothwell and taken to Dunbar. On 3rd May, Lady Bothwell divorced her husband for adultery, citing her maid as co-respondent; on 6th May, Mary and Bothwell returned to Edinburgh; and on 7th May, Bothwell's marriage was annulled in the Consistory Court on account of consanguinity. Be it noted that Bothwell's marriage had been made under dispensation, that Mary knew this, that the dispensation was abstracted, and that Mary thereafter consented to marry Bothwell, knowing the annulment to have been obtained by fraud; finally, she married him by Protestant rites on 15th May. Tolerant in religious matters Mary may have been, but here she cannot have been in control of herself. Two days after her marriage, she is heard to call out for a knife with which to kill herself. Four days later, Drury was saying that she "long had a spice of the falling sickness".

The events which led to Carberry followed swiftly, and, on 15th June, Mary was lodged a prisoner in Edinburgh, where "she came to the window sundry times in so miserable a state, her hairs hanging about her lugs, and her breast, yea, the most part of all her body from the waist up, bare and discovered, that no man could look upon her, but she moved him to pity and compassion" (153).

Mary was removed to Lochleven on 17th June, and there, according to Nau (671): "She remained fifteen days without eating, drinking or conversing with the inmates of the house, so that many thought she would have died". By mid-July, she was in good health Various people heard that she was pregnant, and she said that she took herself to be seven weeks gone with child. On 24th July, she abdicated, and Nau says (672) that "when prevailed upon to sign her abdication, she was lying on her bed in a state of very great weakness, partly in consequence of a great flux, the result of a miscarriage of twins, her issue by Bothwell", Soon after, she had a swelling of one half of her body and one leg, perhaps a '*phlegmasia alba dolens*' or, 'white-leg', a condition of thrombosis, of the deep veins of the leg which occasionally follows delivery. Nine months later, on 2nd May, 1568, Mary escaped from Lochleven. Langside was fought on 13th, and, on 16th May, Mary arrived in England.

From all this, there seems to be no doubt that she had a complete break-down, probably of an hysterical nature, after Darnley's death, and that, from this time until some time before she escaped from captivity, she reacted to stress in such a way that she was frequently not mistress of herself. During the whole of this period, she never emerges into daylight, but is always seen in the shadows of Bothwell and her Council, who managed affairs with little reference to herself, and even bent her to their will.

James Hepburn, fourth Earl of Bothwell, hereditary Great Admiral of Scotland, later Duke of Orkney, and Lieutenant-General of the Marches, was born in 1535 (252). He was, therefore, 31 at the time of Darnley's death. He was educated mainly in France and wrote French with a scholarly hand. His health was good, and, until his injury by Jock o' the Park on 7th October, 1566, we hear nothing of any illness. On that occasion, he received a wound in the thigh, possibly another in the hand, and a sword stroke across the frontal region of his skull which left a scar (276). At first he was thought to be blinded, but this fear was unfounded. Fourteen weeks later, he suffered a serious flux of blood from one of his wounds.

After the affair of Carberry, he fled to the North of Scotland, and, eventually, to Norway, where he was imprisoned and conveyed to Copenhagen, and thence to Malmoe. Here he remained in durance until 1573; in that year, a man "lately out of Sweden reported that the Earl of Bothwell was stark mad, and had long been so" (287). There are some other indications that he became insane at about this time. In the summer of the same year, he was removed to Dragsholm, where he died on 24th April, 1578, aged about 43. He was buried in the church at Faareveijle, his body being exhumed in 1858. He was about 5ft. 6in. tall and looked about 50. His hair was red and streaked with grey; the scar on his head could easily be seen (288).

The immorality of Bothwell's life is notorious, and it would not be surprising if he, too, had contracted syphilis during one of his numerous amours. This hypothesis might account for his subsequent insanity, but there is no other evidence of the disease, save that, in spite of his many 'affairs', history only records one illegitimate offspring.

Mary arrived at Workington on 16th May, 1568. She was 25½ years old, and was to spend the remaining nineteen years of her life in captivity. From Workington she was conveyed to Carlisle, and thence, in July, to Bolton. It was at Bolton that the project for a marriage between Mary and the Duke of Norfolk was first mooted, a project which was to lead the Duke to the scaffold for treason. Bothwell, whom she now believed to have murdered her second husband, was forgotten, and she readily assented to a divorce from him, although that divorce was never, in fact, obtained.

In Feburary, 1569, Mary was removed to Tutbury, the strongest castle in the region. She dreaded the removal, and caused much delay during the journey, complaining of the old pain in her side (462). Three weeks later, she was visited by a Mr. White, when "she laid her hand on her left side, and complained of an old grief newly increased there" (463). Shrewsbury, now Mary's keeper, wrote to Cecil on 13th March, 1569 (464),

"She hath complained almost this fortnight of her grief of the spleen, which my physician, Leveret, informeth me, as he understands by her physician, is 'obstructio splenis cum flatu hypochondriaco', wherewith oft times, by reason of great pains through windy matter ascending unto her head and other parts, she is ready to swoon. On Thursday last, she received pills devised by her own physician, whereof she was very sick that night, but, after the working, amended. She wanteth, as she saith, things necessary touching medicine for her in such needful cases".

In April, Mary was removed to Wingfield, and on 10th May, 1569, Shrewsbury again wrote to Cecil concerning her health (465),

"This Queen, on receipt of pills by her physician for ease of her spleen, became very sick and swooned divers times vehemently, so as they were driven to give her to drink *aqua vitae* in good quanity, but after the pills wrought the same night, she escaped the danger. Her body remains yet still very much distempered".

Mary's account of the attack was (415) that she "was suddenly seized with shivering and vomited and fell several times into convulsions". The Spanish Ambassador thought her illness to be feigned (466). She rapidly recovered but shewed marked symptoms of hysteria on the following day. She now wrote to Norfolk, and speaks of herself as "in pain, being in fever", and signs the letter "from my bed" (467).

At the request of the Bishop of Ross, now Mary's Ambassador in London, Elizabeth sent two physicians (Drs. Cauldwell and Francis) to Mary. On 25th May, 1569, Shrewsbury wrote (468), "Since the arrival of the physicians within these two days, there has grown in the next chamber by her, a very unpleasant and fulsome savour, hurtful to her health, by continual pestering and uncleanly order of her own folks".

The upshot was that the Queen was removed to Chatsworth, but returned to Wingfield before 1st June. At the end of June, she consulted Dr. Francis "for the old grief of her side", and, nearly two months later, she was still troubled with it (469). Shrewsbury wrote to Cecil (469) that Wingfield, "in consequence of the long abode here, and the number of people (more than 240), waxes unsavoury".

In September, on Norfolk's treason becoming known, she was returned to Tutbury; on 8th November, Norfolk was sent to the Tower. On 9th November, Shrewsbury wrote (470),

"This said Queen on Saturday night last complained much of grief and pain of her side, her heart and head, and suffered then a painful fit. And, on the night following, her fit increased, whereat she shewed herself somewhat afraid of her life. Since that time she remains still complaining of faintness at her heart and pain of her head .. Truly, her colour and complexion of her face is presently much decayed".

The term 'fit', of course, must not be interpreted in its modern sense; it means a bout or attack, not a convulsive seizure.

When the revolt of the Northern Earls broke out in November, 1569, Mary was removed to Coventry, returning to Tutbury early in 1570. On 28th February, Shrewsbury writes (471) that she "fell into a fever on

Saturday last, with pain of her head and swelling of her hand. To-day, . . .
while writing, (she) fell into a fit of her fever, and caused her secretary to
finish her letter".

However, Mary seems to have had better health this year, and we hear
of her using her long-bow. The death of her servant, John Beaton, in
October, 1570, caused her much distress, and, although she was suffering
from an inflammation of the eye, the result of a severe cold, she wrote a
long letter of condolence to his brother, the Archbishop of Glasgow (472).
Her health now deteriorated again: on 27th November, she wrote to the
Bishop of Ross (473),

"It is of truth we are not in good health, nor have we not been two
days together since your departing herefrom. For, notwithstanding
the accustomed dolour of our side, there is a rheum (cold) that
troubles our head greatly with an extreme pain, and descends in the
stomach, so that it makes us wholly to lack appetite of eating . . .
Yesterday, thinking the air should have done us good, we walked
forth a little on horseback, and, so long as we were abroad, felt out-
selves in a very good state, but yet since find our sickness nothing
slacked".

Late in November, Mary was removed to Sheffield. Apart from a few
short visits to Chatsworth, Worksop and Buxton Spa, she was to remain at
Sheffield for fourteen years. The convenience of having her at Sheffield
was, to Shrewsbury, immense. With Mary's large retinue, the guards and
Shrewsbury's own household, the place of residence, devoid of sanitation,
soon became 'noisome'. At Sheffield there was a manor house in the Castle
grounds, and a change of residence was thus easy, when one of the places
became too foul.

On 3rd December, 1570, the news reached London that the Queen of
Scots was 'very sick' (474), and, on 11th, the Bishop of Ross who visited
her wrote to Cecil (475),

"We found the Queen's Majesty, my mistress, much molested with
a continued distillation from her head into her stomach, whereof
hath grown such debility and weakness in that part that she neither
hath desire to any meat, neither faculty to retain that long when
she doth eat it. She is troubled also with an incessant provocation
to vomit, by the which she hath and doth void a great quantity of
raw, tough and slimy phlegm, without any great or manifest relief
or release of her pains, likewise she is molested with a great inflammation and tension in her left side, under her short ribs, which
reacheth so far every way that they yet doubt whether it be the inflammation of the stomach, the spleen, the womb, or of all those three
parts together, as rather, by the accidents which follow her Grace,
they gather. Her Grace is likewise troubled with continual lack of
sleep, which hath continued for ten or twelve days past, all which

time she hath kept her bed, and still remains in the same estate, continually afflicted with sighs and pensiveness. Before the coming of the
physicians, her Majesty was much molested with vehement fits of the
mother (womb), with the which she hath been marvellously afflicted
this 10th December in the morning. The 9th December they gave her
Highness a gentle potion to cleanse her stomach and first veins (i.e
the great veins nearest the liver, the inferior vena cava) which through
the great weakness of these parts, she vomited again. The 10th they
proved (tried) afresh, but her Highness could not brook it in any form,
neither yet anything that she received the same morning. Besides the
judgment of the physicians, I do perfectly understand that her disease
proceedth of extreme thought and care, and of want of wonted exer-
cises".

However, the Queen was not thought to be in danger of death, and, by
29th December, she said she was 'partly convalesced" (476).

By 13th January, 1571, the two physicians had left. Mary, who had had
another 'rheum', acknowledged that they had 'taken great pains', but
added that "we are in the same state as they left us in, and does what we
can to obtain quietness" (477). Her health improved, but, on 5th May,
she asked the Bishop of Ross to tell Elizabeth (478), "the state of my person,
how I have been lately vexed by sickness, with a great vomiting, first of
pure blood, and after of congealed blood, phlegm and choler (bile), the
dolour of my side, etc. It may bring about my death at length". She also
asked for two physicians to be sent from France.

In February, 1571, Ridolfi's plot started, but, in April, the Lords of the
Congregation captured Dumbarton Castle, until then held in her interest.
A month after this event, Shrewsbury writes, "she has been very sickly
since and brooks little meat". She was sick again early in June and had
swooned three or four times. Shrewsbury thought that the sickness arose
more from anxiety than from physical causes (479).

In September, 1571, Norfolk, who had been released, was a second time
committed to the Tower, and Mary again began to complain of the old
grief in her side and of headaches. During Norfolk's trial, she kept her room
for a whole week, and, having become very religious, as was natural in
such adversity, she "fell into great contemplation, fasting and prayer,
observing three days of abstinence each week" (480). She remained sickly
throughout the first half of 1572, and, on the execution of the Duke of
Norfolk, fell into what was described as a 'passion of sickness' (481).
Once again, Shrewsbury was not impressed and said that she had "made
overmuch use of physics and baths" (481).

In 1573 and on subsequent occasions, Mary was allowed to visit the
Baths at Buxton; Shrewsbury disapproved: "She seems more healthful
now. She has very much used bathing and herbs of late. What need she
hath of Buxton Well, I know not". It is to be noted that at this time she was

in high hopes of obtaining her freedom. Various plots were on foot, and she feared that, if they should be discovered, she would be poisoned. She wrote to the French Ambassador for a mithridate (an antidote to poison). The fear remained with her, so that, next year, she asks for (482) *terra sigillata* or fine unicorn's horn (both believed to be sovereign remedies against poisoning).

From now until 1580, apart from minor ailments, her health seems to have been good. We hear of a sprained foot and of a bad cough (483) on one occasion, but there is little news of the old grief in her side. There is, however, abundant proof of her increasing religiosity, in letters to the Pope (486) and in such expressions as her 'desire to restore religion to this poor isle'.

In July, 1580, she injured her back by a fall from a horse when starting on one of her visits to Buxton (484) and, in May, 1581, she lost the use of her legs (485) which continued to be afflicted until the end of the year.

In November, 1581, Mary was visited by Beale, an emissary of Elizabeth's Privy Council. Mary staged a full-scale attack of stomach pain, headache, medicines and poultices, which certainly impressed her visitor, in spite of the fact that he and Shrewsbury at first thought she was malingering. He wrote (487),

"Her left side and thigh have long been ill, and to ease the pain she is forced to use continually medicines and poultices, which I have smelled myself, and Lady Shrewsbury has seen applied. She cannot stand or be out of her bed. Ordinarily she eats little and drinks more, but not immoderately. She complains that her nutriment is wholly converted into phlegm, whereof, many times, she casteth up great abundance. She is continually dealing with physic to consume the phlegm and help the distillation which she says falls upon her side".

At the beginning of the following year "she felt herself very weak, but void of pain" (488). In May, 1582, she was visited by two more physicians, Drs. Smythe and Barsdale (489). They recommended another visit to Buxton. In spite of this, she still continued to complain of ill-health (490).

In 1583 her health was better: she visited Worksop on two occasions. Her last visit to Buxton was made in July, 1584 (491). In September, Mary was removed from Shrewsbury's charge and placed under the care of Sadler, once again at Wingfield. He reported that there was little likelihood of her escape, seeing the "tenderness of her body, subject to a vehement rheum upon any cold, which causeth plentiful distillation from above down unto her left foot, wherewith, resting there, she is much pained and is sometimes a little swollen" (492). Soon afterwards, Paulet was made her keeper, and, in December, 1585, she was moved to Chartley.

In 1586, Mary entered into Babington's conspiracy. She was now much stronger and in better health, being also very optimistic of the outcome of the plot. She writes, "I thank God that He hath not yet set me so low, that I am able to handle my crossbow for killing of a deer, and to gallop after the hounds on horseback". In August the Babington Conspiracy was exposed. Mary was not informed, but was removed to Tixall while her papers were rifled. She was brought back to Chartley again and, finding her papers stolen and the whole plot exposed, she became ill and took to her bed. When the Babington conspirators were executed, she was again unable to walk. Five days later she was removed to Fotheringhay.

Her trial for participation in Babington's Conspiracy took place three weeks later. She behaved with great courage and dignity. From the time of her condemnation she remained unwell. When the Commissioners came to announce the date of her execution, they found her in bed suffering from a 'rheum'. However, she arose and dressed herself to receive them. The following day, 8th February, 1587, she was executed. She was so crippled with pain that she had to be helped by her servants down to the Great Hall of Fotheringhay (642), where the scaffold was erected. However, conscious of her dignity and her predicament, she mounted the scaffold without help nor did she shew any difficulty in kneeling and placing her head on the block. The executioner's first blow struck her on the back of the head and probably stunned her. His second severed the head, save for a little gristle, which was divided by a third blow (113). Thus died Mary at the age of 44.

We have, in this account, abundant evidence of Mary's main physical complaint, a gastric ulcer, and it is noteworthy that, as she became more inured to her captivity, the symptoms became less urgent. At the same time, there is also good reason for diagnosing an hysterical diathesis, of which we saw the beginning in her early life, and which shewed itself particularly in an aggravation of all her symptoms at times of stress; in the use she made, either consciously or unconsciously, of her illnesses to further her ends; in the religiosity which developed as adversity thickened round her, so that she even came to believe that she died a martyr to the Catholic faith; in the manner in which she allowed herself to be dominated by any man of strong character who came into contact with her; and in certain specific symptoms, such as the loss of the use of her legs, which disappeared when she was hoping to regain her freedom and when she became the centre of the scene at her execution. That Mary Stewart had undergone a great deal of stress no one will deny, yet, when we consider her broken and spoiled upbringing, and remember, too, that very tall women are often at a psychological disadvantage, we can see that the seeds of hysteria were already sown before adversity overtook her.

The tragedy of Mary Queen of Scots is not lessened when we survey her medical case history. It is apparent that her worldly fortunes were translated with great facility into bodily states, and it is to be doubted if such a person could, even in less tragic circumstances, ever have proved happy. Yet her unhappy temperament should do her this much good in the eyes of posterity: hysterical people are often sexually frigid, so that this diagnosis conflicts with the story of her lustful and adulterous intrigue with Bothwell, and, if she did break down after the death of Darnley as she seems to have done, this again argues her innocence of that assassination; a murderess would have eaten a hearty breakfast after hearing of the success of her schemes and would only have shewn remorse, shame or mental upset when discovery had become inevitable and danger of punishment was imminent.

A diagnosis of an hysterical diathesis is a medical, not a moral, judgment, and it should carry with it no stigma. On the moral side, it may be added that, in moments of supreme crisis, as, for example, after the death of Riccio and at her execution, Mary Queen of Scots displayed a behaviour so courageous as to out-weigh her failings, and this, combined with her beauty, charm, innocence and misfortune, has given her an enchantment wherewith men are still bewitched. Requiescat in pace.

Sir James Balfour

Sir James Balfour was in good credit with Darnley until the time of the latter's death. He returned to Edinburgh secretly some time after that event, but kept a guard about him. He was soon in good correspondence with Bothwell, and became, under his government, keeper of Edinburgh Castle. After Carberry, he was on friendly terms with the Lords of the Congregation, and he finally gave up his governorship on "good composition". This, in spite of the facts that he was trusted by no one, bitterly hated by John Knox, and later came in danger of being tried for the murder of Darnley.

These facts could be explained in the following manner. Balfour was the originator of Darnley's plot to murder Mary at Kirk o'Field. It was he who bought the powder, installed it in the New Provost's House, which belonged to his brother, and prepared the cellar of the Old Provost's House. Shortly before the fatal night, Balfour and Darnley quarrelled, perhaps over the question of rewards. In spite, Balfour betrayed his master to Moray or Morton, thus enabling them to set the ambush in the South Garden, whither Balfour knew that Darnley would excape shortly before the explosion.

Meanwhile, one of the King's servants, Sandy Durham, betrayed Darnley's plot to Bothwell: he received his reward soon afterwards. Presumably, Balfour heard that Durham had seen Bothwell and, putting two and two together, realised that Darnley's plot to kill Mary, Bothwell and the rest of her *entourage* must now fail, and that his position would therefore become impossible. He saved himself by betraying not only Darnley, but also Moray and Morton to Bothwell, who thus received confirmation of Durham's story and learnt of the ambush in which the King was to be killed. We may assume that Balfour did not tell Bothwell that it was he who had opened the plot to Moray; perhaps he blamed another of Darnley's servants. Equally, we may assume that, when Bothwell, after the masque at Holyrood, told Mary of Darnley's plot to blow up Kirk o'Field, he said nothing of the other plot by Moray and Morton to kill the King in the garden. When, therefore, he had prevented Mary from returning to Kirk o'Field and had himself gone thither, following, from Blackfriars, that part of the route which Darnley would have expected Mary to take, he knew that his action would cause Darnley's death, but Mary was ignorant of this, and expected Bothwell to bring the King back to Holyrood to answer for his behaviour.

This explanation would account for Balfour's subsequent actions and for his ability to come to terms with both Bothwell and the Lords of the Congregation. Since his triple treachery might have been discovered at any time, it is not surprising that he kept a guard about himself after he returned to Edinburgh. It would also explain the readiness with which Mary came to regard Bothwell as one of her husband's murderers.

APPENDIX C

Bibliography and References

(1–20) Anderson

Collections Relating to the History of Mary Queen of Scotland. In four volumes. Containing a Great Number of Original Papers never before Printed. Also a few Scarce Pieces Reprinted, taken form the best Copies. Revised and Published by James Anderson, Esq., with an Explanatory Index of the Obsolete Words, and Prefaces shewing the Importance and Usefulness of these Collections. The second edition. London: Fletcher Gyles, etc. 1729.

Vol. I

(1) 24	(5) 41	(9) 87
(2) 36	(6) 43	(10) 107
(3) 38	(7) 45	(11) 111
(4) 40	(8) 48	

Vol. II

(12) 7	(15) 22	(18) 165–191
(13) 10	(16) 49	(19) 173
(14) 18	(17) 70	

Vol. IV part 2

(20) 165

(21) Arnot

A Collection and Abridgement of Celebrated Criminal Trials in Scotland. From A.D. 1536 to 1784. With historical and critical remarks. By Hugo Arnot, Esq., Advocate. Edinburgh: Smellie. 1758.

(21) 385

(22) Bain.

The Hamilton Papers. Letters and Papers illustrating the Political Relations of England and Scotland in the XVIth Century. Formerly in the possession of the Dukes of Hamilton. Now in the British Museum. Edited by Joseph Bain, F.S.A. Scot., etc. Vol. I A.D. 1532–1543. Published by the authority of the Lords Commissioners of Her Majesty's Treasury, under the direction of the Deputy Clerk Register of Scotland. H.M. General Register House, Edinburgh. 1890.

(22) 551.

(23–90) Bain.

Calendar of the State Papers relating to Scotland and Mary Queen of Scots, 1547–1603. Preserved in the Public Record Office, the British Museum, and elsewhere in England. Edited by Joseph Bain, F.S.A. Scot., etc. Published by the authority of the Lords Commissioners of Her Majesty's Treasury, under the direction of the Deputy Clerk Register of Scotland. H.M. General Register House, Edinburgh. 1898.

Vol. 1 (A.D. 1547–1563)

(23) 260	(28) 612	(32) 647
(24) 482	(29) 614	(33) 666
(25) 555	(30) 634	(34) 672
(26) 605	(31) 642	(35) 687
(27) 607		

Vol. 2 (A.D. 1563–1569)

(36) 12	(55) 277	(73) 319
(37) 29	(56) 278	(74) 320
(38) 30	(57) 281	(75) 322
(39) 39	(58) 283	(76) 323
(40) 135	(59) 288	(77) 324
(41) 143	(60) 289	(78) 325
(42) 145	(61) 293	(79) 326
(43) 147	(62) 294	(80) 327
(44) 166	(63) 300	(81) 328
(45) 172	(64) 308	(82) 330
(46) 180	(65) 309	(83) 350
(47) 182	(66) 310	(84) 356
(48) 220	(67) 311	(85) 360
(49) 241	(68) 312	(86) 517
(50) 269	(69) 313	(87) 576
(51) 270	(70) 316	(88) 722
(52) 273	(71) 317	(89) 728
(53) 274	(72) 318	(90) 730
(54) 276		

(91) Berry-Schiern.

Life of James Hepburn, Earl of Bothwell by Frederik Schiern, Professor of History in the University of Copenhagen. Translated from the Danish by the Rev. David Berry, F.S.A. Scot. Edinburgh: David Douglas. 1880.

(91) 407

(92–93) Black.

Andrew Lang and the Casket Letter Controversy by J.B. Black, M.A., LL.D., F.R.Hist.S., Professor of History in the University of Aberdeen. Being the Andrew Lang Lecture delivered before the University of St. Andrews, 11 May 1949. Thomas Nelson & Sons, Ltd.; Edinburgh. 1591.

(92) 20   (93) 33

(94–96) Brown and Bentinck.

Calendar of State Papers and Manuscripts, relating to English Affairs, existing in the Archives and Collections of Venice, and in other libraries of Northern Italy. Vol. 7, 1558–1580. Edited by the late Rawdon Brown and the Right Hon. G. Cavendish Bentinck, M.P. London: Eyre and Spottiswoode, etc. 1890.

(94) 388	(95) 389	(96) 390

(97) Cameron.

The Scottish Correspondence of Mary of Lorraine, including some three hundred letters from 20th February 1542–3 to 15th May 1560. Edited by Annie I. Cameron, M.A., Ph.D. Edinburgh: Printed at the University Press by T. and A. Constable, Ltd., for the Scottish History Society. 1927.

(97) 433

(98) Chauviré.

Etat Présent de la Controversie sur les Letters de la Cassette, by Prof. Roger Chauviré, in Revue Historique, 1935, (janvier-juin): Vol. 175:

(98) 66

(99–100) Clifford—Sadler.

The State Papers and Letters of Sir Ralph Sadler, Knight-Banneret. Edited by Arthur Clifford, Esq. In two volumes. To which is added a memoir of the life of Sir Ralph Sadler with historical notes by Walter Scott, Esq. Edinburgh: Archibald Constable & Co., etc. 1809.

Vol. I

(99) 87	(100) 253

(101–112) Crosby.

Calendar of State Papers, Foreign Series of the reign of Elizabeth, 1566–8, preserved in the State Paper Department of Her Majesty's Public Record Office. Edited by Allan James Crosby, Esq., B.A. Oxon, Barrister-at-Law. London: Longman and Co,, etc. 1871.

(101) 94	(105) 217	(109) 297
(102) 192	(106) 229	(110) 309
(103) 198	(107) 237	(111) 363
(104) 215	(108) 261	(112) 405

(113) Dack-Wynkfeilde.

The Trial, Execution and Death of Mary Queen of Scots. Compiled from the original documents by Charles Dack. Northampton: The Dryden Press: Taylor & Son, etc. 1889.

(113) 16

(114–123) Dickinson-Knox.

John Knox's History of the Reformation in Scotland. Edited by William Croft Dickinson, D.Lit. In two volumes. Thomas Nelson and Sons, Ltd. London. 1949.

Vol. 1.

(114) 260

Vol. 2.

(115) 33	(118) 47–53	(121) 209
(116) 38	(119) 54	(122) 327
(117) 40	(120) 158	(123) 444

(*124–202*) *Fleming.*

Mary Queen of Scots. From her Birth to her Flight into England. A Brief Biography, with Critical Notes, a few Documents hitherto unpublished, and an Itinerary by David Hay Fleming. Second Edition. London: Hodder and Stoughton. 1898.

(124) 1	(151) 158	(177) 427
(125) 27	(152) 163	(178) 428
(126) 28	(153) 164	(179) 430
(127) 29	(154) 165	(180) 432
(128) 31	(155) 169	(181) 442
(129) 38	(156) 171	(182) 443
(130) 39	(157) 222	(183) 444
(131) 51	(158) 236	(184) 447
(132) 52	(159) 238	(185) 449
(133) 108	(160) 270	(186) 452
(134) 109	(161) 272	(187) 454
(135) 110	(162) 307	(188) 463
(136) 115	(163) 314	(189) 477
(137) 117	(164) 352	(190) 481
(138) 128	(165) 359	(191) 485
(139) 131	(166) 364	(192) 504
(130) 132	(167) 374	(193) 507
(141) 136	(168) 380	(194) 510
(142) 137	(169) 381	(195) 517
(143) 140	(170) 386	(196) 537
(144) 141	(171) 403	(197) 539
(145) 144	(172) 405	(198) 540
(146) 145	(173) 413	(199) 541
(147) 146	(174) 414	(200) 542
(148) 148	(175) 416	(201) 543
(149) 153	(176) 419	(202) 544
(150) 157		

(*203–251*) *Goodall.*

An Examination of the Letters, said to be written by Mary Queen of Scots, to James Earl of Bothwell: shewing by intrinsick and extrinsick Evidence that they are Forgeries, also, an Enquiry into the Murder of King Henry. By Walter Goodall. In two volumes. Edinburgh: T. and W. Ruddimans. 1754

Vol. 1.

(203) 274

Vol. 2.

Containing I. The Letters themselves, in Scottish, Latin and French. II. The Conferences at York and Westminster, and other Writings relative to the letters.

(204) 29	(220) 212	(236) 256
(205) 36	(221) 217	(237) 261
(206) 54	(222) 221	(238) 265
(207) 75	(223) 224	(239) 281
(208) 76	(224) 227	(240) 298
(209) 81	(225) 231	(241) 300
(210) 87	(226) 234	(242) 304
(211) 90	(227) 235	(243) 305
(212) 91	(228) 238	(244) 307
(213) 92	(229) 239	(245) 311
(214) 139	(230) 241	(246) 312
(215) 140	(231) 242	(247) 313
(216) 192	(232) 243	(248) 317
(217) 200	(233) 244	(249) 321
(218) 206	(234) 246	(250) 332
(219) 208	(235) 252	(251) 360

(252–288):Gore-Browne.

Lord Bothwell by Robert Gore-Browne. A Study of the Life, Character and Times of James Hepburn, 4th Earl of Bothwell. Collins, London. 1937.

(252) 30	(265) 167	(277) 265
(253) 43	(266) 175	(278) 287
(254) 44	(267) 188	(279) 294
(255) 45	(268) 192	(280) 328
(256) 50–51	(269) 193	(281) 330
(257) 61	(270) 198	(282) 340
(258) 65	(271) 199	(283) 345
(259) 78	(272) 205	(284) 346
(260) 99	(273) 236	(285) 362
(261) 101	(274) 241	(286) 409
(262) 104	(275) 253	(287) 448
(263) 122	(276) 263	(288) 458
(264) 142		

(289–302) Henderson.

The Casket Letters and Mary Queen of Scots. With appendices. By T.F. Henderson. Edinburgh: Adam and Charles Black. 1889.

(289) 14	(294) 47	(299) 163
(290) 17	(295) 48	(300) 169
(291) 19	(296) 92	(301) 177
(292) 41	(297) 153	(302) 182
(293) 45	(298) 156	

(303–314) Henderson

Mary Queen of Scots. Her Environment and Tragedy. A Biography. By T.F. Henderson. In two volumes. London: Hutchinson and Co. 1905.

Vol. 1.

(303) 147	(305) 218	(306) 245
(304) 161		

Vol. 2.

(307) 397	(310) 450	(313) 664
(308) 446	(311) 451	(314) 667
(309) 448	(312) 486	

(315–331) Hosack

Mary Queen of Scots and Her Accusers. Embracing a narrative of events from the death of James V in 1542 until the death of Queen Mary in 1587. By John Hosack, Barrister-at-Law. Second edition, much enlarged. In two volumes. William Blackwood and Sons: Edinburgh.

Vol. 1. 1870

(315) 213 note	(320) 291	(325) 523
(316) 214	(321) 293	(326) 551
(317) 246	(322) 294	(327) 552
(318) 268	(323) 380	(328) 556
(319) 290	(324) 518	(329) 558

Vol. 2. 1874

(330) 583	(331) 584

(332–333) Hume

Calendar of State Papers relating to English Affairs preserved principally in the Archives of the Simancas. Vol. 1. Elizabeth. 1558–1567. Edited by Martin A.S. Hume, F.R. Hist. S. London: Eyre and Spottiswoode. 1892.

(332) 618	(333) 638

(334–338) Hume.

The Love Affairs of Mary Queen of Scots. A Political History. By Martin Hume. London: Eveleigh Nash. 1903.

(334) 112	(336) 349	(338) 416
(335) 298 note	(337) 412	

(339–398) Keith.

History of the Affairs of Church and State in Scotland. From the beginning of the Reformation to the year 1568. By the Right Rev. Robert Keith, Primus of the Scottish Episcopal Church. With Biographical Sketch, Notes and Index, by the Editor. In three volumes. Edinburgh. Printed for the Spottiswoode Society.

Vol. 1. 1844

(339) xcvi	(340) xcvii	(341) ciii

Vol. 2. 1845

(342) 90	(357) 482	(372) 573 note

(343) 91	(358) 482 note	(373) 578 note
(344) 97	(359) 484 note	(374) 579
(345) 326	(360) 486 note	(375) 584 note
(346) 329	(361) 496 note	(376) 585 note
(347) 368 note	(362) 497 note	(377) 610
(348) 405	(363) 517 note	(378) 612
(349) 426	(364) 521	(379) 616 note
(350) 446 note	(365) 532	(380) 617 note
(351) 447 note	(366) 535	(381) 618 note
(352) 448	(367) 554	(382) 644
(353) 458 note	(368) 555	(383) 659
(354) 460	(369) 556	(384) 789
(355) 477	(370) 565	(385) 791 note
(356) 478 note	(371) 569	(386) 797

Vol. 3. 1850

(387) 41	(391) 152	(395) 260
(388) 51	(392) 153	(396) 261
(389) 145	(393) 237	(397) 286
(390) 146	(394) 252	(398) 349

(399–401) Knox.

The Historie of the Reformatioun of Religioun Within the Realm of Scotland, conteining The Manner and be quhat Persons the Lycht of Chrystis Evangell has bein manifested unto this Realme, after that horribill and universal Defectioun from the Treuth, whiche has come be the Means of that Roman Antichryst.

Together with The Life of John Knoxe the Author, and several Curious Pieces wrote by him; particularly that most rare and scarce one, intitled, The first Blast of the Trumpet against the Monstrous Regiment of Women, and a large Index and Glossary.

Taken from the Original Manuscript in the University Library of Glasgow and compared with other ancient Copies. Edinburgh: Robert Fleming and Company, etc. 1732.

(399) 258	(400) 259	(401) 392

(402–421) Labanoff.

Lettres, Instructions et Mémoires de Marie Stuart, Reine d'Ecosse; publiés sur les originaux et les manuscrits du State Paper Office de Londres et des principales archives et bibliothèques de l'Europe, et accompagnés d'un résumé chronologique. Par le Prince Alexandre Labanoff. In seven volumes. Londres: Charles Dolman. 1844.

Vol. 1.

(402) 281	(405) 393	(407) 396
(403) 349	(406) 395	(408) 398
(404) 392		

Vol. 2.

(409) 5	(412) 31	(414) 44
(410) 6	(413) 41	(415) 342
(411) 21		

Vol. 7.

(416) 6	(418) 13	(420) 110
(417) 8	(419) 109	(421) 340

(422–431) Laing.

The History of Scotland from the Union of the Crowns on the accession of James VI to the throne of England, to the Union of the Kingdoms in the reign of Queen Anne. The third edition, corrected. With a Preliminary Dissertation on the participation of Mary Queen of Scots in the murder of Darnley. By Malcolm Laing, Esq. In four volumes. London: Mawman, etc. 1819.

Vol. 1.

(422) 24	(425) 58 note	(427) 82
(423) 35 note	(426) 75	(428) 90
(424) 52		

Vol. 2.

(429) 74	(430) 77	(431) 109

(432–461) Lang.

The Mystery of Mary Stuart. By Andrew Lang. Longmans, Green and Co. London. 1901.

(432) 21	(442) 197	(452) 318 note
(433) 25	(443) 201	(453) 319 note
(434) 61	(444) 208	(454) 323
(435) 84	(445) 209	(455) 354
(436) 108	(446) 210	(456) 393
(437) 109	(447) 211	(457) 414
(438) 126	(448) 226	(458) 416
(439) 135	(449) 257	(459) 418
(440) 171	(450) 291	(460) 419
(441) 180	(451) 292	(461) 422

(462–492) Leader.

Mary Queen of Scots in Captivity; a Narrative of Events from January, 1569, to December, 1584, whilst George Earl of Shrewsbury was the guardian of the Scottish Queen. By John Daniel Leader, F.S.A. Sheffield: Leader and Sons. 1880.

(462) 30	(473) 138	(483) 421
(463) 42	(474) 158	(484) 446
(464) 46	(475) 159	(485) 459 note
(465) 61	(476) 161	(486) 466
(466) 62	(477) 163	(487) 480
(467) 63	(478) 184	(488) 489

(468) 65	(479) 197	(489) 504
(469) 73	(480) 248	(490) 514
(470) 97	(481) 261	(491) 584
(471) 116	(482) 322	(492) 603
(472) 137		

(493–498) Mahon.

The Indictment of Mary Queen of Scots as derived from a manuscript in the University Library at Cambridge, hitherto unpublished. With comments on the authorship of the manuscript and on its connected documents. By Major-General R.H. Mahon, C.B., C.S.I. Cambridge: at the University Press. 1923.

(493) 3	(495) 39	(497) 51
(494) 28	(496) 49	(498) 52

(499–521) Mahon.

Mary Queen of Scots. A Study of the Lennox Narrative in the University Library at Cambridge. With some reflections on her environment in France & on her marriage negotiations. By Major-General R.H. Mahon, C.B., C.S.I., F.R. Hist.S. Cambridge: at the University Press. 1924.

(499) 75	(507) 110	(515) 128
(500) 76	(508) 111	(516) 129
(501) 77	(509) 112	(517) 139
(502) 78	(510) 117	(518) 141
(503) 78 ff.	(511) 122	(519) 142
(504) 84	(512) 126	(520) 143
(505) 93	(513) 126 note	(521) 209
(506) 101	(514) 127	

(522–575) Mahon.

The Tragedy of Kirk o'Field. By Major-General R.H. Mahon, C.B., C.S.I. Cambridge, at the University Press. 1930.

(522) 2	(540) 130	(558) 211
(523) 25	(541) 140	(559) 213
(524) 44	(542) 149	(560) 215
(525) 46	(543) 152	(561) 235
(526) 47	(544) 155	(562) 245
(527) 49 note	(545) 158	(563) 248
(528) 63	(546) 160	(564) 251
(529) 80	(547) 165	(565) 252
(530) 84	(548) 166	(566) 255
(531) 85	(549) 169	(567) 256
(532) 96	(550) 171	(568) 259
(533) 101	(551) 180	(569) 262
(534) 102	(552) 181	(570) 265
(535) 104	(553) 184	(571) 266

(536) 105	(554) 191	(572) 270
(537) 112	(555) 192	(573) 271
(538) 117	(556) 195	(574) 273
(539) 120 note	(557) 205	(575) 277

(*576*) *Macfarlane.*

Personal Communication (1957) from William Veitch Macfarlane, Esq., M.D., Ch.B., D.P.H.; Lecturer in Venereal Diseases at King's College in the University of Durham.

(*577–580*) *Mignet.*

The History of Mary Queen of Scots. By F.A. Mignet, Member of the Institute, and of the French Academy, etc. In two volumes. London: Richard Bentley. 1851.

Vol. 1.

(577) 188	(578) 235 note
	Vol. 2.
(579) 432	(580) 433

(*581*) *Neale.*

Elizabeth I and her Parliaments, 1559–1581. By J.E. Neale, Astor Professor of English History in the University of London. Jonathan Cape. London. 1953.

(581) 149

(*582–583*) *Pearson.*

The Skull and Portraits of Henry Stewart, Lord Darnley, and their bearing on the tragedy of Mary Queen of Scots. By Karl Pearson, F.R.S. Issued by the Biometric Laboratory, University College, London, and printed at the University Press, Cambridge. (From Biometrika, Vol. XXB). No date (1928).

(582) 46	(583) 55

(*584–585*) *Percy.*

John Knox by Lord Eustace Percy. Hodder and Stoughton. London. 1937.

(584) 361	(585) 389

(*586–589*) *Pitcairn.*

Criminal Trials in Scotland, from A.D. 1488 to A.D. 1624, embracing the entire reigns of James IV, and V, Mary Queen of Scots, and James VI. Compiled from the original records and MSS., with historical notes and illustrations. By Robert Pitcairn, Esq., W.S., F.S.A. Scot., Hon. F.S.A. Perth, etc. In three volumes, the first in two parts. Edinburgh: William Tait, etc. 1833.

Vol. 1. Part 1.

(586) 461	(588) 481 note	(589) 489
(587) 480		

(*590–627*) *Pollen.*

Papal Negotiations with Mary Queen of Scots during her reign in Scotland. 1561–1567. Edited, from the original documents in the Vatican

Archives and elsewhere, by John Hungerford Pollen, S.J. Edinburgh:
Printed at the University Press by T. and A. Constable for the Scottish
History Society. 1901.

(590) xxxviii	(603) 187	(616) 354
(591) lxxi	(604) 189	(617) 358
(592) xci	(605) 236	(618) 360
(593) cxxi	(606) 261	(619) 362 note
(594) cxxvi	(607) 263	(620) 365
(595) 49	(608) 278	(621) 369
(596) 54	(609) 313	(622) 386 note
(597) 74	(610) 324	(623) 397
(598) 89	(611) 333	(624) 414
(599) 132	(612) 335	(625) 421
(600) 138	(613) 344	(626) 422
(601) 162	(614) 348	(627) 475
(602) 171	(615) 351	

(628) Polson.

Personal Communication (1957) from Cyril John Polson, Esq , M.D.,
Ch.B , F.R.C.P., M.R.C.S , Barrister-at-Law; Professor of Forensic
Medicine in the University of Leeds.

(629–633) Robertson.

The History of Scotland during the reigns of Queen Mary, and of King
James VI till His Accession to the Crown of England, with a Review of
Scottish History previous to that period; and an appendix containing
Original Papers. In two volumes. By William Robertson, D.D , Principal
of the University of Edinburgh, and Historiographer to His Majesty for
Scotland. The twelfth edition, with alterations and additions. London:
T. Cadell. 1791 (apparently published in 1801).

Vol. 1.

(629) 285 note	(630) 364	

Vol. 2.

(631) 362	(632) 364	(633) 406

(634–641) Robertson.

Inuentaires de la Royne Descosse Douairiere de France. Catalogues
of the jewels, dresses, furniture, books and paintings of Mary Queen of
Scots. 1556–1569. Edinburgh. 1863. (Edited by Joseph Robertson)

(634) xlix	(637) lviii	(640) 93–124
(635) 1 note	(638) lviii note	(641) 177
(636) lvli note	(639) lxxxviii	

(642) *Scott.*

The Tragedy of Fotheringay. Founded on the journal of D. Bourgoing,
Physician to Mary Queen of Scots, and on unpublished MS. documents.
By the Hon. Mrs. Maxwell Scott of Abbotsford. London: Adam and
Charles Black. 1895.

(642) 203

(643–647) Scott-Melville

The Memoires of Sir James Melvil of Hal-Hill: containing An Impartial Account Of the most Remarkable Affairs of State During the last Age, not mention'd by other Historians: More particularly Relating to the Kingdoms of England and Scotland Under the Reigns of Queen Elizabeth, Mary Queen of Scots, and King James. In all which Transactions the Author was Personally and Publickly concern'd. Now published from the Original Manuscript. By George Scott, Gent. London: Robert Boulter. 1683.

(643) 48	(645) 77	(647) 199
(644) 70	(646) 177	

(648–649) Skelton.

Maitland of Lethington and the Scotland of Mary Stuart. A History. By John Skelton, C B , Doctor of Laws of the University of Edinburgh, etc. In two volumes. William Blackwood and Sons, Edinburgh.

Vol. 2. 1888

(648) 226	(649) 233

(650) Spottiswoode.

The History of the Church and State of Scotland, Beginning the Year of our Lord 203, and continued to the end of the reign of King James the VI of ever blessed memory In seven books, wherein are described The Progress of Christiantiy, The Persecution and Interruptions of it, The Foundation of the Churches, The Erecting of Bishopricks, The Building and Endowing Monasteries and other Religious Places, The Succession of Bishops in their Sees, The Reformation of Religion, And the frequent Disturbances of that Nation by Wars, Conspiracies, Tumults, Schisms. Together with great variety of other Matters, both Ecclesiastical and Political. Written By that Grave and Reverend Prelate, and wise Counsellor, J. Spotswood, Lord Archbishop of S. Andrews, and Privy Counsellor to King Charles the First, that most Religious and Blessed Prince and Martyr. The fourth edition, corrected, whereunto is added a Large Appendix. London: R. Royston. 1677.

(650) 71

(651–660) Stevenson.

Selections from Unpublished Manuscripts in the College of Arms and the British Museum, illustrating the reign of Mary Queen of Scotland. 1563–1568. Glasgow: The Maitland Club. 1837. (Edited by Joseph Stevenson).

(651) 120	(655) 163	(658) 176
(652) 130	(656) 167	(659) 178
(653) 152	(657) 173	(660) 234
(654) 159		

(661) Stevenson.

Calendar of State Papers, Foreign Series of the Reign of Elizabeth. 1563. Preserved in the State Paper Department of Her Majesty's Public Record Office. Edited by Joseph Stevenson, M.A., of University College, Durham. London: Longman, Green and Co. 1869.

(661) 355

(662–672) Stevenson-Nau.

The History of Mary Stewart from the murder of Riccio until her flight into England. By Claude Nau, her Secretary. Now first printed from the original manuscripts. With illustrative papers from the secret archives of the Vatican and other collections in Rome. Edited, with historical preface, by the Rev. Joseph Stevenson, S.J. Edinburgh: William Paterson. 1883.

(662) cxxiii	(666) clxxii	(670) 245
(663) cxlviii	(667) 16	(671) 261
(664) cxlix	(668) 30	(672) 264
(665) clxi	(669) 48	

(673–686) Stoddart.

The Girlhood of Mary Queen of Scots, from her landing in France in August 1548 to her departure from France in August 1561. By Jane T. Stoddart. Hodder and Stoughton. London. No date (1913?).

(673) 7	(678) 109	(683) 217
(674) 9	(679) 110	(684) 301
(675) 19	(680) 132	(685) 310
(676) 33	(681) 199	(686) 312
(677) 94	(682) 213	

(687–689) Strickland.

Letters of Mary Queen of Scots and Documents connected with her personal history, now first published. With an introduction, by Agnes Strickland. In two volumes. London: Henry Colburn. 1842. (Volume three appeared in 1843).

Vol. 1.

(687) 21   (688) 35

Vol. 2

(689) 278

(690–697) Strickland

Lives of the Queens of Scotland and English Princesses connected with the regal succession of Great Britain. By Agnes Strickland. In eight volumes. William Blackwood and Sons, Edinburgh

Vol. 4. 1853

(690) 379

Vol. 5. 1854

(691) 8	(694) 149	(696) 195
(692) 14	(695) 184	(697) 261
(693) 52		

(698–713) Stuart.

A Lost Chapter in the History of Mary Queen of Scots Recovered: Notices of James Earl of Bothwell and Lady Jane Gordon and of the dispensation for their marriage; Remarks on the law and practice of Scotland relative to marriage dispensations; and an appendix of documents. By John Stuart, LL.D , Secretary of the Society of Antiquaries of Scotland. Edinburgh: Edmonston and Douglas. 1874.

(698) 2	(704) 17	(709) 91
(699) 6	(705) 18	(710) 92
(700) 6 note	(706) 24	(711) 93
(701) 7	(707) 53	(712) 94
(702) 8	(708) 90	(713) 100
(703) 16		

(714–722) Teulet.

Relations Politiques de la France et de l'Espagne avec l'Ecosse au XVIe siècle. Papiers d'état, pièces et documents inedits ou peu connus, tirés des bibliothèques et des archives de France. Publiés par Alexandre Teulet, Archiviste aux Archives de l'Empire. Nouvelle edition. (In five volumes). Paris: Veuve Jules Renouard, Editeur, Libraire de la Société de l'Histoire de France. 1862. Vol. 2. Correspondances francaises. 1559–1573. (François II, Charles IX—Marie Stuart).

(714) 267	(716) 297	(718) 299
(715) 282	(717) 298	(719) 300

Vol. 5. Correspondances Espagnoles. 1562–1588 (Philippe II–Marie Stuart, Jacques VI).

(720) 13	(721) 21	(722) 23

(723–741) Tytler.

History of Scotland. By Patrick Frazer Tytler, Esq. Third edition. In seven volumes. Edinburgh: William Tait. 1845.

Vol. 5.

(723) 248	(729) 381	(735) 499
(724) 266	(730) 385	(736) 509
(725) 307	(731) 397	(737) 511
(726) 355	(732) 445	(738) 512
(727) 359	(733) 446	(739) 515
(728) 363	(734) 447	(740) 516

Vol. 6.

(741) 36

(742) Tytler.

An Inquiry, Historical and Critical, into the Evidence against Mary Queen of Scots; and An Examination of the Histories of Dr. Robertson and Mr. Hume, with respect to that evidence. By William Tytler, Esq., Vice-President of the Society of Scottish Antiquaries, and F.R.S. Edinburgh. The fourth edition, Containing several additional Chapters, and an Introduction, in two volumes. London: T. Cadell, etc. 1790.

Vol. 2.

(742) 42 note

(743) *Document.*

Letter from Thomas Randolph to the Earl of Leicester, 14th February, 1566. Quoted in the Scottish Historical Review, 1955: Vol. 34 (743) 137.

INDEX